Demonizing the Other

Studies in Antisemitism
Series Editor Dalia Ofer
Chair, Vidal Sassoon International Center for the Study of Antisemitism
The Hebrew University of Jerusalem, Israel

Studies in Antisemitism brings together in one series major worldwide research on this complex phenomenon from which the student and decision-maker as well as the general public may learn. The studies cover antisemitism, ancient and modern, from a broad range of perspectives: historical, religious, political, cultural, social, psychological, and economic.

Volume 1
The Catholic Church and Antisemitism
Poland, 1933–1939
Ronald Modras

Volume 2
Russian Antisemitism, Pamyat, and the Demonology of Zionism
William Korey

Volume 3
Vichy Law and the Holocaust in France
Richard H. Weisberg

Volume 4
Demonizing the Other: Antisemitism, Racism, and Xenophobia
Edited by Robert S. Wistrich

This book is part of a series. The publisher will accept continuation orders which may be cancelled at any time, and which provide for automatic billing and shipping of each title in the series upon publication. Please write for details.

Demonizing the Other
Antisemitism, Racism, and Xenophobia

Edited by Robert S. Wistrich

Published for the
Vidal Sassoon International Center
for the Study of Antisemitism
The Hebrew University of Jerusalem

by

 Routledge
Taylor & Francis Group
LONDON AND NEW YORK

2 Park Square, Milton Park,
Abingdon, Oxon, OX14 4RN

711 Third Avenue, New York,
NY 10017

Routledge is an imprint of the Taylor & Francis Group

First issued in paperback 2011

British Library Cataloguing in Publication Data
A catalogue record for this book is available from the British Library

ISBN13: 978-9-057-02497-9 (hbk)
ISBN13: 978-0-415-51619-8 (pbk)

COVER Frankfurt Judensau, broadsheet, early eighteenth century

EDITING AND COMPOSITION
   Alifa Saadya

Every effort has been made to contact the owners of the copyright of all the works reproduced in this book but if, for any reason, any acknowledgement has been omitted, the publishers ask those concerned to contact them.

Contents

List of Illustrations

Foreword

The original idea for this book came from Mr. Felix Posen — a longstanding supporter and friend of the Vidal Sassoon International Center for the Study of Antisemitism and the Hebrew University of Jerusalem. He had encountered in Japan and Korea a mystifyingly positive response to the antisemitic stereotype of the Jew found in the *Protocols of the Elders of Zion,* which his Asian business colleagues perceived as praising the Jews. Their acquaintance with Jews was limited, and they knew little of Jewish history, including the difficult relationship between Jews and Christians in Medieval and modern Europe, or about antisemitism in general. It became apparent that in order to make antisemitism more comprehensible, it was necessary to suggest other types of demonization more familiar to their own societies, such as the attitude of the Japanese towards Koreans.

It was decided to hold an international conference in order to explore the comparative dimension of antisemitism. Professor Dov Kulka of the Hebrew University and Academic Advisor for the Felix Posen Bibliographic Project on Antisemitism of the Center served as chair of the organizing committee of the conference. Held at the Hebrew University in June 1995, the intention was to better understand the contexts in which the negative image of the outsider was developed, and how this could lead to demonization of the "other." Antisemitism we believe to be the foremost example of this phenomenon which has acquired an all too tragic significance in this century.

The wealth of knowledge and insight in this book (meticulously and skilfully edited by Robert Wistrich) is a testimony to the importance of a comparative scientific endeavor, and this short foreword hardly does justice to it. This book truly provides an indispensable tool for understanding the dynamics of demonization — the first step before any change in attitudes can be intelligently implemented. Let us hope that the combined efforts of the scholars who have presented their findings here in this volume, will have the impact they deserve in future policy and action.

Yehuda Bauer
Dalia Ofer
The Vidal Sassoon International Center
for the Study of Antisemitism
The Hebrew University of Jerusalem, Israel

The Devil, the Jews, and Hatred of the "Other"

Robert S. Wistrich

There has been no hatred in Western Christian civilization more persistent and enduring than that directed against the Jews. Though the form and timing which outbursts of anti-Jewish persecution have taken through the ages have varied, the basic patterns of prejudice have remained remarkably consistent.[1] Particularly striking is the deeply irrational and counter-factual character of most accusations that have been levelled against the Jewish people over the past two thousand years.[2] They have been charged with deicide (the killing of Christ), with piercing holy communion wafers to make them bleed (desecration of the Host), with the ritual murder of Christian children at Easter; they have been held responsible for poisoning wells and for the Black Death during the Middle Ages; for practising witchcraft, forging an alliance with the mythical Antichrist, and conspiring to destroy Christendom.[3] In modern times, new and no less sinister variations have been added to the theme of the "Jewish peril"—that Jews are striving for world domination by achieving control of the international financial system, by promoting revolutionary socialist ideologies, or through the alleged machinations of Zionism and the State of Israel. Modern antisemitism has thrived on irrational Manichean myths like the Judeo-Masonic, the Judeo-Communist, or Zionist-American conspiracies, and the belief in an occult global Jewish power, embodied in the *Protocols of the Elders of Zion.*[4] The litany of stereotypes and accusations seems endless and has acquired a seemingly timeless quality, despite its lack of any empirical basis.

The persistence, longevity, and mythic power of such group hatred makes it an especially revealing barometer of the tensions and conflicts within European Christian culture from which it stemmed. Moreover, the fact that antisemitism culminated in the Holocaust of World War II—the systematically planned mass murder of six million Jewish men, women, and children—has further underlined the extreme irrationality which has been one of its chief distinguishing features. The traumatic, cataclysmic nature of this event has sparked many attempts in the past fifty years to find theories and explanations that could illuminate antisemitism, racism, and the roots of murderous hatreds of the "other" in general.[5] Yet despite the important contributions from historians, political scientists, sociologists, psychologists, theologians, and researchers in many other disciplines, an element of mystery remains. There are factors in antisemitism that both derive from and yet clearly transcend the hatred of the different and the alien, so characteristic of religious bigotry and racism in general.[6] There are certain parallels between Jew-hatred and the persecution of heretics, witches, homosexuals, gypsies, blacks, and many other minorities, yet in the latter cases, the sacral, quasi-metaphysical quality of antisemitism is singularly absent. Moreover, some of the more obvious factors in racist prejudices such as the legacy of colonial oppression, slavery, or economic exploitation have only limited value in understanding the specificity of Judeophobia.

Nevertheless, the emergence of modern racist ideology in the nineteenth century was a decisive turning point in the history of antisemitism which undoubtedly paved the way for Nazi totalitarianism and the "Final Solution." If we define racism in its most basic sense as *heterophobia* (hatred of the other) and the attempt to "essentialize" real or perceived differences so that *fixed* attributes are henceforth applied to human groups, then the consequences are bound to be far-reaching. Race theory not only assumes the existence of distinct, identifiable races each with their own separate "essence" or "character," but it also presupposes a hierarchy of differences.[7] There are "superior" and "inferior" races which supposedly embody higher and lower values. In the racist typology, motivated as it has been since the mid-1850s by anti-egalitarian, doctrines, these differences are deemed to be hereditary, immutable, and "eternal."[8] They serve to justify and rationalize the will to exclusion of the "collective other," defined as alien, different, more primitive, or inferior.

Though racism—as in the colonialist model—may also masquerade under the cover of a "civilizing" mission or even of universalist human values, its postulate is invariably the right of the dominant group to lead, command, subjugate, or exploit others. It can rely on a firm rockbed of ethnocentrism—the seemingly universal tendency of a social groups to see themselves as better than others, to valorize the collective self above all else as a means of group self-preservation, cohesion, and permanence. Virtually every culture exhibits some kind of desire to distinguish itself from others, to assert and maintain its identity, to draw boundaries between "us" and "them." At what point, then, does "normal" ethnocentrism turn into xenophobia, racism, or antisemitism? When does family or group egoism, the tendency to exclude or distrust the other, turn into hatred, aggressive hostility, deliberate persecution, or even massacre? When does ethnocentrism become a xenophobic security belt around a specific cultural identity, or

fanaticism - forgetting what the original objection was

worse still, a racist paranoia directed against the dangers of "pollution" and contamination from without or within? Or, as in the case of Nazism, how do racist fantasies acquire a genocidal dynamic that attributes intrinsically evil qualities to the identity and being of the mythical enemy, whose existence is so threatening that he must be totally destroyed?

This type of extreme Nazi racism sought to annihilate Jews not for what they did, for their faith, their customs, or political opinions, but for what they were alleged to be, for their very *being.* The fatality of birth condemned Jews to death, every Jew and all Jews, everywhere and always. They were the counter-type, the paradigmatic "other" race inassimilable by definition, *inclassable,* outside the natural hierarchy of races, beyond the human pale. Not even a race, strictly speaking (since they were "unnatural"), perverse, demonic, the intrinsically evil "other"—in a word, the Jews were the Devil incarnate in human form.[9] Their extermination—in the worldview of Nazi zoological racism—was the prerequisite not simply to secure German race-purity and "Aryan" hegemony, but ultimately the happiness of all mankind.

The Nazi hatred of the Jewish "other," in its sheer intensity and murderous rage, clearly went far beyond "normal" prejudice, institutionalized racist discrimination, xenophobia, segregation, or the pogromist outbreaks that have filled the annals of Jewish history with monotonous regularity. At the same time it cannot and should not be completely divorced from other types of racism and even less from the long history of antisemitism that preceded it. Despite their underlying Christophobia, for example, the Nazi leaders made a thorough and systematic use of Christian anti-Jewish stereotypes.[10] They could and did build on a rich bimillennial tradition that went back to the Gospels (especially John)[11] and their depiction of the Jews as a pariah people, as the murderers of Christ and of their own prophets, in league with Satan himself; and they could draw on teachings of the Church Fathers who persistently referred to Jews as slanderers, blasphemers, an accursed people, members of the Synagogue of Satan. The Nazis exploited and secularized familiar medieval images of the Jew as Host desecrators, demons, sorcerers, well poisoners, and ritual murderers—as usurers, infidels, and insatiable conspirators seeking the destruction of Christian society. The Protestant Reformation in Germany and Martin Luther's mythologizing of the Jews as completely diabolical, provided an even more powerful arsenal of images for Nazi antisemitism.[12]

Such virulent phobias (which preceded the rise of racist ideologies by many centuries) pervaded Medieval Christianity and dominated the folk imagination in Europe. It was here that seeds of fear and a fanatical hatred were sown, which can only be described as demonological. Long before the Nazis, the Jews had been depicted in theological polemics, in sermons, mystery plays, fiction, and the visual arts as representing mysterious, fearsome, and evil forces.[13] In the lower depths of Western culture, in its collective subconscious, the kinship of the Jew with Satan was firmly established by the late Middle Ages. The Jewish thirst for Christian blood, the infidel Jew, the mysterious Jew practising black magic and deliberately spreading poison—these were stock clichés of popular literature and folk tales. The unspeakable crime of crucifying Jesus was attributed to *all* Jews collectively—and hence for medieval Europe there was no crime of which this enemy of mankind was potentially incapable.[14] He was a creature of a different order, not really human—at least not in the sense that Christians were. Most significant of all, he was constantly linked with the Devil in medieval Christian writing, painting, and sculpture.

One must remember that for the medieval Christian, Satan was a very real personage, the arch-enemy of mankind, who had been at war with the Church from the very beginning of its mission. He embodied all the forces of heresy and revolt against God; he constantly tempted believers with doubt, and most important of all, he sought power over *this* world. From the twelfth century onwards, the Devil in Christian art is an undeniably repulsive figure with an oversized head, bulging eyes, horns, a tail, and long, flamelike hair (symbolizing the fires of hell). These frightening and grotesque images also frequently appeared as symbols of Jews and Judaism. Moreover, in painting and sculpture, the Devil would often be represented as riding on the back of a Jew or of *Synagoga*—herself depicted as a blindfolded young woman, incapable of perceiving the true light of Christian faith.[15] There were, moreover, many parallel characteristics attributed to the Jews and the Devil. Both were depicted as arrogant, full of self-love, and masters of logic (the *ars diaboli*), seeking to ensnare believers with their perverse argumentation.[16]

Jews, like the Devil, were also identified with the sin of unbridled lechery—a stereotype that echoed the fourth century preacher, John Chrysostum, who had described the Synagogue as a bordel and dwelling-place for demons. The billy goat, the devil's favorite animal and a symbol of satanic lechery for the Middle Ages, was not surprisingly associated with the Jew. The notorious image of the *Judensau* suckling her Jewish offspring in the presence of the devil, was another very familiar caricature of the Middle Ages. Here, as in other depictions, the association of Jews and the Devil with dirt and excrement was commonplace.[17] No less potent was the belief in the so-called *foetor judaicus*—a distince and odious stench ascribed to the Jews—and supposedly a mark of the demonic Jew. While such ascriptions are common enough as stigmas designed to bolster the sense of superiority of one group against another in other cultures—in Christian Europe the Jewish stench was seen as punishment for the unbelief of the Jews and their crime against Jesus. Moreover, evil spirits in general and especially Satan were often characterized by a similarly offensive stench.[18]

The Jew-Devil with horns and tail was not only physically repulsive, but also a mortal enemy of Christendom in the *spiritual* realm. Stricken with blindness and stubbornness by Satan after the Crucifixion, the Jew had not only rejected the true doctrine but had supposedly spared no effort to destroy Christian souls. Having made common cause with the Devil, the Jews now looked to Antichrist as their long-awaited Messiah. Portrayed in the literature as the child of a union between the devil and a Jewish harlot, the Antichrist symbolized to the medieval mind the sinister and truly satanic role of the Jews in world history. The Jews were indeed perceived as the spearhead of Antichrist's legions in the coming battle to annihilate Christendom. The apocalyptic threat represented by the Antichrist myth was to become one of the most potent driving forces of medieval antisemitism, and its influence carried over into the modern era.[19]

At the more rarefied theological level—as in highly influential anti-Jewish tracts like Raymond Martini's *Pugio Dei* (written towards the end of the thirteenth century)—the Jewish pact with the devil is no less salient. It was used, for example, to explain why the Jews rejected Jesus so arrogantly, observed the ritual commandments literally and remained willfully blind to the truth of Christianity. The Jews, in effect, were assumed to believe in the revelation of Satan rather than God, and even their *kiddush ha-shem* (sanctification of the Holy Name) was interpreted as a kind of martyrdom for the Devil.[20] In a similar vein, the Spanish theologian Alfonso di Spina in his fifteenth century polemic *Fortalitium Fidei,* suggested that even when Jews preferred to be burned alive at the stake, they were behaving as "damned devil's martyrs."[21] Thus, in their greatest distress, Jews were stigmatized as children of the devil, perversely invoking demons and giving them the honor due to God.

When Luther called for burning their synagogues and for their expulsion from German lands, he, like so many others before him, pointed to the Jews' imagined *demonic* hostility to Christianity. Christians, he contended, were ruthlessly exploited by Jewish usury and would only suffer far more from them if they did not take harsh pre-emptive measures. Abraham a Sancta Clara, the populist seventeenth century Viennese Catholic preacher, was also echoing a widespread sentiment when he claimed that "After Satan Christians have no greater enemies than the Jews.... They pray many times each day that God may destroy us through pestilence, famine and war, aye, that all beings and creatures may rise up with them against the Christians."[22] Thus, at the intellectual heights as in the lower depths of European society, the Jew had by the dawn of the modernity, long ceased to be a living human being—he had been ineluctably transformed into a theological abstraction of truly diabolical perversity and malice.

Clearly, the powerful emotions released by this tradition of Christian antisemitism (even before it became a raging fever under the Nazis) must reflect deep unconscious fears which have profound symbolic significance. Historians have often overlooked this psychological dimension, preferring to deal with the supposedly more "objective" economic, social, and political factors on the surface. Yet we cannot afford to ignore unconscious factors and more hidden sources if we are to come closer to understanding the riddle of antisemitism.

The Viennese founder of psychoanalysis, Sigmund Freud, himself a Jew who suffered acutely from antisemitism, left us some sporadic though valuable hints concerning this enigma.[23] At one level, Freud regarded antisemitism as the displacement of unresolved murderous urges of the sons against their fathers. As a religion which had put the Son in place of the Father (but admitted complicity for his Death), Christianity, according to Freud, had absolved itself of guilt while projecting it onto the Jews. As the "murderers of God," on the other hand, Jews—who had refused to acknowledge the divinity of Jesus—were thereby cast into the role of parricides. At another level altogether, Freud thought that antisemitism might also be a displaced form of *Christenhass* (Christophobia). Christians, who unconsciously resented the exacting (superego) demands of their own faith—its repression of the instincts, moral strictures, etc.—could more easily direct these unacknowledged feelings against Judaism—traditionally stigmatized as a lower form of revelation.[24]

Freud was also alive to the powerful charge of sibling rivalry or jealousy of the Jews as the "chosen people" of God, the favored nation of God the Father. Freud did not elaborate on this point, but there is no doubt that antagonism towards the claim of chosenness has indeed been a constant motif in antisemitism through the ages. One testimony to its force lies in the usurpation of God's promises to the Jews by the Christian churches, as the heirs of ancient Israel, who have superseded it in divine favor. In Islam, too, there is a doctrine of supersession (of both Judaism and Christianity) in which Muslims become the elect people of Allah. Moreover, in many modern nationalisms, the Judaic idea of chosenness has been adopted (often in a secularized and politicized form) and not infrequently has it led to fierce hostility against Jews and Judaism. As the most ancient repositories of chosenness, the Jews are almost inevitably a lightning rod for rival claims of election, whose psychological dynamics can easily trigger an irrational hatred. This, again, seems to me a distinctive feature of antisemitism compared with most forms of hatred towards the "other."

Finally, Freud pointed to the rite of circumcision, with its unconscious meaning of castration and all the dread and anxiety that this may arouse. For Freud it was clear that this was one of the deeper roots of antisemitism "which appears with such elemental force and finds such irrational expression among the nations of the West."[25] In another context, commenting on the misogynist, self-hating Jewish-born philosopher Otto

Weininger—whose book *Geschlecht und Charakter* (Sex and character) caused a sensation in turn-of-the-century Vienna—Freud argued that the common hatred of Jews and women derived from the castration complex. "The castration complex is the deepest unconscious root of anti-Semitism; for even in the nursery little boys hear that a Jew has something cut off his penis—a piece of his penis, they think—and this gives them a right to despise Jews. And there is no stronger unconscious root for the sense of superiority over women."[26]

Elsewhere, Freud noted that Jews, as a comparatively small and powerless cultural group, had provided a perfect target for the instinct of aggression "in the form of hostility against intruders." Evoking with understandable sarcasm the massacres of Jews in the Middle Ages, Freud observed that "the Jewish people scattered everywhere, has rendered the most useful services to the civilizations of the countries that have been their hosts."[27]

Psychoanalytic theory can perhaps help us to understand the unconscious and repressed drives that have so often assumed a murderous character in antisemitism. For example, there is the image of the *carnal,* debauched Jew represented as leading an unbridled sexual life, as being the seducer, rapist, and contaminator of the "blood purity" of innocent Christian maidens. Adolf Hitler's chilling fantasy about the devilish Jew seeking to bastardize the white Germanic race and poison its blood through sexual intercourse, has its parallels, of course, in similar projections about blacks or dark-skinned people in other societies: but in *Mein Kampf,* he specifically evokes the black-haired young Jew lurking for hours, "satanic joy in his face, waiting for the unsuspecting girl whom he defiles with his blood and thereby robs from her people."[28]

If Jews came for many Gentiles to represent the repressed id of European Christian culture (its forbidden lusts) they could also embody the intolerable constraints of its Christian superego, which were unconsciously blamed on Judaism. It is possible, for instance, that in the blood accusations against the Jews, the ambivalence of Gentile Christian feelings against the moral prohibitions ("Thou shalt nots") of the stern Judaic God may have found an outlet. Here, as in so many other demonic fantasies about the Jews, it must be stressed that the specific delusions themselves have no basis at all in fact, logic, or in any real historical situation. What is however common to all the accusations about deicide, ritual murder, Host desecration, poisoning of wells, etc., is their obvious relation to the Jewish rejection of Christianity and to the fantasy about the Jew as a *persecutor* of Christians. Despite the lack of any objective evidence, the blood libels have persisted into the twentieth century as a potent source of antisemitism. Their obsessive repetition and the vehemence with which the deicide myth underlying them has been defended over the centuries, suggests the possibility of powerfully repressed Christian doubts about the divinity of Jesus himself, which are exorcised by projecting guilt onto the Jewish infidel. Indeed, from a psychoanalytical viewpoint, one can regard the tragic martyrdom of the Jews in the Christian world as a testament to all the unresolved and unacknowledged hatred, fear, and aggression buried deep in the recesses of its popular culture. All the negative qualities, dark drives, or crimes attributed to the Jews (and sometimes to other dissidents, outsiders, or marginalized groups) surely represent parts of their own selves that Christians cannot live with and therefore have sought to expunge from their midst. The countless persecutors who have plundered Jewish property, burned and massacred Jews over the centuries have always prepared the ground by first accusing their victims of the crimes they themselves already have and will continue to commit.

Demonizing others is not of course confined only to Jews.[29] It would appear that scapegoating and the projection of evil onto humans who have been demonized is a universal human problem. Not only does it, as we have seen, exorcise unavowed guilt, create boundaries between in- and out-groups, help to define social, religious, and national identity, but it helps construct a moral order against the dangerous, disruptive, defiling Other. The Other (who is generally assumed to share a different moral and social code) must take the blame and responsibility for everything that goes wrong in "normal" human society. Yet, as we have seen in the case of the Jews, he or she is also a reflection of the Self—the flawed and even the wicked Self which is out of control, unable to deal with its own repressed, sadistic impulses.

The demonization of the Other as a means of "ethnic cleansing" has also played an important role in modern nationalisms that prey on ethnocentric group differences to solidify their community against a common enemy. The Bosnian tragedy is a good contemporary illustration of the nexus between nationalism and ethnic paranoia, once the language of blood and belonging takes over. In the ex-Yugoslavia, following the collapse of legitimate state authority, a kind of historical regression to the late Middle Ages occurred. In the ensuing war of all against all, ethnic-national belonging was now defined by common blood and language and involved driving out neighbors assumed to be bent on one's destruction, despite decades of peaceful coexistence. Each side to the conflict saw itself only as blameless victims and the others as "genocidal" killers.[30]

For Serbs, Croats, and Muslims, it would appear that without unrestrained hatred of the other, there was no clearly defined national self. Only the "other" was responsible; *they* behaved like beasts, *they* only understood violence, etc.—how many times has one heard this litany of reproach in territorial and ethnic-national conflicts throughout this century? Almost invariably, the possibility of massacres ensues once the enemy has been metaphorically dehumanized and made to appear beyond the pale of civilization. The more monstrous the image of physical deformity, moral depravity, and general backwardness, the easier it becomes to rationalize killing. This linkage between the awesome power of stereotypes and the inflicting of mass death has been all too obvious in our own century, undoubtedly the bloodiest and most genocidal in all human history.

By contrast, the late eighteenth century with its universalist Enlightenment ideals, its optimistic faith in reason, and belief in a more or less constant human nature, did for a time develop a certain curiosity about the "other" as the royal road to know ourselves. With its cosmopolitan outlook and recognition of the primacy of the individual, its toleration for different faiths and for exotic outsiders, the eighteenth century Enlightenment did seem to offer a rationalist alternative to that fratricidal hatred of the "other" which had torn Europe apart during the wars of religion a century earlier.[31] It was, after all, the French Enlightenment which had paved the way in Europe for Jewish and black emancipation, despite the elitist prejudices which even its best intellectuals had conserved and the more problematic long-term consequences of its philosophical assault on the Judeo-Christian legacy.

In France a century ago, at the height of the Dreyfus Affair, a highly significant battle was fought to preserve this rationalist heritage of the Enlightenment and the French Revolution. Its adherents were faced by an assault from all the conservative forces of the *ancien régime*—the Church, the Monarchy, the Army, and a massed phalanx of integral nationalists and antisemites. At the symbolic heart of this confrontation stood Alfred Dreyfus, a Jewish army officer, falsely accused of betraying his country to the Germans. Dreyfus's guilt was assumed not only by antisemites, but by all those in France for whom the Republic was perceived as a satanic force, irreparably undermining the traditional Christian character of the land. The Affair demonstrated that even in the most enlightened, civilized, modern European state, antisemitism could suddenly erupt with tremendous power, fusing the older Catholic demonology of the Jew with newer modern racial categories.[32] Jews and Freemasons, liberals and socialists, were predictably accused by the Catholic and nationalist Right of orchestrating a demonic conspiracy against France on behalf of Dreyfus and his purported German paymasters.

The myth of the all-powerful Jew (embodied by the Rothschilds and "Jewish" international high finance) acquired a new lease on life: so did the medieval fantasies of the Jew as Antichrist, agent of Satan and corrupter of morals. The traitor Dreyfus as a reincarnation of Judas (the classic Christian symbol of betrayal) became the modern embodiment of the cursed deicidal people. The Affair admittedly ended with a victory for Dreyfus and his supporters, for the rule of law, and the Republican credo of human rights. But it was nonetheless a matrix for the emergence of European fascism, for the fabrication of forgeries like the *Protocols of the Elders of Zion,* and (as

Hannah Arendt long ago pointed out) a kind of dress rehearsal for totalitarian politics and Nazi-style antisemitism.[33]

The tendency to identify Jews and Judaism with great and powerful forces of modernity (democracy, liberalism, the stock exchange, international socialism, artistic modernism, and secularization, etc.) had already emerged in France during the European fin-de-siècle. It was to take on a tremendously heightened form in the Weimar Republic and throughout European society after 1918. These developments could be seen as a response to the growing and visible impact of Jewish emancipation and assimilation, to the general crisis of European civilization after the First World War and fear of the Bolshevik Revolution, as well as to the rise of extremist antisemitic movements that embraced fully-fledged conspiracy theories of history. Some of these antisemitic movements were Christian (Christian-socialist, Christian nationalist, Catholic populist, etc.) and some were anti-Christian, but all believed in the centrality of the Jewish role in Western civilization.

German National Socialism took this widespread belief and totalized it a negative sense, so that the whole of world history came to be seen as a struggle to the death between Nordic "Aryanism" and the "Jewish spirit." In the Nazi *Weltanschauung,* the "otherness" of the Jew now became absolute and all the more ominous because he had penetrated into the very heart of German culture. An otherness which was seemingly indefinable, amorphous, infinitely fluid and capable of endless adaptation while supposedly retaining its own unchanging "racial" integrity. Perceived as the protean carriers of an evil essence, the Jew therefore appeared in Nazi eyes as the incarnation of the powers of darkness. As a superhuman and a subhuman threat, Judaism and Jewry were figuratively transformed into universal carriers of death, whose annihilation was the precondition for the salvation of humanity. This "redemptive antisemitism," as Saul Friedländer among others has suggested, lay at the core of Hitler's program and without it the Holocaust could not have happened.[34]

The Satanic Jew came alive again in Nazism as an apocalyptic and visceral danger to the existence of Germany, of Aryan "pure blood," dreams of vital living space and territorial expansion. His racial otherness had clear echoes of Christian demonology but it had been radicalized, so that the Jew stood completely outside of humanity.[35] The Jews were described as microbes, vermin, a cancer in the bloodstream, the "racial tuberculosis of the peoples," universal poisoners, and parasites. The language of the Nazis was medicalized, hygienized pseudo-science, the vocabulary of pest control and "racial hygiene"—by 1944 the war against the Jewish Satan would indeed be resolved by Zyklon-B.[36] Hitler pursued his relentless *Endlösung* against the phantom Jewish *Weltfeind* ("world enemy") to the bitter end by wiping out six million defenseless Jews who had never even declared war on Germany or sought to harm her!

Since World War II, neither the fear and hatred of the "other," racism, antisemitism, nor genocide have disappeared from the world. We have witnessed massive killing by dictatorial governments of political opponents, autogenocidal experiments in social engineering such as those practised by the Khmer Rouge in Cambodia, fearful tribal massacres in Africa, "ethnic cleansing" in the Balkans, and many other horrors. Neither racism nor antisemitism has been the driving force of any of these killings but their potential is still far from exhausted. Belief in a Jewish world conspiracy remains remarkably tenacious, even when as in Japan, it appears to be relatively benign.[37] The hidden, imaginary power of the Jews as exemplified in the *Protocols of the Elders of Zion* continues to bedazzle antisemites around the world, whether Right or Left wing, religious fundamentalist or secular, whether resident in the West, the East, or the Third World. From Russia and Eastern Europe, through the Middle East to North and South America, the notion of Jews striving for global domination still finds adepts and believers. The allegation that Zionists and Jews "invented" the Holocaust has itself become an important part of this postwar variation on conspiracy theory. Thus the satanic power of the Jews is above all demonstrated by their ability to carry out a gigantic hoax, to generate a "genocide myth" that has brought to them great financial and political power.[38]

The other major source of postwar antisemitic mythology has been the State of Israel and international Zionism. Ideological anti-Zionism whether in the former Soviet Union, among fundamentalist Muslims, in large parts of the Arab world, or among radical and Left factions in the West, has constructed a demonic image of Israel as the incarnation of evil.[39] Adopting the Manichean schemas of classic antisemitism, it portrays Israel and Zionism as a malevolent superpower, operating by corrupt, occult methods to subjugate the Middle East and the entire world. The diabolical Zionist Jews are invariably vilified as "imperialist," "racist," expansionist, and "Nazi"; they engage in relentless persecution of Arabs; they systematically lie and perversely manipulate the Holocaust to whitewash their sins. In the Arab world and Iran, it has become commonplace for radical and fundamentalist opinion to view Israel in a conspiratorial light, as a satanic force plotting against Islam.[40] For the Islamists in particular, the Jews and Israel are seen as controlling the Great Satan, America, and working closely with it to subjugate the entire Middle East.

But this is not only a political and territorial conflict; for believers it is a holy war *(jihad)* and a struggle of civilization, a battle for the soul of Islam.[41] Tragically, the Jew has become the demonic "other" in the new fundamentalist drive to affirm a Muslim self-identity against Israel and the "infidel" West. The wheel has come full circle in a highly paradoxical manner: Zionism intended to solve the "Jewish Question" in Europe by transplanting Jews back to their ancient homeland in the Middle East. It definitely did not cure the age-old pathology of antisemitism, but instead it unwittingly created a new Islamic variety of the same disease, itself imported from Europe. This European-style antisemitism, while appropriately Islamicized and peppered with tendentious quotations from the Quran and *hadith,* has nonetheless appropriated a classically Christian demonology of the Jews. Hence we find Arab and Islamic antisemites incorporating into their propaganda medieval attacks on the Talmud, allegations of Jewish ritual murder, and the notion of an accursed, pariah people—concepts traditionally alien to Islamic religion and civilization.

As if to heighten the paradox, Muslims and Arab immigrants in Europe have found themselves increasingly stereotyped and harassed as their stubbornly particularist diasporic presence arouses xenophobic and racist reactions. To a certain extent, *they* (along with gypsies, guest-workers, and colored immigrants) have replaced the Jews as the feared "other" in a multicultural Europe that has not yet exorcised the demons of its own genocidal and colonialist past.[42] Both in Europe and in the Middle East, the ancient lesson of the book of Exodus has still to be implemented: "And a stranger shalt thou not wrong, neither shalt thou oppress him."[43] In the Hebrew Bible, the commandment to love the stranger is repeated no less than thirty-six times. Clearly, hatred of the "other" can only be a blind alley. It is in recognition of the alien and acceptance of the fact of difference that we are asked to rediscover the true meaning of humanity.

Notes

1. See Edward Flannery, *The Anguish of the Jews* (New York 1985), and Robert S. Wistrich, *Antisemitism, the Longest Hatred* (London 1991).

2. This point is particularly emphasized by Gavin Langmuir, *History, Religion and Antisemitism* (Berkeley 1990).

3. See Wistrich, *Longest Hatred,* 13–42; Judith Taylor Gold, *Monsters and Madonnas: The Roots of Christian Antisemitism* (New York 1988); Robert Moore, *The Formation of A Persecuting Society: Power and Deviance in Western Europe 950–1250* (Oxford 1987); and Rainer Erb, ed., *Die Legende vom Ritualmord: Zur Geschichte der Blutbeschuldigung gegen Juden* (Berlin 1993).

4. On the *Protocols,* see Norman Cohn, *Warrant for Genocide. The Myth of the Jewish World Conspiracy and the Protocols of the Elders of Zion* (London 1967); and Pierre-André Taguieff, ed., *Les Protocoles des Sages de Sion,* 2 vols. (Paris 1992).

5. Shmuel Ettinger, "Jew Hatred in Its Historical Context," in *Antisemitism Through the Ages,* ed. Shmuel Almog (London 1988), 1–12.

6. For useful attempts to compare antisemitism, racism, xenophobia, and other kinds of "heterophobia," see Albert Memmi, *Le Racisme* (Paris 1982); and Daniel Sibony, *Écrits sur le Racisme* (Paris 1988).

7. See Pierre-André Taguieff, *La Force du Préjugé. Essai sur le Racisme et ses Doubles* (Paris 1988).

8. George L. Mosse, *Towards the Final Solution: A History of European Racism* (New York 1975); and Maurice Olender, *Les Langues du Paradis: Aryens et Sémites—un couple providentiel* (Paris 1989).

9. See Robert Wistrich, *Hitler's Apocalypse* (London 1985); and Joel Carmichael, *The Satanizing of the Jews: Origins and Development of Mystical Anti-Semitism* (New York 1992).

10. Michael Lay, *Genozid und Heilserwartung. Zum Nationalsozialistischen Mord am Europäischen Judentum* (Vienna 1993), 213–29.

11. Micha Brumlik, "Johannes: Das judenfeindliche Evangelium," *Kirche und Israel* 4, no. 2 (1989): 102–13.

12. See Heiko A. Oberman, *Wurzeln des Antisemitismus. Christenangst und Judenplage im Zeitalter von Humanismus und Reformation* (Berlin 1983) for a classic analysis of Luther and contemporary Reformation attitudes to Jews and Judaism.

13. See Joshua Trachtenberg, *The Devil and the Jews. The Medieval Conception of the Jew and Its Relation to Modern Antisemitism* (Philadelphia 1961), 11–56; also Natascha Bremer, *Das Bild der Juden an den Passionsspielen und in der bildenden Kunst des deutschen Mittelalters* (Frankfurt a.M. 1986) on the passion plays.

14. See Rosemary Ruether, *Faith and Fratricide: The Theological Roots of Antisemitism* (New York 1971). On the deicide myth, Hyam Maccoby *A Pariah People. The Anthropology of Antisemitism* (London 1996).

15. Robert Bonfil, "The Devil and the Jews in the Christian Consciousness of the Middle Ages," in *Antisemitism Through the Ages,* ed. Almog, 91–98.

16. Ibid., 95.

17. For the equation of Jews with dirt and disease in German medieval folklore and its possible implications, see Alan Dundes, *Life is Like a Chicken Coop Ladder: A Portrait of German Culture through Folklore* (New York 1984).

18. Trachtenberg, *Devil and the Jews,* 47ff, 116.

19. See Hyam Maccoby, *The Sacred Executioner. Human Sacrifice and the Legacy of Guilt* (London 1982), 172; Wistrich, *Longest Hatred,* 30, 38.

20. Bonfil, "Devil and the Jews," 97. For a possible link between *kiddush ha-shem* and the emergence of the blood libel, see Israel Yuval, "Vengeance and Damnation, Blood and Defamation; From Jewish Martyrdom to Blood Libel Accusations" (in Hebrew), *Zion* 58, no. 1 (1993): 33–90.

21. Di Spina was a Franciscan monk whose polemic (written in 1464) denounced heretics, Saracens, and demons as well as Jews. He recommended that Spanish Jewry be expelled, as had already happened to their co-religionists in France. See Alisa Meyuhas-Ginio, "The Expulsion of the Jews from the Kingdom of France in the Fourteenth Century and its Significance as Viewed by Alfonso de Espina [*sic*], author of *Fortalitium Fidei*" (in Hebrew), *Michael* 12 (1991): 67–82.

22. Trachtenberg, *Devil and the Jews*, 42.

23. Robert S. Wistrich, *The Jews of Vienna in the Age of Franz Joseph* (Oxford 1989), 537–82.

24. Some of these ideas concerning the relationship between Judaism and Christianity are more fully developed by Rudolph Lowenstein, *Christians and Jews. A Psychoanalytic Study* (New York 1952), 96ff; Peter Loewenberg, *Fantasy and Reality in History* (New York and Oxford 1995), 172–91.

25. See Sigmund Freud, *Standard Edition of the Complete Psychological Works,* trs. James Strachey et al (London 1964), vol. 11, 95–96 n. The note came in the 1919 addition which Freud made to his essay on Leonardo da Vinci's childhood, originally published in 1910.

26. Sigmund Freud, "Analysis of a Phobia in a Five-year Old Boy" (1909), in *Standard Edition,* vol. 10, 36 n. See also Wistrich, *Jews of Vienna,* 535–56. On Weininger, see Nancy Harrowitz and Barbara Hymens, eds., *Jews and Gender. Responses to Otto Weininger* (Philadelphia 1995).

27. Sigmund Freud, "Civilization and Its Discontents" (1930), in *Standard Edition,* vol.2, 21, 114.

28. Adolf Hitler, *Mein Kampf* (Munich 1927), 357. For the Viennese background to Hitler's sexually-charged antisemitism, see Robert S. Wistrich, *Hitler's Apocalypse,* 15–17; also Wilfried Daim, *Der Mann, der Hitler die Ideen gab. Jörg Lanz von Liebenfels* (Vienna 1994), and Brigitte Hamann, *Hitlers Wien. Lehrjahre eines Diktators* (Vienna 1996).

29. An instructive parallel is provided by the persecution of witches. In the period between 1575 and 1700 (a time of social distress and upheaval) it is estimated that at least a million witches in Europe may have been burned at the stake. Witches, like Jews, were ideal scapegoats for sexually repressed fantasies; they, too, were viewed as allies of the Devil and their defenders were branded as his agents. For the structural parallels, see Adolf Leschnitzer, *The Magic Background of Modern Anti-Semitism* (New York 1956) 97–100.

30. Michael Ignatieff, *Blood and Belonging. Journeys into the New Nationalism* (New York 1993), 19–53.

31. See Hans Meyer, *Außenseiter* (Frankfurt a.M. 1976) for an exploration of Enlightenment attitudes to women, Jews, and homosexuals—especially as they were reflected in nineteenth century European bourgeois society.

32. Stephen Wilson, *Ideology and Experience. Antisemitism in France at the Time of the Dreyfus Affair* (East Brunswick, N.J. 1982), 456–584.

33. On the connection between the Dreyfus Affair, Zionism, and the *Protocols,* see Pierre Nora, "1898. Le thème du complot et la définition de l'identité juive," in Taguieff, *Les Protocoles des Sages de Sion,* vol. 2, 457–74.

34. Ley, *Genozid und Heilserwartung,* 237–39; see also Saul Friedländer, *Nazi Germany and the Jews,* vol. 1: *The Years of Persecution, 1933–1939* (New York 1997), 73–112.

35. Wistrich, *Hitler's Apocalypse,* 30–47.

36. Robert N. Proctor, *Racial Hygiene. Medicine under the Nazis* (Cambridge, Mass. 1988), 131–76.

37. See Ben-Ami Shillony, *The Jews and the Japanese: The Successful Outsiders* (Rutland 1992) for a cultural contextualization of Japanese beliefs about Jewish power.

38. See Gil Seidel, *The Holocaust Denial: Antisemitism, Racism and the New Right* (London 1986).

39. An instructive analysis of the Soviet and post-Soviet Russian case can be found in William Korey, *Russian Antisemitism, Pamyat, and the Demonology of Zionism* (Chur 1995); Deborah Lipstadt, *Denying the Holocaust* (New York 1993).

40. See Ronald Nettler, *Past Trials and Present Tribulations. A Muslim Fundamentalist's View of the Jews* (Oxford 1987), and the essays on Arab and Islamic antisemitism in Robert Wistrich, ed., *Anti-Zionism and Antisemitism in the Contemporary World* (London 1990), 63–84, 102–20; also Bernard Lewis, *Semites and Antisemites* (New York 1986), and most recently, Daniel Pipes, *The Hidden Hand: Middle East Fears of Conspiracy* (New York 1997).

41. On the meaning of jihad and its relevance to contemporary Islamic perceptions of the Jewish and Christian "other," see Bat Ye'or, *Juifs et Chrétiens sous L'Islam. Les Dhimmis face au défi intégriste* (Paris 1994); also Rivka Yadlin, *An Arrogant, Oppressive Spirit. Anti-Zionism as Anti-Judaism in Egypt* (Oxford 1989) for a detailed analysis of the Egyptian case.

42. See Robert S. Wistrich, "Antisemitism in the New Europe," in *Der Umgang mit dem "Anderen." Juden, Frauen, Fremde...*, ed. Klaus Hödl (Vienna 1996), 31–47.

43. Exodus 22:20.

Part I

1

Demonizing the "Other"

Harumi Befu
Stanford University, California and Kyoto Bunkyo University, Japan

The literature on demons and demonization almost invariably and in the same breath makes references to "vampires," "devils," "satans," "witches," "sorcerers," and the like. Together they form a class of beings which threaten "good people." While occupying somewhat different semantic spaces, they also partially share the semantic domain as "demons." Thus "demons" are not always clearly distinguishable from other beings in this class.

When we examine the phenomena of demon and demonization cross-culturally, we immediately run into the problem of identifying the equivalents of demons in different cultures. Is a "demon" in England the same as one in New England, for instance? This problem is compounded when we cross linguistic boundaries. Is a "demon" in English the same as *"exotiká"* in Greek,[1] or *"yakṣa"*[2] or *"devata"*[3] in South Asia?

These are reasonable questions to which we have no neat answer. What we can say from the comparative standpoint is that having faith in the unity of humanity, similar phenomena, judiciously considered, may expose a fundamental commonality of human problems and their solutions. We posit that demons and demonization are part of a widespread, if not universal, human problem. They are simultaneously a means by which humans try to solve problems, misguided and incomplete though such a solution inevitably may be. For the time being, however, let us accept "demon" to mean beings which embody evil, i.e., immorality of various kinds.

Demonic Appearance

Demons as a concrete manifestation of immorality and evil typically assume an imaginary form, part-human, that arouses dread, fear, and horror. In the film, *Demon Lover,* the demon has two horns, fangs, fur all over the body, glittering red eyes, and claws on the fingers. On the island of Naxos in dreaded reptile. They are described as "dragon-like" or "beast-faced," and assume distinct names. *Gorgónes* is half woman and half fish; *Exotiká* may have animal legs or a fish's tail instead of legs. *Spanós,* on the other hand, is a man with no facial hair, a wily and treacherous character.[4]

In Japan demons *(oni)* assume a human form, but are equipped with pairs of fangs in the upper and lower jaws. Often monocular, they are either red-, black-, or blue-green-faced, and have one horn in the middle of the head or a pair of horns. They sometimes leave one huge footprint in snow or mud and subsisting on human blood and human children, they are capable of traveling eighty to ninety kilometers overnight. They are typically large and have extraordinary strength which no human can match.[5]

Demons also assume the forms of dreaded animals, ill-thought of in the local culture. But they are in part feared precisely because of their association with demons. In Greece, a demon often takes the form of a goat (especially female), a snake, a cow, a donkey, a cat, a hare, or a dog. Many of these modes of demonic manifestation share grotesque abnormality and animality as defined by the local culture. It is no wonder, then, that in the Middle Ages in Europe, many of those accused of *maleficia* were ugly or deformed, solitary eccentrics, or had a bad temper and a sharp tongue.[6] These are traits which, being beyond the pale of normalcy, placed these individuals at the symbolic margin of society, suspected of demonic activities.

Demons, on the other hand, may assume a form which totally conceals their evilness, representing the opposite of their heinous character. A Sarakatsanos has encountered a devil who appeared as an Orthodox priest in red robes. The devil often pretends to be an ordinary Sarakatsanos.[7] The heinousness of the demon lies precisely in its treachery, in the ability to disguise itself in an innocent or even a noble character.

The devil appearing in the form of a beautiful woman is a common sight in the demonological landscape of world ethnography. It was a major basis for the great European witch-hunt from the fifteenth to the seventeenth centuries.[8] *Nereids,* a form of female demon in Greece, are beautiful women, impeccable in behavior, good housekeepers, and extremely talented. In India, the female *Yakshini,* is portrayed in sculpture as beautiful, voluptuous, and erotic. Kapferer has argued that this phenomenon is closely related to the ritually rationalized notion of pollution and religiously justified sinfulness of women, which legitimizes the inferior cultural position that women occupy in many societies.[9]

This cultural construction of the demon as having a normal human façade but with evil intentions, allows a logic which enables inference from human appearances to a presumed hidden demonic character and from apparent demonic traits of a person to their presumed demonic substance. It is their ability to transfigure themselves from one form entirely into another and to totally deceive unsuspecting humans, which gives demons a power that is threatening and terrifying to humans.

A demon is not, therefore, a being with specific substance. Instead, it is an abstract entity—with evil will and intentions—which assumes a variety of forms and is capable of transforming itself from one being to another. In Stewart's words, the "abstract concept of evil represented by the Devil is mediated by the plethora of anthropomorphic or zoomorphic exotiká."[10] Herein lies the justification of Kapferer's proposal for the concept of "the demonic" as an attribute, instead of positing a concrete substantive being called "demon."[11]

Doers of Evil

The existence of the demonic is predicated on the definition of morality in the community. Looking at it from the flip side, "the monstrous is an appropriate subversion of whatever the society holds to be aesthetic. It entails an affront to the moral order—society's ideal of what is good, beautiful."[12] A demon is an icon for the bad and the evil of the world. Since evil forces are invisible, demons are a useful means for visualizing the inner obstacles and terrors that a person must overcome. Since demons are symbolized by aberrant behavior, this then becomes proof of the demon's existence.

Demonic manifestations, such as in witchcraft, are grounded in *individuals* who are under attack by demons, suffer mentally and physically, succumb to the Devil's temptations, and traffic with devils. Remedies, such as exorcism, are performed for the benefit of suffering individuals. The organic and psychological aspects of demonology should never be slighted in this process. Nonetheless, we shall focus on the *collective* side of the story, the demonic as a moral issue. If demonic manifestations in illness and suffering are signs of cosmic disorder, then it stands to reason that exorcist ceremonies "actively restore an order and occasion the restructuring of social and political relationships...."[13]

In Japan, demons mislead women, rob travellers on highways, cause crop failure, bring about diseases, and otherwise cause human sufferings of diverse sorts. In Greece, demons may cause disease and illness, leading people astray and causing them to sin. They provoke lewdness, shamelessness, greed, and envy. They stir up illusions, make people lethargic, and promote lies, pride, vanity, evil, idolatry, and covetousness. Demons defile; they delude and pollute. In Greece they can cause abnormal swelling of the penis and make men impotent. They can trick humans into death. *Exotiká* in Greece are blamed for miscarriages, infant mortality, for drying up a mother's milk.[14] In the form of wild exotic women *(nereids)*, they can seduce men, take their brains away, destroy their ability to reason.[15] *Strìngla* in Greece is said to drink the blood of children, eat their entrails, and kill their parents. A *nereid* can harm a woman who marries a man that the *nereid* wanted to marry. In Medieval Europe, witches were believed to kill babies, hence midwives were prime suspects since many newborn babies died in their hands, presumably aiding the witch's insatiable craving for very young flesh.[16]

Sutherland's following summary of the dimensions of evil or "disvalue" as embodied in *yakṣa* and other demons is informative[17]:

1. opposite of the good
2. illusion, delusion
3. impediment to performing ritual
4. abuse of power
5. disturbance of social hierarchies and relationships
6. suffering and frustration of life and death
7. otherness conceived of as enemy and threat.
8. obstacle to union with the gods.

The demonic is thus the anti-structure of the moral community.

Because demons are manifestations of evil and what is bad, in time of social dislocation, when the society is in flux, demons engage in intensified activity and social disruption. Demonic (= witchcraft) activities are thus "a symptom of a sick society."[18] The infamous Salem witch-hunt of 1692, according to Boyer and Nissenbaum, basically resulted from the impossibility of locating an unambiguous center of authority in a divided Salem, due to political, social, and religious strife and changes taking place in late seventeenth-century Salem in an era of upheaval.[19]

Witch-hunts and exorcism may be thus viewed as an attempt to restore homeostasis.[20] The witch-hunt in Orissa, India which Bailey analyzes so deftly, illustrates the homeostatic model. It began when a girl in Bisipara, Orissa, died and was divined to have been killed by *devata* who had possessed her. This devata was kept by a washerman who earned far more income than he should—for reasons I cannot go into here—thereby disturbing the social equilibrium—and more importantly—the moral order of the village. Identifying the washerman and accusing him of witchcraft were ways to restore the moral balance of the community, according to Bailey. "Morality triumphed," as he puts it.[21]

Structural Separation of Good and Evil: Spatial and Temporal

Good and evil are in constant struggle, in which the latter continually tries to make inroads into the good. In the Greek community of Sarakatsan shepherds, "God and the Devil fight a pitiless battle for the souls of men in which the three elements in the struggle are the grace of God, the cunning and subtlety of the Devil, and the will of man."[22] A community must therefore try diligently to prevent the erosion of "the space for the good" by setting up barriers. These barriers are a mode of spatial/temporal separation and ritual/symbolic segregation. The two are often combined. The transitional, temporal and spatial boundaries are interstices of order and disorder, a liminal zone. This liminal zone is dangerous. Sorcery is most potent, as is demonic attack generally, according to Kapferer, at the margins, during moments of transition or at points of hierarchical reordering, where the cosmic unity is momentarily out of joint.[23] Mary Douglas recognized structurally marginal areas as being prone to magical danger, and particularly to witchcraft.[24]

Demons, as a manifestation of ritual pollution, prefer to reside outside the ritually clean and purified community. It thus makes sense that a poster in Athens identifies the Jehovah's Witnesses in Brooklyn, New York, as a political organization of Jews.[25] Both Jehovah's Witnesses and the Jews are outside Greece, and can thus be safely identified as representing the demonic.

In February, throughout Japan to this day, at home and in religious edifices, one throws beans all around the premises while shouting "Happiness inside! Demons outside!" In addition to implying the incompatibility of happiness and demons, this expression defines the place of demons as *outside*. Inside, where people carry on their daily activities and where deities reside, demons are declared off limits.

Temporal separations are of three kinds: diurnal, annual, and life-cyclic. When a day is divided into day and night, and when day, with the sun shining, is defined as the zone in which "the good" presides, then night is necessarily the zone in which demons prowl. In the film, *Interview with a Vampire,* we find that vampires left in the sun are scorched to death. In the film *Demon Lover,* demons and vampires are only active at night.

The annual cycle is punctuated by both celebratory and dangerous times. The Japanese calendar indicates which days are auspicious, so that one may plan a wedding or other happy events without the fear of demonic intervention. Other days may be fraught with magical danger, when one must avoid certain activities: weddings must not be scheduled, for example. The throwing of beans in February to keep demons away from the home illustrates a division of the year in which demons make their appearance as winter leaves and spring comes.

Regarding life cycles, on Naxos island, it is believed that until an infant is baptized, it is vulnerable to evil influences. In addition, *exotiká* attacks are most prevalent on Naxos at the time of transition from unmarried to married status. In Japan, *yakudoshi*—"dangerous years" (thirty-three years of age for women, and forty-two for men)—requires rituals to ward off danger and assiduously to avoid conducting risky activities.[26] The time of death in many societies is also a dangerous period fraught with the possibilities of demonic visitation upon the living. In Greece and in Japan, unnatural deaths are believed to be brought on by demons and other evil spirits.

Structural separation is accomplished also by the creation of hierarchies (as in Indian and Sri Lankan cosmology), with the Buddha at the top and the demonic at the bottom or near the bottom of the hierarchy. Although, as we shall see, these designations of status are not rigidly fixed, the degree of orientation to the Buddha or to the demonic determines one's place in the hierarchy. The Buddha and those close to the Buddha are safely separated from demons.[27]

In making spatial demarcations between "inside" and "outside," it is well to note that "inside" can be the family, the village, the nation, or any kind of group, notably an ethnic group. That is, "inside" is not a fixed space, but a flexible unit which can enlarge or shrink, depending on the issue at stake or the location of the Other.

From the point of view of inhabitants of a community, demons reside outside their own in-group. However, in conceptualizing the worldview of inhabitants, demons must be regarded as an integral part of the cosmology, inasmuch as the good cannot exist without the bad, the moral without the immoral. The world is always made up of "us" and "them"—those who share a moral order and those who do not share it.

Those who bring about danger, trouble, or crisis to the community are of two categories: (1) those who are within the moral community but transgress its moral codes; (2) those outside the moral community who do not share the same moral order and thereby threaten the well-being of the community. As long as humans are imperfect, demons are a convenient explanatory component for this imperfect world, whether inside the community or outside.

The Dynamic Relation of Good and Evil

Good and Evil are not simply juxtaposed side by side. Instead, they are in a constant battle to claim and expand their respective spaces. In this struggle, however, the two adversaries are not equal. Rather, forces of good are basic and prior to forces of evil. The latter constitute an opposition that may sometimes sway people to its side. Diabolical influences of demons are manifested in illnesses and wicked actions. The good, with the aid of God, the Buddha, angels, saints, and gods, must constantly combat the influence of demons. As demons attempt to demonize humans, humans must make the effort to humanize demons.

At the same time, saints refine themselves through the direct, constant challenges by demons. Lust and death are primeval components of the demon *Māra,* and the Buddha is in constant battle with this demon.[28] The devil in the Sarakatsan community tempts villagers with ill-gotten material wealth and illicit sex.[29] Women, in this battle of good and evil, are regarded as agents of the Devil.[30] Among the Sarakatsani, envy is "inherent in the material world of limited resources and numerous contrary wills,"[31] and

> is the great triumph of the Devil; firstly, because it implies a whole complex of vices including enmity, greed, and deceit; and secondly, because...almost all Sarakatsani, in their pursuit of the elusive and competitive ends of prestige with its mixture of spiritual and material values, are necessarily involved in this form of sin.[32]

Demons serve as tests of morality for humans. By being able to resist demonic temptations and other influences, humans prove their fortitude and strengthen their moral fiber.

Demonic Gods and Deified Demons; Humanized Demons and Demonic Humans

Good and evil are not categorical entities clearly distinguished from one another; rather they are ends of a seamless continuum with infinite gradations from one extreme to the other. Stewart maps out the hierarchy of morality in a Greek village from God at the pinnacle, saints below Him, followed by humanity, below which is *exotiká,* and then the devil at the bottom.[33] As noted above, Kapferer, too, recognizes a hierarchy of beings in Sri Lankan Buddhism and Hinduism from buddhas and gods at the top to demons at the bottom, with gradations of beings in between, including humans.[34]

What is problematic in this seamless gradation is that demons do not stay evil, and gods and saints do not remain holy. In the Judeo-Christian tradition, while God is absolved from any fault, saints and angels can be faulted and become demons, as in the expression "a fallen angel." In Hinduism, too, demons and gods are sometimes interchangeable. In the village of Bisipara in Orissa, India, according to Bailey, the deities Shiva and Vishnu are considered *devata,* which he ambiguously "knew to be a divinity, demon, or spirit."[35] The Sinhalese Buddhist goddess called *Pattini,* too, has demonic manifestations.[36] But, says Kapferer, demons can be converted to Buddhism, that is, they can be humanized. If saints and gods can become demons, so too can humans. In Sri Lanka, Oddi Raja is a being of fragmentation and disorder, but he becomes a creature of order through his agreement to subordinate himself to the Buddha.[37]

Speaking of nereids, Stewart says: "For the most part, the nereids exhibit a licentiousness that exactly opposes the reserve and decorum that young maidens should ideally display. In other respects, however, the nereids closely resemble young women." Villagers readily accept them into their own community. "As brides, the nereids are an image of the culturally defined goal of young women."[38]

Regarding the Indian *yakṣa,* Sutherland comments that in some Vedic verses, "*Yakṣa* seems creaturely, animal-like and in others like a god.... The conjunction of the bestial and the celestial is a common motif in Hindu and other religious traditions...."[39] In India, *Yakṣa*'s demonic character is seen in the demon's "peculiar synthesis of vengefulness, sexuality and fecundity, secrecy and magic, the mysteries of birth and death, and the association with the ambiguous figure of the king." Indian guardian spirits are barely tamed demons whose powers of evil have been transformed into positive forces for good. "Fierceness, cruelty, and ugliness [of the *yakṣa*] can be transformed through devotion and consequently seen as vaguely beautiful, benignly powerful."[40] "The Buddhist *yakkha* was a metaphor for the human being gone astray.... the Buddhist *yakkha* was, on the one hand, more demonic but, on the other hand, closer to the human realm, since humans have more in common with demons than they do with gods."[41]

Thus the boundary between the malevolent, the demonic, and the benevolent, protective spirit is not a line but a murky sea, where good and bad commingle, where demons and humans exchange places, and where demons show redeeming features and humans unforgiven qualities. These examples indicate the capacity of the human imagination to turn fellow humans into demons and demons into humans. Herein lies a basis for the demonization of the Other and humanization of demons.

Relativity of the Moral Community

One notes that in these cases, it is the "immorality" of the human which causes the human to become a demon. But whose morality is being used as the standard? It is unquestionably the morality of self which is being used to judge the Other. But to the extent that morality is relative, the morality of one society may well be the immorality of another.

Thus, the morality derived from the Aryan myth in the Third Reich was total anathema to most other nations. This is to caution against privileging the morality of any society or nation as superior to others. Although we have spoken of the "moral community" and its demonized Other (from the perspective of the demonized Other), it might just as well be the moral community which is demonized and the demonized community moralized. This process of mutual demonization is a common practice between two hostile groups, such as the United States and the

Soviet Union during the Cold War. The United States and Japan, in their current trade war have been on the verge of demonizing each other.

Prophylactics against Demonic Power

Every society which acknowledges the existence of demons also provides prophylactic therapies to immunize its members from their effects. At the very least, one should conduct oneself properly and ethically to avoid giving demons opportunities to take advantage. Demons love to enter a person whose moral conduct is less than perfect and whose moral fiber is weak.

Demonic influence, however, can attack anyone, regardless of how they live. Demonology provides an explanation for demonic attacks and prescribes methods of averting them. There are activities, rituals, and symbols that provide effective prevention against demons. Going to holy places and places of worship regularly, receiving holy blessings, baptism and other rituals are all ways of warding off evil spirits and demonic influence. Carrying a cross or other sacred symbols, having a priest read an exorcism, and the recitation of scripture are also ways of preventing attacks by demons.

Dangerous spatial and temporal interstices—liminal zones of life—should be avoided as much as possible, but society also provides various means for resisting demonic attacks—including amulets, tablets, rosaries, the Bible, and the recitation of biblical passages, to name a few examples.

Rituals can transform the definition of the situation (i.e., the meaning of an event) or alternatively a phenomenon can go from being demonic to benign.[42] In monotheism, there is an important cosmic assumption that while the good does come in gradations, the supreme good can overpower the bad and any demonic forces, no matter how evil. This assumption implies that the opposite does not prevail. The worst evil cannot subdue the supreme good. In Christianity, Judaism, and Islam, God is immune from any demonic influence and is capable of subduing demons. So, too, is the Buddha; this bespeaks the ultimate triumph of good over evil.

Scapegoating as Demonization

A number of authors have warned against the danger of a facile use of scapegoating as an explanatory variable.[43] The following remarks, nonetheless, take scapegoating as one important perspective in understanding the demonization process.

Relegating evil doing to other humans-turned-demons has the consequence of exonerating humans from their wrongdoing, since the cause of such action is attributed to demons, who ultimately cause humans to do what humans would not do otherwise. If a woman has premarital sex in Greece, blame is placed on *exotiká:* a devil got inside her.[44] By pinning responsibility for inexplicable phenomena on demons, the world is made explainable and hence more livable. The demon is a scapegoat which allows the self to appear good by eliminating one's evil and transferring it to demons.

Demonization is a form of scapegoating in the extreme. This demonization may be the result of self-perception, of extreme guilt and/or perception of the Other as the source of extreme evil. Heightened hostility and ethnocentrism are often at the base of demonization.

Demonization

To demonize a human is to strip a person or a group of persons of moral pulchritude entirely, ascribing to them all immoral and evil attributes existing in society. Reducing a human to a subhuman or nonhuman demonic form is a drastic psychological process, often requiring special ideological justification. It is this reduction of humans to nonhuman beings which enables annihilation of the Other without guilt or remorse. For the Other to be eliminated is not only subhuman, but he or she is also evil. Annihilation of evil from this world is laudable, not sinful.

Herein lies the structure of the moral cosmology. Humans transfer their own moral weakness to demons—the Other—thereby nullifying any moral blame on themselves. The cultural construction of malevolent and maleficent demons allows scapegoating as a way of ignoring one's moral failings. Demonization is therefore a demonstration of human fallibility and of the inability to be morally strong and to deal honestly with one's own weakness.

In demonizing the innocent Other, immorality is further perpetrated by punishing or destroying the victim as if it were a morally justified action.[45] The demonized Others are not only depicted as a threatening enemy and violator of the fundamental values of one's community, they do not belong to humanity as defined by one's own moral standard.

An entity which is to be defined as "good" may include the self, family, village, nation, or ethnic group. By the same token, the Other to be demonized may be a person, family, nation, or ethnic group. The Other may be an *anonymous* Other, or it may consist of those towards whom one feels animosity or enmity, or it may be an innocent bystander.

I don't think so.

Relatives or friends about whom one feels positive emotions are unlikely candidates for demonization.

At the same time, at another more abstract level, as Raz argues so well, the Other is in reality a reflection of self.[46] It is, however, a reflection, not of the totality of self, but only of selected aspects. Raz quotes Gilman in this respect:

> The Other is invested with all the qualities of the "bad" or the "good." The "bad" Self, with its repressed sadistic impulses, becomes the "bad" Other; the "good" Self/object, with its infallible correctness, becomes the antithesis to the flawed image of the Self, the Self out of control. The "bad" Other becomes the negative stereotype. The former is that which we fear to become; the latter, that which we fear we cannot achieve.[47]

In the present context, the "bad" Other is the demon, and the positive "Other" is a god (or God in the Judeo-Christian context). That we have made God in our image is a common adage; but we have also made the demon in our image.

This Other is the Super Ego (in the Freudian meaning) at the individual level but it is also "the generalized other" in George Mead's sense—at the collective, societal level—but with the following difference: namely, the Super Ego and the "generalized other" are to be split into two dimensions of good and bad. We tend to associate the Super Ego with the embodiment of prescriptive, normative values, i.e., the good. However, the bad as a negation of the good points to it through its negation. To put it more concretely, a demon-fearing person is ipso facto a god- (or God-) fearing person.

The process of demonization is made all the easier because, as we have observed, in the cosmology of the world, gods, saints, angels, and humans can and already do assume demonic forms. For Greeks to demonize Turks and Jews and to label them *exotiká* is merely to extend the application of the available formula of demonization as it exists in the cosmology of the village community to other external enemies. For the Japanese during the Second World War to demonize the British and Americans is simply to apply the terminology available in their traditional folk cosmology to newly-found enemies.

A Greek poster mentioned previously demonizing the Jehovah's Witnesses and confounding the Jews with this sect should be quite understandable by now. Both Jehovah's Witnesses and Jews are outsiders, and as such are an easy prey for demonization. So are the Turks, who for the Greeks represent a perennial enemy. This status is recognized in the definition of *Arménides*, evil spirits which may appear in Turkish costume. Greeks also regard Americans as agents of the Turks. Thus, outsiders who do not share the same cultural and moral code, and at the same time are a political enemy or a competitor for economic resources, are targets of demonization.

At work in this kind of demonization process is a certain definition of normalcy, separating "normal," i.e., good people, from those who are not. One recalls the Nazi definition of perfect physical form, modeled after the Greek ideal. Nazi social policy involved reproduction of this ideal by mating Nordic blond men with Nordic blond women. The flip side of this policy was the categorical elimination and extermination of those who did not fit this ideal, which, as we all know, was systematically carried out against Jews and gypsies.

In the Pacific War, too, demonization of enemies was legion on both sides of the conflict. Ben-Ami Shillony has given us an excellent overview of the Allied demonization of the Japanese in this volume.[48] Equally vehement demonization of the Allies by the Japanese is elaborated upon in *War Without Mercy* by John Dower.[49]

Demonizing the "Other" is a powerful means of cleansing the community. Although good and evil are not engaged in a strict zero-sum game, where the evil within a community may increase or decrease in direct proportion to the exercise of the good, there is some correlation between the two. Demonization of the Other can displace evil from inside the community to the outside. It allows the community to solidify under the banner of "Hate the demonic enemy!" It preys on ethnocentrism, and if the nation is the Self, then demonizdemoning the "Other" appeals to group narcissism while reinforcing nationalist sentiments.

Notes

1. Even in Greece, different terms are used in different regions to refer to demonic phenomena, *exotiká* being only one of them. Charles Stewart, *Demons and the Devil: Moral Imagination in Modern Greek Culture* (Princeton: Princeton University Press, 1991); J. K. Campbell, *Honour, Family, and Patronage: A Study of Institutions and Moral Values in a Greek Community Village* (New York: Oxford University Press, 1974).

2. Stewart, *Demons and the Devil.*

3. F. G. Bailey, *The Witch-Hunt; Or, the Triumph of Morality* (Ithaca: Cornell University Press, 1994).

4. Stewart, *Demons and the Devil,* 253.

5. For further discussion on oni, see Ishibashi, Gaha, *Oni* (Demon) (Tokyo: Shōkabō, 1909); Akiko Baba, *Oni no Kenkyū* (Studies on demon) (Tokyo: San'ichi Shobō, 1971); Yoshihiro Kondō, *Nihon no Oni; Nihon Bunka Tankyū no Shikaku* (Japan's demons: A perspective for the search of Japanese culture) (Tokyo: Ōshōsha, 1966).

6. Norman Cohn, *Europe's Inner Demons: An Enquiry Inspired by the Great Witch Hunt* ([Sussex]: Sussex University Press, 1975), 149.

7. Campbell, *Honour, Family, and Patronage,* 332.

8. Cohn, *Europe's Inner Demons.*

9. Bruce Kapferer, *A Celebration of Demons: Exorcism and the Aesthetics of Healing in Sri Lanka* (Washington, DC: Smithsonian Institution, 1983), chapter 5.

10. Stewart, *Demons and the Devil,* 99.

11. Kapferer, *Celebration of Demons.*

12. Stewart, *Demons and the Devil,* 180.

13. Kapferer, *Celebration of Demons,* 90.

14. Stewart, *Demons and the Devil,* 174.

15. Ibid., 195.

16. Cohn, *Europe's Inner Demons,* 100.

17. Gail Hinich Sutherland, *The Disguises of the Demon: The Development of the Yakṣa in Hinduism and Buddhism* (Albany: SUNY Press, 1991), 158.

18. Mary Douglas, "Introduction," in *Witchcraft: Confessions and Accusations,* ed. M. Douglas (London: Tavistock, 1970), xxi.

19. Paul Boyer and Stephen Nissenbaum, *Salem Possessed: The Social Origin of Witchcraft* (Cambridge, MA: Harvard U Press, 1974); Joyce Bednarski, "The Salem Witch-Scare Viewed Sociologically," in *Witchcraft and Sorcery: Selected Readings,* ed. Max Marwick (Middlesex, England: Penguin, 1970), 151–63.

20. Douglas, "Introduction," xx–xxi.

21. Bailey, *Witch-Hunt,* 3, 205.

22. Campbell, *Honour, Family, and Patronage,* 335.

23. Bruce Kapferer, *Legends of People, Myths of State: Violence, Intolerance, and Political Culture in Sri Lanka and Australia* (Washington, D.C.: Smithsonian Institution, 1988), 106.

24. Mary Douglas, *Purity and Danger: An Analysis of the Concepts of Pollution and Taboo* (New York: Praeger, 1966), 101–103.

25. Stewart, *Demons and the Devil,* 79.

26. Edward Norbeck, "*Yakudoshi:* A Japanese Complex of Supernaturalistic Beliefs" *Southwestern Journal of Anthropology* 11: 105–20.

27. Kapferer, *Legends of People,* 105–106.

28. Sutherland, *Disguises of the Demon,* 3.

29. Campbell, *Honour, Family, and Patronage,* 336.

30. Ibid., 31.

31. Ibid., 340.

32. Ibid., 336.

33. Stewart, *Demons and the Devil,* 153.

34. Kapferer, *Legends of People,* 11.

35. Bailey, *Witch-Hunt,* 19.

36. Kapferer, *Legends of People,* 11.

.37. Ibid., 68.

38. Stewart, *Demons and the Devil,* 176.

39. Sutherland, *Disguises of the Demon,* 71.

40. Ibid., 163.

41. Ibid., 160.

42. Kapferer, *Legends of People,* 82; idem, *Celebration of Demons.*

43. Otto Dov Kulka, "Critique of Judaism in European Thought in the Modern Era. Genuine Factors and Demonic Perceptions" (Paper presented at the conference, "The 'Other' as Threat: Demonization and Antisemitism," The Hebrew University of Jerusalem, Israel, 12–15 June 1995).

44. Stewart, *Demons and the Devil,* 176.

45. Henri Zukier, "The Essential Other, the Jew, and the Western Mind." (Papers presented at the conference, "The 'Other' as Threat: Demonization and Antisemitism," The Hebrew University of Jerusalem, Israel, 12–15 June 1995).

46. Jacob Raz, *Aspects of Otherness in Japanese Culture,* Performance in Culture, no. 6, chapter 1 (Tokyo: Tokyo University of Foreign Studies, Institute for the Study of Languages and Cultures of Asia and Africa).

47. Sander L. Gilman, *Difference and Pathology: Stereotypes of Sexuality, Race, and Madness* (Ithaca: Cornell University Pres, 1985), 20.

48. Ben-Ami Shillony, "The Flourishing Demon: Japan in the Role of the Jew?" (Paper presented at the conference, "The 'Other' as Threat: Demonization and Antisemitism," The Hebrew University of Jerusalem, Israel, 12–15 June 1995).

49. John W. Dower, *War Without Mercy: Race and Power in the Pacific War* (New York: Pantheon, 1986).

2

Why Do Stereotypes Stick?

Yaacov Schul
The Hebrew University of Jerusalem
Henri Zukier
Graduate Faculty, New School for Social Research, New York

The continued existence of stereotypical beliefs that are devoid of truth may seem puzzling. After all, given the importance of accuracy in everyday life, how can people hold a set of beliefs that is totally incorrect and "obviously" inappropriate? Moreover, how can people act upon these beliefs, interact with the stereotyped person and behave as if the belief were true? At first glance it seems that the persistence of stereotypes is contrary to evolutionary principles. Inappropriate beliefs should disappear in the same way that unfit species do. Yet stereotypes thrive almost everywhere at the end of the twentieth century, and more often than not it seems that they are here to stay and even grow. We shall explore the reasons for the seemingly implausible persistence of stereotypes.

The question of the dynamics of stereotypes is, of course, not new, and many conceptions have been offered to explain it since the turn of the century.[1] The early conceptions can be classified into two broad categories: motivational accounts and socio-cultural accounts. We believe, however, that the early accounts are too simple and only give a partial view of the psychological processes involved.

Motivational explanations, particularly psychodynamic accounts like those of Bettelheim and Janowitz, find the origins of stereotyping in the hearts of people, in their emotional needs, frustrations, and fantasies.[2] The stereotyped person is largely a convenient prop for the expression of personal needs, and the stereotypical beliefs are likely to persist as long as the personal needs of the stereotype are active. According to this line of thought, since the stereotyped person is so useful to the stereotyper's emotional life, the latter is highly motivated to discard or distort any contradictory information.

not have powerful emotional needs; instead, they merely adopt the norms and customs prevalent in society, and simply conform to institutionalized forms of discrimination.[3]

Current psychological research has pointed to the limitations of these "classic" approaches, suggesting that stereotypes not only come from the heart or from other people, but also stem in crucial ways from the mind. We emphasize a motivational-cognitive perspective and consider stereotypes as an outgrowth of processes of ordinary thinking. Thus, in order to understand the puzzle of the persistence of stereotypes, we examine their formation and their similarities as well as differences from ordinary beliefs.

The Emergence of Stereotypes

To elucidate the nature of stereotypical beliefs and the reasons for their persistence, consider the following two beliefs:

1. Obese people are prone to heart attacks.
2. Obese people are (or tend to be) lazy.

Both beliefs are equivalent in the sense that they attribute a particular characteristic with high frequency to a class of people—in this case, a group defined by a physical rather than an ethnic attribute. Indeed, as with any natural-language category, as Rosch has argued, the classification of person-beliefs into those that are stereotypic and those that are not, cannot be governed by precise rules or clear-cut criteria.[4] Nevertheless, there are some subtle differences between the two beliefs and the different linguistic formulations reflect structural differences between the two types of beliefs. Thus, the first belief includes a notion about a within-group variation in it. "Obese people are prone to..." suggests that some will have heart attacks but others will not. The second belief implies a sweeping generalization. Although both provide information about group members, the first belief seems to be more factual in the sense that it is more easily falsifiable. There is also a sense in which the first belief is about heart attacks, while the second is about obese people. This is due, in part, to the fact that the linkage between obesity and heart attacks was generated by empirical data, whereas the linkage between obesity and laziness was not. Finally, although the first belief appears to be affectively neutral, the second conveys a devaluation of obese people.

These differences suggest that although stereotypic and nonstereotypic beliefs may not differ in terms of structural properties, the motivations behind each one are different. In the first case ("obese people are prone to heart attacks"), the individual seeks to understand the world and articulates an empirical relationship with few or no evaluative implications. The motivation behind the individual's action is the desire for accuracy.[5] In the second case ("obese people are lazy"), the individual appears to be more interested in saying something about obese people than about the empirical world. Moreover, the motivation behind this belief is a "will to believe," a desire to bolster a prior, private conviction. Stereotypic beliefs, once established, are driven primarily by "the will and affections," by the motivation for a desired conclusion.

We define a *stereotypical belief* as a belief about people that is 1) wholly derived from membership in a special group; 2) disregards the variability within the group; 3) is accompanied and sustained by negative affect. It should be noted that in spite of the negative affect toward the group that the definition requires, the stereotypic belief itself might be positive (as in the case of "Jews are shrewd businessmen"). Equally, although it is easy to think of examples of clear-cut stereotypic beliefs (e.g., "Jews have horns"), in many cases it may be difficult to determine whether a belief is stereotypic. This is because stereotypicality is not only an attribute of the belief, but also *an attribute of the way the belief is held.*

One of the potential consequences of stereotypical beliefs is a prejudicial action (or inaction) toward a person based on his group membership. For example, stereotypers may attempt to exclude those they have stereotyped from an ever-larger circle of life opportunities—from their circle of friends, their neighborhoods and clubs, or even from society as a whole—arguing that they have become "the internal enemy."

Stereotypical beliefs may also *follow from prejudicial action* rather than precede it.[6] For example, once a group is discriminated against, the discriminator may generate a system of beliefs in order to justify discrimination. Stereotypic beliefs, in this situation, serve to justify and support the exploitation of other people. Victims are never simply oppressed. The aggressor often feels psychologically compelled to depict the victims as deserving their lot. In this way, oppressors can both engage in reprehensible actions and preserve their self-esteem. Prejudicial action, then, may give rise to the beliefs that rationalize it.

Stereotypic beliefs may also be constructed to justify negative emotions toward a group, generated for many different and unrelated reasons. The individual may feel fear of and/or guilt toward the group or toward a person within it because they are being exploited by the individual's own group; the individual may have learned early in life that the group as a whole is negative in some fundamental respect (e.g., they killed Christ, they practice immoral sexual acts); the individual's group may be in a conflict with the other group and consequently experience negative feelings toward it; group members may have characteristics that give rise to negative affect (e.g., a handicapping illness). In such cases, people possess a negative attitude toward individuals prior to meeting them, independent of their subsequent stereotypes and for reasons they may not even be aware of. Still, the "free-floating" negative affect needs justification and the stereotypic beliefs may serve this purpose.

Stereotypic beliefs need not be held exclusively by the observers. Not infrequently, they are shared by the victims of these beliefs. For example, there is abundant evidence that many women believe (just as many men do) that women are unfit to handle high-level management positions, or that a woman's success at a difficult task is due to a combination of luck and ability. Yet the same achievement by a man would be entirely credited to his ability.[7] Another point worth noting is that stereotypic beliefs held by the victims may be used by them to justify the fate of the stereotyped group. While exploiters need to explain why they are justified in exploiting another person, those who are exploited need a way to make sense of their condition and explain to themselves why they are being exploited. By internalizing stereotypic beliefs, exploited individuals can impose a sense of order and coherence on the world at the expense of accuracy. This tendency is but one instance of a general principle in human cognition, which suggests that people strive for order, predictability, and control over the events in the world by explaining its more perturbing (and often arbitrary) occurrences with causal theories.[8]

By imposing a causal theory on the victims' plight, people maintain the illusion that bad things generally happen only to people who behave wrongly and that they may be spared misfortune if only they behave appropriately. Stereotypic beliefs, according to this view, are not merely arbitrary associative links that connect particular characteristics to random groups. Rather, stereotypic beliefs are part of mental structures containing assertions about causes and effects.[9] The cause-and-effect nature of these theories makes them more resistant to change.

The Persistence of Stereotypic Beliefs

While a few stereotypic beliefs involve external manifestations of their designated object (e.g., "Jews have horns"), more typically, they concern personality characteristics, characteristics that are hidden and often acccompanied by a potential to do harm. Those who are stigmatized are believed to be sly, lazy, or dishonest. Such characteristics are very functional to stereotypers because it is especially difficult to falsify them.[10]

In order to counter an allegation that he has an undesirable characteristic such as dishonesty or laziness, the victim not only needs to constantly display honesty and industriousness, but must show that this behavior is genuine, not merely an attempt to deceive the observer. This can boomerang when the effort to disprove false beliefs only leads to their reinforcement. For example, viewing a lazy person working hard and conscientiously, the stereotyper may infer that the worker is only acting this way because he or she is being observed. The chain of inferences, however, does not stop at this point. The stereotyper may ask himself (or herself) rhetorically why the worker needs to manipulate the impression. The simple answer is that the worker is actually lazy. As a result, the contrary evidence (industriousness) may be regarded as supporting the stereotypic belief about laziness. In trying "to hide" his undesirable characteristics, the worker has revealed that he is also dishonest. In other words, *stereotypic beliefs manufacture the evidence needed to support them!* Rather than being refuted by disconfirming evidence, they help generate evidence consistent with them, and thereby survive intact.

This is largely because the cognitive system has developed a set of structures and procedures designed to filter all incoming information, to select and interpret the stream of occurrences, whether intentionally or automatically. Consider a person afraid of snakes who is taking a walk in the woods. The person is likely to keep in mind the different snakes he "knows," their shapes, the sounds they generate, and their potential danger. The cognitive structures associated with snakes are highly activated during that time. Consequently, the slightest stimulation which even remotely resembles a snake is likely to attract his attention, and will be interpreted accordingly. Let us term the accessibility of a concept due to the fact that it is under consideration at the moment, *momentary accessibility.*[11] The example illustrates that cognitive structures that have high momentary accessibility may influence selection and interpretation of information, and in this way affect perception.

The accessibility of a construct does not depend only on what the perceiver actively considers at the time the stimulation is received. Cognitive structures differ in the strength of stimulation that is needed to activate them. One needs fairly strong stimulation to think about a white elephant, perhaps because elephants are not very useful in everyday life. One needs only the weakest stimulation in order to notice one's own name. The cognitive structure that corresponds to one's own name has high *chronic accessibility.* Chronic accessibility makes us ready to perceive stimulation that might be culturally important. Think about a Jew and a Chinese watching an array of symbols, one of which is a swastika. The Jew is likely to notice the swastika earlier than the Chinese. This effect would stem from the high accessibility accorded to the swastika symbol in twentieth century Jewish history.[12]

Cognitive structures that correspond to stereotyped groups tend to have high momentary and chronic accessibility. Often group members are salient because they carry or are made to carry cues that distinguish them from the others.[13] The salience is further enhanced because the basis of group classification typically involves some interest or utility to the observer and serves to support exploitation or to classify those who have and those who do not have access to a scarce resource. Such classifications are loaded with affect which, metaphorically, energizes the classification. The cognitive constructs corresponding to such "meaningful" group classification, therefore, have high chronic accessibility. Not only would these structures be activated by any signal of group membership, but the individuals often search for them purposely.

Because of the potential richness of actions, and because any action can be interpreted as corresponding either to a genuine intention, or to an intention to deceive, almost any behavior can be interpreted in line with a stereotype. Thus, regardless of how the stereotyped target responds, if the stereotyper looks for a particular interpretation of the information, he will find it. To quote Francis Bacon, "The human understanding when it has once adopted an opinion...draws all things else to support and agree with it. And though there be a greater number and weight of instances to be found on the other side, yet these it either neglects and despises, or else by some distinction sets aside and rejects" (aphorism 46).

Confirmation of stereotypes is also aided by a faulty process of inference-generation. Observers fail to weigh the power of the situation sufficiently in interpreting actions.[14] Often observers see others in a restricted range of situations. As a result, they have a biased sample of behavior patterns that might be limited by the external conditions and the type of contact between the observer and the individual observed. Ideally, observers should correct for these constraints in generalizing about the cross-situational dispositions of actors.

The fundamental attribution error may have grave consequences for inferences about members of the stereotyped group. Let us remember that stereotypes are often constructed by the dominant group to describe members of groups with a lower status. Contact between the two groups is limited, so that members of the stereotyped group are often observed by members of the dominant group under restricted conditions. For example, in the Middle Ages, authorities in Western Europe excluded Jews from most professions and virtually forced them into money-lending. Encounters with Jews, there-fore, often confused the person with the occupational role. If, as is often the case, the stereotypical belief links the stigmatized person to a less desirable role, then every encounter with a medieval Jew was likely to strengthen the prevailing image of a money-obsessed individual.

We have suggested that through selection, interpretation, and faulty generalization, stereotypic beliefs can be confirmed even when the evidence contradicts them. However, stereotypic beliefs may distort not only how the perceiver *sees* the stereotyped person but also influence the actual *behavior* of the stereotyped individual. Let us consider an individual who is about to meet a person whom he distrusts. The individual is likely to behave cautiously, trying to protect himself from acts of deception. The behavior of the individual, however, also provides cues for the other person. Having sensed that he or she is being mistrusted, that person may either confirm or disconfirm this distrust, depending, in part, on the power relationship between them.[15] When the behavior of the stereotyped person conforms to the stereotypic beliefs, it reinforces these beliefs even more. This is termed *behavioral,* as opposed to *perceptual* confirmation.[16]

Still, counter-stereotypic examples are often numerous and readily available. In spite of believing that women are not fit for high-level executive roles, one might observe a woman Prime Minister. In spite of believing that Jews are mean, one may find out that one's neighbor, a Jew, is a philanthropist. Ideally, encounters like these should mitigate stereotypic beliefs. If such beliefs were simple assertions about category membership (e.g., "Jews are cheap"), even a few counter-examples would be enough to disprove them, but this is rarely the case.

There are situations where people cannot dismiss contradictory information or dissociate the exception from the group. Typically, however, in such cases people are able to explain away the contradiction. Instead of modifying their belief about dispositions or negative potentials, people attempt to attribute contradictory behavior to factors specific to the situation: the stereotyper tries to explain why the particular case does not refute the rule. For example, how would an individual who believes that females are not capable of executive office explain the success of someone like Margaret Thatcher? It is true that there have been several female prime ministers, our stereotyper may contend, but these were not typical or "true" females. In fact, so the explanation goes, Ms. Thatcher was the "boss" at home. In other words, Ms. Thatcher is portrayed as an untypical female, having the characteristics of the "typical" male executive.

Such explanations can paradoxically bolster the stereotype in two important ways. Explanations of this kind often mix the evidence with conjectures and fabrications. However, once generated, the explanation can serve to increase belief in itself, especially when people fail to consider possible counter-explanations.[17] Often, because a story seems to fit so well, it is considered valid.

We argued earlier that stereotypic beliefs might differ from non-stereotypical beliefs in the motivational forces that drive them. The latter are often driven by the need for accuracy and truth. Stereotypic beliefs, by contrast, are motivated by other concerns, especially by a desire for *justification.* However, even when stereotyping individuals are motivated to test the accuracy of their stereotypic beliefs, they often fail. Unlike the external physical world, in which the observer has relatively little impact on the nature of observation, in the social world the beliefs of observers may influence what is being observed.

Contending with Stereotypes

Although awareness is not necessary for learning, it is often facilitated when learners become aware of their mistakes or biases and make some effort to correct them. However, the influence of stereotypical beliefs is often covert, making attempts to overcome them especially difficult. Banaji and Greenwald have distinguished two types of influence which stereotypes may have: *implicit* and *explicit.*

An implicit influence occurs when the stereotyper is not consciously aware of what they are doing at the time he or she processes the information about the stereotyped person. Imagine an individual who believes that whites are incompetent jazz musicians. This belief, as we noted, might influence the perception of an ambiguous performance. Given the same performance by a white and a non-white musician, the individual is likely to see more flaws in the performance of the white person, especially if the musician is not explicitly evaluated. This perception may color how the individual sees reality and lead to perceptual confirmation. As a result, the mental representation of the world will be more similar to the stereotypical beliefs than it would have been without the implicit stereotyping. Furthermore, the biased records of perception will be stored in memory, and are likely to be taken as evidence for the truth of the stereotypical beliefs.

It should be noted that implicit stereotyping may also happen to those who condemn stereotypic beliefs. The implicit impact of the stereotype occurs through a passive, uncontrolled process whether the perceiver likes it or not. The most striking example is when even the stereotyped individual adopts the beliefs of the stereotypers. Many such beliefs are learned almost incidentally at a relatively early age by all members of a given culture. As a result, implicit stereotyping can be quite pervasive and its impact can only be countered with great effort. If one is aware of potential biases in perception, one may try various strategies to overcome them. Differences between those who condone a stereotype and those who condemn it will emerge during these attempts at correction. People who believe in the validity of their stereotypic beliefs will not attempt to correct them and may even try to augment their impact by explicit stereotyping. Those who condemn stereotyping may on the other hand try to overcome its impact on perception. This might be termed explicit de-stereotyping. However, it should be noted that in order to de-stereotype, individuals must be aware that implicit stereotyping has been operating. More often than not, awareness of this process is lacking.

Attempts to correct implicit stereotyping require two preconditions—individuals must have a model of bias and some idea about its direction. When rendering judgments about a stereotyped person, one may become aware of a potential bias in perception. However, awareness is less likely when evaluation is not taking place. Moreover, the individual must also be motivated to overcome his bias and be willing to devote the necessary mental resources in time and capacity.

Accuracy of Stereotypes

One may object to our analysis by challenging the assumption that stereotypes are inaccurate. In fact, it has been argued that, although stereotypic beliefs are not true about all the people in a particular group, they are true about many of them. In other words, there is no smoke without fire, and there must be a kernel of truth in the stereotype.[18] Actually, sophisticated bigots are quite ingenious in eliciting evidence in support of their beliefs. They often strive to appear objective and rational in their attitudes and decisions.[19] But we must point out again that stereotypes do not "reflect" an existing reality; they create a new one out of whole cloth, and then use it as "evidence" in support of itself. Our discussion has suggested three ways in which stereotypical beliefs can "create" the actual behavior consistent with them.

For example, many of the beliefs associated with our stereotype of "Woman" concern her social functions, especially those of nourishment. It could be argued that in order to justify the role imposed on women, the dominant male group invented the stereotypic belief that women are nurturant by nature. The stereotypic beliefs would thereby serve to justify behaviors which then in turn is used to confirm the prior assumptions.

Moreover, once a stereotypic belief becomes widely accepted, society creates various situational constraints and barriers to channel the stereotyped person into behavior fitting these expectations. In such cases it becomes fairly difficult to break out of the vicious circle and to exhibit counter-stereotypic behavior. The cost associated with such a demonstration is often greater than their short-term benefit to the actor. As a result, counter-stereotypic actions will be taken only by those who are willing to sustain a high cost in order to obtain long-term benefits. Women breaking through the barriers of male-dominated professions often have to pay a high price.

Educational pressures may make counter-stereotypic behaviors even less likely. For example, there may be no formal barriers against female students who wish to study mathematics at college level. Still, the proportion of female students is much lower than that of males. This has often been cited to support the belief that females are not as capable as males in the mathematical domain. We do not know whether this is true or false. However, it should be noted that the educational system itself might be responsible for the dominance of males in this area, by shaping women so as to steer them away from the subject.[20] In short, society makes it difficult to engage in counter-stereotypic behavior.

The danger of stereotypic beliefs is not only in promoting claims about groups which are false. A still graver danger, we think, is the acceptance of inequality and exploitation as well as their justification by the dominant group. This can occur because stereotypes attribute phenomena generated by social and economic realities to personal potential and characteristics and completely neglect all other environmental forces.

As societies have become more aware of the nature and dynamics of prejudice, some have attempted to combat it through education, through changing the social norm of publicly acceptable discourse, or by other means. Success, however, has often been limited because one cannot change the stereotype without transforming the social conditions that support it. This has led to an alternative approach in psychology, and in some cases in public policy. In keeping with Festinger's theory of cognitive dissonance, the focus has shifted from trying to modify prejudiced attitudes and beliefs to attempts to modify behavior even by force of law or other means of coercion. Prejudicial behavior, unlike the stereotypes that justify it, is unambiguously public and detectable, and hence more easily controllable. Moreover, psychology suggests that eventually people's opinions and beliefs fall into line with their behavior. Prejudiced individuals do feel the need to justify their (admittedly forced) unprejudiced behavior. As we come to the close of this century, one of the most violent in history, the tenacity of stereotypes has once again become all too apparent and with it the urgent need to re-examine their impact and origins and to combat them one step at a time.

Bibliography.

Ajzen, I. (1977) Intuitive theories of events and the effects of base-rate information on prediction. *Journal of Personality and Social Psychology* 35: 303–14.

Allport, G. W. (1954) *The Nature of Prejudice*. Reading, Mass.: Addison-Wesley.

Anderson, C. A., and Sedikides, C. (1991) Thinking about people: Contributions of typological alternative to associationistic and dimensional models of person perception. *Journal of Personality and Social Psychology* 60: 203–17.

Bacon, F. (1620/1960) *The New Organon*, Book I. Indianapolis, IN: Bobbs-Merrill.

Banaji, M. R. and Greenwald, A. G. (1994) Implicit stereotyping and prejudice. In M. P. Zanna and J. M. Olson, eds., *The Psychology of Prejudice: The Ontario Symposium*, 7: 55–76. Hillsdale, N.J.: Erlbaum.

Bargh, J. A. and Tota, M. E. (1988) Context-dependent automatic processing in depression: Accessibility of negative constructs with regard to self but not others. *Journal of Personality and Social Psychology* 54: 925–39.

Bettelheim, B. and Janowitz, M. (1950) *The Dynamic of Prejudice*. New York: Harper and Row.

Bruner, J. (1957) On perceptual readiness. *Psychological Review* 64: 123–52.

Cantor, N. and Mischel, W. (1977) Traits as prototypes: Effects on recognition memory. *Journal of Personality and Social Psychology* 35: 38–48.

Darley, J. M., Fleming, J. H., Hilton, J. L. and Swann, W. B. (1988) Dispelling negative expectancies: The impact of interaction goals and target characteristics on the expectancy confirmation process. *Journal of Experimental Social Psychology* 24: 19–36.

Deaux K. (1985) Sex and gender. In M. R. Rosenzweig and L. W. Porter, eds., *Annual Review of Psychology* 36: 49–81. Palo Alto, Calif.: Annual Review.

Devine, P. G. (1989) Stereotypes and prejudice: Their automatic and controlled components. *Journal of Personality and Social Psychology* 56: 5–18.

Erdelyi, M. (1974) A new look at the new look: Perceptual defense and vigilance. *Psychological Review* 81.

Gidron, D., Koehler, D. J. and Tversky, A. (1993) Implicit quantification of personality traits. *Personality and Social Psychology Bulletin* 19: 594–604.

Ginosar, Z., and Trope, Y. (1980) The effects of base rates and individuating information on judgments about another person. *Journal of Experimental Social Psychology*.

Hamilton, D. L. and Trolier, T. K. (1986) Stereotypes and stereotyping: An overview of the cognitive approach. In J. Dovidio and S. L. Gaertner, eds. *Prejudice, Discrimination, and Racism: Theory and Research*. Orlando, Fla.: Academic Press, 127–63.

Helmreich, W. B. (1984) *The things they say behind your back*. New Brunswick, N.J.: Transaction books.

Jussim, L. (1990). Social reality and social problems: The role of expectancies. *Journal of Social Issues* 46: 9–34.

Kahneman, D. and Tversky, A. (1973) On the Psychology of prediction. *Psychological Review* 80: 237–51.

Katz, D. and Barly, K. (1935) Racial prejudice and racial stereotypes. *Journal of Abnormal and Social Psychology* 30: 175–93.

Koehler, D. J. (1991) Explanation, imagination, and confidence in judgment. *Psychological Bulletin* 110: 499–519.

Kunda, Z. (1990). The case for motivated reasoning. *Psychological Bulletin* 108: 480–98.

Langer, E. J. (1975) The illusion of control. *Journal of Personality and Social Psychology* 32: 311–28.

Lerner, M. (1980) *The Belief in a Just World: A Fundamental Decision*. New York: Plenum.

Lippmann, W. (1922) *Public Opinion*. New York: Harcourt Brace.

Lord, C. G., Lepper, M. R. and Mackie, D. (1984) Attitude prototypes as determinants of attitude-behavior consistency. *Journal of Personality and Social Psychology* 46: 1254–66.

McCauley, C., Stitt, C. L., and Segal, M. (1980) Stereotyping: From prejudice to prediction. *Psychological Bulletin* 87: 195–208.

Miller, D. T. and Turnball, W. (1986) Expectations and interpersonal processes. *Annual Review of Psychology* 37: 233–56.

Pettigrew, T. F. (1985) New black-white patterns: How best to conceptualize them? *Annual Review of Sociology* 11: 329–46

Renzetti, C. and Curran, D. (1992) Gender socialization. In J. A. Kourany, J. P. Sterba, and R. Tong, eds., *Feminist Philosophies*. Englewood Cliffs, N.J.: Prentice Hall, 31–42.

Rosch, E. (1975) Cognitive representations of semantic categories. *Journal of Experimental Psychology: General* 104: 192–233.

Ross, L. (1977) The intuitive psychologist and his shortcomings: Distortions in the attribution process. In L. Berkowitz, ed. *Advances in Experimental Social Psychology*, vol. 10. New York: Academic Press.

Rothbart, M. and John, O. P. (1985) Social categorization and behavioral episodes: A cognitive analysis of the effect of intergroup contact. *Journal of Social Issues* 41: 81–104.

Snyder, M. L., Tanke, E. D. and Bercheid, E. (1977) Social perception and interpersonal behavior: On the self fulfilling nature of social stereotypes. *Journal of Personality and Social Psychology* 35: 656–66.

Uleman, J. S.,and Moskowitz, G. B. (1994) Unintended effects of goals on unintended inferences. *Journal of Personality and Social Psychology* 66: 490–501.

Notes

1. Two important early contributions: W. Lippmann, *Public Opinion* (New York: Harcourt Brace, 1922). D. Katz and K. Barly, "Racial prejudice and racial stereotypes," *Journal of Abnormal and Social Psychology* 30 (1935): 175–93.

2. For example, B. Bettelheim and M. Janowitz, *The Dynamic of Prejudice* (New York: Harper and Row, 1950).

3. T. F. Pettigrew, "New black-white patterns: How best to conceptualize them?" *Annual Review of Sociology* 11 (1985): 329–46.

4. E. Rosch, "Cognitive representations of semantic categories," *Journal of Experimental Psychology: General* 104 (1975): 192–233.

5. Z. Kunda, "The case for motivated reasoning," *Psychological Bulletin* 108 (1990): 480–98.

6. O. Campbell, "Stereotypes and the perception of group differences," *American Psychologist* 22 (1967): 817–29.

7. For example, K. Deaux "Sex and gender, " in *Annual Review of Psychology*, vol. 36, eds. M. R. Rosenzweig and L. W. Porter (Palo Alto, Calif.: Annual Review, 1985): 49–81.

8. See examples in E. J. Langer, "The illusion of control," *Journal of Personality and Social Psychology* 32 (1975): 311–28; and M. Lerner, *The Belief in a Just World: A Fundamental Decision* (New York: Plenum, 1980).

9. C. A. Anderson, and C. Sedikides, "Thinking about people: Contributions of typological alternative to associationistic and dimensional models of person perception," *Journal of Personality and Social Psychology* 60 (1991): 203–17.

10. D. Gidron, D. J. Koehler and A. Tversky, "Implicit quantification of personality traits," *Personality and Social Psychology Bulletin* 19 (1985): 594–604; M. Rothbart and O. P. John, "Social categorization and behavioral episodes: A cognitive analysis of the effect of intergroup contact," *Journal of Social Issues* 41 (1985): 81–104.

11. Cf. J. A. Bargh and M. E. Tota, "Context-dependent automatic processing in depression: Accessibility of negative constructs with regard to self but not others," *Journal of Personality and Social Psychology* 54 (1988): 925–39.

12. Cf. M. Erdelyi, "A new look at the new look: Perceptual defense and vigilance," *Psychological Review* 81 (1974).

13. G. W. Allport, *The Nature of Prejudice* (Reading, Mass.: Addison-Wesley, 1954).

14. L. Ross, "The intuitive psychologist and his shortcomings: Distortions in the attribution process," in *Advances in Experimental Social Psychology*, ed. L. Berkowitz, vol. 10 (New York: Academic Press, 1977).

15. J. M. Darley, J. H. Fleming, J. L. Hilton and W. B. Swann, "Dispelling negative expectancies: The impact of interaction goals and target characteristics on the expectancy confirmation process," *Journal of Experimental Social Psychology* 24 (1988): 19–36.

16. D. T. Miller, and W. Turnball, "Expectations and interpersonal processes," *Annual Review of Psychology* 37 (1986): 233–56; M. L. Snyder, E. D. Tanke and E. Bercheid, "Social perception and interpersonal behavior: On the self fulfilling nature of social stereotypes," *Journal of Personality and Social Psychology* 35 (1977): 656–66.

17. D. J. Koehler, "Explanation, imagination, and confidence in judgment," *Psychological Bulletin* 110 (1991): 499–519.

18. L. Jussim, "Social reality and social problems: The role of expectancies," *Journal of Social Issues* 46 (1990): 9–34; C. McCauley, C. L. Stitt and M. Segal, "Stereotyping: From prejudice to prediction," *Psychological Bulletin* 87 (1980): 195–208.

19. Z. Kunda, "The case for motivated reasoning," *Psychological Bulletin* 108 (1990): 480–98; T. Pyszczynski and J. Greenberg, "Toward an integration of cognitive and motivational perspectives on social inference: a biased hypothesis-testing model," in *Advances in Experimental Social Psychology*, ed. L. Berkowitz, vol. 20, 297–340 (New York: Academic Press, 1987).

20. C. Renzetti and D. Curran, "Gender socialization," in *Feminist Philosophies*, eds. J. A. Kourany, J. P. Sterba, and R. Tong (Englewood Cliffs, N.J.: Prentice Hall, 1992), 31–42.

3

The Demonization of the "Other" in the Visual Arts*

Ziva Amishai-Maisels
The Hebrew University of Jerusalem

The depiction of the "other" in art is found in all cultures in a variety of ways, depending on how the dominant culture relates to "others" in general. However, the demonization of the "other"—its representation not only with different costumes or facial features, but as a subhuman being with evil overtones—occurs only in certain cultures at certain times. In this essay I seek to analyze the ways in which this demonization has become part of European art and why these stereotypes developed.

Two kinds of the "other" are demonized in art: the "external other" who belongs to a different culture or nation, and the "internal other", a member of a society who differs in race, religion, gender or social class from the dominant part of that society. These "others" have good qualities from which the dominant society can profit, and dangerous qualities from which it must be protected. In the process of demonization, a decision is made— consciously or not—to counter the attraction of the "other's" good qualities by making it frightening or repulsive. This creates clear differences between "us" and "them" and helps bring about "their" defeat, in feeling and in fact, through domination or extinction. As Timothy Long states:

> At the heart of this kind of prejudice lies the conviction that the outsider is in fact inferior to the insider, that he is not the same kind of being as the insider. It is essential that the insider adopt the Aristotelian position that the outsider is subhuman. This clears the way to destruction and grants the insider a natural moral superiority.[1]

The most ancient artistic methods used to stimulate this repulsion are the deformation of the "other" or its combination with animal parts to clarify the differences between such creatures and the "truly human." However, whereas almost all cultures have demons of this kind, this imagery is two-edged: hybrids and monsters awake not only repulsion but awe. They are manifestations of the *non*-human, but can as easily depict the *super*-human as the *sub*-human. Thus many tribal groups identified with totemic animals and combined them with humans in a positive sense, and many religions have gods who are part animal. Even modern Western religions have winged (i.e., part-bird) angels. Therefore, whether a given culture uses such imagery to depict the "other" depends on the implications such hybrids have for it, as well as on how it regards the "other"—whether there is a live and let live attitude or a sharp distinction between "us" and "them."

Most ancient cultures, such as Egypt and Mesopotamia, that believed in gods and/or demons who were portrayed with non-human features, restricted this type of representation to the supernatural. They depicted the human "other"—members of other nations, races, or religions—naturalistically, in the process teaching us a great deal about the costumes and racial composition of various groups.[2] This approach to the depiction of the "other" resulted from an utilitarian attitude: other groups were to be conquered and integrated into the dominant culture as tribute nations or slaves. They were thus different but not frightening. This approach developed in dictatorships which expanded from a fixed center outwards and never felt themselves to be a minority among strangers.

In Greece, however, although gods such as Zeus masqueraded as animals to conceal their identity and had animal symbols, they were human in shape. Whereas minor gods—e.g., Eros, Nike, and Nemesis— had wings, Hermes, a major deity, is depicted with wings only on his sandals or hat.[3] Distorted figures (Cyclops), those who were part bird (Harpies and Sirens), snake (Giants, Gorgons, and Erinyes), or animal (centaurs, satyrs, and Pan), were seen as monsters and awakened fear and repulsion. These creatures did not abide on Olympus, and they were considered sub- not super-human. Always on the brink of chaos, they endangered the innate rationality of Greek culture.[4]

Some of these hybrids were used in art from the Archaic period on to express the view that as a non-Greek, the "other" was only half-human. Although the half-animal quality of creatures such as the centaurs meant that they were especially atuned to nature (e.g., Chiron taught his instinctive wisdom to Achilles and Asklepios), such positive interaction is not used to depict the "other." Instead, at Foce del Sele, a Greek settlement in Italy, the temple of Hera was decorated with scenes of Greeks battling satyrs and centaurs, whose uncivilized behavior includes getting drunk, raping Greek women and destroying property. The Greeks, living on the border of an area dominated by the Etruscans, used these hybrids to warn against intermarriage or friendship with the natives: by representing them as half-human, they were shown to be beyond the pale.[5] This xenophobic approach resulted from the way Greece expanded its empire, establishing small colonies in foreign lands connected by sea. In such a case of "diaspora" mentality, the need to preserve Greek culture against foreign "contamination" was strongly felt.

However, this approach is also found on the west pediment of the Temple of Zeus at Olympia and in the metopes of the Parthenon in Athens, where the attempted rape of Lapith women by the centaurs [fig. 1] and their ensuing battle with the Lapiths is used as an allegory for the Persian-Greek wars: the centaurs represent the Persians, and the human Lapiths—the Greeks.[6] Here the Greeks reacted to attacks on mainland Greece by another high culture by symbolizing it as a barbarian "other." Both here and in Foce del Sele, the incentive is the perceived threat to Greek culture and the result is an animalization of the "other."

The Greeks did not use this symbolism for nations such as the Egyptians, Phoenecians, and Scythians, who did not pose a direct threat. Thus Scythian archers in the Greek police were simply portrayed in their specifying costumes.[7] Moreover, after Alexander conquered the Persians, there was no longer a need to animalize them: they are depicted naturalistically on Hellenistic monuments.[8] However, when Pergamon was invaded by the Gauls, the use of animalization was revived. Although the wars against the Gauls were at first commemorated by human representations of their defeat, in the Gigantomachia on the Pergamon Altar the gods symbolize the Pergamenes and the giants with serpent-bodies, the Gauls.[9]

Although Greek art showed little interest in "others" unless they impinged forcefully upon Greek life, it depicted blacks in a naturalistic manner close to that used in the Near East. The usual explanation is that blacks were so exotically different that it was unnecessary to animalize them. It should be added, however, that since the Greeks did not establish colonies in black Africa, blacks were not felt to be a threat. They were, in fact, at first depicted as allied warriors of Memnon, king of Ethiopia.[10] In the Hellenistic period, they were subject to the exaggeration accorded to members of the lower classes, but their beauty was also often stressed.[11]

Yet this is not the whole story. Greek archaic and classic vases juxtapose black and white heads to stress racial differences and the lack of classical beauty in negroid physiognomy.[12] At the same time, satyrs assume negroid facial features: small upturned noses, wide lips and tightly curled hair [fig. 2].[13] This was purposeful: in a sixth-century kantheros in the form of a black African head, a satyr with such features appears on the defining scene on the vase's neck [fig. 3].[14] In another kantharos, a black satyr's head is juxtaposed to that of a white woman.[15] This link was popular in the Greek colonies in Southern Italy from the late fifth century on: satyrs have negroid features and animal ears, a negress frolics with a satyr, and the exaggerated features of actors' masks in phylax scenes are often negroid, a point stressed with color on a fourth-century vase.[16]

The most revealing Greek representations of the "other" are those of the strange races who were *imagined* to reside beyond the realms of Greek habitation. From the *Odyssey* on, the Greeks were contrasted to the fantastic creatures they discover on their travels. This idea influenced historians: Herodotus in the fifth century and Ktesias and Megasthenes in the fourth century B.C.E. described inhabitants of far-off lands such as India as having two heads, six arms or one foot, a head in their stomachs, etc.[17] Not usually animal in form, these creatures have redistributed human body parts, so that they are humanoid but not human.[18] As Greek culture expanded and Greeks and Romans found, to their surprise, that they kept encountering humans of various races and cultures, not humanoid monsters, they constantly pushed the domicile of these creatures beyond their boundaries. Thus in the first century C.E., Pliny places them between Scythia and the Baltic region or in Africa, in and beyond the Libyan desert.[19] The adherence to such fantasies despite the facts indicates that they stemmed from deep psychological needs within Greek culture and not only from a delight in exercising the imagination, an attraction to the exotic or a fear of the unknown.[20] Taken in conjunction with the use of hybrids to symbolize near neighbors, these creations reinforce the idea of the Greeks' xenophobia and their need to see themselves as superior to all nations: to be Greek was not only to be human, but to be the *only* humans.[21]

Greek art also depicted a type of "other" who was human but engaged in "non-Greek" behavior. Thus the matriarchal Amazons refuse to marry and accept male domination.[22] Although they are described as burning off their right breast in order to shoot their bows more comfortably, this is not shown in art. Instead, they appear as beautiful young women who battle with, and are defeated by, the Greeks.[23] Although the Amazons' domicile, like that of the monstrous races, was constantly moved beyond the range of Greek civilization as it expanded, they were often depicted in Phrygian or Greek clothes, so that they seem part of the expanded Greek nation rather than a true "other."

This is also true of the Maenads, adherents of Dionysus who violated all norms of Greek behavior: in their drunken ecstasy, they danced wildly in savage nocturnal rites outside the city. They were said to have intercourse with satyrs, to hunt and tear animals and humans limb from limb and to devour them raw.[24] Whereas drinking wine at symposia was thought to benefit men, it turned women into murderesses and sexual deviants. They are often portrayed dancing with wild hair [fig. 4], wearing animal pelts on their dresses, handling snakes or brandishing animal or human body parts.[25] Unlike the Amazons, the Maenads actually existed: they were normal Greek women and priestesses who, during the short period of the Dionysian rites, indulged in excesses that were forbidden them in their highly restricted daily life.[26] Dionysius himself, though his mother was from Thebes, was considered a "stranger god" whose worship was said to have been imported from Lydia or Thrace to Greece. Thus the behavior of his Greek adherents was seen as expressing "otherness."[27]

It is important that Amazons and Maenads, *women* who act in ways not acceptable to Greek men, are not represented as hybrids or humanoids, but as *femmes fatales*. This may reflect not only a problem with independent Greek women within a strictly patriarchal society, but—since several heroes loved or married Amazons and Maenads were normal Greek women before and after the rites—a wish not to rule them out of the reckoning of humanity in the same way that foreign men were ruled out as appropriate mates for Greek women. Significantly, one of the oft-depicted norms broken by the Maenads is to frolic and have intercourse with satyrs who had been used to symbolize the forbidden foreign men.

All of these representations of the other in Greek art were determined by a similar mind-set: only Greeks were fully civilized and human. Room might be made for foreign women,[28] but other civilizations were not equally valid. Although the Greeks allowed foreign gods into their Pantheon, albeit in more "civilized" forms,[29] foreigners were tolerated only if they accepted Greek culture. This led both to the spread of this culture in a manner not common to previous dominant civilizations in the Mediterannean region, and to intense conflicts with religions such as Judaism, which had maintained its integrity under Egyptian, Philistine, Mesopotamian, and Persian domination, but was threatened with extinction for refusing to accept Greek gods.

The Romans did not adopt the Greeks' use of hybrids to symbolize their foes, and treated Gauls, Dacians, Parthians, and others naturalistically.[30] They were, however, fascinated by the monstrous races living beyond their realm and depicted them in wall paintings, mosaics, and illuminated manuscripts.[31] This lack of animalization of the other derived from the Roman perception of the hybrid as *super*-human, an approach that allowed them to adopt oriental religions with animal-headed gods.[32]

Italy's most important contribution to the iconography of demonization stems from fourth-century B.C.E. Etruscan depictions of demons in Hades. These demons were winged and either had the face of a bird of prey, the ears of an ass and snake-hair, or a human form with a sharply hooked beak-nose, blue coloring, and two small snakes projecting from their unkempt hair like horns [fig. 5].[33] The Romans applied the hooked nose and wild hair to satyrs and Pan [fig. 6], replacing the negroid features favored by the Greeks but maintaining their rationale of differentiating the satyrs' physiognomy from that of straight-nosed humans and gods.[34] However, the Romans, according to their portraits, often had prominent or hooked noses themselves and may have identified with this feature more than the Greeks did with snub noses.[35] Although they did not demonize real, as opposed to imaginary "others," they did follow the Greek model in persecuting groups who refused to accept their culture, such as Jews and Christians.

Unlike the Romans, Early Christianity relied on its powers of persuasion to convert people to its spiritual message and believed that all nations, women, members of the lower class, and slaves, would be equally worthy once they had accepted Christ. This attitude influenced the way Christianity reacted both to paganism and to early Christian disputes and heresies. Rather than exterminating opposing factions, they wrote tracts to convince them, exiled, or excommunicated them.[36] The situation began to change by the end of Constantine's reign: pagan statues were destroyed and pagan temples and synagogues burnt or converted into churches. This led to pogroms against pagans and Jews and, by the sixth century, to their forced baptism or expulsion.[37] However, despite Julian the Apostate, the Aryan and Monophysite controversies, schisms between the Eastern and Western churches, outbreaks of factional violence in which Christians killed each other and burnt churches, and the invasions of Northern tribes who were in due course converted, no attempt was made in art to demonize opponents.

On the contrary, most figures in Early Christian, early Byzantine, Carolingian, and Ottonian art are depicted with little national differentiation.[38] Even when they are differentiated–as when Melchizedek, the three Hebrews in the furnace, and the three Magi wear Eastern costumes[39]; Jews don phylacteries and prayershawls or have their heads covered[40]; or the Egyptian St. Menas is shown as a black and the Ashburnham Pentateuch adds blacks to portrayals of Biblical Egyptians[41]—the national, religious, or racial "other" is seen in a positive light. Even Lucifer and the monstrous races fared well. According to Origen, the devil was an intelligent being who had fallen, but could repent and be saved.[42] He is often winged and distinguished from ordinary angels only by being blue or purple, the colors of unenlightened night. Demons, such as those Christ expelled from the demoniac [Mark 5:1–20; Luke 8:25–40], were depicted as small angels or men, or as black shadows with unkempt hair like Pan. Both types recall demons common in Etruscan art as well as satyrs and shepherds in Roman wall paintings.[43] In like manner, Augustine postulated that if the monstrous races existed and were human, their condition must result from abnormal births, and they should be converted and saved.[44] Sixth century manuscripts seemingly made them as human as possible, despite their deformities.[45] Moreover, the fourth- to sixth-century Greek Acts of the Apostles which passed to Ireland before the tenth century, tell of dog-headed converts. The most famous, St. Christopher, appears with a dog's head in Eastern church art well into the seventeenth century.[46]

The change in the Christian conception of the "other" began in the ninth century simultaneously in the East and the West in response both to Iconoclasm and various eighth century heresies; and to Islam which had conquered the Near East to the borders of Constantinople in the mid-seventh century, and North Africa and most of Spain by 711. Besieged from within and without on theological and political levels, Christianity turned militant. Although the earlier iconography continued, a new approach evolved in the illustrations of two books which were used to promote mainline Christianity: the Psalter interpreted from a Christological perspective and Beatus' *Commentary on the Apocalypse.*

In the West, during the Carolingian renaissance which opened the Church and the Court to Greco-Roman influences, the *Utrecht Psalter* reflected Carolingian crusades against heretics and Islam by depicting idols and their destruction, while the many demons and pictures of Hell warn what will befall sinners. The connection between these themes is suggested by parallels between idols of the horned Pan holding a spear, and the satyr-like horns and tails of demons who pursue sinners with tridents and spears. Other demons have snake-hair like their Etruscan predecessors.[47]

The *Stuttgart Psalter,* strongly influenced by the Church, added Jews to the groups to be opposed. Since Charlemagne and Louis the Pious protected the Jews, they lived harmoniously with Christians and attracted many to Judaism, including those who had been converted by force. Agobart, archbishop of Lyons, constantly agitated against the Jews whom he called enemies of Christ, and incited mobs to attack them.[48] In the psalter, the dark winged demons have horns, claws, fiery breath, unruly hair and hooked noses [fig. 7], and these last two traits become characteristic of heretics and Jews [fig. 8].[49] Black figures with hooked noses or unruly hair who appear among the ungodly or in hell represent Moors.[50] Jews, heretics and Moors are depicted rejecting or persecuting Christ and the Church, and worshipping idols. To stress the connection of Jews to the devil, they are shown sacrificing their children to demons.[51]

This approach spread to Constantinople in the mid-ninth century, where the battle was against iconoclasts, Jews, and Muslims, since the latter two were blamed for inspiring Iconoclasm.[52] In the monastic psalters, these groups are portrayed in the same new ways as are devils: demons have unkempt hair like satyrs, and Satan either has a hooked nose [fig. 9] or resembles a fat Silenus with a short upturned nose.[53] Iconoclasts, who were seen as sorcerers and heretics inspired by demons, are depicted with the latter's unkempt hair or as monstrous blasphemers with enormous mouths and tongues.[54] The Jews have "demonic" faces—long or hooked noses, thick lips, and/or Silenus-like features—and are shown, as in the *Stuttgart Psalter,* rejecting, torturing, and crucifying Christ [fig. 10], worshipping idols, and sacrificing their children to demons [fig. 11]. In the *Khludov*

Psalter, where this imagery is pronounced, the Jews are further demonized as dog-headed men.[55] This stress on the Jews' diabolical nature reflects John Chrysostom's comment: "A demon abides in the soul of every Jew."[56] Muslims are represented in specific costumes, sometimes—as in the sale of Joseph to the Ishmaelites, who were considered ancestors of the Arabs—in Persian garb with slightly hooked noses.[57] Pagan idols and river gods, who had previously been rendered in a classical mode, are given horned hats to suggest that they are demonic forces unacceptable to Christianity.[58]

In these Eastern and Western psalters, certain bodily features—unkempt hair, horns, Silenus heads, hooked, upturned or long noses—are borrowed from depictions of devils to describe an enemy's demonic qualities and soon assume negative connotations on their own. These characteristics derive from Greek or Roman prototypes, and the multiple symbols chosen indicate an iconography in the process of formation. Yet there is an essential difference between these images and their classical sources. Greek art animalized the "other," making him *sub*-human. Ninth century Christian art began a process of *demonization* in which the enemy has both *sub-* and *super*-human overtones, and elicits fear as well as contempt. Moreover, as in the scenes of Jews slaughtering their children—which recall the blood libels against the Jews that began in Syria in 415 C.E.[59]—the enemy is portrayed as *in*human. These psalters created a Christian iconography of the "other" which penetrated into Christian consciousness long before the eleventh century, when persecution of the "other" became "part of the character of European society."[60]

This iconography did not last long in Byzantium. By the eleventh century, having totally defeated Iconoclasm, Byzantine art returned to the Early Christian approach, passing it on to Russian art. Thus the Eastern dress of the Magi, Daniel, and the three Hebrews in a furnace is preserved even when it is misunderstood and the Phrygian hat merges with the Jewish phylactery box.[61] Although there are remnants of an association with the devil in the unruly locks of hair that suggest horns peeking out from under the Jews' mantles in an eleventh century lectionary, they usually appear simply in typical costumes, their heads covered with striped shawls or "hats" which derive from their phylacteries.[62] Later, in Belorussia, Jews are depicted in "modern" dress: in the seventeenth century they wear tzitzith and turbans, and in the eighteenth—black clothes and brimmed hats.[63] These naturalistic representations of Jews in the intensely antisemitic realm of Tsarist Russia demonstrate that they are not seen as innately demonic: they can be saved through conversion to Christianity.[64]

Blacks in Eastern Church art are also treated naturalistically. They appear as attackers of Christianity, in the process of conversion, or as apostles of their new religion.[65] Since the Coptic church included many blacks, they appear in depictions of Egyptians. As Ishmael's mother was the Egyptian

Hagar, Ishmaelites may also be portrayed as black, and since Ishmael was seen as the father of the Arabs, this symbolism expanded to make blacks represent Islam in Pentecost scenes.[66]

In this atmosphere, devils continue to be human, although they are small, black and winged, their unruly hair now flame-like, and they sometimes have tails.[67] This image combines—with keen logic during classical renaissances—Etruscan demons and satyrs with the Erinyes, the Greek goddesses who punish evildoers.[68] In the Last Judgment, although the serpents surrounding the Devil become fierce, he and the Antichrist in his lap remain human.[69] These images are preserved in Russian icons through the seventeenth century. Horns and monstrous forms occur only when there has been strong influence from the West.[70]

In the West, the *Stuttgart Psalter*'s diabolization of the "other" was reinforced by another major polemic book, Beatus's *Commentary on the Apocalypse,* written ca. 776, around the time that Charlemagne launched his attack on the Muslims, some fifty years after they had conquered Spain. During this period, the minute territory of Christian Spain where Beatus lived was plagued by doctrinal disputes. Williams explains:

> The Apocalypse is primarily taken up with the struggle which will precede that day [of Judgment]. In a country unusually beset by doctrinal disputes, as Spain was in Beatus' lifetime, the Commentary offered a warning about, and a guarantee of victory over, threats to orthodoxy from within the Christian fold. At the same time, however, the struggle could be seen in terms of the battle against enemies outside the Church.... Inevitably,...the Muslims...came to be explicitly identified with the anti-Christian forces of the Apocalypse.... This kind of topical association of the malevolent forces of Revelation with the occupants of Andalucía gave the Beatus Commentary a renewed relevance for Spanish Christians. It was...the Book of the *Reconquista.*[71]

Tenth-century Beatus manuscripts are full of depictions of apocalyptic monsters and the devil has hairy legs and claws.[72] By 1047, in the *Beatus* of Fernando I, a leader of the reconquest, the devil's bestial quality was more fully developed, and soon his face became monstrous as well.[73] The meaning of such figures is suggested by tenth-century manuscripts in which the whore of Babylon sits beneath Muslim symbols, while heretics with unruly hair appear as Death on a pale horse in the eleventh century.[74] This symbolism inspired the sculptors of Santiago da Compostela, a church which became popular because St. James was believed to have aided the Reconquest.[75] In the the left-hand tympanum of the Puerta de las Platerias [fig. 12], finished ca. 1103, Christ is pushed aside and the main figures are devils with combined animal and human traits, who inhabit a city part of whose name is covered by the kneeling demon's single horn. The fact that those who listen to Christ's preaching seem to become more human, suggests that he is not only rejecting their temptation, but converting them. As in the manuscripts, these devils may symbolize the inner (heretical) and outer (Muslim and Jewish) "other."[76]

Islam was also represented in the West from the twelfth to the fifteenth century by black Moors, who were often rendered naturalistically: they combat Christians, play chess, form part of the Sultan's court or listen to Mohammed preaching.[77] The wish to convert Muslims, expressed in Byzantine Pentecost scenes, inspired Western artists to depict blacks as "possessed" men whom Christ cleanses of demons, as well as to portray their lives, conversion, and subsequent resurrection.[78] From the thirteenth century on, St. Maurice—originally portrayed as a Caucasian—appears as a black.[79] The wish to convert Eastern Muslims and blacks from India also led to their representation as one of the Magi coming from the East or as members of their cortège.[80] This positive approach also inspired depictions of the Queen of Sheba and the bride of the Song of Songs as beautiful black women.[81]

Another line of thought occurs in an eleventh-century *Beatus Apocalypse:* two grotesque black heads stick out their tongues above a depiction of Christ presenting the text to St. John [fig. 13], expressing the scorn Spaniards believed their Muslim neighbors had for Christianity.[82] From the start of the Crusades (1096)—which ideologically continue the Reconquest and were influenced by apocalyptic writings[83]—to the fifteenth century, artists developed this idea in different ways. Blacks with negroid features or diabolic hooked noses appear as demonic monsters, the King of Babylon and damned souls in Apocalypse illuminations,[84] as real or apocalyptic executioners and with or instead of Jews as tempters, tormentors of Christ, and worshippers of Antichrist.[85] In a late twelfth-century German manuscript, the artist who lived far from Muslims gave the black a Jew's hat, substituting a known for an unknown "other," and in the betrayal of Christ in a thirteenth-century English manuscript, the Romans are represented as blacks both with negroid features and with hooked noses and Jews' hats [fig. 14], thus representing the two contemporary groups who "betray" Christ–Muslims and Jews.[86]

As this imagery spread in the north, Jews often replaced Muslims as Apocalyptic evildoers. While continuing their role as Christ's torturers and deniers, from the thirteenth century on they also appear—identified by the Jew's hat—as Apocalyptic riders, false prophets, worshippers of Antichrist, and companions of the heretics in Hell. In such works, Antichrist, demons, apocalyptic killers, heretics, and Jews often have hooked noses [fig. 15].[87] This originally demonic feature became associated specifically with Jews by the thirteenth century, and has remained an accepted stereotype to this day.[88] Thus many depictions of Christ's Passion and other scenes of his life display hooked-nosed Jews, and the demonic meaning thus given the Jew is indicated by the thirteenth century drawing in the Forest Roll of Essex of a hooked-nosed Jew labeled "Aaron fil diaboli."[89]

The Beatus manuscripts also contributed to the new iconography of the devil that developed in Europe in the twelfth century.[90] Imagination ran riot in concocting novel forms: to the usual horns, claws, tails, flame-like hair and wings, were added monstrous or animal faces and fish, reptile, animal or corpse-like bodies, traits which were also given to the vices.[91] This imagery could be used to preach against any group's "evil enemy," including Jews, kings, bishops, burghers, and heretics.[92] It was popular in both Catholic and Protestant broadsheets during the religious wars of the sixteenth and seventeenth centuries [fig. 16].[93] The potency of this approach is seen in its continued use today in caricatures and works of popular art in which the enemy is given animal-like, monstrous or diabolical forms.[94] It was used to maximal damage during World War II: Jews were visually likened to lice and rats to dehumanize them and legitimize their slaughter, and the Japanese were called "Yellow Devils" and dehumanized in cartoons. This method is used today in Islamic anti-Western propaganda, ironically turning this Western mode of symbolization against its originators.[95]

As part of their identification of "enemies" with the devil, medieval artists often turned idols in scenes of idol worship into devils, as had been suggested in the *Utrecht Psalter,* where demons resemble statues of the horned Pan.[96] This imagery could be used to attack any "lapse of faith," from the practices of heretical cults to those of other monastic orders, classes or people out of favor.[97] Moreover, all non-Christians by definition were seen as idol worshippers whether they had idols or not.[98] Thus as Jews had been portrayed in ninth-century psalters *sinning* by worshipping idols and sacrificing Jewish children to Moloch [fig. 11], the practice of Judaism became equated with idol worship and in the fifteenth century Jews were shown sacrificing Christian children to the devil. A thirteenth-century Bible Moralisée portrayal of the devil directing Jews to circumcise a child held by a tonsured priest can also be read as the devil ordering Jews to kill a Christian child.[99] Muslims too were depicted worshipping and sacrificing children to idols who are often human-headed animals [fig. 17].[100] From the fifteenth century on, Jews were also shown cavorting with the devil in depictions of the *Judensau* [fig. 18].[101] Worshippers of idols soon assumed the guise of their gods: Mohammed and Saladin become animal-headed preachers, and the Jews not only worship the devil, but *are* devils.[102]

This approach led to a strange phenomenon: Moses, David and the Jews developed horns. Whereas Moses' horns derived in the eleventh century from Jerome's purposeful mistranslation of Exodus 34: 29 which states that the skin of Moses' face radiated light, the biblical sources of David's horn reveal the origins of this imagery and its meaning.[103]

1. Deidameia and Eurytion, detail of the West Pediment of the Temple of Zeus, Olympia, c. 460 B.C.E. Courtesy of the Olympia Archaelogical Museum.

2. Head of a Satyr, detail from a krater from Bari, fourth century B.C.E. Courtesy of the Department Classical & Near Eastern Antiquities National Museum, Copenhagen.

4. Polygnotos Painter, Maenads in Orgiastic Dance, krater, c. 440–430 B.C.E. Museo Nazionale Archeologico di Spina, Ferrara.

3. Kantharos in the shape of a Negro head, Black-figure head vase, c. 530 B.C.E. H: 0.177 m. Henry Lillie Pierce Fund, Courtesy, Museum of Fine Arts, Boston.

5. Painter of the Vanth group, Charon and the dragon, amphora, end fourth century B.C.E. Museo Faina, Orvieto.

6. Head of the God Pan, detail of a mosaic pavement from Genezzano, third-fourth century C.E. Courtesy of the Museo Nazionale Romano, Rome.

7. Sick and afflicated souls being rescued from the devil, detail of fol. 16v of the *Stuttgart Psalter*, early ninth century. Courtesy of the Württembergische Landesbibliothek, Stuttgart, Cod. bibl. fol. 23.

8. The Flagellation of Christ, from Psalms 34: 15, detail of fol. 34v of the *Stuttgart Psalter*, early ninth century. Courtesy of the Württembergische Landesbibliothek, Stuttgart, Cod. bibl. fol. 23.

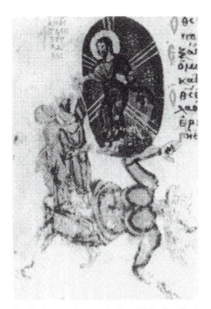

9. Christ rescuing souls from Hell, detail of fol. 63v of the *Khludov Psalter*, illustrating Psalm 67:7, mid-ninth century. Courtesy of the State Historical Museum, Moscow.

10. Arrest of Christ and Jews disputing with Christ, detail of fol. 54v from the *Khludov Psalter,* mid-ninth century. Courtesy of the State Historical Museum, Moscow.

11. Israelites sacrificing their children to Moloch, detail of fol. 109v from the *Khludov Psalter,* mid-ninth century. Courtesy of the State Historical Museum, Moscow.

12. Tympanum of the Puerta de las Platerias, c. 1103, Cathedral of Santiago de Compostela.

13. Christ delivering the Apocalypse to St.
John, detail of fol. 4v of the *Beatus of St.
Sever*, 1028–1072. Courtesy of the
Bibliothèque Nationale, Paris. Ms. Lat 8878.

14. Betrayal and arrest of Christ, fol. 150v from
the *Chichester Psalter*, c. 1250. John Rylands
University Library Ms. Lat. 24. Reproduced by
courtesy of the Director and University
Librarian, the John Rylands University Library
of Manchester.

15. The Beast grabs the Witnesses before the enthroned Antichrist, fol. 17r
from an English Apocalypse, c. 1245–1255. Courtesy of the Bibliothèque
Nationale, Paris. Ms. fr. 403.

17. Child Sacrifice to Mohammed, detail of fol. 185r of the Duc de Berry's *Livre des Merveilles du Monde*, c. 1413. Courtesy of the Bibliothèque Nationale, Paris. Ms. fr. 2810.

16. Pope Alexander VI as the Devil Unmasked, woodcut with trick fold, second position, sixteenth century. © The British Museum, reprinted by permission.

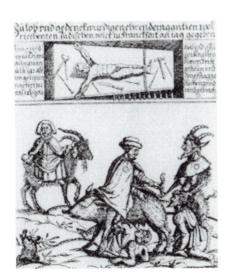

18. The Frankfurt Judensau, broadsheet, Frankfurt, early eighteenth century.

19. Samuel anointing David, detail of fol. 79r of the *Khludov Psalter*, mid-ninth century. Courtesy of the State Historical Museum, Moscow.

21. David being anointed by Samuel and crowned by Humility, detail of fol. 6v from a mid-thirteenth century manuscript. Courtesy of the Bayerische Staatsbibliothek, Munich. clml. 17403.

20. The destruction of the horns of the wicked, detail of fol. 74r of the *Khludov Psalter*, mid-ninth century. Courtesy of the State Historical Museum, Moscow.

22. The Exodus, Moses receiving the Law and the Worship of the Golden Calf, detail of fol. 16r of *Cursus Sanctae Mariae*, 1215. Courtesy of the Pierpont Morgan Libary, New York. M. 739, f. 16 (det.). Ms. 739.

23. Wantons with devil lovers, part of the archivolts of a doorway, c. 1120, Ste. Croix, Bordeaux.

24. Salome's Dance, detail of page from the *Aachen Gospels of Otto III*, 983–1002. Aachen, Cathedral Treasury.

25. Hans Baldung Grien, *Witches Sabbath*, 1510, woodcut, Private Collection.

26. Edvard Munch, *The Vampire*, 1900, lithograph.

27. The Monstrous Races, woodcut illustration from C. van Megenberg, *Buch der Natur*, Germany, 1475, fol. 284v.

28. Wild Man, detail of fol. 70 from the *Luttrell Psalter*, 1335. By permission of The British Library, London. Ms. Add. 42130.

In Jewish and early Byzantine art, Samuel anoints David out of the narrow end of the horn,[104] but in ninth century psalters, the horn is turned upside down on his head so that he appears to have a single horn [fig. 19]. The ways this new scheme was used elucidate its meaning. In the *Stuttgart Psalter,* God anoints David and Aaron with an inverted horn whose wide mouth tends to cover their heads.[105] These pictures conflate textual descriptions of anointing with nearby passages. David's anointing (fol. 104r) illustrates Psalms 89: 21–22, which is preceded by verse 18: "You will raise our [the Israelites] horn," and followed by verse 25: "Through My name will his [David's] horn be raised."[106] Aaron's anointing (fol. 149v) illustrates Psalms 133: 2 closely following Psalms 132: 17, which can be literally translated: "There I will cause David to grow a horn."[107] The term "horn" is used in these Psalms figuratively to mean strength and power, but it is depicted literally in the psalter, conflated with the horn of anointing.

This conflated meaning reappears in the *Khludov Psalter,* where Samuel twice anoints David by placing a horn on his head.[108] Whereas on fol. 89r, this motif illustrates Psalm 89 as in the *Stuttgart Psalter,* its use on fol. 79r and the placement of the horn there directly on David's head with no space between them [fig. 19] adds new meaning. This is one of a group of interrelated images illustrating Psalms 78–79, which deal with God's choice of David and Jerusalem and with that city's destruction. The illustrations interpret the text as referring to Christian Jerusalem and its conquest by the Muslims, symbolized by the ruler in a high hat directing the slaughter below.[109] David "receives his horn" between images of the holy city and its destruction, suggesting a causal relationship. The artist's understanding of this image is clarified by the way he had just illustrated Psalms 75: 11 which describes the "horns" (might) of the wicked being cut off: on fol. 74r, he portrays the literal horns of the wicked being bloodily hacked off [fig. 20]. Such a literal interpretation of the raising of the "horn" of David and of the people of Israel led to the belief that both David and the Jews had at least one horn. Thus these psalter illustrations develop one way in which Jews would be demonized from then on.

This imagery soon disappeared from Byzantine art: later psalters return to depicting the horn used to anoint David as being held narrow end down.[110] In the West, twelfth- and thirteenth-century German artists, conscious of the new motif's meaning, felt a need to reinterpret David's election to kingship so as not to demonize Christ's ancestor: Samuel seems to be removing David's horn, while Humility sets a crown on his head. In the thirteenth century version, the horn is an elongated version of the traditional Jew's hat [fig. 21].[111]

In fact, the literal understanding of horns in the Psalter inspired the horned hat *(pileum cornutum)* that Jews were forced to wear from the thirteenth century on. It too began to appear in art in the ninth century and is visually derived from late versions of the Magi's hats and from the Phrygian caps worn by deniers of Christ in the *Stuttgart Psalter*.[112] These hats vary in form but have one thing in common: a single point or hump which simultaneously covers and calls attention to the horn the Jew was believed to have [figs. 14–15, 22].[113] That these hats denote an identification with the devil is shown in thirteenth century illuminations in which there is no clear differentiation between a demon's single horn and pointed hats.[114] By revealing the horn the Jews skillfully hide, these pointed hats acted as a mark of Cain. The latter was itself sometimes interpreted as a horn since Cain was thought to be the son of the devil or to consort with him. He and his descendants often have horns or wear Jews' hats.[115] Such hats are depicted well into the sixteenth century, when they may no longer have been worn.[116]

In view of this tradition, Moses' horns, which were very popular from the twelfth century on, would have been read as negative symbols that turn him into a satanic figure.[117] This image originated simultaneously in two forms. The single-horned Moses who appears in early eleventh- and twelfth-century German manuscripts and in a twelfth-century Spanish sculpture is clearly connected to the imagery discussed above.[118] The double-horned Moses is closer to accepted images of the devil, and the way his horns grow—out of his head, cheeks or just below his pointed Jews' hat—has clear parallels in the horns of the hooked-nosed demons in the early twelfth-century *Oxford Apocalypse*.[119] In thirteenth-century Bible Moralisées both the devil and the men he directs have horns identical to those of Moses. In other manuscripts Moses' horns parallel those of the golden calf [fig. 22] or he is depicted as a horned idol.[120] From the thirteenth century on, Moses has horns already as an infant, indicating that his demonic quality—like that of the Jews—is inborn.[121]

Western Christianity's total rejection of the Jews led artists to give their pointed hat to the Patriarchs, the Prophets, Jesse the father of David, Joachim the father of Mary, and her husband Joseph.[122] Clearly there is no difference between good and bad Jews—they are all horned like the devil. This approach differs from Christian ambivalence towards Muslims who were not "Christ-killers." One reason for this difference—the Jews' refusal to convert—was expressed by Peter the Venerable in 1146:

> If the Saracens are to be detested...how much more are the Jews to be execrated and hated who, utterly insensible to Christ and the Christian faith, reject, blaspheme, and ridicule the virgin birth and all the sacraments of human redemption?[123]

Emile Mâle connected the proliferation of devils in the twelfth century to a different "other": women who tempted monks in erotic visions. He saw the monastery as an "entrenched camp besieged by the enemy," an apt metaphor after reforms stiffened monastic rules.[124] To help monks withstand temptation, women were depicted as Luxuria or as wantons. Both images often have wild hair and snakes or toads suckling at their breasts [fig. 23]. Their demonic origin, stated in the proverb "It takes the help of a devil to make a woman," was illustrated on a fifteenth-century French misericorde.[125] However, in medieval art, St. Anthony and Theophilus are tempted by demons, not women.[126]

It was Salome who epitomized evil sensuality for medieval man since her lascivious dance led to the death of John the Baptist. In the fifth century, Petrus Chrysologus described her dance in animalistic terms based on depictions of Maenads [fig. 4]:

> She moves like a tiger, not a woman;... she shakes her mane, not human hair; she bows and stretches her body; she grows with increasing fury, rising over the mass of men in her horribleness.... A serpent was hidden in this woman, whose unholy gift overflowed her whole body and dominated the guests, so that their bodies and souls thrilled madly; she turned them into beasts who longed to eat human flesh and drink human blood.[127]

The earliest extant depiction of Salome's dance dates from the early ninth century, during which many images of the demonic "other" were developed.[128] At the end of the tenth century, she dances like a Maenad, half-nude with wild hair [fig. 24]; by the eleventh, when the story became popular, she performs acrobatics, pliant as a snake. In a twelfth-century poem, her dance is compared to that of a bacchante, and in the fourteenth century in San Marco in Venice, she dances with the Baptist's head like a Maenad dancing with the head of Pentheus.[129] Another twelfth-century poem describes her "innocent" decadence: in love with the Baptist, she kisses his lips when his head is delivered to her. To expose her demonic nature, contemporary depictions set Satan behind her and the Baptist's execution or the bringing of his head to her nearby.[130] This presentation began to change in the fifteenth century. Salome's dance was moved into the background or eliminated, and she is posed watching St. John's execution or holding his head to stress that she is a femme fatale.[131]

Fifteenth and sixteenth-century artists were also interested in other deadly women: Judith, who had personified virtue, became a femme fatale, Eve turned into a sensual seductress, and the snake became a semi-nude Lilith. Even St. Anthony's demons were replaced by diabolical women.[132] At this time witches entered the realm of art, replacing the magician Simon Magus who had once symbolized the heretic.[133]

From the thirteenth century on, the Church increasingly used accusations of witchcraft against heretics, scientists, Jews, and politically problematic figures (e.g., Joan of Arc), regardless of sex. However, from the late fifteenth century on, books on witchcraft stated that women were more inclined to sorcery than men as they were impressionable and had erotic malice.[134] Although men and women can be shown worshipping Satan and depictions of sorcerers continue,[135] most artists from Dürer to Callot preferred to portray erotic witches [fig. 25].[136] Dürer also drew Maenads and women sporting with satyrs and other hybrids.[137] In fact, witches are the Christian version of the Maenads: they break all norms of behavior, dance and cohabit with satyr-like devils, and sacrifice their children to Satan. However, unlike the Maenads, they did not return to normalcy having rid themselves of their aggressions, but were burnt at the stake by a society which both feared and was attracted to the release of such urges during a period in which the church was riven by strife and secular culture was on the ascendant.

A similar feeling of crisis was caused at the beginning of the modern period by political revolutions and the emergence of a women's rights movement. From 1798 on, Goya depicted devil worship in a frightening rather than an erotic guise.[138] In the mid-nineteenth century, the Amazon was resurrected in Bachofen's theory on early matriarchal societies, and cartoons depicted "bloomer girls" assuming male roles while men care for the home.[139] The tension between the sexes led artists to stress female "otherness", and finally to demonize them. Whereas in the first half of the nineteenth century, women were shown as victims of male violence, in the second half, as the women's liberation movement spread, they were depicted as erotic monsters, emasculating and killing men [fig. 26].[140]

As women succeeded in their struggle for equality, the European need to demonize the "other" focused on old demonic images of Jews and blacks, and on the monsters of modern technological civilization. The demonization of these new groups had its source in the Greek concept of monstrous races who live beyond the limits of civilization. These creatures remained popular in medieval Greek, Latin and Arabic encyclopedias and "scientific" books [fig. 27].[141] As in Early Christian times, they appear in twelfth century scenes of the Mission to the Apostles as redeemable peoples, thus expressing the Crusaders' zeal to convert everyone to Christianity.[142] However, from the eleventh to the fourteenth centuries they also appear as moral allegories for the virtues and vices, and their physical deformity is often seen to reflect moral depravity.[143] Several of these races were said to be cannibalistic, the cursed children of Cain or Ham, or the outcome of couplings with the devil or with animals.[144] Since on medieval maps Jerusalem is the center of the world, their habitation of the ends of the earth was seen as expressing their distance from salvation.[145] The monstrous races thus became images of evil, who lend their characteristics to demons and are portrayed worshipping Antichrist.[146]

From the thirteenth century on, these creatures influenced the image of the "wild men" with hairy clothes or bodies who walk erect or on all fours, live in the woods and share many features with satyrs [fig. 28]. The wild men may have been based on the "Tafurs" who took part in the Crusades, or on poor social misfits who lived in the woods. For civilized Europeans, this image embodied a freedom from confining laws and an indulgence in natural appetites which did not reach the dangerous pitch exemplified by witches.[147] Wild men became especially popular in the fifteenth century: they could be shown fighting with civilized men and devouring children, or living quietly with their families in the woods, converting to Christianity, and becoming saints.[148] The idea that they were "noble savages" became increasingly popular due to greater contact with China, whose people were regarded as wise and peaceful.[149]

Slowly, the wild man was replaced by the American Indian, the black African and the Polynesian "discovered" by European explorers. However, existing attitudes to the wild man colored the way these tribes were perceived and depicted. They too were seen as attacking and devouring white men, or living in harmony with nature and converting to Christianity, while their women became objects of erotic fantasy. Only rarely did artists document their true nature and refrain from fitting them into prepared categories of the demonic "other" or the noble savage.[150]

Belief in the monstrous races lasted into the seventeenth century despite the scientific exploration of the world. Pilgrims and explorers—primed to find such races by fictional travel books—reported having seen them.[151] Although they were discredited in the eighteenth and nineteenth centuries, their impact on Western culture survives: depictions of these races seem like sketches for *Star Trek*. Like the monstrous races, space creatures can be good or evil: they can be wise, with superhuman traits such as telepathy, or they can be dangerous and deceitful, interested in conquering or killing humans. Once again, as in Hellenistic and Roman times, they have simply been moved to new realms, just hovering beyond man's reach.

In conclusion, cultures demonize "others" in art under conditions of insecurity which turn them ethnocentrically and xenophobically inwards in self-defense and militantly outwards to expand their boundaries. This art is both an expression of a mindset and a way of inculcating it: the appearance of demonic "others" in art "proves" their existence to the public. The Greeks initiated the depiction of the demonic other from the archaic period on, and Christian Europe and Byzantium adopted it in the ninth century along with the Greek world view: the only way to be fully human is to accept white, patriarchal Christian culture.

Yet there are innate differences between the Greek and Christian approaches. The Greeks animalized national and religious external others, but used human forms to represent their non-conformist women. Christians demonized both the internal and external "other", developing rigid cultural and religious definitions that they applied to real or imagined enemies. The measure of their success is both the twelve centuries these ideas have been in force, and the degree to which they are still believed to be true. The genocides and suppressions perpetuated by this approach haunt us to this day.

List of Illustrations

1. Deidameia and Eurytion, detail of the West Pediment of the Temple of Zeus, Olympia, ca. 460 B.C.E. Olympia Archaeological Museum.
2. Head of a Satyr, detail from a krater from Bari, fourth century B.C.E. Copenhagen, National Museum.
3. Kantharos in the shape of a Negro head, second half of the sixth century B.C.E. Boston, Museum of Fine Arts.
4. Polygnotos Painter, Maenads in Orgiastic Dance, krater, ca. 440–430 B.C.E. Ferrara, Museo Nazionale Archeologico di Spina.
5. Painter of the Vanth group, Charon and the dragon, amphora, end fourth century B.C.E. Orvieto, Museo Faina.
6. Head of the God Pan, detail of a mosaic pavement from Genezzano, third–fourth century C.E. Rome, Museo Nazionale Romano.
7. Sick and afflicted souls being rescued from the devil, detail of fol. 16v of the *Stuttgart Psalter,* early ninth century. Stuttgart, Württembergische Landesbibliothek, Cod. 23.
8. The Flagellation of Christ, from Psalms 34: 15, detail of fol. 34v of the *Stuttgart Psalter,* early 9th century, Landesbibliothek, Stuttgart.
9. Christ rescuing souls from Hell, detail of fol. 63v of the *Khludov Psalter,* illustrating Psalm 67:7, mid-ninth century. Moscow, State Historical Museum.
10. Arrest of Christ and Jews disputing with Christ, detail of fol. 54v from the *Khludov Psalter,* mid-ninth century. Moscow State Historical Museum.
11. Israelites sacrificing their children to Moloch, detail of fol. 109v from the *Khludov Psalter,* mid-ninth century. Moscow State Historical Museum.
12. Tympanum of the Puerta de las Platerias, ca. 1103, Cathedral of Santiago dE Compostela.
13. Christ delivering the Apocalypse to St. John, detail of fol. 4v of the *Beatus of St. Sever,* 1028–1072. Paris, Bibliothèque Nationale Ms. Lat 8878.
14. Betrayal and arrest of Christ, fol. 150v from the *Chichester Psalter,* ca. 1250. Manchester, John Rylands University Library Ms. Lat. 24.
15. The Beast grabs the Witnesses before the throned Antichrist, fol. 17r from an English Apocalypse, ca. 1245–1255. Paris, Bibliothèque Nationale Ms. fr. 403.

16. Pope Alexander VI as the Devil Unmasked, woodcut with trick fold, second position, sixteenth century. London, British Museum.

17. Child Sacrifice to Mohammed, detail of fol. 185r of the Duc de Berry's *Livre des Merveilles du Monde,* ca. 1413. Paris, Bibliothèque Nationale Ms. fr. 2810.

18. The Frankfurt Judensau, broadsheet, Frankfurt, early eighteenth century.

19. Samuel anointing David, detail of fol. 79r of the *Khludov Psalter,* mid-ninth century. Moscow State Historical Museum.

20. The destruction of the horns of the wicked, detail of fol. 74r of the *Khludov Psalter,* mid-ninth century. Moscow State Historical Museum.

21. David being anointed by Samuel and crowned by Humility, detail of fol. 6v from a mid-thirteenth century manuscript. Munich, Bayerische Staatsbibliothek clm. 17403.

22. The Exodus, Moses receiving the Law and the Worship of the Golden Calf, detail of fol. 16r of *Cursus Sanctae Mariae,* 1215. New York, Pierpont Morgan Library Ms. 739.

23. Wantons with devil lovers, part of the archivolts of a doorway, ca. 1120, Ste. Croix, Bordeaux.

24. Salome's Dance, page from the *Aachen Gospels of Otto III,* 983-1002. Aachen, Cathedral Treasury.

25. Hans Baldung Grien, *Witches Sabbath,* 1510, woodcut. Private Collection.

26. Edvard Munch, *The Vampire,* 1900, lithograph.

27. The Monstrous Races, woodcut illustration from C. van Megenberg, *Buch der Natur,* Germany, 1475, fol. 284v.

28. Wild Man, detail of fol. 70 from the *Luttrell Psalter,* 1335, London, British Library, Ms. Add. 42130.

Notes

* I would like to thank Elizabeth Revel-Neher, Silvia Rozenberg, Sonia Klinger, Suzy Dufrenne and Moshe Barasch for their helpful comments while I was writing this paper.

1. Timothy Long, *Barbarians in Greek Comedy* (Carbondale 1986), 163.

2. W. Stevenson Smith, *The Art and Architecture of Ancient Egypt* (Harmondsworth 1981), figs. 13–14, 234, 239–241, 330–332, 337, 365; Jean Vercoutter, Jean Leclant, Frank M. Snowden Jr. and Jehan Desanges, *L'Image du Noir dans l'Art Occidental* (Fribourg 1976), figs. 1–135; Henri Frankfort, *The Art and Architecture of the Ancient Orient* (Harmondsworth 1970), figs. 182–184, 190–191, 200–208, 418, 436, 439.

3. Even when heroes were given animal qualities, the Greeks refrained from hybridization: Heracles wears a lion skin which is not part of him, and Alexander wears the ram's horns of Ammon as part of a hairband or an animal-head hood; J. J. Pollitt, *Art in the Hellenistic Age* (Cambridge 1986), figs. 13–15.

4. Apollo flaying the satyr Marsyas for competing with him in music has been seen as an allegory on the god of reason punishing a foray into his domain by the irrational. Robert Hughes, *Heaven and Hell in Western Art* (London 1968), 237.

5. Silvia Rozenberg, "The Silenomachy and the Centauromachy on the Temple of Hera at Foce del Sele," (Ph.D. diss., Hebrew University, Jerusalem, 1989). See also the statement by Edith Hall, *Inventing the Barbarian: Greek Self-Definition through Tragedy* (Oxford 1989), 50: "Colonization myths expressing conflict with the ethnically other often conceptualize the enemy as subhuman, bestial or monstrous."

6. J. J. Pollitt, *Art and Experience in Classical Greece* (Cambridge 1972), 80–82; V. J. Bruno, "The Parthenon and the Theory of Classical Form," in *The Parthenon,* ed. V. J. Bruno (New York 1974), 55–97, and esp. 91–92; Elizabeth G. Pemberton, "Review of R. Ross Holloway, A View of Greek Art," *Art Journal* 33 (Summer 1974): 372; John Barron, *An Introduction to Greek Sculpture* (London 1981), 78.

7. John Boardman, *The Greeks Overseas* (London 1980), 256, figs. 296–297. For other naturalistic depictions of foreigners in native costumes, see François Lissarrague, *L'Autre Guerrier: archers, peltastes, cavaliers dans l'imagerie attique* (Paris 1990), chs. 1, 5–7.

8. Pollitt, *Hellenistic Age,* 3–4, 38–40, 43–46, 89–90, 94.

9. Ibid., 79–110.

10. Vercoutter, et al., *Noir,* 136–59; Lissarrague, *Guerrier,* 21–29, figs. 1–6, 100–101, 103–104, 106.

11. Compare Vercoutter et al., *Noir,* figs. 184–185, 201, 203–205, 220, 268, 298, 312, with John Boardman, *Greek Art* (London 1964), figs. 149, 171, 183–184. See also Vercoutter et al., figs. 241–242, 251–255, 265, 282.

12. Vercoutter et al., *Noir,* figs. 159–160, 174, 193, 196–197. This juxtaposition also takes place in depictions of blacks as allied warriors (e.g., Lissarrague, *Guerrier,* figs. 1–6).

13. Boardman, *Greek Art,* figs. 94, 96, 100, 104, 154; John Boardman, *Athenian Red Figure Vases: The Archaic Period* (London 1975), figs. 6, 14, 21, 39, 69, 73, 85, 106, 113, 139–140, 207, 252, 299, 313. Compare even the lines of the forehead and the heavy eyebrows in Boardman, *Greek Art,* fig. 100 with those in Vercoutter et al., *Noir,* figs. 161–163.

14. Boardman, *Greek Art,* fig. 150; Vercoutter, et al., *Noir,* figs. 154, 208–209, 214.

15. Vercoutter et al., *Noir,* figs. 178–179.

16. Ibid., fig. 204–206, 212, 219–220; A. D. Trendall, *Red Figure Vases of South Italy and Sicily* (London 1989), figs. 11, 13, 22, 64, 72, 74, 83, 85, 105, 120, 271, 339–340, 350, 357, 364, 370, 372, 374, 379.

17. Rudolf Wittkower, "Marvels of the East: A Study in the History of Monsters," *Journal of the Warburg and Courtauld Institutes* 5 (1942): 159–66; John Block Friedman, *The Monstrous Races in Medieval Art and Thought* (Cambridge, Mass. 1981), 5–21.

18. One exception, the dog-headed cynocephali who bark rather than talk, derive from a merging of the Egyptian god Anubis with the idea that non-Greeks babble "bar bar" rather than speaking Greek, the only acceptable human language; Wittkower, "Marvels," 160; Friedman, *Monstrous Races,* 29. Friedman (24–25) sees these creatures as based on apes, an idea also discussed by Wittkower, 190–92, pl. 48.

19. Friedman, *Monstrous Races,* 9–10, 12, 16, 24. Friedman (34–36, 52) sees living at the edges of human habitation as a negative characteristic: since Greeks believed that they lived at the center of the universe, their love of the mean led them to think poorly of those living at the extreme limits of the earth.

20. Ibid., 24–25; these are the reasons Friedman suggests.

21. Ibid., 34. Since hybrids could symbolize a developed urban society such as Persia, whether a nation was organized into city states, a distinction Friedman suggests (30), could only be a minor factor in the concept of Greek superiority. Friedman also links Greek "humanity" to customs, eating habits, costume, and language (26–29). Hall, *Barbarian,* 4–8, states that the geographic dispersion of the Greeks led them to pick language as a culture module. This is true in literature and theatre (Long, *Barbarian,* 162–63), but not in the visual arts.

22. Hall, *Barbarian,* 53 derives the Amazons from the matriarchal Lycians described by Greek ethnographers, without realizing that ethnographers, like historians, had hidden agendas in describing other peoples. See E. Fantham, H. Peet Foley, N. Boymel Kampen, S. B. Pomeroy, and H. A. Shapiro, *Women in the Classical World: Image and Text* (New York 1994), 128–34; Bernice Schultz Engle, "The Amazons in Ancient Greece," *Psychoanalytic Quarterly* 11 (1942): 512–54.

23. Dietrich von Bothmer, *Amazons in Greek Art* (Oxford 1957).

24. They killed Orpheus whose singing calmed the beasts but not the Maenads; and Pentheus, who is torn to pieces by Maenads led by his mother in Euripides' *Bacchae.*

25. For depictions of Maenads, see Thomas H. Carpenter, *Dionysian Imagery in Archaic Greek Art* (Oxford 1986); Sheila McNally, "The Maenad in Early Greek Art," in John Peradotto and J. P. Sullivan, eds., *Women in the Ancient World: The Arethusa Papers* (Albany 1984), 107–38; Boardman, *Red Figure,* figs. 136, 218, 277, 311, 313, 317, 374, 380; Trendall, *Sicily,* figs. 11–12, 158, 162, 271, 339; Charles Daremberg and Edmond Saglio, *Dictionnaire des Antiquités Grecques et Romaines,* vol. 3 (Paris, n.d.), pt. 2, 1479–1493.

26. E. R. Dodd, *The Greeks and the Irrational* (Berkeley 1971), 270–78; Fantham et al., *Women,* 87–91; Ellen D. Reeder, *Pandora: Women in Classical Greece* (Princeton 1995), 381.

27. Euripides, *Bacchae,* ed. E. R. Dodd (Oxford 1960), xx–xxv; Albert Henrichs, "'He Has a God in Him': Human and Divine in the Modern Perception of Dionysius," in *Masks of Dionysus,* eds. Thomas H. Carpenter and Christopher A. Faroane (Ithaca 1993), 31–36.

28. This could also prove dangerous: Medea, like the maenad Agave, was said by Euripides to have killed her children.

29. E.g., Horus and Osiris were depicted in human form rather than as a bird and a mummy as they were in Egyptian art.

30. Donald Strong, *Roman Art* (Harmondsworth 1988), figs. 40, 79, 81, 84–85, 87–88, 94, 132, 135, 138–140, 143, 145–146, 153–154, 163.

31. Wittkower, "Marvels," 166–67, 171, 174–76; Friedman, *Monstrous Races,* 7–8.

32. Zofia Ameisenowa, "Animal-headed Gods, Evangelists, Saints and Righteous Men," *Journal of the Warburg and Courtauld Institutes* 12 (1949): 21–24, fig. 16b; Boston Museum of Fine Arts, *Romans and Barbarians* (1976–1977), nos. 22, 42–43, 48.

33. Otto J. Brendel, *Etruscan Art* (Harmondsworth 1978), 337–39, 348–49, 412–14; Massimo Pallottino, *Etruscan Painting* (Geneva 1952), 111–18; Arturo Stenico, *Roman and Etruscan Painting* (London 1963), 23–24, pl. 49; Ranuccio Bianchi Bandinelli and Antonio Giuliano, *Etruschi e Italici primo del Dominio di Roma* (Milan 1979), fig. 318; Jeffrey Burton Russell, *The Devil: Perceptions of Evil from Antiquity to Primitive Christianity* (Ithaca 1977), 155–57, 159. Stenico, p. 24, says these demons emphasize "those qualities of terror and repulsiveness which the Greeks did not care to see exhibited even for religious purposes."

34. Stenico, *Roman*, pl. 155. In a fourth-century vase shaped as the head of a hooked-nose demon (J. D. Beazley, *Etruscan Vase-Painting* [Oxford 1947], pl. 40, nos. 1–2), a tiny head of a satyr with upturned nose and negroid features appears under the handle. This juxtaposition of non-classic physiognomies suggests the line of thought behind the new treatment of the satyr.

35. Brendel, *Etruscan*, fig. 308b; Strong, figs. 8, 96; Ludwig Goldscheider, *Roman Portraits* (London 1945), pls. 2, 14–17, 22, 28, 31, 34, 36, 40, 48, 50–51, 53, 59, 67, 82, 84, 88, 92, 96, 101, 106.

36. Henry Chadwick, *The Early Church* (Harmondsworth 1967), passim. Tertullian, who intolerantly conceived of his task "as a conflict with diabolical forces" (pp. 91–92), ended his days outside the official Church.

37. Ibid., 153, 167–68, 170–71; Simon Dubnov, *History of the Jews*, vol. 2 (New York 1968), 185, 190–93, 208–209, 213–14, 480, 484, 495–500, 510–27.

38. Elizabeth Revel-Neher, *The Image of the Jew in Byzantine Art* (Oxford 1992), 44–50.

39. E.g., Michael Gough, *The Origins of Christian Art* (London 1973), figs. 34, 87, 156; Revel-Neher, *Image of the Jew*, 47–50, figs. 4, 6–7; David Talbot Rice, *Art of the Byzantine Era* (London 1963), fig. 15; Gertrud Schiller, *Iconography of Christian Art*, vol. 1, (Greenwich, Conn. 1971), figs. 144, 146–147, 149, 151, 168, 246–247, 249–253, 255–260; John Beckwith, *Early Medieval Art* (London 1964), figs. 55, 58.

40. Revel-Neher, *Image of the Jew*, 50-51, 58, states that this began to occur in the sixth century and brings examples from the seventh to the fourteenth centuries (pls. V–VII, IX, figs. 12, 29, 30); see Beckwith, *Early Medieval*, fig. 29, for a Carolingian example.

41. Jean Devisse, *The Image of the Black in Western Art* (Switzerland 1979), 38–46, esp. figs. 2, 5–8. Although Paulinus of Nola stated that the Ethiopians' skin had been burned black by their sins, they were not represented as evil in Early Christian art, and theologians stated that blacks could be made white by conversion to Christianity (Friedman, *Monstrous Races*, 65).

42. Chadwick, *Early Church*, 106–07; Jeffrey Burton Russell, *Satan: The Early Christian Tradition* (Ithaca 1981), 125–27.

43. Jacques Levron, *Le Diable dans l'Art* (Paris 1935), 14–19; *The Rabbula Gospels*, eds. Carlo Cecchelli, Giuseppe Furlani, and Mario Salmi (Olten 1959), fol. 8b; Schiller, *Iconography*, vol. 1, 143–44, 173, figs. 390–392, 525; Suzy Dufrenne, *Les Ilustrations du Psautier d'Utrecht: Sources et Apport Carolingien* (Paris 1978), 127 n. 367, fig. 60; Russell, *Devil*, 230; idem, *Satan*, 169. Compare these images with Stenico, *Roman*, pls. 49, 52, 84, 106–107, 118, 154–155.

44. Friedman, *Monstrous Races*, 59, 90–92.

45. These manuscripts are known only through copies; Wittkower, "Marvels," 167–68, 171–72, figs. 42a, 48a.

46. Friedman, *Monstrous Races,* 69-75; Ameisenowa, "Animal-headed," 42–45, fig. 20c.

47. Dufrenne, *Utrecht,* 99–119, 126–28, 138–39, pl. 74, esp. nos. 4, 9–10, pl. 75, esp. nos. 1, 10–12, 19–20, 22, 24, 28, 31, 34–35, 38–39; Russell, *Devil,* 156–57.

48. Dubnow, *History,* vol. 2, 542–53.

49. Ernest T. de Wald, *The Stuttgart Psalter* (Princeton 1930), fols. 4v, 10v, 16v, 29v, 38r, 45v, 56r, 70v, 88v, 102v, 107r-v, 122r, 126r-v, 147v, to fols. 2r, 4r-5v, 11r, 25r-v, 31r, 34r, 43v, 45v, 46v–47v, 52r, 53r, 64v, 66v–67r, 79v, 140r, 141v, 145v, 155r, 156r. Some of the choices are indicative: a hooked-nosed Absalom chases a straight-nosed David (fols. 3v, 66v), but David made ill by his sins has a hooked nose and unruly hair (fol. 6r). Judas sometimes has a hooked nose (fol. 53r), and the wicked who spurn Christ point to their eyes which cannot see him (fol. 67r). Those of Christ's adherents who have hooked noses (fols. 3r, 31v) may depict forcibly converted Jews who were constantly suspected of returning to Judaism.

50. Ibid., fols. 15r, 29v.

51. Ibid., passim, esp. fol. 122r.

52. Kathleen Corrigan, *Visual Polemics in the Ninth-Century Byzantine Psalters* (Cambridge 1992), 6, 31.

53. M. V. Shchepkina, *Miniaturi Khlodovskoii Psaltiri* (Moscow 1977), fols. 8v, 35v, 63r-v, 92v, 96v, 102v, 109v-110r, 113r, 140r; Mt. Athos Pantocrator 61, fol. 130v.

54. Corrigan, *Polemics,* 27–30, 122, figs. 14, 16–17, 38–39, 41–43; Revel-Neher, *Image of the Jew,* 108; Mt. Athos Pantocrator 61, fols 16r, 98v.

55. Corrigan, *Polemics,* 30–32, 34–37, 43–61, figs. 25, 32, 48–49, 56–57, 59–60, 94; Revel-Neher, *Image of the Jew,* 79; Shchepkina, *Miniaturi,* fols. 2v, 17r, 19r-20r, 31r, 35r, 45v, 54v, 66r, 67r, 77r, 78r, 84v, 85v, 108v, 109v-110r; Mount Athos Pantocrator 61, fols. 29r, 68v, 69r, 87r.

56. Dubnov, *History,* vol. 2, 187–88.

57. Corrigan, *Polemics,* 78–103, figs. 90, 95–96; Shchepkina, *Miniaturi,* fols. 78v–79r, 106r, 135r; John Williams, *Early Spanish Manuscript Illumination* (London 1977), 27. Muslims thus wear the traditional "Eastern" costumes that continued to characterize the Magi, the three Hebrews, etc. Ishmaelites are also depicted with hooked noses in the *Stuttgart Psalter,* fol. 119r.

58. Compare Shchepkina, *Miniaturi,* fols. 41v, 106v, 116v, 135r; Corrigan, *Polemics,* figs. 31, 33; Mount Athos Pantocrator 61, fol. 164v; with Schiller, *Iconography,* vol. 1, figs. 355, 358, 360–361. For the demonic meaning involved, see Corrigan, fig. 49. This feature may have derived from depictions of the satyr Onnaseuas in Greco-Etruscan art (Trendall, *Sicily,* fig. 22) or from Athena's helmet with horn-like plumes found in a sixth century C.E. work (Boston, *Romans and Barbarians,* no. 205).

59. Dubnow, *History,* vol. 2, 191.

60. R. I. Moore, *The Formation of a Persecuting Society* (Oxford 1987), 99. This negative approach to the "other" is often seen as a product of the religious and social crises in the late eleventh or twelfth century caused by thwarted expectations of an apocalyptic second coming and by the rise of the towns. In reaction, the Church consolidated its power and became a persecuting society (Moore, 67–91, 98–99, 102–12).

See also Jeffrey Burton Russell, *Dissent and Order in the Middle Ages: The Search for Legitimate Authority* (New York 1984), 39–40. Although these factors helped spread this approach, artistic developments indicate that its sources were the traumas of the eighth and ninth centuries, when Christianity, attacked from without and within, reacted exactly as had the Greeks to similar threats.

61. Schiller, *Iconography*, vol. 1, figs. 157, 159, 269–270; Athens, National Gallery and Alexandros Soutzos Museum, *Gates of Mystery: Treasures of Orthodoxy from Holy Russia* (Athens 1994), pls. 21, 32, 36; G. Vzdornov, *Art of Ancient Vologda* (Leningrad 1978), 78–79; Tamara Talbot Rice, *A Concise History of Russian Art* (London 1963), fig. 98; Revel-Neher, *Image of the Jew*, 69, fig. 27.

62. Revel-Neher, *Image of the Jew*, passim, esp. 79, pls. VIII, X, figs. 13–17, 19, 22–26, 28, 31–34, 37, 39, 45; Athens, *Gates of Mystery*, pls. 15, 17a, 18, 59; Schiller, *Iconography*, vol. 1, fig. 342. Compare Revel-Neher, *Image of the Jew*, fig. 45 to Brendel, *Etruscan*, fig. 271, for the demonic meaning involved.

63. N. F. Visotskaya, *Icon Painting in Belorussia 15th–18th Centuries* (Minsk 1992), pls. 26, 44, 72.

64. Despite the widespread blood libels in Eastern Europe and Russia, all depictions of ritual murder were based on Western European models. See, e.g., [Ierom. Alexii], *Evrei i Krovavii "Izvet"* (Pochaev 1913).

65. Devisse, *Black*, 96–108, figs. 56–75, 95–96.

66. Ibid., 105–107, figs. 76–78; Friedman, *Monstrous Races*, 62–64. This is not due simply to the black Moors, as most of the Muslims the Byzantines met were light-skinned.

67. A.-M. Cocagnac, *Le Jugement Dernier dans l'Art* (Paris 1955), 17, 19; Selma Jónsdóttir, *An 11th Century Byzantine Last Judgement in Iceland* (Reykjavik 1959), pls. 5–6, 19, 21, 30; Kurt Weitzmann, Manolis Chatzidakis, Krsto Miatev, and Svetozar Radojcic, *Icons from South Eastern Europe and Sinai* (London 1968), pl. 19; Devisse, *Black*, fig. 79; Adolf Katzenellenbogen, *Allegories of the Virtues and Vices in Mediaeval Art* (New York 1964), fig. 23.

68. See Oskar Seyffert, *Dictionary of Classical Antiquities* (New York 1969), 224. For other suggestions on the origin of the fiery hair, see Devisse, *Black*, 68.

69. Jónsdóttir, *Last Judgment*, pls. 2, 4, 14, 20; Emile Mâle, *Religious Art in France: The Twelfth Century* (Princeton 1978), fig. 99. The exceptions are those manuscripts which copy ninth-century psalters, e.g., Schiller, *Iconography*, vol. 1, 182, fig. 568; Sirarpie der Nersessian, *L'Illustration des Psautiers Grecs du Moyen Age*, vol. 2: Londres, Add. 19.352 (Paris 1970), figs. 16, 133vn-134.

70. E.g., Athens, *Gates of Mystery*, pls. 3, 16, 21, 29, 35a, 36, 47; Vzdornov, *Vologda*, 19, 21, 51; Rice, *Russia*, figs. 54, 119. For examples of demons influenced by the West, see Visotskaya, *Icon*, pl. 38; Weitzmann, et al., *Icons*, pl. 137; and the restoration of the devils over the doorway at Torcello (Jónsdóttir, *Last Judgment*, pl. 2).

71. Williams, *Spanish*, 27. The Visigoths were intolerant before the Islamic invasions. Chadwick, *Early Church*, 171, stated: "The worst persecution suffered by the Jews occurred under the Visigoths in seventh-century Spain.... Isidore of Seville remarked that the Visigothic kings, in the enthusiasm of recent conversion, had a zeal not according to

knowledge." For a review of the early *Reconquista,* see Pedro de Palol and Max Hirmer, *Early Medieval Art in Spain* (London 1967), 27–30.

72. Williams, *Spanish,* pls. 15–16, 18, 29; Gertrud Schiller, *Ikonographie der christlichen Kunst* (Gütersloh, 1991), vol. 5, figs. 121, 698.

73. Williams, *Spanish,* 29, pl. 32; de Palol and Hirmer, *Spain,* 64, 128. Compare Williams, pl. 32 with an earlier version in Schiller, *Ikonographie,* vol. 5, fig. 121, and see also her fig. 696.

74. Williams, *Spanish,* 20, 77, pl. 19a; Schiller, *Ikonographie,* vol. 5, figs. 122, 612.

75. De Palol and Hirmer, *Spain,* 28, 152, fig. 110.

76. For the Jewish context, see the late twelfth-century Moses with a single horn above the portal of the south transept of the Cathedral of Ciudad Rodrigo (Ruth Mellinkoff, "More about Horned Moses," *Journal of Jewish Art* 12–13 [1986–1987]: 187), and the discussion of the single horn below in the text.

77. Devisse, *Black,* 86–87, figs. 43–45, 47–50, 94; Jean Devisse and Michel Mollat, *The Image of the Black in Western Art* (Lausanne 1979), figs. 73–76, 84, 100, 154–157; Ruth Mellinkoff, *Outcasts: Signs of Otherness in Northern European Art of the Late Middle Ages* (Berkeley 1993), vol. 2, fig. III.28. In contrast, in fifteenth-century Venice, where the main Islamic contacts were with the Turks, Muslims were depicted as turbaned whites, as were Egyptians and Jews (Bernard Berenson, *Italian Pictures of the Renaissance: Venetian School* [London 1957], vol. 1, pls. 82, 184, 189; Patricia Fortini Brown, *Venetian Narrative Painting in the Age of Carpaccio* [New Haven 1988], pls. XI, XV, XXXI–XXXIV, figs. 2, 26, 37, 39, 76–77, 118, 120–123, 131, 144). See also Joan Evans, *Life in Medieval France* (London 1969), fig. 72.

78. Devisse, *Black,* figs. 24, 51–53, 84, 87, 110–113; Devisse and Mollat, *Black,* figs. 16, 85, 89, 105–106, 114, 119, 122, 135, 146, 148, 205–207, 216, 244–247.

79. Devisse, *Black,* 149–205, 270–71, figs. 114–168; Devisse and Mollat, *Black,* fig. 25. This change repeats that undergone by St. Menas in Early Christian art. See also St. Gregory the Moor (Devisse and Mollat, fig. 27).

80. Devisse, *Black,* fig. 105; Devisse and Mollat, *Black,* figs. 30–40, 44, 111–112, 118, 126–127, 137–138, 140–141, 143–145, 158–187.

81. Devisse, *Black,* fig. 103; Devisse and Mollat, *Black,* figs. 11, 26, 42, 136.

82. Devisse, *Black,* fig. 19. For the meaning of this gesture in medieval times, see Mellinkoff, *Outcasts,* vol. 1, 198–201, vol. 2, figs. IV.14, VI.57, VII.38 (where one of the mockers is black), X.1–5, 7, 9–12, 15–16.

83. Norman Cohn, *The Pursuit of the Millennium* (London 1970), 61–88.

84. Devisse, *Black,* 69–72, figs. 18, 22–23; Devisse and Mollat, *Black,* figs. 46–48, 64–66; Schiller, *Ikonographie,* vol. 5, figs. 272, 314, 1027, 1047, 1049.

85. Devisse, *Black,* 72–80, figs. 25, 27–38; Devisse and Mollat, *Black,* figs. 67, 69, 72, 107, 211, 239; Mellinkoff, *Outcasts,* vol. 1, 67, 126–27, vol. 2, figs. I.12, 30–34, 38–40, 42–43, III.41, VI.24–27, 31, 35, 42–43, 57, VII.34–40, VIII.5–6, IX.4–5.

86. Mellinkoff, *Outcasts,* vol. 2, fig. VII.34; Devisse, *Black,* fig. 29. The heretic's flame-like hair also influenced images of Islam: it was translated into the winged ears of the Ishmaelites in a fourteenth-century German *Biblia Pauperum* (Ruth Mellinkoff, *The*

Devil at Isenheim: Reflections of Popular Belief in Grünewald's Altarpiece [Berkeley 1988], 49, 55, fig. 32).

87. E.g., Schiller, *Ikonographie*, vol. 5, figs. 138, 279b, 283–285, 306, 309–310, 376–377, 385–386, 464, 473–474, 479–480, 483, 542c, 592, 647, 736, 738, 742, 1023, 1026, 1031, 1035, 1048; Mellinkoff, *Outcasts*, vol. 2, figs. III.124, VI.34, VIII.25–26.

88. Bernhard Blumenkranz, *Le juif médiéval au miroir de l'art chrétien* (Paris 1966), 20–22, 29–33.

89. E.g., Mellinkoff, *Isenheim*, fig. 41; idem, *Outcasts*, vol. 2, passim, esp. pls. I.44, 49, II.22, III.24, VI.57, VIII.16; Joshua Trachtenberg, *The Devil and the Jews* (New Haven 1943), 27.

90. Fernando I (1037–1065) may have helped this imagery spread outside Spain. He made a large donation to the Burgundian monastery of Cluny, which became a leader both in promoting the new image of the devil, and in supporting the Reconquista and the pilgrimage to Santiago (Williams, *Spanish*, 29; Kenneth John Conant, *Carolingian and Romanesque Architecture 800–1200* [Harmondsworth 1974], 158, 190; Mâle, *Twelfth Century*, 364–66, 370–72). There the demons of the Puerta de las Platerias would have forcibly struck the pilgrims.

91. Mâle, *Twelfth Century*, figs. 17, 20, 108, 153, 186, 256, 260–261, 264, 288, 290, 292, 301–302; Beckwith, *Early Medieval*, figs. 189, 194; Cocagnac, *Last Judgment*, 37, 51, 63, 65, 81, 97; Devisse and Mollat, *Black*, figs. 240, 242; de Palol and Hirmer, *Spain*, fig. 238; Henri Focillon, *The Art of the West*, vol. 1, *Romanesque* (London 1969), pls. 100, 103, 111–112; Michael Camille, *The Gothic Idol: Ideology and Image-Making in Medieval Art* (Cambridge 1992), figs. 7, 28; Schiller, *Ikonographie*, vol. 5, passim, esp. figs. 151, 153, 289, 539.

92. E.g., Trachtenberg, *Devil*, 30; Schiller, *Ikonographie*, vol. 5, figs. 153, 684, 689, 691, 1034, 1036, 1039–1040.

93. For anti-Papist and anti-Lutheran uses of demonic imagery, see Cohn, *Millenium*, pl. 2; Hughes, *Heaven and Hell*, 230–31.

94. E.g., Cohn, *Millenium*, 285–86; S. Nilus, *Förlaten Faller...* (Hangö 1924), cover; Norman Cohn, *El Mito de la Conspiración Judia Mundial* (Madrid 1983), cover, figs. 14, 18; Wiktoryn Grabczewski, *Diabel Polski w Rzezbie i Legendzie* (Warsaw 1990), 32.

95. Islamic representations of the other had in the past been naturalistic without apparent "evil" overtones (Devisse, *Black*, figs. 40–42; David Talbot Rice, *Islamic Art* [London 1965], figs. 19, 115, 219, 227).

96. Dufrenne, *Utrecht*, pl. 74, nos. 4, 6, 10; Camille, *Gothic*, figs. 1, 9–10, 14, 33–36, 41, 56, 65, 67, 70–72, 89, 91.

97. Camille, *Gothic*, 258–81, figs. 39, 140–141, 144.

98. Ibid., figs. 82–85, 90, 106, 161; Friedman, *Monstrous Races*, fig. 52. This Christian belief led Gauguin to view Tahitian religion incorrectly as idol worship (Ziva Amishai-Maisels, *Gauguin's Religious Themes* [New York 1985], 340–99).

99. Shchepkina, *Miniaturi*, fols. 109v–110r; Camille, *Gothic*, 165–94, figs. 35–36, 53, 78–79, 92, 94–95, 100, 105, 136; Trachtenberg, *Devil*, 136; Schiller, *Ikonographie*, vol. 5, 103, fig. 417b.

100. Camille, *Gothic*, 129–64, figs. 76, 79–80, 87–88; Schiller, *Ikonographie*, vol. 5, fig. 458.

101. Trachtenberg, *Devil*, passim, esp. 62; Isaiah Shachar, *The Judensau: A Medieval Anti-Jewish Motif and its History* (London 1974).

102. Camille, *Gothic*, fig. 77; Schiller, *Ikonographie*, vol. 5, fig. 724; Trachtenberg, *Devil*, 195. For links between Jews with devils, see Schiller, vol. 5, fig. 134; Blumenkranz, *Juif*, figs. 55, 57.

103. Ruth Mellinkoff, *The Horned Moses in Medieval Art and Thought* (Berkeley 1970), 1–2, 77–78. Jerome used the correct translation in his Commentary on Ezekiel, but incorrectly adds that the Hebrew states that Moses was "horned." Mellinkoff's benign approach ignores the fact that Jerome had a Christian agenda in translating the Bible. See my forthcoming article on David's horn.

104. See its earliest depiction at Dura Europos (Revel-Neher, *Image of the Jew*, fig. 9); the early seventh-century rendering (Steven H. Wander, "The Cyprus Plates: The Story of David and Goliath," *Metropolitan Museum Journal* 8 [1973]: 91, fig. 4; and ninth-century versions (Henri Omont, *Les Miniatures des plus anciens, Manuscrits grecs de la Bibliothèque Nationale du VIe au XIVe siècle* [Paris 1929], pl. 37).

105. Compare these versions to the other renderings of the anointing in the *Stuttgart Psalter* (fol. 24r), in the *Utrecht Psalter* (Dufrenne, *Utrecht*, pl. 88, nos. 1–7), and in the *Golden Psalter of St. Gallen* (Theodor Ehrenstein, *Das Alte Testament im Bilde* [Vienna 1923], 539).

106. The Psalms are numbered according to the Hebrew Bible. The Hebrew verb "rum" (inf.) is often translated "exalt" which is its correct meaning in this context, but the literal meaning is "raise." In the Vulgate, the translation differentiates in this Psalm between "elevabis" applied to the Israelites' horn and "exaltabur" for David's horn.

107. Here the Hebrew verb is "atzmiah" rather than a variation on "rum."

108. See also Mt. Athos Pantocrater 61, fol. 125r.

109. Corrigan, *Polemics*, 52. This high hat is a variation on the Persian hat of the Magi (Shchepkina, *Miniaturi*, fols. 106r, 160v), and is used here to symbolize Islam.

110. See e.g., Anthony Cutler, "A Psalter from Mar Saba and the Evolution of the Byzantine David Cycle," *Journal of Jewish Art* 6 (1979): 42–44, figs. 4–5, 20; Kurt Weitzmann, "The Psalter Vatopedi 761. Its Place in the Aristocratic Psalter Rescension," *Journal of the Walters Art Gallery* 10 (1947): 24; Ernest T. De Wald, *The Illustrations in the Manuscripts of the Septuagint*, vol. 3 (Princeton 1942), pl. 23; Rainer Stichel, "Ausserkanonische Elemente in byzantinischen Illustrationen des Alten Testaments," *Römische Quartalschrift für christliche Altertumskunde und Kirchengeschichte* 69, nos. 3–4 (1974): pl. 7b. The idea that Jews have horns is, however, suggested by the treatment of the Jew's hair in an eleventh century manuscript (Revel-Neher, *Image of the Jew*, fig. 45), a treatment later used in the West for the horns of Abraham and Moses (Mellinkoff, "More Moses," 192–93, figs. 15–17; idem, *Outcasts*, vol. 2, pl. I.11).

111. Adolf Katzenellenbogen, *Allegories of the Virtues and Vices in Mediaeval Art* (New York 1964), fig. 55; Mellinkoff, "More Moses," 188, fig. 7. See also Ehrenstein, *Alte Testament*, 541, nos. 20–21.

112. Mellinkoff, *Outcasts*, vol. 1, 62, 89–91, vol. 2, pls. III.114–115; Schiller, *Iconography*, vol. 1, figs. 168, 250–251, 256, 260–261, 289, 291, 293, 296; de Wald, *Stuttgart*, fols. 2v, 3v as compared with the Magi's hat on fol. 84r.

113. Trachtenberg, *Devil*, 44–47, 227 n. 5.

114. Mellinkoff, *Outcasts,* vol. 2, pls. III.41, 121, 124; idem, *Moses,* fig. 61; Camille, *Gothic,* fig. 110. Demons and apocalyptic beasts have single horns well into the fifteenth century (Schiller, *Ikonographie,* vol. 5, figs. 464, 466, 1059). For the negative meaning of single-horned men whose "moral deformity...is reflected in their physical appearance," see Friedman, *Monstrous Races,* 54–55, 125.

115. Ruth Mellinkoff, "Cain and the Jews," *Journal of Jewish Art* 6 (1979): 16–38, figs. 11, 13–20, 26, 32–33; idem, *Outcasts,* vol. 2, VI.50; Friedman, *Monstrous Races,* 95–98, fig. 32.

116. E.g., Blumenkranz, *Juif,* figs. 15, 32–41, 44–47, 50–52, 76–77, 88–93, 95–115, 132, 135–141, 153–158; Mellinkoff, *Moses,* 128–31, 135–36, figs. 50, 57, 59, 61, 71, 73, 75, 80, 90–91, 117; idem, "Cain," 22, 33, 36, figs. 6, 30, 34; idem, *Outcasts,* vol. 1, 59, 61–75, 91–94, vol. 2, pls. III.37, 41, 43, 60, 64, 78, VII.40; Henry Kraus, *The Living Theatre of Medieval Art* (Philadelphia 1967), figs. 106–109.

117. For a positive meaning of Moses' horns, see Mellinkoff, *Moses.* In her last chapter, she deals with this symbol's ambivalence, but cannot believe that the artists intended a negative meaning. This despite her suggestion that Cluny, which was a major disseminator of devil images, may have been "an important intermediary for horned Moses" (p. 67), and her article on the perjorative meaning of the Tablets of the Law (Ruth Mellinkoff, "The Round-Topped Tablets of the Law: Sacred Symbol and Emblem of Evil," *Journal of Jewish Art* 1 [1974]: 28–43).

118. Mellinkoff, "More Moses," 186–88, figs. 4–6. This wide diffusion in time and space suggests that this imagery was more common than is now known.

119. Mellinkoff, *Moses,* figs. 47–88 passim, 107–110, 116–118; Schiller, *Ikonographie,* vol. 4, figs. 279–281, 285, 295, vol. 5, passim, esp. figs. 129, 299, 714, 718. For similarities between Moses and demons, compare Mellinkoff, "More Moses," figs. 8, 9–14 and idem, *Moses,* figs. 51, 56 with Schiller, vol. 5, figs. 455, 132.

120. Schiller, *Ikonographie,* vol. 5, fig. 60; Mellinkoff, *Moses,* figs. 61, 65, 69, 75; Camille, *Gothic,* fig. 136. See also the demonic Moses who appears as a background to the Ten Commandments in a thirteenth-century manuscript (Camille, fig. 20).

121. Mellinkoff, "More Moses," 195–96, figs. 19–23.

122. Schiller, *Iconography,* vol. 1, figs. 33, 140–141, 171, 173, 175, 183; idem, *Ikonographie,* vol. 5, figs. 97, 718; Blumenkranz, *Juif,* figs. 135, 139–140, 143, 145, 150–151; Mellinkoff, "Cain," fig. 24; idem., *Outcasts,* vol. 1, 79–82, 233, vol. 2, pls. III.80, 93.

123. Mellinkoff, "Cain," 18. Christians doubted whether even baptism could rid Jews of their diabolical qualities (Trachtenberg, *Devil,* 50).

124. Mâle, *Twelfth Century,* 365–66; Evans, *Life,* 59–67; Jeffrey Burton Russell, *Lucifer: The Devil in the Middle Ages* (Ithaca 1984), 130. Solomon being led to idol worship by beautiful women shows how they lead even wise men astray (Devisse and Mollat, *Black,* figs. 43, 45; Camille, *Gothic,* fig. 162).

125. Mâle, *Twelfth Century,* 372–76; Katzenellenbogen, *Allegories,* 58–59, fig. 56; Kraus, *Theater,* figs. 17, 20, 131; Camille, *Gothic,* fig. 175.

126. E.g., Focillon, *West,* fig. 111; Emile Mâle, *The Gothic Image: Religious Art in France of the Thirteenth Century* (New York 1958), 260–62, fig. 135; Jean Seznac, "The Temptation of St. Anthony in Art," *Magazine of Art* 40 (March 1947): 87–90.

127. Hugo Daffner, *Salome* (Munich 1912), 30–31. Compare his words also to depictions of the Maenad's dance in Boardman, *Red Figure*, figs. 132.2, 136, 218; Pollitt, *Hellenistic Age*, figs. 175–177; and Daremberg and Saglio, *Dictionnaire*, vol. 3, pt. 2, fig. 4768.

128. Daffner, *Salome*, 43. In the sixth-century Codex Sinopensis, Salome wears a sheer dress but does not dance (ibid., 35).

129. Ibid., vi, 46–47, 50–52, 57, 59, 61, 63, 73, 88, 97; Euripides, *Bacchae*, ed. Dodd, xxxiv; Mira Friedman, "The Metamorphoses of Judith," *Jewish Art* 12–13 (1986–1987): 245–46, fig. 30. Salome dancing with the Baptist's head appears in a drawing of a silver relief which Daffner, *Salome*, 69, dates to the tenth century. For the connection to the Maenad, compare esp. Daffner, 46–47 with Daremberg and Saglio, *Dictionnaire*, figs. 4768, 4770, and with Russell, *Devil*, 140. This last–a sixth-century Coptic ivory incorporated into the Ambo of Henry II at Aachen–suggests the way the tradition of the maenads was conveyed.

130. Daffner, *Salome*, passim, esp. 54, 61, 72, 74.

131. Ibid., 99–363 passim. Exceptions occur mainly in fifteenth-century Italian and late nineteenth–early twentieth century art (ibid., 101, 104, 106, 108, 113, 126–27, 129, 131, 253, 285, 332–33, 341, 348, 353–54, 356, 358, 364–65).

132. Friedman, "Judith," 232–46; Ehrenstein, *Alte Testament*, 53–75, nos. 73, 75, 88–93, 95, 97, 114, 140–41; Seznac, "Temptation," 90–93; Enrico Castelli, *Le Démoniaque dans l'art* (Paris 1959), pls. 6–13, 24, 36, 41, 48–51, 53–57, 59–63, 65–66, 70–74.

133. E.g., Corrigan, *Polemics*, 2, 27–29, 131–32, fig. 38; Kraus, *Theater*, fig. 130.

134. Julio Caro Baroja, "Witchcraft and Catholic Theology," in *Early Modern European Witchcraft, Centres and Peripheries*, ed. Bengt Ankarloo and Gustav Henningsen, (Oxford 1990), 23–43. For the Jew as sorceror, see Trachtenberg, *Devil*, 57–155.

135. Folke Nordström, *Goya, Saturn and Melancholy* (Stockholm 1962), figs. 79–80; Schiller, *Ikonographie*, vol. 5, figs. 876–877; Paris, Bibliothèque Nationale, *Les Sorcières* (Paris 1973), 10–12, 16–21, 55, 59–61, 78–80, 95–96, 124–28, 130–34.

136. Erwin Panofsky, *The Life and Art of Albrecht Dürer* (Princeton 1971), 70–72, figs. 97–98; Paris, *Sorcières*, 31–33, 40–49, 62–63, 66–71.

137. Panofsky, *Dürer*, figs. 48–49, 107–108, 122–23.

138. *The Complete Etchings of Goya* ([New York], 1943), *Capriccios* 44–48, 51, 60, 62, 64–72; Nordström, *Goya*, 153–71, 213–21.

139. J. J. Bachofen, *Das Mutterrecht* (Stuttgart 1861); Ayelet Shefer, "The Bird in the Cage: A Study in Pre-Raphaelite and Victorian Iconography" (Ph.D. diss., Hebrew University of Jerusalem, 1981), 146–67, 560–64.

140. Mario Praz, *The Romantic Agony* (New York 1956), 93–286; Bram Dijkstra, *Idols of Perversity* (Oxford 1986).

141. Wittkower, "Marvels," 166–78, pls. 42–49; Devisse and Mollat, *Black*, figs. 18–23, 238; Friedman, *Monstrous Races*.

142. Wittkower, "Marvels," 176–77; Mâle, *Twelfth Century*, 326–32; Friedman, *Monstrous Races*, 60–62, 66–86.

143. Wittkower, "Marvels," 177–78, figs. 46a,c; Mâle, *Twelfth Century*, 323–26; Friedman, *Monstrous Races*, 93, 122–30, 205–206, figs. 59–62.

144. Friedman, *Monstrous Races,* 95–107, fig. 3; Wittkower, "Marvels," fig. 44a; Timothy Husband, *The Wild Man: Medieval Myth and Symbolism* (New York 1980), 21.

145. Friedman, *Monstrous Races,* 43–46, figs. 19–20, 22–23, 30–31.

146. Schiller, *Ikonographie,* vol. 5, figs. 539, 575, 1027, 1036, 1059–1060; Castelli, "Démoniaque," pl. 62; Centro Internazionale di Studi Umanistici, Cristianesimo e Ragion di Stato, *L'Umanisimo e il Demoniaco nell'Arte,* ed. Enrico Castelli (Rome 1953), tav. XIX. Friedman's earliest visual example of cannibalism among the monstrous races is from the eleventh century (fig. 8), but he derives the negative approach to them from the eighth century (pp. 149–53).

147. Cohn, *Millenium,* 65–67; Husband, *Wild Man,* 9–17.

148. Devisse, *Black,* fig. 106; Husband, *Wild Man,* passim.

149. Friedman, *Monstrous Races,* 60, 163–70; Hugh Honour, *Chinoiserie: The Vision of Cathay* (London 1973), 5–29.

150. Hugh Honour, *The European Vision of America* (Cleveland 1976); idem, *The Image of the Black in Western Art* (Cambridge Mass., 1989), compare vol. 1, figs. 4–5, 21, 34, 39, 45, 53, 71–74, 93, 118–123, 186, 189, 191 and vol. 2, figs. 2, 12, 20, 102, 112, 119–124, 133, 136–137, 171, 173, 179, 181, with vol. 1, figs. 15–19, 22–28, 40–42, 70, 96 and vol. 2, figs. 29–38, 90–98, 164–170.

151. Wittkower, "Marvels," 191–97; Friedman, *Monstrous Races,* 1, 141–48, 154–62, 199–200, figs. 8, 10, 13–14, 16–17, 42–43, 46–52, 54–56. A minority of travellers from the thirteenth century on stated that these races did not exist (Wittkower, 191–93; Friedman, 197–99).

4

Antisemitism and Other -ism's in the Greco-Roman World

Daniel R. Schwartz
The Hebrew University of Jerusalem

The "Jerusalem School of Jewish History" placed great store on elements of historical continuity throughout all the existence of the Jewish people.[1] It is, therefore, remarkable that the School's central survey of antisemitism should open with Menahem Stern's "Antisemitism in Rome,"[2] with only the briefest review of the biblical and Hellenistic background. Of course, the Jerusalem School attempted to turn this debit into an asset, from a Zionist point of view, frequently asserting that antisemitism was simply a corollary of the Diaspora, which originated only after the biblical period. Thus, in Ettinger's introduction to the volume on antisemitism, he deals as follows with the question as to when a fundamentally adverse attitude to the Jews first appeared in history:

> An attempt to answer this question brings us back to the Hellenistic Era when a widespread diaspora came into being—either as a result of immigration or proselytism—and a monotheistic minority took its place among the nations as a fixed factor and, in the course of time, as a competitor.[3]

A. Tcherikover, one of the School's prominent scholars of antiquity, in a popular survey of our theme, offered the following elaboration:

> It seems we shall not err if we define the inner essence of antisemitism as follows: Antisemitism is hatred of the Jews resulting from the very existence of the Jewish people as a foreign body among other peoples. According to this definition, the inner essence of antisemitism remains the same in all times and places. It is the Jews' strangeness which is the basic reason for the appearance of antisemitism. And this strangeness has two aspects: the Jews are strange to other peoples because they are foreigners and came from another land, and the Jews are strange because their ways and customs are strange—in the eyes of the local residents.[4]

Undeniably, there is some truth to this postulate, but it nonetheless leaves a serious problem. The Jewish Diaspora originated in the sixth century B.C.E.—Nebuchadnezzar and the Babylonian Exile having preceded Pompey by more than half a millennium.[5] Of course, the fact that Stern's essay is the first to open the collection might be fortuitous, and there is no dearth of scholars who have devoted serious attention to antisemitism in the Hellenistic period.[6] Indeed, one could even point to a few data from the Persian period, i.e., the very end of the biblical period, which might fall under the rubric of antisemitism[7]: Esther 3:8 has Haman expressing hatred for Jews because they follow their own laws; the Elephantine Papyri (ed. Cowley, no. 27) report that an aroused mob of Egyptians destroyed the Jews' temple there in 410 B.C.E.; and Hecataeus of Abdera (c. 300 B.C.E.), according to Josephus (*Against Apion* 1.191–192 = *GLA* I, no. 12), reported that the Jews were tortured by Persian governors due to their refusal to disobey their laws, and punished by Alexander the Great for their refusal to participate in the restoration of a pagan temple. But this is not much, and it is also problematic: the Jews of Elephantine attacked by Egyptian nationalists were not just any Jewish community but, rather, a military outpost of the Persian empire[8]; the historicity of Esther is highly questionable and its date is probably Hellenistic[9]; and Josephus' "Hecataeus" was probably a Pseudo-Hecataeus, a Jewish writer of the Hasmonean period—so the persecutions which he reports might be no more than literary reflections of those of the days of Antiochus IV Epiphanes.[10] In general, moreover, it is hard to see how or why the basically closed Jewish community of the Persian period could arouse much opposition. Finally, concerning the Greek and Roman world, which shall be our focus here, it is clear that the very fact of the Jews' existence was unknown, or virtually unknown, prior to the end of the fourth century B.C.E.[11]

But what of the Hellenistic period? Here too, it seems, the cupboard is nearly bare, although this assessment is more controversial. The usual picture of ancient Greek attitudes toward the Jews, once they came to be aware of them, moves from a basically positive attitude, in the first two or three generations (Aristotle, Theophrastus, Hecataeus of Abdera, Megasthenes, Clearchus and Hermippus), according to which the Jews are idealized as philosophers, to a negative attitude thereafter.[12] The difference is usually chalked up to the Hasmoneans, whose conquests, and destruction of outposts of Hellenistic civilization in Palestine, aroused antipathy. However, this hardly stands up to criticism. On the one hand, even the earliest Hellenistic accounts of the Jews are not free from negative comments,[13] and, on the other hand, the earliest thoroughly anti--Jewish account in Greek, by Manetho (Josephus, *Against Apion* 73-105 = *GLA* I, nos. 19–20), may well precede the Hasmonean period.[14] Moreover, as I. Shatzman has recently shown,[15] apart from Poseidonius, who was a Syrian and hence particularly close to the issue, it is difficult to find much evidence for anti-Jewish attitudes as a result of the Hasmonean conquests. Rather, it seems that Greek observers would likely view the Hasmoneans as doing what they themselves would do: building a state, and expanding its borders, when the opportunity arose.

Thus, for example, even Nicolaus of Damascus apparently reported without venom that the Jews expanded their state beyond its natural borders during the Hasmonean period, and were restored to the latter by the Romans.[16] Indeed, Strabo (Josephus, *Antiquities* 13.319 = *GLA* I, no. 100)—quoting Timagenes, an Alexandrian writer—is positively laudatory about Aristobulus and the way he conquered the Ituraeans and forced circumcision upon them.[17] Although some modern scholars have assumed that this policy (evident in at least one other case as well)[18] was viewed as extreme barbarism and must have aroused non-Jewish hostility (perhaps even more than the conquest itself), Strabo and Timagenes seem to have taken it for granted: conquerors impose their law on conquered territories and their inhabitants.[19] Thus, while no one would suggest non-Jews in the environs of the Hasmonean state enjoyed the fact or the circumstances of Hasmonean conquest, it appears that the latter will not take us far in explaining ancient antisemitism. Indeed, apart from Manetho and Poseidonius we have yet to see much of that.

Alexandrian Antisemitism

> The libels upon us originated with the Egyptians.
> Josephus, *Against Apion* 1.223

It is only in Alexandria that the story really begins. Here, in a Diaspora minority situation similar to that depicted in the Book of Esther, the fact that the Jews were different did lead to hostility. But even here—and this is our main point—this was not always the case. While we have mentioned Manetho, an Egyptian priest of the third century B.C.E. who may have evinced a sharp hostility toward the Jews, we have also recalled Timagenes, an Alexandrian philosopher and historian of the first century B.C.E. who had only good things to say about them; similarly, an earlier writer associated with Alexandria, Apollodorus, is known to have taken the Jews' side in his account of Antiochus Epiphanes (Josephus, *Against Apion* 2.83–84 = *GLA* I, no. 34). From such sporadic testimony no one should make rules. Similarly, although we have some scattered reference to Ptolemaic kings who were hostile toward Jews, we also have references to other Ptolemies who were on good terms with them. It seems clear that, as with the Egyptians' attack on the Jews of Elephantine, such cases of Ptolemaic hostility, on a few occasions derived only from their supporting opposing candidates for the royal throne.[20]

Thus, it is only in the Roman period that the antisemitic dossier becomes fuller, and more uniformly negative. This is the period, especially the first century C.E., which supplied us with such rabid Jew-haters as the Alexandrians Lysimachus, Apion, and Chaeremon, as well as the authors of the *Acta Alexandrinorum* (Acts of the Pagan Martyrs).[21] Moreover, this literature was also paralleled, and partly occasioned by real events. What is usually and justifiably termed the first "pogrom" in history took place in Alexandria in the summer of 38, followed by additional fighting over the next few years, and then later at the time of the Judaean revolt (66–73 C.E.). Similar events were to transpire in Antioch, the other major Greek city of the Roman East.[22] Despite Roman attempts, in both centers, to separate the combatants and protect the Jews, they did not succeed. Similarly, the end of the Greco-Roman Diaspora was to come, early in the second century, when such hostility between Jews and their neighbors—and not primarily against Rome, although that too played a role—broke out in a series of rebellions around the eastern Mediterranean.[23] Significantly, it is by no means clear that Palestine was included among the scenes of Jewish rebellion at that time.[24]

Thus, it would appear that the explanation of ancient antisemitism lies less in the acts of a Jewish state than in the diasporic context, but only when that Diaspora came to be included in the Roman empire. One might conceivably explain the matter simply as a result of the "unnaturalness" of Diaspora existence. Just as it was natural, and by no means reprehensible, for the Jews of Hasmonean Judaea to expand as far as they could, so was it unnatural for *Ioudaioi* (Judaeans) to live outside of Judaea and yet go on calling themselves *Ioudaioi*.[25] People normally fear or hate things which are unnatural. But this alone cannot explain why this anti-Jewish hatred first appears, to a real extent, in the Roman period and not earlier. Why were the Jews of Egypt and Syria tolerated under Ptolemaic and Seleucid rule, but so troubled under Roman rule?

Evidently, the explanation lies in the fact that the Roman period brought great insecurity to the Greeks of the East. Not only did they lose their kings and their kingdoms; in Alexandria, they even lost their city. Constitutionally, Alexandria was hardly a *polis* anymore. Deprived of its municipal council *(boule)*, it was not much more than just another part of the Roman province of Egypt.[26] Of course, Alexandria and the Alexandrians still existed, but under foreign rule. They went on existing as Alexandrians largely due to their attachment to an idea concerning their past history and future hopes.

Thus, during the Roman period the Alexandrians were engaged in a struggle to define themselves, a situation very similar to that of the Jews in their midst. For the Jews of the Diaspora were long used to defining themselves by virtue of their affiliation to an -ism—in this case Judaism.[27] In the Roman period, much as the Romans established Diaspora conditions for the

Jews in Judaea, it established them in Alexandria, for the Alexandrians.[28] This created a special problem for the Alexandrians, who had been used to looking at a whole class of residents of Egypt as being simply *laoi,* or "natives." Now, with the constitutional death of Alexandria, the Greeks of the city were threatened with being just like the natives—namely, residents of a place but lacking any legal status. Hence, the Greeks of Alexandria were threatened not only with the loss of their Alexandrian identity, but, also with the loss of their edge over the rest of the population in Egypt. In this situation, the Jews, who had enjoyed a privileged status as a protected minority within Alexandria, which continued under Roman rule, posed a real threat for the Greeks of Alexandria.[29] Those who had previously been protected guests remained protected by the foreign power who had dispossessed the master of the house.

It is this struggle for Alexandrian identity which is echoed in Apion's complaint that "if they are citizens [of Alexandria] why do they not worship the same gods as the Alexandrians?" (Josephus, *Against Apion* 2.65 = *GLA* I, no. 169).[30] The gods here are substituted for municipal independence as the criterion of "Who is an Alexandrian?" The Alexandrians' claim before Claudius Caesar that the Jews ought to be classed with the *laoi* (natives), and should pay the taxes required for *laoi* while Alexandrians were still exempt, was another way to say that there are still differences which make a difference.[31] But although the Alexandrians apparently won that case, and Claudius confirmed that for the Jews Alexandria is a "foreign city" (*CPJ,* no. 153, line 95),[32] the basic grounds for the conflict still remained. The resentment of the Alexandrians would soon find extralegal outlets—Claudius' decision was followed by street fighting—and a generation later there was massive anti-Jewish violence in Alexandria.

The situation can be clarified by comparing it with that prevailing in another Mediterranean port, Caesarea Maritima in Judaea. During the middle decades of the first century C.E. there was a protracted dispute in Caesarea about whether the city belonged to the Jews or to its non-Jewish inhabitants.[33] The precise import of the dispute escapes us, but what is important is that the dispute did not break out under Herod, but only after direct Roman provincial rule had been established in Caesarea as in the rest of Judaea. As in Alexandria, the issue concerning the previous relationship between the master of the house and the "guests" still obtained. Here too, the dispute worked its way up to the imperial court—only this time it was the Jews who, under Nero, lost their case. So it was Jewish resentment which on this occasion had to find other outlets. Indeed, the great rebellion against Rome, which culminated in the destruction of Jerusalem and the Second Temple (70 C.E.), began shortly after Nero's verdict, a causal nexus emphasized by Josephus.

Rome

On the other hand, the position of the Roman Jews contrasts neatly with the situation in both Alexandria and Caesarea.[34] Here we find a community which had lived over the centuries more or less peacefully, and without special problems with its Gentile neighbors. In her survey of Roman attitudes to the Jews, M. Pucci Ben Zeev noted that there was no "Jewish problem" under the Republic.[35] The heyday of Roman antisemitism largely corresponded to that in Alexandria—from Augustus to the mid-second century.[36] This period included not only a number of nasty literary references to the Jews, but two expulsions of Roman Jewry.[37]

It should be noted that the Alexandrian literature itself played a certain role in these developments. Apion, who created a lot of noise around himself (Tiberius called him "cymbalum mundi"), was widely read in first-century Rome, which explains Josephus' focus upon him in his apologetic tract *Against Apion*.[38] However, much more is involved than simply literary influences and Roman reflections of the Alexandrian situation. Any explanation for the rise of antisemitism in Rome during the first and second centuries must be based upon two factors. First, there was widespread Jewish proselytism—whether fostered or not by active missionizing[39]—which aroused resentment among those devoted to the maintenance of Rome's own traditions. Secondly, there were the Jewish revolts against Rome, especially those of 66–73, 115–117, and 132–135. Proselytism led directly to the expulsion from Rome of 19 C.E. and drew the worst barbs from first-century writers[40]; but it was the rebellions which provided the general background for anti-Jewish feeling and as Tacitus emphasized, this factor increased Roman anger against them. Proselytism and rebelliousness had a significant dialectical relationship since the former gained in intensity and success as a result of the Jewish rebellions and their failure,[41] while eliciting ever greater frustration and anger. As Seneca famously expressed it: "the accursed race...the defeated gave their laws to the victors"—and no one likes to see his hard-earned victory turned on its head.

What is significant here is that proselytism is predicated, by definition, upon the Jews being adherents of Judaism. Previously we postulated that Jews as adherents of Judaism had aroused fear and hostility in Alexandria only once Alexandria lost its status as a city which granted identity, turning Alexandrians into willful devotees of Alexandrianism. But why should proselytism have aroused such hostility in Rome, which, after all, remained Rome? The answer is that Rome did not in fact remain Rome—it became the center of a many-hued empire, of which even the basic language, at least in the East (where the Jews came from) was not Roman but Greek. Moreover, the capital city itself became more and more the home of foreigners. The more Romans could feel threatened by the foreign cultures with which they were forced to deal at home as well as abroad, the more easily an ideology of "Romanism" developed in response.[42] The same historical dynamic which operated in Alexandria and Caesarea existed in Rome as well.

A student of Roman literature in the first and second centuries might have expected Roman hostility to the Jews to become increasingly serious, yet it tapered off from the mid-second century. This happened despite the fact that while the Jewish rebellions against Rome ceased, proselytism did not. Indeed, recent research has shown that conversion to Judaism remained widespread for centuries after the Bar-Kochba rebellion.[43] What saved the Jews, ironically enough, was the appearance of Christianity. The growth of Christianity not only put the Jews into the shade; it also helped them insofar as the Romans (in need of anti-Christian ammunition) could point to them as authentic and condemn the Christians as deviants even from their own tradition. History did not have to wait until Julian to find pagans who favorably contrasted Jews to Christians from this point of view.[44]

We have suggested that ancient pagan Jew-hatred, in its two best-documented varieties, is best understood as a function of the denaturalization of Alexandrian and Roman existence. Roman rule over Alexandria first made the Alexandrians creatures of an -ism alone; then, when the Roman empire threatened to do the same to the Romans themselves, they found themselves competing with others who were equally defined by reference to their -isms. All -isms are, by their nature, universal and compete with one another. Judaism was, by all accounts, quite a successful competitor. Roman protection of the Jews in Alexandria and the Roman wars against the Jews in their different ways exacerbated the problem. But at its core lay the fact that the Romans, by creating diaspora conditions for the Alexandrian Greeks, and by threatening to do the same to themselves, had put them into the same rink as the Jews. People in the same rink normally fight each other, especially if one or more is angry.

Christian Antisemitism

This explanation, may help to account for Christian antisemitism as well. For Christians, like post-Hasmonean Jews defined themselves not by virtue of their relationship to any place—but by their beliefs—by their adherence to a new -ism called Christianity.[45] Moreover, their competition with Judaism was not only an example of the general competition of all -isms, exacerbated—as in Alexandria—by the fact that the Christians were persecuted by the Roman Empire while the Jews were protected by it. Christian-Jewish competition was especially vicious precisely because it was between two -isms which were very close to one another.[46] Unlike Alexandrianism, Christianity did not claim merely to be better than its rival—it claimed to supplant it as the true Judaism. The continued existence of its predecessor posed a special threat to Christianity, since Judaism could be conceived as more authentic (especially if the Christian claim, that the first covenant had been abrogated, was not accepted), and it therefore competed in a very real way. The most vicious *Adversus Judaeos* texts, those by John Chrysostomus, are best understood against the background of Judaization among the Christians of fourth-century Antioch, against which he angrily fulminated.[47]

The aetiology of Alexandrian and Christian antisemitism is similar in yet another, related manner. As we have argued, antisemitism first appeared in Alexandria following the challenge posed by Rome to its essential identity. As long as there were Jews and Alexandrians alone, but no Romans, host-guest relationships were clear and there were no serious problems. It was the addition of the third party, the Romans who were now in control, which complicated matters. Henceforth, Jews and Greeks, whether of Alexandria or Caesarea, had to argue before the imperial tribunal that they were to be favored and their claims allowed. It was natural, in such competitive situations, that this would entail bringing the competition into disfavor. One relevant result was that any difficulties with Rome were most readily projected onto the Jews. Thus, Alexandrian antisemites could tell themselves that Claudius Caesar, who was friendly with the Jewish king Agrippa I and somewhat favorable to the Jews,[48] was in fact a bastard son of a Jewess[49]; and that his council was full of Jews.[50] Later, Alexandrians and Antiochians would resentfully term the emperor Alexander Severus an "archisynagogus."[51]

Similarly, some of the worst anti-Jewish passages of the New Testament can only be understood in terms of Christian relationships to the third party, the Romans.[52] Such considerations no doubt explain the frequent underlining of Paul's Roman citizenship, or Jesus' need to reassure Pilate that his kingdom—which might otherwise compete with Rome—was in fact in heaven. The darker side of this syndrome was the desire to explain away all Christian difficulties with Rome as a product of Jewish machinations. If Roman officials crucified Jesus, it could only be because of jealous and troublemaking Jews. The terrible New Testament scene of Jews screaming "crucify him, crucify him" was required to gloss over the fact that the Roman governor, who had found no guilt in Jesus nevertheless had him crucified. The other option, that Pilate had Jesus killed because he was convinced he was indeed a rebel, was intolerable for minority historiography in the Roman empire.

Again, if officials of a Roman colony flogged and imprisoned Paul, it was allegedly because of Jewish machinations and we have the Romans apologizing at the end of the story,[53] just as when the early Church was persecuted in Jerusalem, the Jews are said to have enjoyed it (Acts 12:3). The point of this statement is made clear by the end of the same chapter, where Caesarea, the Roman capital of Judaea and seat of the Roman governor, will be the place where the Church is vindicated. Later this becomes the place which protects Paul from Jerusalem and where the Roman governor found no guilt in him. In all of these cases, the vilification and incrimination of the Jews and Jerusalem is required to shift responsibility away from Rome for all the Church's troubles, in the hope of reconciling these two players in what is a three-player show.[54] The same dynamics later governed the respective roles of Rome and the Jews in early patristic literature as well.[55]

Conclusion

In his classic survey of the "Second Temple Period in the Light of Greek and Latin Literature," Johanan (Hans) Lewy underlined the fact that ancient antisemites usually considered themselves to be on the defensive with regard to the Jews. He identified three perceived fronts, along which the Jews were thought to be threatening non-Jews: (1) the Hasmonean wars of expansion; (2) the growth and spread of the Diaspora communities, which remained separate and aloof from their non-Jewish neighbors; (3) Jewish proselytism and propaganda on its behalf.

About each of these themes, one could write volumes.[56] We shall confine ourselves, however, to three glosses on Lewy's summary. First, we shall underscore that all three developments depend upon the Jews' self-understanding as adherents of Judaism, rather than as Judaeans. This is obviously clear regarding Jewish separatism and proselytism. For the very existence of Diaspora Jewry and the willingness to consider as Jewish, people who were born neither in Judaea nor of Jewish parents, was based upon the notion that being Jewish was a function of culture, not of place or race. But even the Hasmoneans' expansion of Judaea's borders beyond the regions of Jewish habitation, would have been impossible had they not first become convinced that being Jewish was not bound up with any particular place. That is, the Jews' religion (Judaism) and their land (Judaea) need not coincide. This recognition was paralleled and given full constitutional expression, in the days of the greatest Hasmonean conquerors, by the formal separation of religion and state. Beginning with Aristobulus I, the Hasmoneans were both kings and high-priests.[57] The case of Salome Alexandra (76–67 B.C.E.), who was queen but not high-priest, shows that the separation was very real. It was the Jewish self-perception of being adherents of Judaism—fostered especially by interaction with Hellenism (culture, not place or race defining the Greek) which, in the Hasmonean period allowed for the appearance of Jewish sects, and differing attempts to define Judaism.[58] So, too, it was that same self-perception which allowed for Hasmonean expansion.

But it was not enough for the Jews to define themselves as adherents of Judaism. What engendered serious antisemitism was the redefinition of non-Jews too as adherents of -isms, and as direct competitors with the Jews. When Diaspora Jews (or Jews of Judaea after the Hasmonean period, who had lost their land and defined themselves as adherents of "Judaism") came face to face with Alexandrians who having lost their polis had become adherents of Alexandrianism; or when they confronted Romans who had to consciously and tenaciously adhere to Romanism, the Jews had to compete in a way that was previously unnecessary or even impossible. Similarly, when Jews defined by their Judaism came up against Christians defined by their Christianity, they too had to compete, especially in light of the close linkage between the two religions which exacerbated all distinctions.

Finally, we have also emphasized that the Alexandrian/Jewish and Christian/Jewish competition was heightened and nuanced by the fact that it took place in the presence of an omnipresent and all-powerful Rome; far from merely observing and listening in on these debates, Rome gave them their point. Whenever one side said something to or about the other, it had to do so with an eye to what the Romans would think. Correspondingly, Roman/Jewish competition abated when the Jews could be placed on the sidelines, or even positively viewed in the light of Christian/Roman competition. Of course, in the first instance, it was Rome itself which forced upon Jews, Alexandrians, and Christians alike the need for self-definition by -ism. In a world in which all territory was Roman, all other self-definitions, if not to be treated as hostile and subversive, had to be "not of this world."

Notes

Two corpora were especially useful in the preparation of this study: *Corpus Papyrorum Judaicarum* [CPJ], 3 vols., eds. V. A. Tcherikover, A. Fuks, and M. Stern (Cambridge, Mass. 1957–1964); and M. Stern, *Greek and Latin Authors on Jews and Judaism* [GLA] 3 vols. (Jerusalem 1974–1986).

1. For the main document of this school, see H. H. Ben-Sasson, ed., *The History of the Jewish People* (Cambridge, Mass. 1976); the three-volume Hebrew original, appeared in 1969; see also D. N. Myers, "Was there a 'Jerusalem School?'...", in *Reshaping the Past: Jewish History and the Historians, Studies in Contemporary Jewry,* ed. J. Frankel, 10 (Jerusalem 1994): 66–92; and D. R. Schwartz, (in Hebrew) *Cathedra* 73 (September 1994): 148.

2. Shmuel Almog, ed., *Antisemitism Through the Ages* (Oxford 1988), 13–25. For a much more detailed study by Stern, see below, n. 15. The Hebrew original of Almog's volume appeared in Jerusalem in 1980.

3. See S. Ettinger, "Introduction," in ibid., 9.

4. A. [V.] Tcherikover, "Antisemitism in Antiquity," (in Hebrew; emphasis in original) *Molad* 16 (1958): 361.

5. Actually, the Jewish Diaspora could have begun in the eighth century B.C.E., when the Assyrians exiled the ten tribes of Israel. However, those tribes were lost, apparently because their identity was mainly territorial; that is, they failed to develop a self-understanding as adherents of an ethnic group, or a religion, which could maintain itself abroad. As we shall argue, it was especially the development in the Hellenistic period of the latter option, "Judaism," which would threaten Gentiles and hence elicit antisemitism; the ethnic option, by definition closed to others (Ezra 9:1-2), did not pose any threat. See D. R. Schwartz, *Studies in the Jewish Background of Christianity* (Tübingen 1992), 5–15.

6. See especially, E. Gabba, "The Growth of anti-Judaism or the Greek Attitude towards Jews," in *Cambridge History of Judaism,* vol. 2, eds. W. D. Davies and L. Finkelstein (Cambridge 1989), 614–56.

7. On terminological issues, see S. J. D. Cohen, "Anti-Semitism in Antiquity: The Problem of Definition," in *History and Hate: The Dimensions of Anti-Semitism,* ed. D. Berger (Philadelphia, New York, and Jerusalem 1986), 43–47.

8. See B. Porten, *Archives from Elephantine* (Berkeley and Los Angeles 1968), 287; J. Meleze Modrzejewski, *The Jews of Egypt from Ramses II to Emperor Hadrian* (Philadelphia and Jerusalem 1991), 39–40; J. Yoyotte, "L'Egypte ancienne et les origines de l'antijudaisme," *Revue de l'histoire des religions* 163 (1963): 133–43.

9. M. V. Fox, *Character and Ideology in the Book of Esther* (Columbia, S.C. 1991), 131–40.

10. On Ps.-Hecataeus, see Stern, GLA I, 22–24; C. R. Holladay, *Fragments from Hellenistic Jewish Authors,* vol. 1 (Chico, Calif. and Atlanta 1983), 277–90; M. Pucci Ben Zeev, "The Reliability of Josephus Flavius: The Case of Hecataeus' and Manetho's Accounts of Jews and Judaism: Fifteen Years of Contemporary Research (1974–1990)," *Journal for the Study of Judaism* 24 (1993): 217–24.

11. See E. Gabba, *Greek Knowledge of Jews up to Hecataeus of Abdera,* Protocol of the Fortieth Colloquy, Center for Hermeneutical Studies (Berkeley 1981); A. Momigliano, *Alien Wisdom* (Cambridge 1975), 74–80.

12. For the listed writers, see *GLA* I, nos. 4, 11, 14, 15, 25. For the common picture of a move from a basically positive attitude in the early Hellenistic period to hostility in later generations, see, inter alia, Th. Reinach, *Textes d'auteurs grecs et romains relatifs au Judaïsme* (Paris 1895), x–xi; J. H. Levy [Lewy], "The Second Temple Period in the Light of Greek and Latin Literature," (in Hebrew) in: idem, *Studies in Jewish Hellenism* (Jerusalem 1960), 3–14. See also J. G. Gager, *The Origins of Anti-Semitism* (New York and Oxford 1983), 39–41.

13. Theophrastus (*GLA* I, no. 4) says the Jews' sacrificial cult is reprehensible, and Hecataeus of Abdera (apud Diodorus Siculus 40.3.4 = *GLA* I, no. 11) refers to their "unsocial and intolerant mode of life."

14. For the debate whether the antisemitic passages in Manetho are authentic (third century B.C.E.) or late, see L. H. Feldman, "Pro-Jewish Intimations in Anti-Jewish Remarks Cited in Josephus' 'Against Apion,'" *Jewish Quarterly Review* 78 (1988–1989): 188–189 n. 2, 194–95 n. 14; Ben Zeev, "Reliability of Josephus," 224–34.

15. "The Hasmoneans in Greco-Roman Historiography," (in Hebrew) *Zion* 57 (1991–1992): 5–64.

16. For the assumption that the detailed passage in Josephus, *Antiquities* 14.74–76 derives from Nicolaus, see D.Schwartz, "Josephus on Hyrcanus II," in *Josephus and the History of the Greco-Roman Period: Essays in Memory of Morton Smith,* eds. F. Parente and J. Sievers (Leiden 1994), 217–19.

17. See M. Stern, "Timagenes of Alexandria as a Source for the History of the Hasmonean Dynasty" (in Hebrew), in *Jews and Judaism in the Second Temple, Mishna and Talmud Period: Studies in Honor of Shmuel Safrai,* eds. I. Gafni, A. Oppenheimer, and M. Stern (Jerusalem 1993) 3–15; Shatzman, "Hasmoneans," 32–34.

18. The Idumeans: Josephus, Ant. 13.257, 15.254; Ptolemy, apud GLA I, no. 146. Cf. I. Shatzman, *The Armies of the Hasmonaeans and Herod* (Tübingen 1991), 58–59 n. 90; 83, n. 179.

19. See B. Stade, *Geschichte des Volkes Israel,* vol. 2, pt. 1 (Berlin 1888), 388; E. Schurer, *The History of the Jewish People in the Age of Jesus Christ,* vol. 1, ed. eds. G. Vermes et al. (Edinburgh 1973), 228; V. A. Tcherikover, *Hellenistic Civilization and the Jews* (Philadelphia 1959), 247.

20. For the various data, especially concerning the period between the death of Ptolemy VI Philometor (145 B.C.E.) and the beginning of Ptolemy IX Lathyrus' rule in Alexandria (88 B.C.E.), see V. A. Tcherikover in *CPJ,* I, 19–25; Stern, *GLA* I, 404–407; II, 445–46. We ignore III Maccabees, which claims to report events of the third century B.C.E. but might better be taken as evidence of the Roman period; see F. Parente, "The Third Book of Maccabees as Ideological Document and Historical Source," *Henoch* 10 (1988): 143–82.

21. *Acts of the Pagan Martyrs,* ed. H. A. Musurillo (Oxford 1954); *CPJ,* II, nos. 154–59. For the three writers listed see, respectively, *GLA* I, nos. 158–62, 163–77, 178; Parente, "Third Book of the Maccabees."

22. For events at the time of the Judaean rebellion, see, for Antioch, Josephus, *War* 7.41–62; E. M. Smallwood, *The Jews Under Roman Rule,* corrected ed. (Leiden 1981), 358–64; on Alexandria: *War* 2.487–498; Alexandria in 38–41 C.E., for which there is much more material (especially Philo's In *Flaccum and Legatio,* Josephus' *Antiquities* 19.278–91, and Claudius' letter to Alexandria *[P. London* 1912 = *CPJ* II, no. 153]), see Tcherikover, CPJ I, 65–74; W. Bergmann and C. Hoffmann, "Kalkül oder 'Massenwahn': Eine soziologische Interpretation der antijüdischen Unruhen in Alexandria 38 n. Chr.," in *Antisemitismus und jüdische Geschichte: Studien zu Ehren von Herbert A. Strauss,* eds. R. Erb and M. Schmidt (Berlin 1987), 15–46; D. R. Schwartz, *Agrippa I* (Tübingen 1990), 74–76, 96–106; Meleze Modrzejewski, *Jews of Egypt,* 161–83. On the whole period 38–117, see A. Kasher, *The Jews in Hellenistic and Roman Egypt: The Struggle for Equal Rights* (Tübingen 1985), 20–28 and passim.

23. See Smallwood, *Jews under Roman Rule,* 389–427; M. Pucci, *La rivolta ebraica al tempo di Traiano* (Pisa 1981); idem, "Greek Attacks Against Alexandrian Jews During Emperor Trajan's Reign," *Journal for the Study of Judaism* 20 (1989): 31–48.

24. See Stern, *GLA* II, 618; M. Pucci, "Il movimento insurrezionale in Giudea (117–118 d.C.)," *Scripta Classica Israelica* 4 (1978): 63–76, and the exchange between A. Oppenheimer and M. D. Herr (in Hebrew) *Cathedra* 4 (July 1977): 58–63 and 67–73, respectively.

25. See Aristotle apud Clearchus apud Josephus, *Against Apion* 1.179 (*GLA* I, no. 15); Schwartz, *Studies,* 8, 125; cf. S. J. D. Cohen, "Religion, Ethnicity, and 'Hellenism' in the Emergence of Jewish Identity in Maccabean Palestine," in *Religion and Religious Practice in the Seleucid Kingdom,* eds. P. Bilde et al. (Aarhus 1990).

26. On Augustus' deprivation of Alexandria of its *boule,* see P. M. Fraser, *Ptolemaic Alexandria,* vol. 1 (Oxford 1972), 94–95; Shatzman, "The Hasmoneans," 62–63) in another context shows that abrogration of a city's institutions was often taken as tantamount to destroying it. For the resultant hatred of Rome on the part of the Greeks of Egypt, given vent in such literature as the *Acta Alexandrinorum,* see M. P. Charlesworth, "The Fear of the Orient in the Roman Empire," *Cambridge Historical Journal* 2 (1926–1928): 14.

27. The term is first found, in tandem with "Hellenism" in II Maccabees; Y. Amir, *Studien zum Antiken Judentum* (Frankfurt am Main, Bern, and New York 1985), 101–13; Schwartz, *Studies,* 11; and Cohen, "Religion, Ethnicity, and 'Hellenism.' "

28. See Schwartz, *Agrippa I,* 82 n. 59.

29. Whether or not this was formulated in an overriding charter or, rather, in ad hoc decisions; see T. Rajak, "Was there a Roman Charter for the Jews?," *Journal of Roman Studies* 74 (1984): 107–23. Rajak emphasizes that the Jews' privileges generally amounted to Roman protection of Jews against the Greeks of the cities in which they lived.

30. As Cohen, "Anit-Semitism in Antiquity," 46, notes, this is "an excellent question" from an Alexandrian point of view.

31. Musurillo, ed., *Acts of the Pagan Martyrs,* no. IVc = *CPJ* II, no. 156c.

32. For Claudius on the Alexandrian "Jewish question," and the argument that his pro-Jewish edicts in Josephus (*Ant.* 19.280–91) are of Jewish origin and should not guide us, see Schwartz, *Agrippa I,* 96–105; cf. Modrzejewski, *Jews of Egypt,* 173–83.

33. See L. I. Levine, "The Jewish-Greek Conflict in First Century Caesarea," *Journal of Jewish Studies* 25 (1974): 381–97; A. Kasher, "The Isopoliteia Question in Caesarea Maritima," *Jewish Quarterly Review* 68 (1977–1978): 16–27; D. R. Schwartz, "Felix and Isopoliteia, Josephus and Tacitus" (in Hebrew) *Zion* 58 (1992–1993): 265–86.

34. See H. J. Leon, *The Jews of Ancient Rome* (Philadelpha 1960).

35. M. Pucci Ben Zeev, "Cosa pensavano i Romani degli Ebrei?," *Athenaeum* n.s. 65 (1987): esp. 336–41, 352–55.

36. See Tcherikover, *CPJ,* I, 93–111.

37. Under Tiberius (*GLA* II, nos. 284, 419; Josephus, *Antiq.* 18.81–84), and Claudius (*GLA* II, nos. 307, 422; Acts 18:2). On Tiberius, see Stern, *GLA* II, 68–73; on Claudius, ibid., 113–17. On the Jews of Rome in this period, see Smallwood, *Jews under Roman Rule,* 201–19.

38. The work's original title seems to have been "On the Antiquity of the Jews"; see L. Troiani, *Commento storico al 'Contro Apione' di Giuseppe* (Pisa 1977), 25–26, 29. On the popularity of Apion's writings, see Feldman, "Pro-Jewish Intimations," 238–39, 244–45. Stern notes (*GLA* I, 148–49) that Apollonius Molon of Rhodes, the only major Greek anti-Jewish writer (*GLA* I, nos. 46–50) influenced Cicero and other Romans of the late Republic.

39. A controversial issue lately; see L. H. Feldman, "Was Judaism a Missionary Religion in Ancient Times?" in *Jewish Assimilation, Acculturation and Accomodation*, ed. M. Mor (Lanham, Md. 1992), 24–37; E. Will and C. Orrieux, *"Proselytisme juif": Histoire d'une erreur* (Paris 1992); and M. Goodman, *Mission and Conversion: Proselytizing in the Religious History of the Roman Empire* (Oxford 1994). Feldman basically answers in the affirmative, the others in the negative.

40. Such as Seneca (cited below), Tacitus (*Historiae* 5.5.1–2 = *GLA* II, no. 281) and Juvenal (*Saturae* 14.96–106 = *GLA* II, no. 301).

41. H. Graetz pointed out the striking fact that Jewish proselytism was most widespread during the two generations following the Roman destruction of the Second Temple; see: *Die jüdischen Proselyten im Römerreiche unter den Kaisern Domitian, Neron, Trajan und Hadrian,* in Jahres-Bericht des jüdisch-theologischen Seminars "Fraenckel'scher Stiftung" (Breslau, 1884); so too: L. H. Feldman, *Jew and Gentile in the Ancient World* (Princeton 1993), 332. The explanation might be a psychological need of the Jews to compensate for their defeat (à la L. Festinger et al., *When Prophecy Fails* [Minneapolis 1956]), or perhaps the fact that the now spiritualized Jewish religion, freed of Temple and sacrificial cult, was more marketable; see M. Simon, "Saint Stephen and the Jerusalem Temple," *Journal of Ecclesiastical History* 2 (1951): 132–37).

42. See G. La Piana, "Foreign Groups in Rome During the First Centuries of the Empire," *Harvard Theological Review* 20 (1927): esp. 226–34 and (for the conflict between universal Judaism and universal Romanism) 384–85; Charlesworth, "Fear of the Orient," 9–16. On Roman contempt for Greeks, who often were orientals or lumped together with them, see N. Petrochilos, *Roman Attitudes to the Greeks* (Athens 1974).

43. See Feldman, *Jew and Gentile,* ch. 11, also published in *Journal for the Study of Judaism* 24 (1993): 1–58.

44. On Celsus, Porphyry, and Julian, see D. Rokéah, *Jews, Pagans and Christians in Conflict* (Jerusalem and Leiden 1982), 58–61.

45. The term *christianismos* was in use already by the late first century, appearing several times in the writings of Ignatius (d. ca. 110); see: R. Schafer, "Christentum, Wesen des," in *Historisches Wörterbuch der Philosophie,* vol. 1, ed. J. Ritter (Darmstadt 1971), cols. 1008–1009.

46. See G. Simmel, *Conflict [and] The Web of Group-Affiliations* (Glencoe, Ill. 1955), esp. 42–43, also in general, A. Davies, ed., *Antisemitism and the Foundations of Christianity* (New York, Ramsey, N.J. and Toronto 1979).

47. See W. A. Meeks and R. L. Wilken, *Jews and Christians in Antioch in the First Four Centuries of the Common Era* (Missoula, Mont. 1978), 30–36; Johannes Chrysostomus, *Acht Reden gegen Juden,* tr. V. Jegher-Bucher, commentary by R. Brandle (Stuttgart 1995).

48. Schwartz, *Agrippa I,* 90–91 n. 3.

49. See *CPJ* II, no. 156d = Musurillo, *Acts of the Pagan Martyrs,* no. IVa, col. 3; and 128–30.

50. Musurillo, no. VIII = *CPJ* II, no. 157, col. 3.

51. See *Scriptores Historiae Augustae, Alexander Severus* 28.7 (GLA II, no. 521). The fact that there was some basis for this claim would only make things worse; see Stern ad loc. and A. Momigliano, "Severo Alessandro Archisynagogus: Una conferma alla Historia

Augusta," *Athenaeum* n.s. 12 (1934): 151–53 = idem, *Quarto contributo...* (Roma 1969), 531–33.

52. In the nature of things, much of this came in connection with the allocation of responsibility for the execution of Jesus. See, for what follows, P. Winter, *On the Trial of Jesus,* 2nd ed. (Berlin and New York 1974, 70–83; and D. Rokéah, "The Church Fathers and the Jews in Writings Designed for Internal and External Use," in *Antisemitism Through the Ages,* ed. Almog, 41–43; for other anti-Jewish themes in the New Testament, see Davies, ed., *Antisemitism and Foundations.*

53. See D. Schwartz, "The Accusation and the Accusers at Philippi (Acts 16,20–21)," *Biblica* 65 (1984): 357–63.

54. It should be emphasized that this reconciliation worked both ways: Luke attempted not only to convince the Romans that the Christians were harmless and, indeed, loyal subjects of Rome, but also to convince the Christians that coexistence with Rome was possible and positive. See P. W. Walaskay, *"And So We Came to Rome": The Political Perspective of St. Luke* (Cambridge 1983).

55. See R. Kampling, "Neutestamentliche Texte als Bausteine der späteren Adversus-Judaeos-Literatur" in *Christlicher Antijudaismus und jüdischer Antipaganismus,* ed. H. Frohnhofen (Hamburg 1990), 121–38; Winter, *On the Trial,* 83–89; Rokéah, "Church Fathers," 44–46; idem., "Anti-Judaism in Early Christianity," *Immanuel* 16 (Summer 1983): 50–64.

56. On the first, see Shatzman, "The Hasmoneans." The second, Jewish separatism, is often taken to be at the heart of ancient antisemitism. So, for example, J. N. Sevenster, *The Roots of Pagan Anti-Semitism in the Ancient World* (Leiden 1975), ch. 3, concludes (p. 144) that "In this seldom disowned strangeness, emanating from the way of life and thought prescribed by the Torah, lies the profoundest cause for the anti-Semitism of the ancient world." Already the same was said by Reinach, *Textes d'auteurs grecs et romains,* xi–xv, who concluded that the Jews' religious and social "particularism" is the root cause of ancient pagan antisemitism; see also Tcherikover, quoted at n. 5 above. As for the third point, see the references above, nn. 44–46.

57. See Josephus, *War* 1.70; *Antiq.* 13.301. For the connection with Hellenism and with Judaea's expansion to include non-Jewish regions, see Schwartz, *Studies,* 12–13, 38–39.

58. Jewish sects (Pharisees, Sadducees, and Essenes) are first mentioned in the context of the tenure of Jonathan the Hasmonean (Josephus, *Antiq.* 13.171–73), i.e., within a generation of the appearance of the term "Judaism" (see above, n. 31); see Schwartz, *Studies,* 12–13.

5

Jews and Christians in the Middle Ages: Shared Myths, Common Language

Israel Jacob Yuval
The Hebrew University of Jerusalem

Any historian concerned with Jewish-Christian relations in medieval Europe comes face to face with a rather perplexing paradox. On the one hand, he must draw a gloomy picture of persecution and humiliation, intolerance and fanaticism; on the other, he should not forget or obscure the fact that the Jews were the only tolerated non-Christian minority. The very same political and religious culture that hounded Jews was also careful to protect and preserve them.

I intend to discuss one aspect of this paradox: the existence of a language shared by Jews and Christians—the language of myths and historical typologies. Interreligious disputation focused on conflicting interpretations of the shared myths rather than on mutual denial. This dialogue was an outcome of the fact that Jews and Christians lived side by side, sometimes even intermingled. Just as the other's myth was not denied, its physical existence was not under threat. I would like to illustrate this common language, demonstrating its power and the very intimate ties that it created.

Herein lies the difference between the Middle Ages and modernity. The symbolic and typological thought of medievalism gave way in modern times to historical realism, rationality, and secularity; these new patterns of thought obliterated the shared mythical foundation of Jewry and Christendom or rendered it irrelevant. The modern Jew was still an "other" but in a quite different sense from his medieval position; perhaps it would be better to say that the "other" had now become the "stranger."

The content of this medieval mythical language reconfirms what we have long known—the profound and vital presence of Judaism in the Christian world. But it also demonstrates something that generally goes unnoticed, that Christianity, too, maintained a very profound presence in the Jewish world. In order to illustrate the intensity of this common language and its polemical power, I shall trace the development of several legends common to Jews and Christians, from late Antiquity until the High Middle Ages. These legends constitute some of the most important myths of medieval politics and religion. In Christianity, they endeavored to establish and justify both the papacy's claim for primacy and the imperial response; while the Jewish versions sought to explicate the Jews' position as a distinct minority in a time of exile. Common to all the stories is the fact that they were "foundation legends," hence looking back to a primeval, formative phase and attributing the legitimation of later claims—political or religious—to an event from that distant past.

My point of departure is the document named *Donatio Constantini*.[1] In brief, this document describes a "gift" that the emperor Constantine was supposed to have made to Sylvester, Bishop of Rome, recognizing the latter as the senior bishop in the church hierarchy. It thus seeks to justify the claim of the Catholic pope in the West for supremacy over his eastern rival, the Bishop of Constantinople. The emperor even presented the pope with his palace, the Lateran, which became the papal seat during the Middle Ages. He also relinquished some of his privileges to the pope. Such an act was of far-reaching significance in the context of the tense relations between the empire and papacy during the Middle Ages. The popes cited *Donatio Constantini* as documentary proof that the priesthood *(sacerdotum)* was supreme over the empire *(imperium)*. According to the church, the "gift" created a new situation, making the emperor henceforth subordinate to the pope. It was the pope's privilege to choose the emperor and to anoint him.

The document was ascribed to Constantine, though in fact it was written at the papal court in the second half of the eighth century. Formally speaking, it was a forgery, though it should more appropriately be labeled as pseudepigraphic literature insofar as it ascribes its composition to a prestigious figure of Antiquity. Political pretensions tend to seek support in ancient myths about primeval founders and leaders.

The Legend of Sylvester

As usual in those times, the motive for this weighty political decision is described in a narrative, known as the *Actus Sylvestri*.[2] The story is told in the first person by Constantine himself, who recounts an event in his life that inspired him to give up his absolute rule and share it with the pope. *Actus Sylvestri* is the primeval seed from which *Donatio Constantini* grew. First committed to writing in the second half of the fifth century, the legend was apparently current in earlier, oral versions around the end of the fourth century.[3] The following summary is based on B. Mombritius's edition[4] and the summary by W. Levison,[5] though have at some points preferred R. J. Lorentz's précis.[6]

The Story of Constantine's Leprosy

Constantine was punished with leprosy for persecuting the Christians. Many physicians tried in vain to cure him. Then the priests of the Capitolium presented themselves before him and told him to set up a basin, fill it with the blood of three thousand innocent children and bathe in the still-hot blood. This would cure him. Accordingly, many innocent children were assembled, but when the pagan priests prepared to slaughter them and pour their blood into the basin, the emperor heard the distressed cries of the mothers and had pity on them. Having ordered the proceedings to be stopped, he restored the children to their mothers and sent them home in chariots, gifts in their hands.

That night, Peter and Paul came to Constantine in a dream and told him that in view of his refusal to spill innocent blood, Jesus had sent them to him to show him a cure. He was to summon Sylvester, the bishop of the city [Rome], who was hiding from Constantine's persecutions in the caves of Mount Seraftim together with his priests. Sylvester would baptize him and thereupon his leprosy would lose its power. He was then to rebuild the churches that had been destroyed during the persecutions and renounce idol worship.

The emperor did as he was bid and summoned Sylvester to appear before him. Sylvester baptized him, and when Constantine left the water he found himself cured. Sylvester taught him the basic tenets of Christianity. Constantine, in gratitude for his recovery, promulgated laws for the benefit of the Christians. He laid the cornerstone for St. Peter's Cathedral, in honor of the Apostles, and also intiated the construction of a basilica in the Lateran Palace [the papal seat].

The *Actus Sylvestri* also includes the story of Helena and the story of the Dragon, which may be summarized briefly as follows:

The Story of Helena

At the time Constantine converted to Christianity, his mother Helena was visiting the East with her grandsons Constans and Constantius. Very favorably inclined toward Judaism, she almost became a proselyte. She corresponded with her son Constantine, each trying to persuade the other of the superiority of his faith, Helena championing the cause of Judaism and Constantine that of Christianity. In order to reach a final decision they decided to hold a public debate. Sylvester was chosen to represent the Christian side; opposing him were twelve Jews led by a magician named Iambri. By magical use of the devil's name, Iambri was able to kill a wild bull, but he could not raise the bull from the dead. Sylvester, using God's ineffable name, successfully did so. This achievement was seen as proof of

Christianity's victory, and more than three thousand Jews—among them Helena herself—decided thereupon to convert to Christianity.

The Story of the Dragon
Paganism had yet to be defeated. Till then, on each New Moon the Vestal Virgins had always brought a votive offering of fine flour to a dragon whose lair was in a cave at the foot of the Capitoline Hill. After Constantine's conversion they were forbidden to do so. The dragon, in retaliation, slew hundreds of people with blight. The priests of the Capitolium demanded that the emperor renew the sacrifice to Vesta, but Sylvester warned him not to do so, pointing out that not one Christian had been among the dead. Calpurnius, the city Prefect, challenged Sylvester to descend to the dragon's lair and subdue it. He promised that if Sylvester could pacify the monster for just one month, he and the pagan priests would become Christins. Sylvester fasted for three days before his encounter with the dragon. He then entered the cave, accompanied by two pagan priests, descending 150 steps till he reached the dragon's lair. The two pagan priests were killed, but Sylvester prevailed over the dragon, sealed its jaws and locked it up in the cave, where it will remain concealed until the Last Trump. The dragon's reign of terror had come to an end, and twenty thousand Romans converted to Christianity.

There is a partial symmetry between the Story of Helena and the Story of the Leprosy. After the Christian victory in the public debate, three thousand Jews converted to Christianity—the same number as that of the children whom Constantine was told to slaughter for his cure. The same number of Jews were baptized on the Feast of Pentecost (Acts 2:40). The typological feature brings out the propagandizing aspect of the entire legend of Sylvester—the endeavor to present Constantine's conversion as a concrete proof of Christianity's supremacy over both paganism and Judaism.[7] Indeed, as early as the middle of the fourth century, an anti-Christian version of the story of the emperor's baptism was current in polytheistic circles. This account held that Constantine had indeed sinned grievously—he had ordered the execution of his wife Fausta and his son Crispus; instead of being punished, he assuaged his conscience by converting to Christianity and thus undeservedly received absolution. The legend of Sylvester was the answer of Christian propaganda to that story.

The Legend of Yavneh

The talmudic story of the foundation of Yavneh contains several elements similar to those in the Christian legend. Constantine's conversion was indeed a marginal event as far as the Jews were concerned; hence the Jewish counterpart of the story was not concerned with proposing a reverse interpretation of the facts of the Christian story, as did the pagan version.[8] The Jewish story resorted to the narrative genre, as represented by the Sylvester legend, in order to formulate its explication of another, very significant issue; the status of the Jewish leadership under Rome after the destruction of the Temple—an issue that aroused considerable conflict between Christians and Jews. The Jewish story survives in several versions[9]; here I shall analyze that incorporated among the legends of the destruction in the Babylonian Talmud, Gittin 56a–56b. The story of Yavneh opens with R. Yohanan b. Zakkai's decision to flee the besieged city of Jerusalem during the Great Revolt in 70 CE. R. Yohanan, sure that the city would fall to the Romans, resolved to save the last remnant of the nation. The Zealots, however, were not allowing anyone to leave. R. Yohanan, feigning death, escaped the city in a coffin. Upon reaching the Roman camp, he presented himself to the Roman commander Vespasian, and a conversation ensued between the two. R. Yohanan hailed him as emperor. Vespasian, at that time not yet crowned, expressed amazement. R. Yohanan predicted that he would soon be appointed king, for the Temple would fall into his hands, and according to tradition, only a king could destroy it. After R. Yohanan's prediction of the destruction of the Temple and Vespasian's imminent accession to the imperial throne, the following dialogue takes place:

(Vespasian): If I am a king, why have you only now come to me?

(R. Yohanan): Biryonim [Zealots] among us did not allow me.

He said to him (V. to R. Y.): If there were a barrel of honey [Jerusalem] and a dragon [the Zealots] were wrapped around it, would one not smash the barrel on account of the dragon?

He (R. Y.) was silent.

Rav Joseph—some say: R. Akiva—recited the following verse in relation to him [to R. Y.]: "Who turns sages back and makes nonsense of their knowledge" [Isaiah 44:25]. He should have answered him: We take pincers and remove the dragon and kill it, leaving the barrel [intact].

In the meantime there came an emissary from Rome, who told him: Rise, for the emperor is dead, and the nobles of Rome wish to seat you at their head.

At that moment Vespasian was wearing only one shoe, and he tried to don the other, but his foot would not enter. He tried to take off the other, but could not. Said he: What is this?

He [R. Y.] said to him: Do not be upset, you have received good news, as Scripture says, "Good news puts fat on the bones" [Proverbs 15:30]. But what should be done to remedy the matter? Let some person whom you dislike come and pass before you, as Scripture says, "Despondency dries up the bones" [Proverbs 17:22]. He did so, and the foot entered....

Said he [to R. Y.]: Request something of me.

He said to him: Give me Yavneh and its sages, and the dynasty of Rabban Gamliel, and physicians to cure R. Zadok.

This complex narrative is a fabric woven from several separate stories: R. Yohanan's escape from Jerusalem, his prophecy to Vespasian, the fable of the dragon, the cure. All stories were similarly motived and for that reason appear together in the Talmud: they were designed to describe how Yavneh took Jerusalem's place, and to legitimize the office of the Jewish patriarch (the dynasty of Rabban Gamliel) as having secured official recognition from the Roman emperor. Vespasian's "infirmity" and his "cure" by R. Yohanan explained the emperor's gift to the Jewish sage.

The similarity between the legend of Yavneh, on the one hand, and *Donatio Constantini* and the legend of Sylvester, on the other, is obvious. Both leaders, Sylvester and R. Yohanan, are confined before their meeting with the emperor in a closed space, oppressed and suffering: R. Yohanan is in Jerusalem under siege; Sylvester in a cave in Rome. In both stories there is an abrupt, extreme transition, which must be explained, from confinement to an audience with the ruler. The persecuting emperor becomes a gracious emperor who grants a "gift" in recognition of his cure. In a variant version in *Abot de-Rabbi Nathan* (version B), the emperor says to R. Yohanan: "It [Yavneh] is hereby given to you as a gift"—a term parallel to *donatio.* the two stories, therefore, are foundation legends, each aiming to base religious leadership on imperial recognition, as a "gift" granted personally by the emperor to the religious leader. The "gift" also includes a geographical territory for the new leadership—the Lateran in Rome, Yavneh in Palestine.

R. Yohanan was indeed the founder of the center at Yavneh and the predecessor of R. Gamliel as leader, during the first post-destruction generation, although he himself was not a scion of the patriarchal family. His request, "Give me Yavneh and its sages," is quite logical and understandable; not so the other request, "the dynasty of Rabban Gamliel," uttered by R. Gamliel's predecessor in office. The logic becomes clear only if we see this request as representing a late bid, after the fact, to obtain imperial recognition for the patriarchate. Later we shall try to conjecture when and under what circumstances this might have been necessary.

Thus, the role played by Constantine for the Christians was played by Vespasian for the Jews as the source of supreme secular authority. Sylvester was for the former what R. Yohanan was for the latter—the mythical founder of a new religious leadership—the papacy in one case, and the patriarchate in the other. Accordingly, *Donatio Constantini* tells us of the move from Constantinople to Rome, the Talmud of the move from Jerusalem to Yavneh.

Another point of contact between the legend of Yavneh and the legend of Sylvester is the fable of the dragon, which does not seem to play any logical role in the Talmudic legend. Gedaliah Alon, who devoted considerable attention to the historicity of the episode, clearly sensed the incongruity: "The matter of the barrel and the dragon wrapped around it...was inserted in the wrong place and its intent has become obscured."[10] Removing the dragon story and reconnecting the remaining two sections does not affect the narrative sequence. What, then, was the function of the story? I suggest that the presence of the dragon in the Talmudic story points to an affinity with an early version of the legend of Sylvester, which, as we remember, included a story of a dangerous dragon, symbolizing paganism, which demanded the restoration of the sacrifice denied it by the emperor.[11] This motif recalls the Talmudic dragon, which enwrapped the barrel as if hungering for the honey therein. One dragon was in the Capitolium, the other in the Temple. The first endangered Rome, the second, Jerusalem. Rome was saved by the defeat of "its" dragon, but Jerusalem, which did not slay "its" dragon (i.e., the zealots), was destroyed. The idea that Jerusalem could have been saved by slaying the dragon is advanced in the Talmud by Rav Joseph, as "wisdom after the event." This may also have been the motive behind R. Yohanan's curious request for help in curing R. Zadok, a semi-mythical figure described elsewhere as having attempted to save Jerusalem from destruction by lengthy fasting. Sylvester, too, hoped to save Rome from the dragon's wrath by a long fast.[12]

These similarities seem to imply that the Talmudic narrator made polemical use of an ancient version of a foundation legend similar to the *Actus Sylvestri*. His purpose was to name the Roman emperor as the source of the Jewish Patriarch's authority. To that end he resorted to the same language of symbols and stories, but with different content and meaning. Constantine's conversion was a formative event in Christianity; the destruction of Jerusalem was a formative event in Judaism.

Behind the scenes we sense the conflicting interpretations of the meaning of the destruction of the Temple. Christianity saw the destruction as signifying the demise of the Jewish nation, in retribution for their rejection of God; while Judaism considered it a catastrophe, tempered nevertheless by a "slight salvation," in R. Yohanan's words.[13] The Jews did not entirely lose political power; they still had a political leader, who had received his mandate from the emperor.

Perhaps one can identify the precise historical context in which the legend of Yavneh was wielded as a polemical weapon against Christian views. On the assumption that the Talmudic narrative was created in the fifth century, it was most likely aimed at attempts on the part of the Byzantine rulers to limit the authority of the patriarchate.[14] It is indeed known that the patriarchate was abolished in the fifth century as part of a general drive to deprive the Jews of the last vestiges of political independence. The story purports to demonstrate early imperial recognition of the patriarchate, and it does so by adopting the common language of Christian Rome, presenting a Jewish version whose plot superficially resembles a parallel Christian story, which had, however, quite different inner content.

The Legend of Josephus

Up to this point we have been comparing two legends, that of Sylvester and that of R. Yohanan b. Zakkai. Juxtaposing their various components, one gets the following picture:

Yavneh	*Sylvester*
Prophecy	—
Infirmity	Infirmity
Cure	Cure
Gift: patriarchate	Gift: papacy

One component of the legend of Yavneh is clearly seen from this table to lack a parallel in the legend of Sylvester—the prophecy. But there is a parallel elsewhere: Josephus, in his *Jewish War,* relates how, after the fall of Jotapata, he was captured and brought before the Roman commander Vespasian, who intended to send him to Rome.[15] Knowing that this meant inevitable death, Josephus appealed to Vespasian and told him that he wished to tell him a secret: he would soon be appointed successor to Nero as emperor. Doubts were expressed in the Roman camp as to the reliability of this prophecy, coming as it did from someone who had not predicted his own defeat and capture at Jotapata. Vespasian, however, believed Josephus and spared his life. As in the story of R. Yohanan b. Zakkai in the Talmud, here too a Jewish leader leaves a besieged city and appears before Vespasian. He predicts the latter's accession to the imperial throne; while Vespasian in both cases is at first dubious, he finally honors the Jewish leader and, expecting the realization of the prophecy, grants his request.

Another popular medieval version of Josephus's prophecy expressed the standpoint of yet another party in the political arena, namely, the emperor himself. This imperial legend sought to deny the legitimacy of the papal claims; it was not concerned with the Jewish positions. The point at stake was an internal Christian controversy as to the status of the Jews in medieval Christian society; who should be considered their protector, pope or emperor? A hint of the existence of such an imperial legend may be found in the German legal code *Sachsenspiegel,* written in the thirteenth century by Eike von Repgow, where we read the following law:

> Should a Christian slay a Jew or do him injustice, he shall be brought to trial for having violated the king's peace. This peace was purchased for

them [for the Jews] by Josephus from King Vespasian, after he had cured [Vespasian's] son Titus of gout.[16]

The purpose of this law was to protect the Jews by virtue of the principle of *pax regis.*[17] The king was responsible for the welfare of his subjects, and the law extended this responsibility to the Jews as well. However, the popes claimed the Jews for themselves; the Jews were subservient to the church and its leader, insofar as their servitude and exile were a punishment for the crucifixion of Jesus. Thus the notion that the emperor was the Jews' overlord clashed with the papal claim.[18] In order to proclaim the king's authority over the Jews as well, the law proposed that their right of physical security had been granted them immediately after the destruction of the Temple by the Roman emperor of the time, Vespasian. The same person who had brought calamity upon the Jews also preserved a small remnant of their nation. Josephus in this context has become the representative of the Jewish people for all time, both before the Roman emperor and before his heirs in the Middle Ages, namely, the German emperors.

The author of the *Sachsenspiegel* was writing a law-book, not legends. He was indifferent to the details of the myth through which the law was justified. At any rate, his phrasing hints at the existence of a historical legend about Josephus, who not only predicted Vespasian's impending coronation but also cured his son Titus of his gout. We have already encountered the same motif in the legend of Yavneh. A more direct allusion to the imperial legend may be found in a work named *Historia miscella,* written ca. 1000 by Landolphus Sagax:

> When Titus received word from Rome that his father had become the ruler of the empire, his joy was so great that his right leg swelled up and he could not put it into his sandal. His leg was restored to the shape of his left leg thanks to the advice of Josephus, dux of the Jews, who advised him to let a person who harbored him much hate pass by him.[19]

Titus's "infirmity" in this account closely resembles that of Vespasian in the Talmud. It should also be noted that Josephus is described here as "dux of the Jews." Thus, the stories are similar as regards not only what happened to him and R. Yohanan b. Zakkai, but also their positions— both are described as leaders of the Jews. A later and more elaborate version of the same legend appears in *Legenda Aurea,* written by Jacob of Voragine in the thirteenth century:

> Titus, at the news of his father's honour, was so overjoyed that his nerves were contracted and one of his limbs was paralysed. Learning of this, Josephus divined the real cause of the malady, and taxed his wits to find a remedy, deeming that contrary should cure contrary. Now Titus had a slave whom he so hated that he could not bear the sight of him, not even hear his

name uttered, without suffering. Therefore Josephus said to Titus: "If thou wilt be cured, give courteous greeting to all whom thou seest in my company!" Titus promised to do so. And immediately, Josephus prepared a banquet, at which he seated the hated slave opposite Titus, and at his own right side. And as soon as Titus saw him, he felt a surge of revulsion which heated his sinews, that were chilled with the excess of his joy, and cured his paralysis. Thenceforth he treated this slave with favour, and admitted Josephus to his friendship.[20]

This legend also recalls another familiar episode from the "Destruction Legends" in the Talmud—the tale of Kamtza and Bar Kamtza—but the similarity and its significance are outside the scope of this paper. Our interest is aroused here by the birth of a new, Christian version, which seems to show the undoubted influence of the Talmudic story. One should also note a fundamental difference between all the Latin versions of the story and the Talmudic text. The patient in the Christian legend is Titus, whereas in the Talmudic version it is Vespasian who is cured and grants his gift. The Talmud, in addition, describes Vespasian, not Titus, as laying siege to Jerusalem. Seemingly, neither Jew nor Christian could face the thought that Jerusalem and the Temple had been destroyed by anyone other than an emperor. For the Christian, Jesus' prophecy, "For the days shall come upon you, when your enemies will cast up a bank about you and surround you, and hem you in on every side, and dash you to the ground, you and your children within you, and they will not leave one stone upon another in you; because you did not know the time of your visitation" (Luke 19:43–44), should be realized by the emperor of Rome himself. Indeed, one also finds very early Christian variants which tell of Titus being crowned emperor even before the occupation of Jerusalem, alongside his father Vespasian. An example is the Christian historian Orosius, in his work *Historia adversus paganos,* written in 417:

> When Vespasian heard of the death of Nero, he proclaimed himself emperor. He hastened to do so according to the counsel of many kings and commanders, and also on the strength of the words of Josephus, leader of the Jews. This person, when captured and bound in chains, had declared in the most believable way, as Suetonius tells us, that he would be released by the same person who had captured him, and that that person would be emperor.[21]

Further on Orosius tells us that even before Titus destroyed Jerusalem, he was crowned emperor by the army, in a ceremony called *acclamatio.* Clearly, it was of major importance for Orosius that the destroyer of Jerusalem should have been an emperor. In Jewish eyes, too, the destroyer of the Temple of the supreme King of Kings had to be an earthly king, the emperor of Rome. We have already shown that this idea also figures in the legend of Yavneh: R. Yohanan knew of Vespasian's imminent coronation owing to the tradition that the Temple would be destroyed only by a king.

The conflict between papacy and empire over the servitude of the Jews was part of a far broader struggle for hegemony in the Christian world, which reached its peak in the thirteenth century. In 1236 the German emperor Frederick II, granted the Jews of his kingdom protection by virtue of their being *servi camerae nostrae.* Salo Baron proved that this recognition concerned the relationship not only between the crown and the Jews but also between the pope and the emperor.[22] The emperor was challenging the doctrine of the Jews' "apostolic servitude" to the pope. The dispute had its political and legal manifestations, but at the root of the matter was a theological conflict. Jews could exist in a Christian society only on the strength of their role as "witnesses to the faith," living proof of the truth of Christian origins in the Old Testament scriptures. Christian tolerance of the Jews, the only aliens surviving in medieval European society, was contingent on their servitude. The question was, to whom did the Jew owe allegiance—to the pope or the emperor, to religious or temporal authority?

Jewish and Christian legends dressed up this theological controversy in a system of "historical" myths. The *Actus Sylvestri* and *Donatio Constantini* presented the papal viewpoint, while the legend of Josephus expressed the imperial position. The Jewish view of the matter, too, had both religious-theological and political implications. On a religious level, the Jews never denied that the destruction had been a punishment for sin; but they preferred to belittle the sin, attributing the catastrophe to "hatred without reason," an outcome of internal rifts and civil war.[23] The message of the legend of Yavneh was that the destruction of the nation was not final and eternal, as the Christians claimed. Jerusalem had indeed been destroyed, but the Jews still had Yavneh, and hence "the scepter shall not depart from Judah, nor the ruler's staff from between his feet" (Genesis 40:10), for the patriarch was a scion of the Davidic line, of the tribe of Judah. This gave the lie to the Christian interpretation of the verse, predicting the loss of Jewish political independence.

The Slaughter of the Innocents

The legend of Sylvester has a visible plot: a repentant Constantine prefers the Christian remedy (bathing in water=baptism) to the pagan (bathing in blood). Underlying this plot, however, is an implicit course of action—the one rejected by Constantine: the slaughter of innocent children and bathing in their blood as a cure. This is essentially the rejection of Constantine's own past. The emperor at first persecuted Christians and Sylvester was forced to hide from him in the cave; the emperor was therefore stricken with leprosy, a recognized punishment for sin. If the story has followed its "expected" course, Constantine would have been branded as a child murderer. This was, as we have seen, indeed the accusation leveled at him by pagan propaganda—the murder of his son Crispus.

The source of the "untold story" about Constantine is, of course, the story of the Slaughter of the Innocents at Bethlehem (Matthew 2). In both stories the monarch—Herod in one, Constantine in the other—is hostile to Christianity and its representative, Jesus or Sylvester. Like Jesus, who was born in a cave, Sylvester hid in a cave—symbolizing concealment, salvation that remains hidden till its revelation. In both stories the ruler tries to save himself or his regime by murdering children. Constantine, however, recoils, thus becoming, as it were, a repentant Herod. The similarity of plot thus stresses the difference.

The story of Jesus' birth, the Nativity, is modeled on that of Moses.[24] The character of Herod parallels that of Pharaoh, who commanded his people, "Every boy that is born you shall throw into the Nile" (Exodus 1:22); Jesus Christ [the Messiah] is the counterpart of Moses, the Savior; so that the last redemption is made in the image of the first. In the world of Christian associations the negative figure of Pharaoh reflects on that of Herod, and both are offset by the positive figure of Constantine, the converted pagan. The Exodus has become a typological model. The only difference between the two religions concerned the question whether the last redemption had already taken place or whether it was still far in the future.

The Legend of Pharaoh

The midrashic literature offers echoes of both Christian legends, the Nativity and the *Actus Sylvestri*. The Jewish reaction to the Nativity and the Slaughter of the Innocents may be found in several late midrashic collections. Here is the story as rendered in Midrash ha-Gadol:

> When Moses' mother became pregnant, wicked Pharaoh dreamed of a crouching ewe which gave birth to a lamb. He saw a balance suspended between heaven and earth. The lamb was brought and placed in one scale of the balance, and all the silver and gold of Egypt was brought, and even more silver and gold was added, but the lamb outweighed them all. In the morning Pharaoh sent for his sorcerers and astrologers and told them his dream. They told him: the crouching ewe that you saw is that nation now living in Egypt, and the ewe that gave birth—[this means that]—a son shall issue therefrom, and he shall destroy Egypt and conquer all countries for this nation.[25]

This legend does not dispute the facts related in the New Testament, but only places them in a different context. The polemical thrust is based not on denial but on appropriation. Jochebed is the counterpart of Mary; the crouching ewe recalls the manger of the Nativity; the lamb is of course the Lamb of God, Agnus Dei, the Christian appellation of Jesus which here denotes Moses; and Pharaoh is Herod. Pharaoh charges his people to throw the children into the Nile, not as a means of controlling the Israelite population, as told in the Bible, but in order to kill Moses, the Israelites' savior—just as Herod ordered the children slaughtered in Bethlehem.

Pseudo-Jonathan cites an almost identical version, with one additional detail: the names of the Egyptian astrologers, Iannis and Iambris (or Jannes and Jambres), a pair of magicians mentioned quite frequently in Christian and Jewish sources (the Talmud calls them Johana and Mamre).[26] It will be remembered that Iambri(s) was also the name of the leading Jew in the legend of Sylvester—proof positive of the link between the latter and the Jewish legend of Pharaoh. A homily even more similar to the legend of Sylvester may be found in *Exodus Rabba:*

> "The king of Egypt died"—he was smitten with leprosy and a leper is considered as if dead.
>
> "The Israelites were groaning"—Why were they groaning? because the Egyptian astrologers were saying: You shall never be cured unless you slaughter Israelite infants, 120 in the morning and 120 in the evening, and bathe twice a day in their blood. When the Israelites heard this cruel decree, they began to groan and mourn.... A miracle occurred and he was cured of his leprosy.[27]

According to this version, Pharaoh was cured not by bathing in the blood of Israelite babes but through a miracle. This is precisely what happened to Constantine, except that in his case, the miracle occurred in recognition of his acceptance of the new faith, whereas Pharaoh owed his miraculous cure to the groaning of the Israelites! Clearly, the midrashic legend entangled itself in this absurdity because of its desire to adhere to the plot of the Sylvester story: Pharaoh, like Constantine, did not, in the end slaughter the children; and just as the Israelite's groaning in Egypt brought on Pharaoh's miraculous recovery, thus the cries of the mothers for their children being led to slaughter prompted Constantine to change his mind and he was thus cured by the miracle of baptism.

In this version we read of 120 infants to be slaughtered twice a day. Another variant lists 150—a variation easily explained on the basis of the similarity of the Hebrew letters kaf, whose numerical value is 20, and nun, equal to 50. May we compare this number to the 150 steps leading down to the dragon's lair in the legend of Sylvester? Or should we compare the number of infants to be slain daily—300—with the number of children in the Sylvester story—3,000? Even if this is a coincidence, the Jewish midrash is clearly engaged in an intimate dialogue with the Christian legend and twists it for its own purposes. Yet another version tells the story of Pharaoh slightly differently:

> When Pharaoh became a leper he had three advisors. He asked the physicians, what would cure him? Balaam advised him to take the Jews, slaughter them and wash in their blood, whereupon he would be cured. Job heard that advice silently, as if agreeing. Jethro heard and fled. He who advised was slain, he who remained silent was afflicted, and he who fled was considered worthy of adding a letter to his name: at first he was Jether, and lastly, Jethro.[28]

Balaam's advice resembles that of the priests in the Capitolium; but instead of slaughtering children, he advises Pharaoh to slaughter the Jews.[29] Perhaps Jethro, the Midianite high priest, was introduced into this legend to replace Sylvester, the Roman high priest. Thus, instead of refuting the offending story, one could offer a Jewish alternative. Both legends have it that Pharaoh, like Constantine, intended to commit murder but did not. However, a whole series of other legends explicitly speak of Egyptian murder of Hebrew infants. The richest source appears in *Pirkei de-Rabbi Eliezer,* consisting of two legends that purport to explain the link (mentioned in the Passover Haggadah) between the verse "I saw you wallowing in your blood" (Ezekiel 16:6) and the slavery in Egypt:

> R. Akiva says: Pharaoh's overseers would beat the Israelites so that they would make their quota of bricks, as Scripture says, "the same quota of bricks," etc. And the Egyptians did not give the Israelites straw.... The Israelites would gather the stubble in the wilderness, and they would trample it with their asses and their wives and sons and daughters. And the stubble in the wilderness pierced their heels, and the blood issued forth and mingled with the mortar.[30]

The picture emerging here describes bricks used for building in Egypt as mixed with the Israelites' blood. There is still no accusation of child murder. That comes in the next legend:

> And Rachel, the granddaughter of Shuthelah, was about to give birth, when she was trampling in the mortar with her husband. And the baby came forth from her belly and was mixed into the brick structure. And her cries ascended to the Throne of Glory. The angel Michael came down and took the brick structure with its mortar, and brought it up before the Throne of Glory. That same night the Holy One, Blessed be He, appeared and smote all the firstborn of Egypt.

Here we have the explicit connection between a child's spilt blood and the redemption. Recalling the passage from Midrash ha-Gadol cited above, in which Pharaoh dreams of the crouching ewe (the Hebrew name Rachel means "ewe") giving birth to a lamb, one is tempted to suggest that in this midrash, too, "Rachel, the granddaughter of Shuthelah" is a counterpart of Mary the mother of Jesus. As in the Christian story, the child dies, and the death brings on the redemption. In this source the common language of midrash and Christian legend creates very similar plots. The Jewish interpretation departs from the Christian in one point only: it insists that the myth of the dead child and the redemption was realized not in Jesus but in Egypt.

Blood and Blood Libels

Myths also infiltrated the world of religious custom. The Jerusalem Talmud (Pesachim 10:3) prescribes that the *haroset* eaten at the Passover seder "should be soft, the reason being to commemorate the blood." That is, the *haroset* should be made soft enough to recall blood. Which blood we are not told but the midrashic sources cited previously clearly imply that the blood of the infants was mixed into the mortar.

The tradition of mixing wine into the *haroset* in order to recall the mortar mixed with infants' blood is referred to in medieval Ashkenazi halakhic works. In *Minhagei Maharil* (fifteenth century), we read: "*Haroset* is first made thick, but when [the bitter herbs] are dipped in it, it is thinned out, to commemorate the blood."[31] Ashkenazi custom followed the Jerusalem Talmud, which considered *haroset* a symbol of the mortar, and the wine mixed with the *haroset,* a symbol of the blood. One cannot but be struck by the amazing resemblance between the symbolic language of Christianity—the sacrament of the wine transformed into Jesus' blood—and that of Judaism—the wine in *haroset* as a symbol of the Israelite children's blood in Egypt.

We have thus made an abrupt leap in time. The world of Ashkenazi custom subsisted in an environment that accused the Jews of the blood libel, that is, the ritual murder of Christian infants as part of the Passover ceremonial—to be precise, to obtain their blood for the preparation of *matzot* (unleavened bread). This allegation, so repulsive and strange to modern eyes, may now be considered in a new context. The Jews, like the Christians, indeed ascribed a mythical significance to red wine and the human blood it symbolized in their religious ritual. When the Christians accused the Jews of using blood to bake *matzot,* they might have been thinking of the *haroset,* in which, as we have seen,there was an important role for "wine" (=blood) which, together with nuts (=bricks), symbolized the mortar. Such thought may not have been far from the imagination of a devout Christian, for whom, in any case, wine symbolized (or actually was) the blood of the Savior, and bread, his body.[32]

The shared language of Christian and Jewish myths also played a part in the world of art. David Malkiel has recently investigated illustrations from Ashkenazi haggadot from the fifteenth century and later, in which Pharaoh is depicted bathing in a bath full of Israelite blood.[33] The accompanying words are "We cried to the Lord, the God of our fathers," in keeping with the aforementioned midrash on the verse "The Israelites were groaning." A comparison of illustrations from the fifteenth and sixteenth centuries reveals a marked increase in details associated with the slaughter of the infants. The fifteenth-century haggadot show Pharaoh bathing and the Israelites mourning and praying to God. The murder of the children is almost ignored, or introduced in a minimal fashion. Only in the sixteenth century does this motif move to center stage.

The *Mantua Haggadah* shows the scene in its entirety.[34] On the right, the mothers lament the loss of their children. The central panel shows the children laid out face down on what looks like an altar, being slaughtered from behind, in keeping with the laws of ritual slaughter; one discerns an obvious attempt to picture the slaughtered children as sacrifices. The spilt blood is being collected in a vessel at the foot of the altar. On the left Pharaoh is seen, bathing in the blood brought to him.

The fact that these illustrations first appear in the fifteenth century does not prove that this midrash came only then to the foreground of Jewish consciousness, for there exist almost no illuminated haggadot from before that time. On the other hand, it is striking that they appear exclusively in the Ashkenazi-German world and its offshoots (northern Italy and Eastern Europe).[35]

Martyrdom, as we know, was in important part of the Ashkenazi religious experience, and cases of massacred children were given particular prominence. Historians and *paytanim* wrote with awe and admiration of the devotion of parents who slew their children rather than see them converted. At first glance, one might think that the inclusion of the Pharaoh legend in haggadah illustration was an internal Jewish development, inspired by the ideology of martyrdom. However, such a development does not explain the essential and abrupt shift in the portrayal of Pharaoh as the would-be child murderer, rather than the parents themselves, who were specifically lauded as such in tales of Ashkenazi martyrdom. Emotionally and ethically, the blame for such acts was laid on the Christians, whose coercion brought Jewish parents to the point of killing their own children. Nevertheless, there is still a considerable distance between Pharaoh's crimes and the medieval Ashkenazi acts of martyrdom—a distance that was surely obvious to haggadah illustrators and readers. Moreover, the children in the midrashic story of Pharaoh are not murdered in the final analysis, while the illustrations in the haggadot give no indication that the "sacrifice" was not actually carried out. As David Malkiel suggested, it is plausible, therefore, to consider such illustrations as attempts to counter the Christian blood libel.[36] One might have expected the reaction to be out-and-out denial of the calumny that Jews needed Christian blood. However, the illustrations, instead of doing so, deliver a different message: the Jews, too, have children who died martyrs' deaths at villainous hands.[37] Thus, the illustrations constitute a Jewish response to the propaganda of the Christian illustrations of the Slaughter of the Innocents at Bethlehem.[38]

These illustrations, then, constitute a visual expression of a principle found to pervade both myth and custom. The two sides to the Jewish-Christian confrontation were not engaged in a process of mutual denial or rejection of one another's religious symbols; rather, each side adopted and reinterpreted part of the other's repertoire. Exposure of this common language, with its manifold expressions, depth, and broad scope, demonstrates not only the central position of the Jew and Judaism in medieval Christianity, but also the centrality of Christianity in Jewish self-consciousness. It has long been customary to view the relationship between Judaism and Christianity as one of mother and daughter; in actual fact, it would be better to compare them to two sisters, daughters of the same mother.[39] To be a Christian necessarily meant to be anti-Jewish, to reject any alternative interpretation other than Christianity. The opposite was also true: to be a Jew in the Middle Ages meant to be anti-Christian, because Christianity offered an alternative interpretation to Judaism. Negation of the "other" was an indispensable stage in the process of defining one's own identity.

At the same time, Judaism was an essential, indispensable part of the common language, landscape, and self-consciousness of Christian Europe. Herein lies a unique feature of medieval antisemitism in comparison with its modern version. For by the beginning of the modern age that symbolic, mythic language had lost its vigor and religious feelings had waned. Paradoxically, the image of the Jew as an alien "other," foreign and incomprehensible, became far more common in modern times.

Notes

1. W. Levison, "Konstantinische Schenkung und Silvester-Legende," *Miscellanea Francesco Ehrle: Scritti di storia e paleografia* (Rome 1924), 159–247, reprinted idem, *Aus rheinischer und fränkischer Frühzeit: Ausgewählte Aufsätze* (Düsseldorf 1948), 390–465; for an English translation of the legend, see Henry Bettenson, *Documents of the Christian Church* (Oxford 1989), 98–101. See also Wolfgang Gericke, "Wie entstand die Konstantinische Schenkung?" *Zeitschrift der Savigny-Stiftung für Rechtsgeschichte: Kanonische Abteilung* 43 (1957): 75–88; Horst Fuhrmann, "Konstantinische Schenkung und Silvesterlegende in neuer Sicht," *Deutsches Archiv* 15 (1959): 523–40; Williams Schafer, "The Oldest Text of the 'Constitutum Constantini' " *Traditio* 20 (1964): 448–61; Nicolas Huyghebaert, "La Donation de Constantin ramenée à ses véritables dimensions," *Revue d'histoire ecclésiastique* 71 (1976): 45–69.

2. Wolfgang Gericke, "Das Constitutum Constantini und die Silvester-Legende," *Zeitschrift der Savigny-Stiftung für Rechtsgeschichte: Kanonische Abteilung* 44 (1958): 343–50; R. J. Lorentz, "Actus Sylvestri. Genèse d'une légende," *Revue d'histoire ecclesiastique* 70 (1975): 426–39.

3. Garth Fowden, "The Last Days of Constantine: Oppositional Versions and Their Influence," *Journal of Roman Studies* 84 (19940: 146–70.

4. Boninus Mombritius, *Sanctuarium seu Vitae Sanctorum* (1478; reprint Paris 1910), 508–31.

5. Levison, "Konstantinische Schenkung."

6. Lorentz, "Actus Sylvestri" (a critical edition by Wilhelm Pohlkamp is soon to appear); idem, "Textfassungen, literarische Formen und geschichtliche Funktionen der römischen Silvester-Akten," *Francia* 19 (1992): 115–96.

7. Arnold Ehrhardt, "Constantine, Rome and the Rabbis," *Bulletin of the John Rylands Library* 42 (1959–1960): 288–312; E. Bammel, "Heidentum und Judentum in Rom nach einer christlichen Darstellung des fünften Jahrhunderts," *Augustinianum* 34 (1994): 437–46.

8. An allusion to the Christian legend and to the leprosy of Constantine can be found in Tanhuma, Tazria, no. 11. I thank Oded Irshai for this reference.

9. *Midrasch Echa Rabbati,* ed. Salomon Buber (Vilan 1899), parasha A, pp. 65–68; *Aboth de Rabbi Nathan,* ed. Solomon Schechter (New York 1967), version A, ch. 4; ibid., version B, ch. 6; BT Gittin 56a–56b.

10. Gedaliahu Alon, *Studies in Jewish History in the Times of the Second Temple, the Mishna and the Talmud* (in Hebrew) (Tel Aviv 1967), 243 n. 69.

11. See also Wilhelm Pohlkamp, "Tradition und Topographie: Papst Silvester I. (314–335) und der Drache vom Forum Romanum," *Römische Quartatschrift für christliche Altertumskunde und Kirchengeschichte* 78 (1983): 1–100.

12. On a typological analysis of the defeat of the dragon, see Mircea Eliade, *The Myth of the Eternal Return* ( ), 37–38; for a literary analysis of the myth, see Pohlkamp, "Tradition und Topographie."

13. On the destruction of Jerusalem in Christianity, see S. G. F. Brandon, *The Fall of Jerusalem and the Christian Church* (London 1951); L. Gaston, *No Stone on Another. Studies in the Significance of the Fall of Jerusalem in the Synoptic Gospels* (Leiden 1970); Zvi Baras, "The Testimonium Flavianum and the Martyrdom of James," in *Josephus, Judaism, and Christianity,* eds. L. H. Feldman and G. Hata (Detroit 1987), 338–48; S. K. Wright, *The Vengeance of Our Lord. Medieval Dramatizations of the Destruction of Jerusalem* (Toronto 1989); G. W. H. Lampe, "AD 70 in Christian Reflection," in *Jesus in the Politics of His Day,* eds. E. Bammel and C. F. d. Mouse (Cambridge 1984), 153–71.

14. This assumption was raised by Yitzhak Baer, "Jerusalem in the Times of the Great Revolt," (in Hebrew) *Zion* 36 (1971): 185. Concerning older, Jewish versions of the legend, see Menachem Kister, "Avot de-Rabbi Nathan. Studies in Text, Reduction, and Interpretation" (in Hebrew) (Ph.D. diss., Hebrew University of Jerusalem 1993), 233–36.

15. Josephus, *De Bello Judaico*, III, §392–408; ibid., VI, §313; A. Schalit, "The Prophecies of Josephus and of Rabban Yohanan ben Zakkai on the Ascent of Vespasian to the Throne" (in Hebrew), in *Salo Wittmayer Baron, Jubilee Volume on the Occasion of His Eightieth Birthday* (Jerusalem 1974–1975), 397–432.

16. K. A. Eckhardt, ed. *Landrecht*, vol. 3, *Fontes Iuris Germanici Antiqui*, 7, 3 (Hannover 1933), 92.

17. Guido Kisch, "A Talmudic Legend as the Source for the Josephus Passage in the *Sachsenspiegel*," *Historia Judaica* 1 (1938–1939): 105–18; Hans Lewy, "Josephus the Physician: A Medieval Legend of the Destruction of Jerusalem," *Journal of the Warburg Institute* 1 (1937–1938): 221–42.

18. Salo W. Baron, "'Plenitude of Apostolic Powers' and Medieval 'Jewish Serfdom,'" *Yitzhak F. Baer Jubilee Volume On the Occasion of his Seventieth Birthday*, ed. S. W. Baron et al (Jerusalem 1960), 102–24.

19. Landolfus Sagax, *Historia miscella*, in *Monumenta Germaniae historica: Auctores antiquissimi*, ed. by H. Droysen, vol. 2 (n.p. 1889), 304. See also Baer, "Jerusalem in the Times," 181–84.

20. Jacobus de Voragine, *The Golden Legend*, tr. Granger Ryan and Helmut Ripperger (New York 1941), 267.

21. Irving W. Raymond, *Seven Books of History against the Pagans. The Apology of Paulus Orosius* (New York 1936), 337–38. See also Baer, "Jerusalem in the Times," 182–83.

22. Baron, "Plenitude."

23. This is the lesson of the story on Kamtza and Bar Kamtza in BT Gittin 55b–56a.

24. R. E. Brown, *The Birth of the Messiah* (London 1977).

25. *Midrash Haggadol On the Pentateuch: Exodus*, ed. Mordechai Margulies (Jerusalem 1967), 22–23.

26. *Pseudo-Jonathan* to Exodus 1:15, ed. M. Ginsburger (Berlin 1903), 99.

27. *Exodus Rabba* 1, 34, ed. A. Shinan (Jerusalem 1984), 99–100.

28. *Midrash Haggadol*, 37–38; see also *Sefer Hayashar*, ed. Joseph Dan (Jerusalem 1986), 283–89; Louis Ginzburg, *The Legends of the Jews*, vol. 2 (Philadelphia 1910), 296–300.

29. In several sources Balaam appears to be a typological figure for Jesus. See Abraham Geiger, "Bileam und Jesus," *Jüdische Zeitschrift* 6 (1868): 31–37; J. Lauterbach, "Jesus in the Talmud," in *Rabbinical Essays* (Cincinnati, Ohio 1951), 545ff; David Berger, "Three Typological Themes in Early Jewish Messianism, Rabbinic Calculations, and the Figure of Armilus," *AJS Review* 19 (1985): 159–62.

30. *Pirkei de-Rabbi Eliezer* (reprint Jerusalem 1970), ch. 48.

31. *The Book of Maharil (Customs by Rabbi Yaacov Mulin)*, ed. Shlomo J. Spitzer (Jerusalem 1989), 91. R. Isaac ben Moses (thirteenth century), *Or Zarua* (Zhitomir 1982), fol. 117b also explains that only red wine is used for the four cups in order to evoke the memory of the infants' blood of Egypt.

32. Ram ben Shalom has recently discovered a text in a Hebrew manuscript which confirms this assumption, according to which Jews in fifteenth-century southern France were accused of having murdered a Christian in order to use his blood for the preparation of *haroset* (in press). Accusations concerning a possible connection between haroset and

the use of Christian blood, were also raised by the Frankists; see Abraham Y. Brawer, *Studies in Galician Jewry* (in Hebrew) (Jerusalem 1965), 239–40. I thank Israel Bartal for this reference.

33. David Malkiel, "Infanticide in Passover Iconography," *Journal of the Warburg and Courtland Institutes* 56 (1993): 85–99. Cf. Chone Schmeruk, "Sefer divrei ha-adon shel Yacov Frank" (in Hebrew), *Gil'ad* 14 (1985): 34–35.

34. Malkiel, "Infanticide," plate 10b.

35. Ibid., 91.

36. Ibid., 98–99.

37. A similar Jewish response to Christian accusations is to be found in the apocalyptic *Tefilat Rashbi,* in which Christians were depicted as killers of Jewish children during the eschatological war "for the name of Jesus." Adolf Jellinek, *Bet ha-Midrash* 4 (1967 reprint): 123.

38. Cf. Mary Minty, "*Kiddush ha-Shem* in German Christian Eyes in the Middle Ages," *Zion* 59 (1994): 209–66.

39. Alan F. Segal, *Rebecca's Children. Judaism and Christianity in the Roman World* (Cambridge, Mass. 1986).

6

Jews and Christians in Medieval Muslim Thought

Hava Lazarus-Yafeh
The Hebrew University of Jerusalem

I

The definition of the "other" in classical Islam—and to a certain extent even today, is unambiguous: he is the unbeliever *(kafir),* the one who did not embrace the religious message of Islam and did not join the community of believers. According to Muslim law there are two different kinds of unbelievers: those who are not monotheists and possess no divine revelation or holy book, and those who are considered to be monotheists and possess Holy Scriptures. In theory, those who were not considered to be monotheists had to choose between conversion to Islam or death (sometimes also slavery). In practice, large numbers of unconverted Zoroastrians (who were sometimes also taken to be monotheists), Indians, or Buddhists continued to live unharmed under the rule of Islam. This is an important factor to be remembered in the context of our discussion here: there is, in many fields, a wide divergence in Islam between rules and behavior. It seems sometimes as if this great civilization did possess an inner awareness of the impossibility of achieving unity between its theory and practice in its widely divergent parts. This made for a basically lenient, flexible attitude in many spheres, and for turning a blind eye to many practices which diverged from the desirable theory of holy law.[1]

Jews, Christians, Samaritans, and sometimes other religious groups (such as the Sabians mentioned in the Qur'an) were, however, treated differently in both theory and practice. They had received a truly divine revelation from the same heavenly source as the Qur'an and were therefore considered to be the "People of the Book," members of the early monotheistic forerunners of Islam. As such, they were "Protected People" *(Ahl Al-Dhimma),* and accorded personal safety, freedom to practice their respective religions, and even a certain measure of communal autonomy. But as Islam considered itself to be the one final and true divine revelation which abrogated both Judaism and Christianity, it expected Jews and Christians to join the ranks of Islam, as in fact many of them did. Others, however, refused to do so, and according to Muslim tradition, some even betrayed the Prophet Muhammad himself. Therefore, Jews and Christians could not be and were never regarded as equals to Muslims. Many humiliating restrictions attributed to the Caliph 'Umar I (634–644) were imposed upon them, such as the payment of a special poll-tax *(Djizya)* and wearing specifically marked garments; or the prohibitions against building new monasteries, churches, and synagogues or to repair old ones; or to bear arms and to mount saddles on horses, etc. These restrictions are enumerated in many different versions of the so-called "Pact of 'Umar." Most scholars think that these regulations were consolidated about a hundred years after 'Umar I, perhaps during the reign of 'Umar II (717–720). Many of the restrictions themselves stemmed from pre-Islamic Byzantine Christian anti-Jewish legislation. One scholar, A. Noth, has recently tried to show that most of them could and should be understood as defensive regulations which were meant to protect the early Muslims from any missionary Christian (or Jewish) efforts and to maintain a clear division between conqueror and conquered.[2] In early times the Muslim conquerors were often a minority, while the so-called "minorities" were in fact greater in number.

One cannot ignore the humiliating character of many of these restrictions, such as the duty incumbent on every *Dhimmi* to let a Muslim pass first on a narrow road or bridge, or to greet him first whenever they meet. Some later less well-known rulings of Muslim doctors of law seem to corroborate this, such as the rule "Let him who has no property (from which to pay the alm-tax)—curse the Jews instead."[3]

We know that the restrictions of the "Pact of 'Umar" (except for the collection of the progressive poll-tax) were only very rarely enforced in early Islam, usually by an especially fanatical ruler such as the Fatimid Al-Hakim bi-Amr Allah (d. 1021).[4] In ordinary times the *"Muhtasib"* (market supervisor, the Muslim equivalent of the Greek *agoranomos* or Roman *aedile*), was entrusted with the task of keeping the *Dhimmis* in their place and enforcing the regulations of 'Umar. This was, of course, one of the reasons for the fact that Jews or Christians themselves could not function as market supervisors, the other and more important reason being, according to Al-Ghazzali (d. 1111):

> Preventing a Muslim from doing evil [which is the main task of the market supervisor] means exercising control over him... therefore an admonition of this kind is forbidden to an unbeliever, not in contents but because it is a manifestation of the wish to dominate and judge the Muslim. Every admonition of this kind involves humiliation of the person admonished, and

although every evil-doer deserves humiliation, it should not be inflicted by an unbeliever, who deserves even greater humiliation.[5]

And yet, the office of *Muhtasib* presents us also with a very serious methodological problem: we do not know whether the *Muhtasib* actually enforced the humiliating restrictions of the Pact of 'Umar or was only described so because he should have enforced them! We do not know to what extent the many *Hisba* manuals, describing the tasks and activities of the market supervisor actually reflect conditions of everyday life in medieval Muslim cities or merely draw a picture of wishful thinking. Most scholars have unhesitantly relied upon them as historical sources and there can be little doubt that very often these manuals do in fact relate to what actually happened. There are, however, many other examples to the contrary, which prove again the wide divergence between theory and practice in early Islam. Thus, for example, with regard to the *Ghiyar,* the obligation of Jews and other *Dhimmis* to wear specific clothing, S. D. Goitein writes:

> The most conspicuous discrimination against non-Muslims was the obligation to be distinguished from Muslims by their wearing apparel. They were forced to wear a badge of a certain color, a particular type of belt or headgear, and, in general, to be content with modest clothing as befitting a subject population. Countless references to this imposition are found in Arabic literary sources. The Geniza proves, however, that during the Fatimid and early Ayyubid periods practice must have differed widely from theory. Perhaps no subject is referred to in it so frequently as clothing, but nowhere do we meet in these periods any allusion to a specific Jewish attire. On the contrary, there is much indirect evidence that there was none.[6]

But it is not only the problem of theory and practice which should concern us here with regard to the so-called "Pact of 'Umar." One should also pay attention to a basic characteristic of this pact: it is in a way a legal contract in which *both* sides take upon themselves certain obligations: Jews and Christians (the *Dhimmis*) to keep the restrictions imposed upon them; and Muslims to safeguard the lives, property, and a certain freedom of religion for the *Dhimmis*. This made for some kind of stability in the relationship between Muslims and non-Muslims. There were rules to the game, and no provocation against either Jews or Christians could be launched without proving first that they had "broken the contract" and did not stick to the restrictive regulations imposed upon them. Muslim literature contains many stories and sayings, usually attributed to the first Caliph 'Umar, which point to this dual obligatory character of the Pact, often stressing the economic advantages which Muslims would gain from keeping their part of the contract with regard to the *Dhimmis*.[7] They also reflect rather accurately early Muslim attitudes towards the "People of the Book" *(Ahl Al-Kitab)* or the "Protected People" *(Ahl Al-Dhimma)*—mainly Jews and Christians living under Muslim rule. These complicated attitudes usually contain elements of exploitation and humiliation mixed with those of protection and the need to keep promises made in the so-called "Pact of 'Umar."

It also important to remember that the Islamic Empire was from its very beginnings a pluralistic society, in which a great variety of different ethnic and religious groups lived, prospered, and flourished. This stood in clear distinction to medieval Europe where Jews were the only existing non-Christian group, deeply and negatively associated with the crucifixion of Christ. In contrast, the first formative centuries of Islam were times of great success—temporal as well as spiritual—an era of quick conquests and a flourishing creative civilization which spread from Spain to India and established a new order in the world, unified by a common religious law. Several religious minorities became part of this new order under the supremacy of Islam, and most of them soon began to use the Arabic language even for their own religious purposes. They were never forced to live in special quarters (unless they chose to), with some rare late exceptions as, for example, in North Africa. Nor were they forced out of any productive occupation. Indeed, they took part in and contributed much to the flourishing Islamic civilization.

In fact, there was a profound religious-cultural alliance among these three monotheistic religions in their common confrontation with the pagan cultural legacy which threatened the existence of all three revelations to the same extent. The depth of their spiritual collaboration is remarkable and has probably never been matched in any other period of Jewish history. It seems that such a spiritual alliance could spring up and develop only against the special cultural background of medieval Islam in the Arab East. The rich Arabic language with its advanced religious and philosophical terminology, in which the scholars and thinkers of all three religions wrote, was an additional factor.[8]

This spiritual collaboration, the common Arabic language and frequently shared living quarters may help to explain the fact that Muslims never attributed to Jews (or to Christians) any demonic characteristics. It is true that in one Qur'anic story and in Islamic folklore Jews are associated with sorcery, monkeys, and pigs, as well as with other animals.[9] The great historian Al-Tabari (d. 923) also reports that the 'Abbasid Caliph Al-Mutawwakil (d. 861), when enforcing 'Umar's restrictions upon the protected people, ordered them (Jews and Christians) to nail "wooden images of devils" on their doors so that their houses could be easily distinguished from those of Muslims.[10] This information, however, is an exception to the rule. Even in later times, when relations between Muslims and *Dhimmis* deteriorated, nobody ever connected Jews with Satan (whose presence in Islamic thought and folklore is generally less powerful then in medieval Christianity) or with demons, or attributed to them any devilish intention. Thus, there was no equivalent in the medieval Muslim East to the charge that Jews had poisoned the water-wells—an accusation that spread in fourteenth-century Christian Europe following decimation by the great plague. Yet, Muslims had been no less stricken by the epidemic.[11]

II

Medieval Islamic pluralistic society was pluralistic and relatively open-minded, providing a convenient setting for personal encounters and theological discussions between the followers of different religions and sects. These discussions were often described in detail in literary compilations, and show the fascination of Muslim authors with the study of other religions, despite the evolving orthodoxy of Sunni Islam. Muslim authors asked non-Muslims for information about their beliefs and Scriptures, and Qur'anic verses were often compared to alleged or true Biblical ones. Their similarities were pointed out, tenets of belief were analyzed rationally in a fairly free intellectual atmosphere, and members of different sects or religions participated in these discussions. Islam, of course, always had the last word. It was always dangerous (indeed strictly forbidden) to express any criticism of Muhammad and the Qur'an; yet these discussions were very different from the medieval disputations between Jews and Christians in Europe.[12]

Judaism and Christianity loom large in medieval Arabic sources and the arguments against them which recur in the discussions, can be divided into two groups: arguments pertaining to both Jews and Christians as the two "Peoples of the Book"; and arguments pertaining to Christianity alone. There are no specific arguments against the Jewish religion as such, although Arabic literature has many derogatory remarks about the Jewish people being stubborn and untrustworthy, breaching covenants, etc., as well as information about Jewish religious customs relating to prayer, dietary laws, and similar matters.[13] However, the great affinity between Judaism and Islam as the two strictly monotheistic religions of law left little space for specific theological disagreement, except for the Jewish rejection of Muhammad as a prophet. Muslim authors connected this with the earlier rejection of Jesus by the Jews. This represented a clear contrast to the dogmas of Christianity, which Muslim authors could neither accept nor understand.

One theological argument pertaining to *both* Judaism and Christianity is that of *Naskh,* abrogation or supersession. This well-know motif stems from late antiquity and was also used by Christian authors against Judaism. Muslim authors accepted Christian arguments that Christianity had abrogated Judaism by God's decree, but they argued that Islam—containing God's final and eternally valid dispensation for mankind—abrogated Christianity as well.[14]

More important is the Muslim argument of *Tahrif*—the accusation that both Jews and Christians had falsified their respective Scriptures—a widespread motif in pre-Islamic times used to discredit various opponents and their holy texts (Samaritans and some Christian authors used it against the text of the Hebrew Bible). In the Qur'an it became a central theme, used mainly to explain away the contradictions between the Bible and the Qur'an and to establish that the coming of Muhammad and the rise of Islam had indeed been predicted in the lost, uncorrupted, "true" Bible. Jews and Christians were accused of having concealed or deleted verses from their Scriptures as well of having distorted and rewritten others. Jewish oral tradition, seen as an unauthorized addition to Scripture, was also considered to be part of this falsification (as are the later Greek "translations" of the "originally" Hebrew gospels).

Following the Qur'an, Muslim authors accepted the Hebrew Bible and the New Testament as truly divine revelations, but never considered the existing texts of both as sacred. This ambiguous attitude brought about a very special kind of scholarly polemic against both Old and New Testaments. While Christians usually accepted the holiness of the Old Testament but accused Jews of misunderstanding and misinterpreting it, alledgedly reading it in a purely literal way (the "letter" as against the "spirit")—Muslim authors put the Biblical text itself under polemical scrutiny. In the first case a commonly shared divine text is differently expounded; in the second, the text itself and its transmission are studied and refuted. Some Muslim authors set out to prove the falsification of the Biblical text and its unreliable transmission in an almost scientific manner. They based themselves on higher as well as on textual criticism, using much pre-Islamic material from anti-Christian, Gnostic, and other authors. They pointed out chronological and geographical inaccuracies in the Hebrew Bible or contradictions between the four gospels, as well as theological impossibilities in both, focusing, inter alia, on the anthropomorphic language of the Bible, or the attribution of sins to the Patriarchs and prophets. This was as unacceptable to Muslim authors as the stories of fornication and whoredom inserted into the most important genealogies of the Bible. Such stories could not possibly be of divine origin.

This kind of polemical literature in Arabic flourished especially between the eleventh century (starting with Ibn Hazm in Spain) and the fourteenth century (Ibn Taymiyya, Ibn Qayyim Al-Djawziyya in Syria). Later authors up to the present continue to repeat the same Muslim arguments against both the Hebrew Bible and the New Testament. In this way they not only kept alive and developed ancient pre-Islamic and anti-Biblical traditions, but transmitted them to Europe, where they may have helped to foster early modern Western Bible criticism.[15]

In the Middle Ages, the bulk of interfaith polemical activity took place, however, between Islam and Christianity. A vast polemical literature exists in Arabic, Greek, Syriac, and Latin which reflects not only the political and military rivalry between Christianity and Islam, but deals specifically with their different concepts of monotheism, prophecy, and scripture. Each religion claimed to possess a universal truth, and each made attempts to convert the whole world to its banner.[16] But in a more profound way, the followers of both Christianity and Islam were deeply convinced that they alone possessed the true version of monotheism to the exclusion of all others, and they set out to prove it in hundreds of books and treatises of all kinds.

Many medieval Muslim authors felt that they shared nothing with Christianity, not even the basic belief in one God. They looked upon it as a religious civilization cherishing totally different values from their own. Some saw its dogmas as unbelief *(Kufr)*, others as a form of paganism and polytheism *(Shirk)*. It was not lack of information that brought about these attitudes, nor was it sheer misunderstanding, Muslim authors knew much more about Christianity than medieval Christian writers in Europe knew about Islam.[17] They had a rather good knowledge of the three Eastern Christian denominations (Jacobites, Nestorians, and Melkites) and of the hairsplitting theological debates of the first ecumenical councils (Muslims considered Arius and the Nestorians to be closest to the true monotheism of Islam). Apparently they also had before them Arabic translations of the Gospels, though not of the Hebrew Bible.[18] Much of their information derived from Christian converts to Islam, some of whom were learned priests, physicians ('Ali b. Rabban, Pseudo-Ghazzali and many others), and perhaps also high-ranking officials in the churches.[19] Of course, Muslim authors also misunderstood many details, sometimes perhaps deliberately. For example, they equated the Trinity with belief in three Gods, or included Mary (instead of the Holy Ghost) among the three. But on the whole, Christianity was taken to be a very serious theological challenge, obliging Muslim authors to wrestle for generations with concepts like the Trinity, Incarnation, Crucifixion, and Redemption. They rejected all these beliefs as inconsistent with their commitment to the idea of a totally transcendent single God. Moreover, Christianity was based on a clergy and monasticism, on liturgy, music, icons, festivals and processions, symbols, and emotions; Islam, on the other hand, saw tiself as rational and egalitarian (without clergy and with all believers equal before God!) as well as puritan or Spartan, avoiding festivals,[20] music, icons, liturgy and even visual symbols. Islam dedicated itself completely to the endless search after the true meaning of *Tawhid,* the unity and transcendence of God. It seemed to many Muslims like a fundamentally different religious civilization from Christianity.

By comparison, the faith of Judaism occupied a middle position, closer to Islam, but perhaps somewhat more relaxed with regard to its own monotheistic belief, leaving some space for festivals and religious symbols. It will come as no surprise, therefore, to find that Jewish authors since the ninth century used Muslim arguments in their polemics against Christianity, even transmitting them from the world of Islam (especially in Spain) to southern France and the German lands.[21]

III

In the later Middle Ages social and cultural cooperation between members of the three monotheistic faiths declined under the steady pressure of the Muslim Doctors of Law. Separation and even segregation of the three communities from each other became more frequent and the restrictions of the Pact of 'Umar were more systematically enforced. Humiliations and degradation, though not actual persecution, became normal. With the decline of the Muslim Empire and the fading of the economic initiative that characterized the bourgeois society of earlier centuries, came a kind of centralized military feudal order. Tolerance, openness, and diversity were replaced by intolerance and conformity, though there were still sporadic exceptions to this trend in some Muslim countries at various times.[22]

The most important change came to the Middle East with the importation of European antisemitism by Christian priests and translators during the nineteenth century.[23] In this way, the blood libel came to be known in the Middle East, as well as anti-Jewish polemics condemning Captain Dreyfus, anti-Talmudic tracts, etc., and later the *Protocols of the Elders of Zion*. Even typically Christian motifs such as the charge of Deicide, which the Qur'an flatly rejects,[24] together with other antisemitic motifs and caricatures, began to appear in Arabic literature. Ironically, these same motifs were (and still are) often accompanied by parallel anti-Christian arguments, nursed by fear and resentment of Western Christian supremacy and colonialism. All of these themes were, of course, fuelled by the political conflicts in the area.

One must, however, be careful to distinguish between such modern forms of antagonism towards Jews (and Christians) and the generally more favorable attitudes to the "other" in classical Islam of the early and later Middle Ages.

Notes

1. See Hava Lazarus-Yafeh, "Minorities under Islam and Islam as a Minority," in: *Perspectives in Israeli Pluralism,* eds. K. O. Cohen and J. S. Gerber (Israel Colloquium 1991), 23–33.

2. A. Noth, "Abgrenzungsprobleme zwischen Muslimen und Nicht-Muslimen: Die Bedingungen 'Umars (as-Shurut al-'Umariyya) unter einem anderen Aspekt gelesen," *JSAI* (Jerusalem Studies in Arabic and Islam) 9 (1987): 219–35. For a more general view cf. B. Lewis, *The Jews of Islam* (Princeton 1984), esp. chapter 1; N. Stillman, *The Jews of*

Arab Lands (Philadelphia 1979), "Introduction"; M. R. Cohen, *Under Crescent and Cross, The Jews in the Middle Ages* (Princeton 1994).

3. Ibn Hajar Al-'Asqalani (d. 1449), *Fatawa Hadithiyya* (Cairo? 1307 A.H.), 120.

4. See J. van Ess, *Chiliastische Erwartungen und die Versuchung der Göttlichkeit* (Heidelberg 1977).

5. See Hava Lazarus-Yafeh, *Studies in Al-Ghazzali* (Jerusalem 1975), chap. 7: "Jews and Christians in the Writings of Al-Ghazzali," 444.

6. S. D. Goitein, *A Mediterranean Society*, vol. 2 (Berkeley 1971); vol. 7, A2, 286; and see the example that follows; cf. also vol. 6, 380 ff.

7. See, for example, B. Lewis, ed. and tr., *Islam from the Prophet Muhammad to the Capture of Constantinople* (New York 1974), vol. 2: "Religion and Society," 223–24.

8. See one striking example in Hava Lazarus-Yafeh, *Some Religious Aspects of Islam* (Leiden 1981), 75–76.

9. See Sura 2:60, Sura 5:60, and Sura 113 with their commentaries. Jews are usually designated as monkeys; Christians as pigs.

10. Al-Tabari, *Ta'rikh Al-Rusul wa-l-Muluk*, in *Annales*, ed. M. J. de Geoje and I. J. Barth, 3rd series (Reprint Leiden 1964), 1390; a full translation of the text is available in Lewis, *Jews of Islam*, 48–49.

11. See M. Dols, *The Black Death in the Middle East* (Princeton 1977).

12. See Hava Lazarus-Yafeh, *Intertwined Worlds, Medieval Islam and Bible Criticism* (Princeton 1992), chap. 6, esp. 134–35.

13. Cf. G. Vajda, "Juifs et Musulmans selon le Hadit," *JA* (Journal Asiatique) 1937: 57–137; M. Kister, "Do not Assimilate Yourselves..." *JSAI* 12 (1989): 231–321.

14. See C. Adang, *Muslim Writers on Judaism and the Bible from Ibn Rabban to Ibn Hazm* (Nijmegen 1993), chap. 6; and Lazarus-Yafeh, *Intertwined Worlds*, chap. 2.

15. Ibid., chap. 6.

16. Cf. B. Lewis, *Islam and the West*, 2nd ed. (Oxford 1993); idem, *Jews of Islam*, 58–62.

17. See N. Daniel, *Islam and the West: The Making of an Image*, rev. ed. (Oxford 1993).

18. See S. H. Griffith, "The Monks of Palestine and the Growth of Christian Literature in Arabic," *The Muslim World* 78 (1988): 1–78; idem, "The Gospel in Arabic: An Inquiry into its Appearance in the First Abbasid Century," *Oriens Christianus* 69 (1985): 126–67; cf. also Lazarus-Yafeh, *Intertwined Worlds*, chap. 5.

19. Other authors were less learned; see, for example, I. Sourdel, "Un pamphlet musulman anonyme d'époque 'Abbaside contre les chrétiens," *REI* 34 (1966): 1–33.

20. See Lazarus-Yafeh, *Some Religious Aspects of Islam*, chap. 3: "Muslim Festivals."

21. This becomes very clear through D. J. Lasker's work, although he himself does not explicitly point out the Muslim origins of some Jewish arguments against Christianity. See, for example, his "The Jewish Critique of Christianity under Islam in the Middle Ages," *PAAJR* 57 (1991): 121–52; and idem, "The Influence of Jewish Christian Polemics under Islam on Jewish-Christian Polemics under Christianity," in *W. Z. Brinner Jubilee Volume* (Berkeley forthcoming); ibid., (in Hebrew) *Pe'amim* 57 (1994): 4–16. Cf. also Hava Lazarus-Yafeh, "Appendix" (in Hebrew) to these articles of Lasker, *Pe'amim* 62 (1995): 49–56. One must remember that some of the Muslim arguments against

Christianity may have been taken in the first place from Jewish polemics against Christianity.

22. See Lewis, *Jews of Islam,* 57–58.

23. See B. Lewis, *Semites and Anti-Semites* (London 1986), esp. chap. 5.

24. See Sura 4:157 and the enormous number of Arabic commentaries and modern studies of it. The notion of Deicide is, of course, totally incompatible with the Islamic view of Jesus as a prophet. It is also important to remember in this context that Islam knows of no sacraments and never really developed any kind of liturgy. The verbal aspect of its prayer is almost negligible.

With profound regret, the Center announces the death of
Prof. Hava Lazarus-Yafeh on September 8, 1998.

7

The Transformation of Hatred: Antisemitism as a Struggle for Group Identity

Henri Zukier
Graduate Faculty, New School for Social Research, New York

Towards the end of 1927, Freud confided to his friend Arnold Zweig his consternation at the phenomenon of antisemitism. "With regard to antisemitism," Freud remarked: "I don't really want to search for explanations; I feel a strong inclination to surrender to my affects in this matter and find myself confirmed in my wholly non-scientific belief that mankind...by and large are a wretched lot."[1] Freud's pessimism was quite untypical among the thinkers of the eighteenth and nineteenth centuries. Edward Gibbon, who wrote a landmark history of Rome that was also a meditation on the destructive forces of barbarism, foresaw no such possibility for the West. Four thousand years of European experience, he noted, "should enlarge our hopes and diminish our apprehensions.... [I]t may safely be presumed that no people, unless the face of nature is changed, will relapse into their original barbarism." Thus, he concluded, "every age of the world has increased and still increases the real wealth, the happiness, the knowledge, and perhaps the virtue of the human race."[2] Or, as Herbert Spencer put it: "Progress...is not an accident, but a necessity...so surely must evil and immorality disappear; so surely must man become perfect."[3]. From the vantage point of our own fin-de-siècle, Freud's silence on antisemitism seems particularly striking, an expression not of ignorance but of helpless foreboding. In a process he described at length, old enmities have erupted everywhere yet again in a "return of the repressed" and have torn apart many countries and peoples.

The end of the twentieth century dispels all illusions about any easy reconciliation between peoples. The old-new conflicts of ethnicity, race and class are here to stay, and will be a central issue for all human societies in the next century. It is clear that the mid-century crisis was but the first paroxysm of the new age. The "other" is likely to become an ever more insistent and troubling presence in society, rooted in its fundamental needs, tensions, and entanglements.

I. Conflict and the Essential "Other"

Throughout the ages, many thinkers have observed how humankind, in its state of nature, was driven by selfish motives and, hence, that people were naturally inclined to clash with other individuals and groups. Saint Augustine already observed in his most important political work how strife was endemic in human society. "The city of man," he wrote, "for the most part is a city of contention with opinions divided by foreign wars and domestic quarrels and by the demands for victories which either end in death or are merely respites from further war...the city of man is divided against itself."[4] (In addition, of course, the city of man also was in conflict with the city of God). Hobbes famously depicted pre-political society as a condition of war of every man against his neighbor. By their passions, "men have no pleasure, but on the contrary a great deal of grief, in keeping company." William James put it even more concretely: "The baiting of the Jews, the hunting of the Albigenses...the massacring of the Armenians, express...that aboriginal human neophobia, that pugnacity of which we all share the vestiges, and that inborn hatred of the alien and of the eccentric and non-conforming men as aliens."[5] Thus the most divergent accounts of the origins of humanity, or of particular groups, typically hark back to an aboriginal conflict between significant others. Freud stressed the antagonism between parents and children, leading to the inevitable crime (historical or psychological) of parricide, which spawned the formation of conscience and civilization. The Oedipal conflict was, according to Freud, the early nexus of such struggles. Many other accounts of the dawn of humanity also depict a family struggle marked by fratricide (such as Cain and Abel, or Romulus and Remus).

Conflict is, however, not only destructive. Psychologists concur that personality does not develop linearly but is shaped through a succession of confrontations with real and imagined others. In the Freudian view, the self emerges out of the unremitting clash between repressive strictures from parents and society, which crystallized in the super-ego, and the instinctual stirrings of the id. Erik Erikson described the course of individual development as marked by a series of conflicts between basic attitudes involving self and other, the ontogenetic source of both strength and maladjustment. Piaget's view of intellectual development and numerous other psychological theories are likewise rooted in a conflictual perspective.[6]

For the natural world, the Darwinian account of evolution evokes the continuous struggle for existence of plants and animals, resulting in natural selection and the survival of the fittest. Social philosophers have also seen conflict as an essential moving force in history and in the development of society. Vico and Hume in the eighteenth century, later followed by Comte and Saint-Simon, argued that social and intellectual advancement were furthered by social and economic, even military conflict. Historians such as Tilly, have also noted that wars were the engine for the rise of European states and that preparations for war shaped their internal structure. Tilly argued that the central paradox of European state formation was that "the pursuit of war and military capacity, after having created national states as a sort of by-product, led to a civilianization of government and domestic politics."[7] For Adam Smith, a particular form of economic conflict—the competition between self-interested actors in the market place—was the core dynamic of capitalism and material progress. The opening lines of the Communist Manifesto remain perhaps the most famous expression of the *agonistic* view of history: "The history of all hitherto existing society is the history of class struggles...a fight that each time ended either in a revolutionary reconstitution of society at large or in the common ruin of the contending classes."[8] Or as Engels put it: "Life itself...is a contradiction that is objectively present in things and processes, and is constantly asserting and resolving itself."[9]

Religious identity is also strengthened by conflict. Tocqueville already noted on his voyage to America that "there is no country in the world where the Christian religion retains a greater influence over the souls of men than in America," and the same holds true a hundred years later. This is due, so Tocqueville and modern observers suggested, because established religion was abolished in the United States and replaced by a voluntaristic and sectarian religious tradition that encouraged many denominations, which were inevitably in competition and in conflict with each other.[10]

This explains three remarkable features of the "other." Although he is an outsider to society, he remains such a faithful and dependable presence in it because he is a creation of that society which contrives him in times of need. Also, in spite of their different geographical and temporal origins, outsiders typically display a remarkable family resemblance, a similarity of features and behavior that would befit members of an international brotherhood. These regularities across time and place suggest that the outsiders' genealogy is rooted as much in the mind as in history. Finally, the outsider does not possess just any features, nor does he simply represent alien values. He embodies central and intimate features of his host society, which, like the outsider himself, have often been disavowed and repressed. Hence the figure of the outsider is doubly fearful, due to his imagined destructive powers and the weaknesses of society for which he is the perpetual reminder and cover.

In his role as the polar opposite of society, the "other" easily acquires awesome unnatural features. He embodies the "daemonic" principle which Goethe described at the end of his autobiography: This "fearful" principle "was only manifested in contradictions...seemed to step in between all other principles, to separate them and to unite them...forming a power which, if not opposed to the moral order of the world, yet crosses it so that one may be regarded as the warp and the other the woof...all united moral powers are of no avail against it."[11] The "other" as a kind of demon in human form is an ineluctable, indeed essential presence in society. His significance was captured by Einstein when he allowed that "faith in the influence of demons is probably at the root of our concepts of causality."[12]

II. Categorization and the Imaginary Jew.

I would like to argue that the Jew in modern times has become the privileged and essential "other" in the Western mind; that the imaginary Jew is therefore doomed to an eternal afterlife in the West, unlikely to fade anytime soon; that this evolution is not due to his actual behavior or to socio-economic and political conditions. Rather, the imaginary Jew arose from the Western mind. His inexorable endurance is linked to two factors: the universal psychological dynamics of categorization and the particular historical encounter of the Jew with medieval Christianity. The Church's entanglement with antisemitism did not occur, however, on account of its "teachings of contempt" toward the Jews. Higher Church authorities in the Middle Ages typically took pains to protect the lives of the Jews from popular violence. Instead the origins of modern antisemitism are rooted in the Church's most revolutionary and compassionate teachings, in its special kind of universalistic doctrine, coupled with an insistence on associating salvation with the adoption of a set of dogmatic beliefs. The turning-point occurred around the twelfth century, when the Church's ecumenical beliefs introduced a new element of sensibility into the Western mentality, a revolutionary "mindframe" for intercourse with the "other." This mindframe generated a new overarching category of humanity, as well as a new threat of deviance, which led to a modern logic of exclusion of the "other" that would become the hallmark of modern antisemitism and find its ultimate expression in Nazism.

The most fundamental building block of human thinking is the ability to organize objects and events into discrete classes or categories. Categorization is an act of discrimination, separating those things which belong together from those which do not. Categories thus define the nature of things by stipulating the necessary and sufficient qualities for group membership. Categories often also intimate a hierarchy of differences: they specify relations between classes of objects and a hierarchical organization among them. Categories may also suggest a theory about the origins of hierarchical differences. Thus assertions about the hierarchy and the biological origins of differences in human qualities constitute the core of the racist argument. In contrast to Darwin, theories of racist evolution claim that differences between the races are so large and intractable that the races constitute different species and not merely human diversity.

One may be tempted, of course, to try and transcend or shatter the pernicious binary oppositions constructed by such categorization. To do so, however, one would first have to abolish thinking. For categorization is to the mind what breathing is to the body. Discrimination and prejudice are inherent in the very act of perception. At the social level, this means that to be human is to have an essential "other."

The outsider in Antiquity.

In the ancient Western world, societies were organized as small, rather personalized groups, whose members were united by a common ancestry or territory. The kinship bonds created family, tribal, or ethnic communities, which emphasized their autonomy, and were marked by a sense of exclusiveness and impenetrable group boundaries. This was reflected, for instance, in the conflict between Sparta and Athens, or in the adamant opposition of cities like Athens to granting citizenship to outsiders, even if they came from other Greek cities and even if this led to a majority of non-citizens in some of the larger *poleis*. It was not until the Persian wars that some of the Greek city-states overcame their political fragmentation and for the first time in their history, formed a military union to repel the invader.

Ancient individualism paradoxically led to a measure of tolerance toward the outsider. In a universe divided into many groups which could never come together because they were separated by objective and unchangeable characteristics, there was an awareness of the local dimensions of identity and of the inherent multiplicity of conditions for group belonging. The rejection of the outsider in antiquity was more pragmatic and less principled than in later times. To be sure, he was excluded from society and subjugated, but it was a "negative" exclusion of "not belonging" to the "in-group." Kinship social organizations imply some measure of incommensurability between groups, and thereby a limit to invidious evaluative comparisons. The differentness of the outsider has none of its modern moral or metaphysical meaning. For instance, there is no resentment at the outsider's failure to belong, nor any temptation to force him back into a (non-existent) social or ideological class. The outsider may evoke a concrete conflict of interests or the temptation of exploitation, but not of extermination. His status was one of limited humanity, rather than of inhumanity. Since the category of humankind did not yet exist, the outsider could not be excluded from it.

The circumscribed exclusionary policies of antiquity are exemplified in the cultural tolerance often displayed by ancient conquerors. They were ruthless in enforcing political conformity, but did not seek to impose their beliefs and gods on their conquered subjects. Not infrequently, they even displayed remarkable sensitivity to their subjects' religious feelings. For instance, in Judaea the occupying armies avoided the display of idolatrous images on their coins or army standards, in order not to offend the Jewish population. When Jerusalem acquired the status of a Greek polis in 175 B.C., this political transformation did not inhibit or modify the Jewish religious cult. The ancient religious policy resulted not in total segregation, but in some measure of reciprocal influence. Ancient polytheism was quite flexible, and unlike the *polis,* the pantheon incorporated foreign gods; deities, unlike citizens, could move pretty freely between cities and mythologies, often requiring only a quick change of name. Thus, when Antiochus Epiphanes, the second century B.C. Seleucid ruler of Judaea, suddenly moved against the cult of Jerusalem, imposed the worship of the Olympian Zeus in the Temple, and banned Jewish practices such as circumcision, the Sabbath, or the study of Torah, he shocked not only his Jewish subjects—who quickly rose against him in the revolt of the Maccabees. Antiochus's behavior also confounded many modern historians, some of whom compared him to Nero or Caligula.[13]

The Outsider in Christian Universalism.

Christianity introduced a new way of thinking in the West, which was to renew the fabric of human relations. Christianity fused all local kinship groups into one overarching, universal and all-inclusive category of humanity. For the first time in Western history, the outsider was incorporated into the moral scheme of society. The beginnings of the Christian approach to the outsider can already be discerned in the Hellenistic period. The military conquests of Alexander the Great in the fourth century B.C., when his troops defeated the Persian empire, and pushed on to northern India, brought the Greeks into contact with many other peoples and cultures. This intercourse for the first time generated a recognition that the differentiation between Greeks and barbarians was not as great or as insurmountable as commonly assumed. This new cosmopolitan awareness is reflected in Alexander's decision to grant the subjugated Persians a measure of equality with the Greeks.[14] It would find its full development and expression in Christian universalism.

Christianity founded its vision of human social organization on the radical renunciation of all kinship bonds of blood and territory that were decisive in antiquity. As Paul proclaimed (Galatians 3:28): "There is neither Jew nor

Greeek, there is neither slave nor free, there is neither male nor female; for you are all one in Christ Jesus." Group membership was open to all people, regardless of origins; henceforth, it was a manifestation of personal choice, not of an impersonal (divine or historical) election. People were all equal, for they all were at least potentially the recipients of salvation. Thus Christianity introduced in the West the idea of one all-encompassing and unbounded category of hu(mankind), uniting all people in a common sphere of fellow-feeling and fellow responsibility. Christian inclusiveness even transformed family relations, as the gospel's account of Jesus's relations with his family suggests. When Jesus's mother and brothers (who had previously clashed with him) came to see him while he was preaching to a crowd, Jesus instead turned to the gathering: "'Who are my mother and my brothers?' Looking around at those who sat about him, he said: 'Here are my mother and my brothers! Whoever does the will of God is my brother, and sister, and mother'" (Mark 3:33–35). The "other" had become a brother.

By the seventeenth century, the Christian ecumenical revolution was completed and hu(mankind) had become a universal category, deeply affecting the fabric of human relationships. The secularized idea of the intangible quality of humanity, and of the rights attached to this invisible quality was developed in the works of Locke, Hobbes, and Kant. Kant called this human feature "dignity": it was grounded in man's rationality and capacity for moral choice, and it commanded respect for the integrity of the person. The universal dignity of man was expressed in Kant's categorical imperative, and in his "practical imperative": "Act so that you treat humanity, whether in your own person or in that of another, always as an end and never as a means only." Things only had a relative worth, reflected in their price, but people had an absolute worth.[15] Locke's *Second Treatise* formally developed the idea of natural rights, the precursor of contemporary human rights. This fundamental right was initially called "natural," because it derived, not from controvertible moral claims, laws or custom, but from the "self-evident truth" (as the American Declaration of Independence put it) of man's nature and the requirements of "natural law."

The Christian idea of a realm of inclusion, and the invention of an overarching category of humankind, were, however, vitiated by the incorporation of the exclusionary clause of "justification by faith." In the Kantian system, on the other hand, man's absolute value was simply a function of his humanity and he is owed basic respect, regardless of his behavior: "Humanity itself is a dignity.... I cannot deny all respect to even a vicious man as man; I cannot withdraw at least the respect that belongs to him in his quality as a man, even though by his deeds he makes himself unworthy of it."[16] Christian full-fledged group membership was, however, predicated on the adoption of a core doctrine. Any universalism linked to conformity in belief and salvation, and especially one committed to spreading its doctrine, is likely to engender conflict and the coercion of non-conforming groups.

Christianity had not, in fact, abolished the exclusionary categorization of the ancient world, but reversed its defining characteristics. Ancient rulers were primarily concerned to enforce *political conformity*, and left their subjects considerable room for diversity of belief. Christianity, which aspired to transcend political boundaries, was uninterested in people's ethnic past and bonds of kinship, but pressed instead for *belief conformity*. A conflict over beliefs is psychologically far more momentous, containing the potential of far more and far greater violence than the kinship conflicts of antiquity. Belief conflicts have a greater moral significance and higher stake: in contrast to the fixed kinship boundaries, the outsider was given the possibility to join society, hence his obstinate "otherness" became a matter of choice and rejection of the dominant values. The "other" for the first time presented a moral challenge, contradicting the perception of self-evident truth of society's convictions. Conflict with the outsider acquired an unprecedented metaphysical dimension. He evoked resentment by his refusal to put an end to his marginality and be incorporated into the group. In antiquity, kinship and territorial criteria of group belonging were largely visible, easily detectable and enforceable. The demand for belief conformity, however, created a new form of *invisible deviance*—the counterpart of the invisible quality of humanity. Invisible deviance is far more difficult to detect, to enforce and to contain. It requires a permanent state of vigilance (a paranoid style and/or an Inquisition), a concern to identify and publicly mark the deviants, and perpetual skepticism about the allegiance of many group members. Since an invisible threat cannot be easily confined, there is a much greater temptation to put an end to it once-and-for-all. The potential outcome of the conflict also is more devastating than in antiquity. With the introduction of the universal category of humanity, deviants could be excluded—not only from kinship groups or society—but from humankind and from the sphere of human fellow feeling and obligations. In antiquity the outsider was relegated to a status of limited humanity. In a doctrinal universalism, he could be excluded from humanity altogether.

Crossing Boundaries

In the Middle Ages, the Jew became the first target of the new style categorical exclusion. The conflict between the Church and the Synagogue was essentially over membership in the privileged category of God's chosen people, the old-new identity of *Verus Israel*. In this struggle for identity, the Jews became the most eligible and indispensable participants in Christian society. Jewish non-affiliation was not simply a measure of Christendom's residual incompleteness; it was a repudiation of Christian claims, and thereby challenged the Church's legitimacy. In response, the Church contrived a positive exclusion and a new ontological status for the Jews, decisively removing them from the group of potential or necessary member. The move was amplified by the popular imagination, which assigned Jews to a "counter-group" of the Devil or the Antichrist. The Jew became the prototype of a perversion of the mind, best exemplified by his inhuman blindness to the manifest Christian truth.

The dynamics of category inclusion and exclusion can be clearly seen in the popular image of the Jew. The imaginary Jew obsesses society as one who crosses boundaries, combines contradictory features, breaches the barriers of the natural species and otherwise violates the order of nature. He is "other" because he is a hybrid, transitional figure who exposes society's vulnerabilities and the precariousness of its boundaries, introducing chaos in the structure of the universe. Anthropologists have extensively described how societies structure their understanding of the universe around symbolic objects . As O'Keefe put it, "the organization of these objects falls into place as a classification system that is a cosmological map projecting social morphology onto nature like a magic lantern"[17] With the demise of more primitive ritual symbolism, the Jew became the magic lantern of the modern West. He is a contrivance bearing traces of the major incertitudes and basic polarities of society. His hybrid nature is expressed in many ways. Mythologies typically include beings which, like centaurs, the Minotaur, or mermaids straddle the animal and the human realm. The medieval imaginary Jew often had animal features, such as horns, a tail, or a goat's beard (some of these characteristics he shared with the Devil). The link to the animal world was not simply an eccentricity of the medieval visual imagination, or of the Vulgate translation of Exodus. The association had profound psychological and then historical consequences. In the Middle Ages, a number of authorities required the Jews to wear a form of the animal horn as a distinguishing mark on their garb. The Nazis completed the fusion, casting the Jews as the lowest forms of the animal realm, as unicellular organisms like bacteria. The imaginary Jew is also an intermediary being in other ways. He straddled the realms of sexuality (menstruating men) and of life-and-death (the Eternal Jew). In the Middle Ages, Guibert of Nogent relates the story of a Jew who arranged a meeting between a monk and the Devil, and that Jew had many associates in the medieval imagination.[18] The Jews' historical involvement as intermediaries in international commerce, creating contacts between medieval Europe and the Far East, also became symbolic of their essential homelessness, their internationalism or cosmopolitanism. The intermediary status was equally expressed in the imaginary Jew's privileged association with money. The power of the image far exceeded anything generated by their historical role, and does not spring from Jewish involvement in moneylending or capitalism. Rather, money is the foremost medium of circulation and exchange, accumulated by middlemen, which creates classes of equivalence without regard for the origins or nature of things. The Jew, so Proudhon noted in the nineteenth century, "is by temperament unproductive.... He is an intermediary, always fraudulent and parasitical, who operates in business as in philosophy by forging, counterfeiting...he is the evil element, Satan."[19] Or, in Marx's terms, money has an "overturning power" which "turns individualities and the bonds of society into their contrary" and "the world upside-down—confounding and compounding all natural and human qualities." Money, he famously noted in his *Jewish Question,* was "the jealous god of the Jews" whose "god is only an illusory bill of exchange."[20] The Nazi preoccupation with this kind of category of belonging and their aversion to intermediary beings was a factor in their frenzied antisemitism. Their perplexity throughout the war in their dealings with *Mischlinge,* individuals of mixed Jewish and non-Jewish descent was a symptom of their obsession with boundary crossing.

The conceptions of the hybrid Jew and related myths created mental representations midway between the historical and an inner psychic reality. In 1233, Pope Gregory IX wrote to the bishops of France, asking them to protect the Jews against popular excesses, "no matter how perverse their midway position may be."[21] The "perverse midway position" cogently describes the condition of the outsider, whose being violates traditional distinctions and crosses established categories of thought. The midway position also describes a crucial aspect of the manner in which the outsider is apprehended, his psychological distance. This enabled medieval people to accept the demonization of the Jew without reservations and the Nazis to overcome their natural moral inhibitions and act on the myth and against its victims. As an intermediary reality, the "other" becomes an object, which "triggers" action in a rather unreflective way. As in many sociopathic and impulsive conditions, the decision-making process is shortened and short-circuited in favor of a more "mechanical" reaction provoked by the mere presence of the object.[22] Moral objections are obscured and fudged in this Manichean universe of light and darkness.

Two centuries after Kant, the Nazis reversed his metamorphosis of man by stripping their victims of any distinctive human status and turning them back into objects with a price tag attached to them. In the camps, the Nazis were careful to extract all use-value from their lives and then from the deaths of Jewish "objects." The SS Economic and Administrative Central Office, which administered the concentration camps, produced the following forecast:

> The hiring of concentration camp inmates to industrial enterprises yields an
> average daily return of 6 to 8 RM, from which 70 pf. must be deducted for

food and clothing. Assuming the inmate's life expectancy to be 9 months, we must multiply this sum by 270.... This profit can be increased by rational utilization of the corpse, i.e., by means of gold fillings, clothing, valuables etc., but on the other hand every corpse represents a loss of 2 RM, which is the cost of cremation."[23]

The "midway" position of the "other" also shields the myth, and the perpetrators, from any possible refutation. Any seeming refutation from reality could be dismissed as a failure to penetrate the multiple shapes and appearances of the demon.

The psychological reality of intermediary beings and processes is common in children. Piaget has described children's "animism" in their conception of the world. The young child endows things and the world of nature with consciousness, believing that objects are moved by forces of intentionality. The sun and the moon follow the child, or watch it, just as a bird might above the roofs; the night was created so that children could sleep.[24] The child also "creates" objects which are affectively charged. These are the "transitional objects" described by D. W. Winnicott.[25] The objects have a psychological reality not unlike that of the "other." Early in life, a teddy bear, a worn blanket, or another soft object, often acquire particular importance for the infant. The teddy bear stands for the object of the first relationship—the breast and the mother— and comes to fulfill some of its emotional soothing functions. It may become indispensable at bedtime, or in times of anxiety or deprivation. The objects are "transitional" by the manner of their mental representation and their experience. The child realizes that the object is not "real," but neither is it a mere "thing," or an abstract symbolic representation (of the mother). The object triggers powerful emotions, "as if" it were real. It provides genuine comfort, is affectionately cuddled, loved, or harmed. As the child grows, the objects lose their meaning, and their affective charge, yet the outlook on life need not disappear entirely. The Greek gods and heroes were such adult "transitional objects." The Homeric gods are depressingly human in their failings, follies and longings. The ordinary Greek, it seems, neither fully accepted nor rejected these myths. The humanization of the gods in ancient Greece is mirrored, psychologically, in the demonization of the "other," particularly the Jew. The intermediary quality of the "other's" presence in the mind spawns a very flexible being, freed of reality constraints, which can be manipulated, preserved and called up at will. The imaginary Jew was endowed with such an intermediary psychological quality; his also was a transitional reality in yet another sense, framed by the knowledge of past and future expulsions and slaughters. Like the teddy bear, the imaginary Jew, ever "on call," could provide solace, understanding and release in times of need, and also trigger passions and actions. The Jew was cast in this role in the Middle Ages, and not by mere chance or an unfortunate historical accident. Although his contemporaries did not fully understand their creation nor its origins, they called to life—and death—a being which embodied a new psychological sensibility, a new preparedness to believe and to act which first became conceivable in the Middle Ages and then virtually irresistible in modernity. The Holocaust was not a sudden eruption of new or very old impulses, an uncontrolled reaction on the spur of the historical moment which short-circuited ordinary moral sensibilities. For no new ideas or behavior can occur "spontaneously," unless they "fit" pre-existing mental categories. German moral restraints were not overwhelmed overnight by a whipped up frenzy of Nazi destruction. The inhibitions were tamed over a long period of time, as befits any deeper human quality.[26] Their modern antisemitic themes and calls for action were unprecedented but they did not thereby establish a new beginning. They were the culmination of the new mindset and conception of humankind which gradually came to permeate Western culture and influence relations with the outsider. The Jews were the classic victims of the inability of this culture to come to terms with diversity.

Notes

I am grateful to Joseph Greenbaum and Daniel R. Schwartz for their comments on the paper.

1. Sigmund Freud, *Letters of Sigmund Freud and Arnold Zweig,* ed. Ernst Freud (London 1970), 2 December 1927.

2. Edward Gibbon, *The Decline and the Fall of the Roman Empire* (1776–1778) (New York), 443–44.

3. Herbert Spencer, *Social statics* (New York 1914), 32.

4. Augustine, *City of God,* XV: 4, 5.

5. Thomas Hobbes, *Leviathan* (1651) (Oxford 1946), 289; William James, *The Varieties of Religious Experience* (Harmondsworth 1967), 338.

6. Jean Piaget, *The Origins of Intelligence in Children* (New York 1952); Erik Erikson, *Childhood and Society* (New York 1963).

7. C. Tilly, *Coercion, Capital, and European States, AD 990–1992* (Oxford 1990), 76, 206.

8. Karl Marx and Friedrich Engels, *Manifesto of the Communist Party,* in *Collected Works* by Karl Marx and Friedrich Engles, vol. 6 (New York: International Publishers, 1976), 482.

9. Friedrich Engels, *Anti-Dühring,* in *Collected Works,* Karl Marx and Friedrich Engels, Part I, ch. 12 (New York: International Publishers, 1987), 112.

10. Alexis de Tocqueville, *Democracy in America,* vol. 1 (New York 1963), 314; S. M. Lipset, *Continental Divide* (New York 1984), 75, 80; idem, *American Exceptionalism* (New York 1995), 60 sq.

11. J. W. von Goethe, *Poetry and Truth from My Life* (London 1932), 682–84.

12. Albert Einstein, *Tagebücher,* ed. H. Kessler (Frankfurt am Main 1961), entry 14 June 1927, p. 521

13. V. Tcherikover, *Hellenistic Civilization and the Jews* (Philadelphia 1959), ch. 5.

14. M. Hadas, *Hellenistic Culture* (New York 1959), ch. 3; W. F. Albright, *From the Stone Age to Christianity* (Baltimore 1946), 304.

15. Immanuel Kant, *Foundations of the Metaphysics of Morals,* (Cambridge 1993), 428, 429.

16. Ibid., the doctrine of virtue, par. 38, 39, p. 255.

17. D. L. O'Keefe, *Stolen Lightning. The Social Theory of Magic* (New York 1967, 1982), 187–88; and of course M. Douglas, *Purity and Danger* (London 1966).

18. Guibert of Nogent, in *Self and Society in Medieval France,* J. Benton, 115.

19. P. J. Proudhon, *Césarisme et christianisme* vol. 1 (Paris 1883), 139, cited in Léon Poliakov, *Histoire de l'antisémitisme,* vol. 3 (Paris 1968), 386.

20. Karl Marx, *The Economic and Philosophic Manuscripts of 1844* (New York), 165–69; idem, "On the Jewish Question," in *Early Writings* (New York 1964), 31, 21.

21. Gregory IX, in Solomon Grayzel, *The Church and the Jews in the XIIIth Century* (New York 1966), no. 70.

22. D. Shapiro, *Neurotic styles* (New York 1965).

23. Quoted in N. Davies, *God's Playground: A History of Poland* (New York 1982), 463.

24. Jean Piaget, *The Child's Conception of the World* (Savage, Md. 1951).

25. D. W. Winnicott, *Playing and Reality* (London 1990).

26. Henri Zukier, "The twisted road to genocide: On the psychological development of evil during the Holocaust," *Social Research* 61 (1994): 423–56.

8

The Borrowed Identity: Neo-Pagan Reactions to the Jewish Roots of Christianity

Shmuel Almog
The Hebrew University of Jerusalem

The term "identity" we so often use nowadays is of quite recent coinage, particularly in its sociological and psychodynamic connotations.[1] It tends to play a growing role in current parlance in the wake of two phenomena, namely the so-called "cult of the individual" and, conjointly perhaps, the increasing importance of previously peripheral groups "who have some shared identity," such as ethnicity, culture, or gender.[2] The search for a common identity understandably leads towards past experience and collective memory. It may even induce the "invention of tradition."[3]

All this seems to have started in the 1960s. The linkage between identity and history enjoyed some reputation for about two decades, thanks to Erik Erikson and his school of psychohistory. Thus, for example, Erikson spoke of a "transformation in the overall sense of identity" when referring to the "polarization of the Greco-Roman Empire and the Christian kingdom" in the history of Christianity.[4]

Identity Transformation

The concept of "identity transformation" may be applicable, for instance, to the gentiles who joined the early Church through baptism. Religious conversions are sometimes the result of an inner personality change and more often than not entail a new way of life. William James, in his classic analysis of religion, furnished a psychological explanation to the idea of a new life, which is implied by religious conversion.[5] Subsequently, historians have shown the transformation of identity to apply in many instances, including the case of converts to Christianity in the Greco-Roman era.[6]

Through the act of baptism, converts shed their previous identity and assumed another self; they were even given new names.[7] Joining the Church meant much more than merely accepting a certain set of beliefs and rites. It actually forced the convert to forego previous social ties and join an oppressed and despised, but closely-knit group, that could serve as a substitute family. This "family," dispersed throughout the Roman Empire, was united "in Christ" [Romans 12:5]. The gospel of Jesus was absorbed by believers and his life served as a model and symbol. Moreover, his country and kinfolk were also adopted by them to some extent.

Unlike any religion familiar to the pagan world, the new faith was based on a Holy Book. Initially, this consisted of the Hebrew Scriptures, which told the story of a particular people.[8] Even though Pauline Christianity catered to the gentiles and promoted a universal message, it did not sever its ties with the Jewish background. On the contrary, ingenious hermeneutics rescued the Jewish heritage from the hands of unbaptized Jews and bestowed it upon the "true Israel."[9] Christians became the spiritual children of Abraham, Isaac, and Jacob.

But Christian theology did not pardon the Jews for the death of Jesus and was rather reluctant to recognize its debt to Judaism. Moreover, numerous attempts were made, through sophisticated exegesis of Scripture, to reduce the importance of the Jewish contribution to Christianity.[10] In this spirit, Christian scholars delved into the remote past and came up with a modified sacred history, of which James Parkes, a pioneer researcher in this field, said: "Christian history was shown to be older than Jewish History in that it dated from the Creation."[11]

Nevertheless, despite the tendency to reduce the impact of the Old Testament and disclaim the indebtedness to Judaism, the basic tenet of historical continuity between the two Testaments was kept intact. Mainstream Christianity held onto the major tradition, that upheld the Church as successor to the People of Israel.[12] At the other end stood certain Gnostic sects, which abounded on the periphery of Christianity, sometimes even reaching its core, as did the Marcionite heresy and Manicheism, in the second and third centuries.[13]

"Metaphysical Antisemitism"

As is well known, antinomian traditions do not easily die out: they seem to hide or go under for a while, and then resurge elsewhere in a new shape, as if defying the limitations of time and place.[14] They are less prone to become established structures and often lack clear-cut distinctions. No wonder then that early Gnostic notions were transmitted to later sects and were kept alive for ages. These heresies within Christendom often shared the rejection of the Old Testament. Gershom Scholem, the great historian of Jewish mysticism, labelled them "metaphysical antisemitism."[15]

Take for example the early heretic Marcion (died c. 160 C.E.). He was probably inspired by a rigid rationalism to reject any allegorical interpretation of Scripture. If the brunt of his hatred was borne by the Old Testament, it could well be due to the obvious reason that the New Testament had not yet been canonized.[16] Marcion's adversaries fought against his extreme dualism by resorting to a figurative continuity between the Bible and the Christian dispensation. Judaism was not the bone of contention here, but it retained a highly symbolic significance, personifying the ambivalent image of the Jew as the living protagonist of the Old Testament.[17] Jews were held in contempt yet they also represented a hallowed tradition.[18]

While Christians vied with Jews for the biblical heritage, heretics rejected it for their own doctrinal reasons. Some even interpreted it in a subversive manner, condemning the biblical heroes and praising the rejects, such as Cain for instance.[19] So far no mention was made here of the well-known motif that negates the Bible because it is alien. Yet this argument, for all its modern trappings, can be found in the earliest Gnostic writings.[20]

Considering this background, one could imagine how difficult it might have been for a new Christian to adopt the particular lineage going back to the Jewish Pentateuch. The "borrowed identity" was undoubtedly a heavy burden on their shoulders. Notwithstanding the difficulty, whoever embraced the idea of the "true Israel" had to contend with the burden as best they could.

On the other hand, this perpetual tension enabled the Jews to remain, though humiliated and despised, as a virtual exception to the exclusive reign of Christianity in Europe.[21] This tension also served, however, as a constant incentive to uphold the Jewish identity. Survival owes its staying power to a dynamic equilibrium between centripetal and centrifugal forces.[22] It is not fortuitous perhaps that Judaism survived as a living faith among its competitors—Christians and Muslims—and not among the more tolerant and indifferent Asians.[23]

New Trends

No doubt the highly complex involvement of Christianity with Jews and Judaism defies any simplistic explanation. Christianity has been fraught with a dual attitude to its Jewish heritage. Whereas the negative aspect would come to the fore most of the time, the background would still be tinged by the positive tone, namely by the normative role allocated to Judaism in salvation history. As against this duality, though, numerous attempts were made to steer clear of the Jewish origins. This applies in large measure to the various Gnostic avatars, yet each new trend within the Church also challenged the traditional balance between its divergent sources.

It is noteworthy that a renewed interest in the Old Testament did not signify mere scholarly curiosity, nor did it necessarily promote better understanding between Christians and Jews. In fact, the study of the Old Testament was often inspired by a more intense critique of Judaism.[24] This applies in particular to the Middle Ages, but it recurred time and again in the Early Modern Period. The Renaissance and the Reformation gave rise to a great many innovations and to an abundance of outstanding individuals.[25] New types—humanists, reformers, Hebraists, cabbalists—stirred the theological status quo with their own beliefs, usually accompanied by a matching evaluation of the Jewish heritage.[26] The Early Modern Period was apparently impregnated with a deeper sense of ambivalence towards Judaism than were the preceding centuries.[27] This was after all a period of transition, though slow and uncertain in many respects.

The ambivalence came out, for instance, in the writings of the well-known humanist, Erasmus of Rotterdam, who was most critical of Judaism. Even he did not hesitate to apply to Christians and Christianity the terms "Israel" and "Jews."[28] He rebuked the Jews for their exclusivity and for their claiming to monopolize salvation and keep it from the rest of humanity. The great scholar kept in line here with the oldest Pauline tradition.[29] Indeed, the identity confusion may have troubled Erasmus as it might have bothered St. Paul: now, as then, Christians had to forge an identity for themselves under the impact of a changing world.

The focal point lay in the role attributed to the Old Testament. This changed during the Reformation, which transcended the medieval use of the Pentateuch as a political and constitutional paradigm.[30] The Hebraic texts were usually interpreted in the Middle Ages in a purely legalistic fashion, inspired by Roman Law concepts.[31] This started changing to a considerable extent with the great controversy between Henry VIII of England and Pope Clement VII, on an issue of intense emotional resonance—the annulment of the King's marriage. The Bible in the vernacular was by then already available and wider circles could be drawn into the sphere of the legal fight, based on the Pentateuch. Here was one of the starting points for the enormous impact that the Bible had in England.[32]

From beyond the imbroglio of dogmatic factions and fanatic dissenters the Old Testament arose as a storehouse of political and religious ideas that came alive in seventeenth-century England.[33] This was no longer historical precedent carefully sifted through expert opinion, but a palpable identification with the world of the Bible.[34] The central themes of Puritan England evolved around such Old Testament ideas as the Chosen People, the Covenant, and Messianic hope.[35] These forceful ideas grew even stronger in the American colonies, where the adoption of Hebrew names symbolized the self-image of the "founding fathers" as the "new Israel."[36]

Reason and Enlightenment

The English deists were the harbingers of a profound change in European mentality. Their heyday did not last long, but their message fell on fertile ground, particularly on the Continent. Their success was no doubt facilitated by the winds of change that had reached European shores in the wake of the great discoveries overseas. Exploration and travel widened European horizons and tended to undermine the traditional world-view.[37] The mere awareness of exotic cultures and hitherto unknown human beings gave way to a trend of comparison and self-criticism. This became rather corrosive and undermined the doctrinal interpretation of the Creation, the story of Genesis, and the centrality of Christian civilization.[38]

It was a long and multifarious process that led among other things to a growing dissociation from the Old Testament tradition. It owed much no doubt to the insidious influence of Spinoza, who treated the Bible as the particular heritage of the Jews and not as a universal road to salvation.[39] In Spinoza's footsteps followed the very influential Pierre Bayle, whose harsh judgement of Judaism, though rational in approach, also contained a grain of Gnostic dualism.[40] The upshot of such criticism was an ever-expanding notion that the significance of biblical history had been highly overrated. The preoccupation with the Jews and their Bible appeared as a vestige of doctrinaire Christianity, now subjected to a merciless scrutiny by enlightened modern minds.

The self-distancing of many eighteenth-century *philosophes* from the biblical tradition was concomitant with a pronounced preference for alternative sources of inspiration, such as the Greco-Roman culture or the exotic cultures of China, India, or Persia.[41] Their criticism of Christianity and its Jewish roots was far from being academic or detached. Beside the fashionable neo-classicism and the appeal to reason, the *philosophes* often displayed a close personal relationship with religion. Criticizing the Judeo-Christian tradition, they tended to sever the umbilical cord that had held together the Old and the New Testaments.[42]

Moreover, they implicitly tended to shed their previous identity and assume a new one. The Enlightenment gave birth to the intellectual *avant la lettre,* a free spirit of independent means, who no longer identified with the powers that be, and started forging a new identity for himself.[43] The void that opened up before this new type was to be filled with a feeling of belonging to a tradition of his own making. The intellectual elite quite easily replaced the worn-out Christian identity with a Greco-Roman lineage.[44] Less obvious, but no less important, was its identification with a plethora of pagan traditions, as Voltaire revealed when depicting his ideal type: "He has brothers from Peking to Cayenne and regards all sages as his brothers."[45] A new bond—or if you will, a new Covenant—came to replace outdated loyalties and invested the community of men of letters with ultimate universal wisdom.

Some of the best-known figures of the Enlightenment were most adamant about the biblical heritage. They never missed an opportunity to show that they wanted no share in the Jewish origins of European civilization, that indeed it was alien to Europe and to civilization as such. This attitude applies primarily to the French *philosophes,* such as Diderot and Voltaire, the latter mockingly distancing himself from the biblical Patriarchs.[46] Yet even the great historian Gibbon spoke contemptuously of the ancient Jews, a narrow-minded, hateful tribe, claiming to be the favorites of their national God.[47]

Tom Paine, the radical Englishman who played a historical role in both the American and French revolutions, was a nontypical specimen of the Enlightenment. His lowly origin and Quaker upbringing combined to produce an ideology of representative democracy and anticlerical rationalism. Paine may be classified as a new type of international revolutionary that was still rare in his own time, but would abound in the following century. He may have felt the need to establish his own identity, in a similar fashion perhaps to his sensitivity towards the manifestation of a new American identity.[48] Paine's diatribe against the ancient Jews and their claim to be "the chosen people" befitted his own search for an alternative lineage, based on a mythical construct of the past.[49]

The rationalists could not but attack the Old Testament, but they were generally more lenient toward the New Testament. Their writings reflect an underlying note of estrangement from the Jewish roots of Christianity. This is a general mood among eighteenth-century thinkers, not just the more radical ones. It even affected Gotthold Ephraim Lessing, Voltaire's sharpest critic, whose name has become a favorite household word in German-Jewish history.[50] In his important "Education of Humanity," Lessing portrayed the election of Israel as an exemplary choice of the crudest, most unsophisticated people on earth, to be the first in the process of education.[51] Lessing did endorse this election, but only as a means to a higher end.

The Search for Natural Parents

If the Enlightenment managed to call into question the "borrowed identity," it still left open the quest for Europe's genuine progenitors, the natural parents of European civilization. These were found in the nineteenth century, with the rise of modern Orientalism.[52] The central event was the discovery of Sanskrit, soon to be portrayed as the mother tongue of European culture.[53] This could be fully appreciated if seen as a delayed response to a long-felt need. Sanskrit became the keyword for the liberation of the European identity from the shackles of Judeo-Christian tradition. Romantic longings that had spread out in many directions found their fulfillment in Indian mythology.[54]

The rejection of the biblical heritage, now decried as alien, in favor of some imaginary Asiatic ancestors was not without irony, though this does not seem to have been appreciated by the European adherents of the Aryan myth. The myth continued to grow from an intellectual pastime into a popular idea that would change history in the twentieth century. Even the confusion between its divergent variants—Indo-Germanic, Indo-European, Indo-Celtic, Caucasian, Aryan etc.—or between its manifold facets (language, culture, religion, and race) did not hinder its diffusion and popularity.[55]

The infatuation with the "Aryans" was a purely European affair, confined to people who had been raised as Christians. No Asians were invited to enjoy the glorification of their ancient ancestry.[56] The Aryan myth and its many derivatives, fascinating as they may have been to Romantics and scholars, were all the same manipulated by them for some purpose. These intellectuals were well placed to inspire a larger public and gradually, almost unobtrusively, their brainchildren entered mainstream opinion. Insidiously perhaps, some notions derived from the Aryan myth filtered into general parlance and had a particular resonance when attached to group identity or race.[57]

The discovery of Sanskrit may have been fortuitous, but its implications and consequences were not. The longing for the real identity of Europe had been there before, but now for the first time was approaching its goal. The search would be over as soon as the new identity was found and publicly recognized as the legitimate contender.[58] Where it did not replace the traditional roots of European civilization, it could graft on to them some Indian or so-called Oriental elements.[59]

This coincided with the changing historical perspective that took place in the nineteenth century. Modern historiography had more means at its disposal to approach Voltaire's ideal of universal history, as opposed to a narrow Eurocentrism.[60] The scope of history expanded to include India and China, but European prejudices were not removed in the process. Thus the great philosopher Hegel could relegate Judaism to the fringes of the Oriental world and by the same token minimize its universal role in history.[61] This looks like the typical Hegelian "cunning of history": from Voltaire to Hegel, via Romanticism, Judaism becomes obsolete or insignificant.[62]

Judaism Resurfaces

There was some poetic justice in the recurrent need to demonstrate the insignificance of Judaism. Hegel himself was a case in point. He would refer to the Jews far more than they deserved according to his own system. This discrepancy became even more pronounced in some of the leading Young Hegelians. They were as much preoccupied with religion as was their master, but they gave it a radical twist or explained it away.[63] The Young Hegelians were immersed in the attempt to interpret religion as anthropology, symbol, and myth.[64] Their main criticism was directed against Christianity, but they came up with some of the crudest charges against Judaism, as for instance: explaining Jesus' crucifixion as emanating from a Jewish rite of human sacrifice.[65]

This heterogeneous group radicalized the interpretation of Scripture and, in turn, propagated a new idiom in the critique of society and religion. They had their share in the dawning of a new era, sometimes called the New Enlightenment or the Age of Ideology.[66] On the whole, they had a considerable impact on the midcentury discourse of European intellectuals.

The involvement of Karl Marx in this debate has aroused much interest. Many critics have branded him as an antisemite, while others regard the whole affair as irrelevant to the canonical Marx.[67] His major premise was that "Christianity sprang from Judaism," soon to be followed by the suggestive phrases: "It has now dissolved back into Judaism," and "Christianity overcame real Judaism in appearance only."[68] Marx converted the term "Judaism" into a symbol of bourgeois society. Here again appeared the familiar contradiction between the apparent insignificance of Judaism and its centrality. Despite his invective against Judaism, Marx made it the essence of modern society, the members of which were all in the process of turning into "Jews."[69]

Marx attempted to interpret the theological controversy from a social and political vantage point. "Judaization" meant to him that the trends attributed to Jews, such as egotism and materialism, were becoming dominant in modern society. The specter of "Judaization," though, had long haunted Christianity. Every doctrinal dispute would raise the charge that the other party was guilty of judaizing.[70] The Marxian version added a dynamic dimension to the old accusation, it superimposed on the religious fears the secular myth of Jewish domination. Needless to say that this is also a central theme of modern antisemitism.[71]

Let us take Ernest Renan, for example. He combined two strands of thought, a diluted Young Hegelianism and the Aryan myth. Renan was regarded as the leading French intellectual during the second half of the nineteenth century.[72] His gift for dramatization and genuine scholarship boosted his ideas and made them respectable. His attitude to Christianity had Young Hegelian underpinnings and contained an ambivalent evaluation of its Jewish origins. He assumed a genealogical relationship between Sanskrit sources and European civilization, in contrast to the Semites with their biblical, or for that matter, Islamic traditions.[73] Renan saw Europeans as the offspring of Aryan stock, converted through Christianity to Jewish ideas and overreaching themselves in adopting the Old Testament.[74] This also established a link between Renan and the German School of Bible criticism.[75]

German Biblical scholarship enjoyed high prestige thanks to Julius Wellhausen, whose ideas dominated the field from the last quarter of the nineteenth century onwards. Wellhausen believed the early Israelites to be different in essence from their successors, the legalistic Jews. On the other hand, he tried to establish a link between the original Israelites and Christianity, both differing from the rigidity of the Jewish Torah.[76] He regarded the Israelites as well as the Christians as being full of originality, freedom, and naturalness, whereas the Jews were identified with the artificial, the secondary, and the schematic—imprecise terms, but evocative and powerful.[77] Wellhausen left intact the major tenets of the Christian tradition: the Bible was salvaged after being purified. The election of Israel, though, was no longer relevant.[78]

Latter-Day Prophets

These scholarly works were apparently written in a "value-free" atmosphere, detached from the hustle and bustle of current affairs. Yet the rising tide of antisemitism could be felt already and may have affected the growing radicalization of some scholars and academics. Ordinarily, the lines of communication between the intellectuals and the general public tended to be convoluted and rather covert. The relevance of biblical studies for society and culture in general is likely to vary from one setting to another. Biblical criticism in nineteenth-century Germany, however, belonged to an important tradition that may even go back to Luther himself.[79]

Now, in the nineteenth century the Lutheran tradition was challenged, this time by a movement towards a German national religion, inspired by the philologist and Old Testament scholar Paul de Lagarde.[80] In contrast to many critics, Lagarde did not reject the Old Testament, but like Wellhausen, sought to dispossess the Jews of it.[81] Lagarde, an antisemitic crank, undermined the validity of conventional Christianity that had absorbed the "Jewish principle" through St. Paul, whom he loathed as a Pharisee.[82] Lagarde attempted to construct a Christianity purged of both its Jewish and classical elements, relying on pre-Christian Germanic paganism.[83]

Here was already a tangible link between biblical scholarship, though marginal as yet, and the *Völkisch* ideology of the time. Concurrently, however, radical notions informed the academic scene as well and gradually acquired respectability. Adolf von Harnack, for example, an important historian of religion, acknowledged his debt to the English Deists in vindicating the ancient heretic Marcion.[84] His dissociation from the Jewish roots of Christianity became in time all the more pronounced, thus legitimizing a similar attitude on the part of more extreme Lutheran groups.[85] In his footsteps followed another eminent scholar, Friedrich Delitzsch, whose *Bibel und Babel* challenged the authenticity of the Bible and abetted antisemitism.[86]

Both these scholars belonged to the generation that had achieved status and fame under the Empire, but continued its work well into the Weimar period. Their successors, however, were already integrated into the Nazi orbit and modified their writings accordingly. Thus Gerhard Kittel, a onetime supporter of Judeo-Christian understanding, tried after 1933 to expropriate the Old Testament, claiming once again that it was not Jewish in essence.[87] He may have borrowed here from the idiosyncratic Lagarde, or even relied on such authorities as Wellhausen and the venerable Eduard Meyer.[88]

Extricating the Bible from Jewish hands could have averted the danger that Christianity be decried as Jewish. At the same time the Nazi theorist and leader Alfred Rosenberg went much further in extirpating the Jewish traces and attacking Christianity itself.[89] The so-called Germanic religion bestowed upon Nazism a superior spiritual quality. Now Christians were dethroned from their coveted status as "a holy people," in a language highly charged with biblical allusions.[90] The ancient idea had come full circle: from the Jewish concept of the "chosen people," via Christianity as the "true Israel," to the Aryan "chosen race."

Such tendencies had their advocates not just in Germany, but elsewhere, too—noticeably in France. In that country appeared two most dissimilar thinkers, who attacked the Jewish roots of Christianity from almost diametrically opposed viewpoints. The first was the royalist and antisemitic politician Charles Maurras, who admired Roman Catholicism for its regime, although he saw himself as a pagan.[91] In Judaism he detected the archenemy—namely, individualism—that had permeated Protestantism too.[92] Maurras and his movement were censured in 1926 by Rome, but he held fast to his views against the Bible, the Jews, and even the Jewish Jesus Christ.[93]

At the other end stood Simone Weil, a French-Jewish woman who in the thirties dabbled in leftist politics and then drew close to Christianity. She never baptized, because she abhorred the Jewish origins of Christianity, as well as the Roman tradition of the Church.[94] In some respects this philosopher and martyr was the opposite of Maurras: she was a social reformer and he was a staunch conservative. She was open toward unknown worlds and he hated the foreign and the alien; she detested Rome and he adored it; she was a Gaullist and he a collaborationist. Yet two things they had in common: love for Greece and repugnance towards Israel. He did not even share her love for Jesus. It is quite amazing how these two, so very far from each other, could come to similar conclusions about the Jewish ingredient in Christianity, apparently without relying on contemporary German influences at all.

Finally, I have to mention two great figures of the recent past, who should be remembered here in passing: Sigmund Freud's Swiss associate and rival Carl Gustav Jung, and the Romanian-born Mircea Eliade, an internationally known historian of religion. Their respective connections with Nazism and Fascism and their neopagan and anti-Judaic activities warrant further research into a new kind of intellectual antisemitism, that retained its apparent respectability even after the Holocaust.[95]

Concluding Remarks

I have tried here to survey the historical attitudes to the Jewish component in Christianity, as perceived from the standpoint of Gentile identity.

My contention is that the "true Israel" theology imposed an alien lineage upon the Christian world and that this was often resented by gentiles. Inasmuch as normative Christianity established itself, it was able to transmit a sense of identification with the Old Testament genealogy. Yet numerous countercurrents revolted, through the ages, against the symbolic adoption by Christians of the Biblical Hebrew identity.

This revolt gained much momentum in the wake of the Reformation, when the unity of the Western Church broke down. Subsequently the evaluation of the biblical heritage underwent far-reaching changes: it grew in stature in certain instances, but was rejected in others. Concurrently, biblical scholarship became less dogmatic and applied a more thorough critique to sacred texts, including the analysis of the Jewish contribution to Christianity. All this came to a head in the eighteenth century, but it was still confined to the intellectual elite and did not much affect the other layers of society.

With the advent of the nineteenth century and since then, the individual sense of identity has become more and more pronounced. Gone was the natural sense of belonging to one's habitat, in its place arose the recognition of an individual need for self-determination. A certain order of things that could long be taken for granted had been visibly shaken. Personal identity, including religious background, was fundamentally challenged and reshaped.

Modern Western society took pride in being more open-minded than its predecessors. Religious doctrine was criticized, reformed, sometimes neglected, or simply aired in the light of new ideas. The old theology of the "true Israel" could no longer satisfy the awakened sense of belonging to one's group, culture, and country. The "borrowed identity," long ago imposed on the Gentile world, seemed redundant. The need for a more genuine identification with the "real self" had awakened with a vengeance.

I have depicted the syndrome of the "borrowed identity" as an ongoing process, portraying the accumulating tradition of canonical Christianity, as against the heretical neopagan trends. Whereas the normative tradition tended towards historical continuity, no such conclusion could be drawn from the portrayal of the opposing antinomian traditions. To my way of thinking, it is not really important whether the early Gnostics were in this respect the spiritual forefathers of *Völkisch* neopagans. What is important is the growing sense of revolt against the imposition of the "borrowed identity" and the utilization of ideas and images from the past to uphold the validity of this upsurge.

It seems that official Christianity was more accommodating to the survival of Jews than were its contenders. This may not be borne out in all cases, but there could be no conclusive evidence, historically speaking, to prove the contrary. At the same time, there is not much doubt that modern neo-paganism has been far less tolerant to Jews and Judaism than was conventional Christianity.

Notes

1. Ken Plummer, "Identity," in *Twentieth-Century Social Thought,* eds. William Outhwaite and Tom Bottomore (Oxford 1993), 270–72.

2. Ray Porter, "Personal Happiness and the Cult of the Individual," in *Dictionary of Ideas,* ed. Anne-Lucie Norton (Oxford 1994), 266; Tim O'Sullivan et al., *Key Concepts in Communication and Cultural Studies* (London and New York 1994), 107–108.

3. See Eric Hobsbawm and Terence Ranger, eds., *The Invention of Tradition* (Cambridge 1984).

4. Erik S. Erikson, *Dimensions of a New Identity* (New York 1974), 47–49.

5. William James, *The Varieties of Religious Experience* (New York and London 1977), 165–66, 198.

6. Erick Robertson Dodds, *Pagan and Christian in an Age of Anxiety* (Cambridge 1994), 76–77.

7. S. G. F. Brandon, "Ritual in Religion," in *Dictionary of the History of Ideas,* ed. Philip P. Wiener, vol. 5 (New York 1973), 102b; René Girard, *Des Choses cachées depuis la fondation du monde* (Paris 1991), 45.

8. Henry Chadwick, *The Early Church* (London 1990), 42; Ernst Robert Curtius, *European Literature and the Latin Middle Ages* (Princeton 1990), 310.

9. Christopher Dawson, *The Making of Europe* (New York 1956), 43.

10. Marcel Simon, *Verus Israel, Etudes sur les relations entre chrétiens et juifs dans L'Empire romain (135–425)* (Paris 1983), 106–11.

11. James Parkes, *The Conflict of the Church and the Synagogue, A Study in the Origins of Antisemitism* (New York 1969), 100.

12. F. Gilbert Dahan, *Les Intellectuels chrétiens et les juifs au Moyen Age* (Paris 1990), 516.

13. Steven Runciman, *The Medieval Manichee, A Study of the Christian Dualist Heresy* (Cambridge 1988), 8–10, 16–18, 22.

14. David Christie-Murray, *A History of Heresy* (Oxford and New York 1989), 19.

15. Gershon Scholem, *The Messianic Idea in Judaism* (New York 1971), 104–105.

16. David Rokéah, *Jews, Pagans and Christians in Conflict* (Jerusalem and Leiden 1982), 90–91.

17. John G. Gager, *The Origins of Anti-Semitism, Attitudes Toward Judaism in Pagan and Christian Antiquity* (New York and Oxford 1983), 171–72.

18. Jean-Claude Bologne, *Les Allusions bibliques* (Paris 1991), 25.

19. Gager, *Origins of Anti-Semitism,* 171–72.

20. Hans Jonas, *The Gnostic Religion, The Message of the Alien God and the Beginning of Christianity* (Boston 1963), 95–96; Benjamin Walker, *Gnosticism* (Wellingborough 1983), 44–45.

21. Robert Chazan, "Medieval Anti-Semitism" in *History and Hate,* ed. David Berger (Philadelphia 1986), 53–54.

22. Shmuel Almog, "Between Zionism and Antisemitism," *Patterns of Prejudice,* 28, no. 2, (1994): 55.

23. E.g., Michael Pollak, *Mandarins, Jews and Missionaries, The Jewish Experience in the Chinese Empire* (Philadelphia 1980); Leon Poliakov, *Jewish Bankers and the Holy See, From the Thirteenth to the Seventeenth Century* (London 1977), 225.

24. E.g., Jeremy Cohen, *The Friars and the Jews, The Evolution of Medieval Anti-Judaism* (Ithaca 1983), 171–91.

25. Giorgio de Santillana, ed., *The Age of Adventure, The Renaissance Philosophers* (New York 1956), 9–10.

26. See Jerome Friedman, *The Most Ancient Testimony, Sixteenth-Century Christian-Hebraica in the Age of Renaissance Nostalgia* (Athens, OH 1983); Frances A. Yates, *The Occult Philosophy in the Elizabethan Age* (London 1983).

27. Hans-Martin Kirn, *Das Bild vom Juden im Deutschland des frühen 16. Jahrhunderts, dargestellt an den Schriften Johannes Pfefferkorns* (Tübingen 1989), 193–94; Heiko A. Oberman, *Wurzeln des Antisemitismus, Christenangst und Judenplage im Zeitalter von Humanismus und Reformation* (Berlin 1981), 190.

28. Shimon Markish, *Erasmus and the Jews* (Chicago and London 1986), 53, 63; Guido Kisch, "Erasmus' Stellung zu Juden and Judentum," *Philosphie und Geschichte,* 83/84 (1969): 5–39.

29. Markish, *Erasmus and the Jews,* 48–50.

30. Étienne Gilson, *La Philosophie au moyen age,* vol. 1 (Paris 1976), 331–32.

31. Walter Ullmann, *A History of Political Thought: The Middle Ages* (Harmondsworth 1965), 21.

32. George Gordon Coulton, *Medieval Panorama, The English Scene from Conquest to Reformation* (New York 1955), 701–704; Christopher Hill, *The English Bible and the Seventeenth Century Revolution* (London 1994), 10–12.

33. Basil Willey, *The Seventeenth Century Background, The Thought of the Age in Relation to Religion and Poetry* (Garden City, NY 1953), 229–30.

34. Harold Fisch, *Jerusalem and Albion, The Hebraic Factor in Seventeenth-Century Literature* (New York 1964), 166.

144 *Demonizing the Other: Antisemitism, Racism, and Xenophobia*

35. Hans Kohn, *The Idea of Nationalism, A Study in its Origins and Background* (Toronto 1969), 168.

36. Kohn, *Idea of Nationalism*, 664, n. 13; H. L. Mencken, *The American Language, An Inquiry into the Development of English in the United States* (New York 1963), 650; Frederic Cople Jaher, *A Scapegoat in the Wilderness, The Origins and Rise of Anti-Semitism in America* (Cambridge, MA 1994), 91–92.

37. Paul Hazard, *La Crise de la conscience européenne (1680–1715)* (Paris 1935), 6–15.

38. Norman Hampson, *The Enlightenment* (Harmondsworth 1976), 25–27.

39. Frank E. Manuel, *The Broken Staff, Judaism Through Christian Eyes* (Cambridge, MA 1992), 164.

40. Myriam Yardeni, *Anti-Jewish Mentalities in Early Modern Europe* (Lanham, Md. 1990), 202, 219.

41. E.g., Peter Gay, *The Enlightenment, The Science of Freedom* (New York 1977), 391.

42. J. H. Brumfitt, *The French Enlightenment* (London 1972), 151.

43. Louis A. Coser, "Intellectuals," in *Twentieth Century Social Thought*, eds. Outhwaite and Bottomore 289; Thomas J. Schlereth, *The Cosmopolitan Ideal in Enlightenment Thought* (Notre Dame, Ind. 1977), 11–14.

44. Schlereth, *Cosmopolitan Ideal*, 9; cf. Liah Greenfeld, *Nationalism, Five Roads to Modernity* (Cambridge, MA 1992), 80.

45. Voltaire, *Dictionnaire philosophique* (Paris 1964), 361 [Théiste].

46. Arthur Hertzberg, *The French Enlightenment and the Jews, The Origins of Modern Antisemitism* (New York 1970), 302–303.

47. Edward Gibbon, *The History of the Decline and Fall of the Roman Empire*, vol. 2, ed. J. B. Bury, (New York 1946), 350–53, 355–56.

48. James H. Billington, *Fire in the Hearts of Men, Origins of the Revolutionary Faith* (London 1980), 56; Greenfeld, *Nationalism*, 411–12, 420.

49. Billington, *Fire*, 103; Alfred J. Ayer, *Thomas Paine* (Reading 1988), 147–48.

50. E.g., Wilfred Barnes, "Vorurteil, Empirie, Rettung, der Junge Lessing und die Juden," in *Juden und Judentum in der Literatur*, eds. Herbert A. Strauss and Christhard Hoffmann, (Munich 1985), 52–77; Franklin Kopitzsch, "Lessing und seine Zeitgenossen im Spannungsfeld von Toleranz und Intoleranz," in *Deutsche Aufklärung und Judenemanzipation*, ed. Walter Grab, (Tel Aviv 1980), 29–85.

51. Gotthold Ephraim Lessing, *Freimäuresgespräche und anderes, Ausgewählte Schriften* (Munich 1981), 83–85, 87, 93; cf. Johann Gottfried Herder, *Auch eine Philosophie der Geschichte zur Bildung der Menschheit* (Frankfurt a.M. 1967), 54.

52. Edward W. Said, *Orientalism* (New York 1979), 22, 42–43.

53. Jacques Barzun, *Race, A Study in Superstition* (New York 1965), 97–100.

54. Burton Feldman, "Myth, Eighteenth and Nineteenth Centuries," in *Dictionary of the History of Ideas*, ed. Wiener, vol. 3, 305–306.

55. Maurice Olender, *Les Langues du paradis, Aryens et Sémites: un couple providentiel* (Paris 1989), 27.

56. Said, *Orientalism*, 153–55.

57. George L. Mosse, *Toward the Final Solution, A History of European Racism* (London — 1978), 39–45.

58. Whitney F. Bolton, "Aryan," "The Indo European Languages," in *Oxford Companion to the English Language,* ed. Tom McArthur (New York 1992), 84, 512–14.

59. Raymond Schwab, *La Renaissance orientale* (Paris 1950), 493–95.

60. Schlereth, *Cosmopolitan Ideal,* 69; Ernst Breisach, *Historiography, Ancient, Medieval and Modern* (Chicago 1983), 318–19.

61. Hans Liebeschütz, *Das Judentum im deutschen Geschichtsbild von Hegel bis Max Weber* (Tübingen 1967), 39, 43.

62. Georg Wilhelm Friedrich Hegel, *The Philosophy of History* (New York 1956), 195–98.

63. Owen Chadwick, *The Secularization of the European Mind in the Nineteenth Century* (Cambridge 1979), 54.

64. Leszek Kolakowski, *Main Currents of Marxism,* vol. 1, *The Founders* (Oxford 1987), 84, 89.

65. Shmuel Ettinger, "The Young Hegelians—a Source of Modern Anti-Semitism?" *Jerusalem Quarterly* 28 (Summer 1993): 76–77; Shlomo Avineri, *Moses Hess: Prophet of Communism and Zionism* (New York 1985), 131–32.

66. Franklin L. Baumer, *Modern European Thought, Continuity and Change in Ideas, 1600–1950* (New York 1977), 262–63, 302 seq.; Henry D. Aiken, ed., *The Age of Ideology, The 19th Century Philosophers* (New York 1956), 265–66; cf. Georg Lukàcs, *Von Nietzsche zu Hitler, oder Der Irrationalismus und die deutsche Politik* (Frankfurt a.M. and Hamburg 1966), 11, 56.

67. Julius Carlebach, *Karl Marx and the Radical Critique of Judaism* (London 1978), 261–79.

68. Karl Marx, *A World Without Jews,* tr. Dagobert D. Runes (New York 1959), 43.

69. Ibid., 38. See also Robert S. Wistrich, *Socialism and the Jews. The Dilemmas of Assimilation in Germany and Austria-Hungary* (London 1982).

70. Friedman, *Most Ancient Testimony,* 182–85.

71. E.g., Stephen Wilson, *Ideology and Experience, Antisemitism in France at the Time of the Dreyfus Affair* (East Brunswick, N.J. 1982), 150–51; Alfred D. Low, *Jews in the Eyes of the Germans, From the Enlightenment to Imperial Germany* (Philadelphia 1979), 251–53, 375.

72. Hans Kohn, *Making of the French Modern Mind* (New York 1955), 46–47.

73. Shmuel Almog, "The Racial Motif in Renan's Attitude to Jews and Judaism," in *Antisemitism Through the Ages,* ed. Shmuel Almog (Oxford 1988), 268–71.

74. Ernest Renan, *Judaïsme et Christianisme, textes présentés par Jean Gaulnier* (Paris 1977), 138–39, 141.

75. George P. Gooch, *History and Historians in the Nineteenth Century* (Boston 1962), 484.

76. R. E. Clements, "The Study of the Old Testament," in *Nineteenth Century Religious Thought in the West,* eds. Ninian Smart et al., vol. 3 (Cambridge 1988), 128–30.

77. Christhard Hoffmann, *Juden und Judentum im Werk deutscher Althistoriker des 19. und 20. Jahrhunderts* (Leiden 1988), 161–62.

78. Cf. Almog, "Racial Motif," 262–65.

79. Manuel, *Broken Staff,* 249–54.

80. Hoffman, *Juden und Judentum,* 166.

81. Fritz Stern, *The Politics of Cultural Despair, A Study in the Rise of the Germanic Ideology* (New York 1965), 91.

82. Karl Löwith, *Von Hegel zu Nietzsche, Der revolutionäre Bruch im Denken des 19. Jahrhunderts* (Hamburg 1978), 399; George Mosse, *The Crisis of German Ideology, Intellectual Origins of the Third Reich* (New York 1964), 33.

83. Löwith, *Von Hegel,* 401; Stern, *Politics,* 75.

84. J. C. O'Neill, "Study of the New Testament," in *Religious Thought,* ed. Smart, vol. 3, 147.

85. Hans-Joachim Krauss, "Die Evangelische Kirche," in *Entscheidungsjahr 1932, Zur Judenfrage in der Endphase der Weimar Republik,* eds. Werner E. Mosse and Arnold Pauker (Tübingen 1966), 253.

86. Uriel Tal, "Theologische Debatte um das Wesen des Judentums," in *Juden im Wilhelminischen Deutschland 1890–1914,* eds. Werner E. Mosse and Arnold Pauker (Tübingen 1976), 627.

87. Leonore Siegele-Wenschkewitz, "Protestantische Universitätstheologie und Rassenideologie in der Zeit des Nationalsozialismus, Gerhard Kittels Vortrag, 'Die Entstehung der Judenfrage,' von 1936," in *Antisemitismus, von religiöser Judenfeindschaft zur Rassenideologie,* eds. Günter Brakelmann and Martin Rosowski (Göttingen 1989), 66–67; Robert P. Ericksen, *Theologians under Hitler* (New Haven 1986), ch. 2.

88. Hoffmann, *Juden und Judentum,* 257–59; Hans Liebeschütz, *Das Judentum im Geschichtsbild von Hegel bis Max Weber* (Tübingen 1967), 282–83.

89. E.g., Walther Hofer, ed., *Der Nationalsozialismus, Dokumente 1933–1945* (Frankfurt/M 1957), 150–51, 160–61. Klaus Scholder, "Judaism and Christianity in the Ideology of National Socialism," in *Judaism and Christianity under the Impact of National Socialism,* eds. Otto Dov Kulka and Paul R. Mendes-Flohr, (Jerusalem 1987), 103ff.

90. Uriel Tal, "Political Theology and Myth Prior to the Holocaust" in *The Holocaust as Historical Experience,* eds. Yehuda Bauer and Nathan Rotenstreich (New York 1981), 51–52.

91. Jean-Christian Petitfils, *L'Extrême droite en France* (Paris 1988), 20–21.

92. Michael Sutton, *Nationalism and Positivism, The Politics of Charles Maurras and French Catholics 1890–1914* (Cambridge 1982), 56–57.

93. Pierre Pierrard, *Juifs et catholiques français, Du Drumont à Jules Isaac (1886–1945)* (Paris 1970), 172–74.

94. Simone Weil, *La Pesanteur et la grace* (Paris 1991), 183, 187–91. It has been claimed that Weil did receive baptism on her deathbed; see *La Terra Santa* (Jerusalem), March–April 1994, excerpted in *Hebrew Catholic* (Highland, NY), November–December 1994, 14.

95. See Aryeh Maidenbaum and Stephen A. Martin, eds., *Lingering Shadows, Jungians, Freudians and Anti-Semitism* (Boston 1991); Leon Volovici, *Nationalist Ideology and Antisemitism, The Case of Romanian Intellectuals in the 1930s* (Oxford 1991), 145–47;

Daniel Dubuisson, "Métaphysique et politique. L'ontologie antisémite de Mircea Eliade," — *Genre humain,* 26 (1992): 103–17.

9

Exploring the Other: The Enlightenment's Search for the Boundaries of Humanity

Shulamit Volkov
Tel Aviv University

In December 1799, some sixty scholars—naturalists, geographers, philosophers and medical men—established the Société des Observateurs de l'Homme in Paris. This was yet another scientific group among various short-lived associations at the time, thereafter quickly forgotten and ignored by almost all later commentators. Standard historiography is understandably absorbed by the drama of contemporary politics and the study of more illustrious personalities. At the turn of the century, indeed, politics provided a great deal of excitement. On the international scene, the members of the Second Coalition—England, Austria, and Russia—pressed the French backwards on widely separated fronts. In France itself, Napoleon had given the Republic a final blow on the 18th Brumaire of the year VIII—barely a month prior to the launching of the society. Everywhere in Europe, moreover, the major intellectual figures of a coming new age were already formulating their creeds: Joseph de Maistre's *Considérations sur la France* was published anonymously as early as 1797; by 1799 Novalis had completed his *Christenheit oder Europa,* Hölderlin his *Hyperion,* and Schlegel—his fragments on poetry. Immanuel Kant was by then publishing his last works and the young Hegel wrote his first political essay. Nevertheless, it may be instructive to take a look at that rather obscure group of ideologues at the very end of a glorious century, striving—as they then believed—to accomplish what their predecessors repeatedly failed to do, namely to establish a true "Science of Man."[1]

In order to appreciate their efforts and evaluate their success or failure, a quick review of the relevant intellectual strands, finally joining together by the end of the eighteenth century, is indispensable. After all, "the question of Man" and its various moral, aesthetic and political implications has always been a major philosophical issue in Western thought.[2] Despite the great fascination with the physical world and the nature of the universe since the seventeenth century and despite the euphoria surrounding the discoveries of Galileo, Newton, and Leibnitz, this question was "never very far from the center of attention."[3] In 1674, Nicolas de Malebranche declared in his *De la recherche de la Vérité* that "Of all human knowledge the knowledge of man is the most deserving of his study"[4] and, indeed, soon afterwards, John Locke's *Essay Concerning Human Understanding* (1690) gave the much needed impulse to this sphere of investigation. It never ceased to preoccupy the men of the Enlightenment. Half a century after Locke, David Hume, setting out to write "A Treatise of Human Nature"—to be later followed by his *Inquiry Concerning Human Understanding*—found it necessary to explain the fascination of his topic: after all, he explained in the famous "Abstract" (1740), it alone promises the "satisfaction of being acquainted with what most nearly concerns us" and besides "it may be safely affirmed" that "almost all the [other] sciences" were comprehended in what he then decided to name "the science of human nature."[5] In the mid-eighteenth century, Diderot gave an even sharper expression to this idea in a programmatic entry of the *Encyclopédie:* "Man is the sole and only limit whence one must start and back to whom everything must return, if one wishes to please, interest, touch, even in the most arid considerations and the driest details." And he then adds in a characteristic fashion: "Setting aside my own existence and the happiness of my fellow beings, what does the rest of nature matter to me?"[6]

The search for the essence of man was likewise a major element in the work of David Hume, Jean Jacques Rousseau, and a host of minor thinkers throughout the eighteenth century. Though they differed in many important details from each other, their theories served to substantiate the claim that what made man human was his reason, and that in his capacity as a free agent he was rationally bound to decide—for whatever motives—to enter into a more or less orderly political society, namely into a Social Contract. Virtually all state of Nature theories stressed human rationality and freedom. All Social Contract theories claimed that individuals were born free and equal to each other.[7]

Nevertheless, hints of the *exclusive* potential of these presumably all-*inclusive* theories and of their inherent susceptibility to notions of hierarchy and *in*equality are easy to detect. They are apparent, for instance, in Locke's implicit assumption of differential rights and rationality, or in various comments on the rudimentary culture and language of the American Indians.[8] But of all eighteenth-century philosophers it was perhaps David Hume, who, in one of his most brilliant and amusing political essays, best displayed the contradictory nature of the Enlightenment's view of Man. Though in his major works Hume always championed the belief that "there is great uniformity among the actions of men in all nations and ages" and that "human nature remains still the same, in its principles and operations," he was repeatedly drawn to history, to the particular and the unique in human affairs.[9] In a footnote to one of his shorter essays, "Of national Character," indicated by the small letter "f," Hume writes the following:

> I am apt to suspect the Negroes, and in general all the other species of men (for there are four or five different kinds) to be *naturally inferior to the whites*. There scarcely ever was a civilized nation of any other complexion than white, not ever any individual eminent either in action or speculation. No ingenious manufactures amongst them, no arts, no sciences. On the other hand, the most rude and barbarous of the whites, such as the ancient Germans, the present Tartars, have still something eminent about them, in their valour, form of government, or some other particular. Such a uniform and constant difference, could not happen, in so many countries and ages, *if nature had not made an original distinction between these breeds of men.*[10]

Eighteenth century men, it is true, were occasionally embarrassed by such incongruities. They sometimes debated the conflicting consequences of their thought when applied to the case of slavery or in the discussion about the status of wage-laborers. But notions of inherent inequality and natural hierarchy were also taken for granted. These were essential, to take an often neglected example, in enlightened theories about the position of women. In fact, the case of women is a particularly good example of the way in which universalism could be jeopardized by the belief in natural hierarchy, serving as an ordering and exclusive—rather than inclusive—principle. With the exception of Hobbes, all major thinkers at the time—Pufendorf, Locke, and Rousseau alike—considered the subordination of women perfectly justified. It was a natural phenomenon, they believed, already present in the state of Nature, prior to the introduction of any social contract, and one that ought therefore to be upheld under any kind of political arrangement.[11]

With the approach of the eighteenth century, the familiar discussion of the Renaissance, "ob die Weiber Menschen Seyn oder nicht" no longer seemed pertinent. The language of the *Querelle des femmes,* in which women had then taken an active part too, was now replaced by the language of Natural Law, the exclusive domain of male philosophers.[12] Accordingly, women—though human—were *naturally* subordinate to man. "The male surpasses the female in strength of body and mind" explains Pufendorf in his celebrated *De jure naturae et gentium* of 1672, and though this was not sufficient for him to ensure men's natural mastery over women, it was enough to underwrite their mastery in marriage, so that "they cannot stand as free equals...[and] cannot become civil individuals when the passage is made into civil society."[13] For Locke, too, women were quickly relegated to a subservient position. At the very outset, he thought, like Pufendorf, women *were* in a position to enter as free agents into "conjugal society," but since husband and wife may occasionally have "different understandings" and "different wills" and "since the last determination—i.e., the rule—should be placed somewhere," Locke explains, "it *naturally* falls to the man's share, as the abler and the stronger."[14] We know, he postulates elsewhere, that wives should be subjected to their husbands, since "the Laws of mankind and customs of Nations have ordered it so; and there is, I grant"—he significantly adds—"a *Foundation in Nature* for it."[15] J. J. Rousseau was, if anything, even more adamant on this point, despite his great emphasis on the idea of equality. Paternal supremacy, explains Judith Shklar, "was the one form of inequality that he did not even recognize as such," and it was, according to him too that "the law of nature bids women obey men."[16] It is perhaps somewhat less well-known that Kant followed Rousseau steadily on this point too. Both Rousseau and Kant were committed to human equality and to the basic and inherent capacity of all humans to act in freedom. Like their predecessors, indeed, both of them never denied women's humanity. But they had little difficulty in relegating them to the margin. Women, Kant tells us, know "nothing of must, nothing of due, nothing of ought."[17] They are equal in humanity, to be sure, but, like other categories of dependents, have "no civil personality and their existence is...merely inherent."[18] Strangely, they are "individual" enough in Kant's eyes to enter into a marriage contract, but thereafter they are no longer anything but their husbands' "property." The husband's power over his wife, Kant explains, can*not* be regarded as "contrary to the natural Equality of the human pair," since such legal supremacy is based—so Kant—"upon the *natural* superiority of the faculties of the Husband compared with the Wife."[19] Thus, no doubt, a measure of *natural* human hierarchy was intuitively acceptable at the time, even to the best minds of the century. The most universalist and egalitarian theories of the Enlightenment were never meant to supply an absolute barrier against the introduction of hierarchy within humanity or against delegating the various categories of the "others" such as blacks, women, or Jews—to its margins.

Hierarchy and diversity were thus inherent to eighteenth century thought about humanity. A contemporary publication on diverse human social and political institutions across the globe was Montesquieu's *Esprit des Lois,* first published in 1748. Twenty-two editions immediately followed and the book soon turned into a bestseller. It was greatly admired not only for its method and originality but for its outstanding "lyricism of prose" as well.[20] To be sure, Montesquieu was by no means yet another theorist of Natural Law or of the Social Contract. Though he briefly recognizes a state of Nature, he does not make use of it in order to construct either a particular human nature or one type of ideal political order. Instead, Man for Montesquieu is a *social* being from the outset, subject to laws which can be both observed and analyzed. For diverse physical or moral reasons, these vary greatly in time and in space but they all can be evaluated on the basis of some uniform, scientific rules. Montesquieu's search for such rules made him a pioneer of political science.[21] His insistence on the empirical observation of humanity—despite his deficient "groundwork"[22]—entitle him to be called a pioneer anthropologist. From this perspective, what counts is neither his methodological sophistication, nor his apparent political conservatism, but his straightforward acceptance of human diversity and the nascent historicism of his thought. By its success and popularity, *Esprit des Lois* provided legitimation for this approach to the study of Man. It has never since been absent from the discourse of the Enlightenment.

Nevertheless, some clearly felt ill at ease with Montesquieu's empiricism. In his *Discours sur l'origine de l'inégalité,* Rousseau, having declared that "It is of man that I have to speak," hastens to add: "Let us therefore begin by putting aside all the facts, for they have no bearing on the question."[23] But in his famous note no. 10, appended to the *Discours,* he too seems to be pointing in another direction: "The entire earth is covered with nations of which we know only the names, and we dabble in judging the human race!" Only with the help of a comprehensive natural, moral and political history of mankind, to use his own categories, would we be able to see "a new world sally from our pen, and we would thus learn to know our own."[24] At the same time, Voltaire, equally critical of Montesquieu, though perhaps more especially annoyed by his politics, also made his own effort at a study of human pluralism. His *Essai sur les moeurs* exposes the inner tension between the belief in universality, which he had never abandoned, and fascination with cultural and human diversity. It is precisely this tension that best reflect the purpose of the work, manifesting both its author's unwillingness to choose between two different approaches as well as his inability to mediate between them. Lessing, for one, was impatient with Voltaire's lack of consistency. In a review of the *Essai,* following its first appearance in German, he succinctly stated the dilemma: "Either one considers man in particular or in general...."[25] It was precisely this alternative that Voltaire refused to address.

Parallel to the discourse of philosophers or historians, the world of learning since the last two decades of the seventeenth century was also debating matters concerning the physical and physiological aspects of Man. Man had now finally lost his privileged position in the center of creation. Galileo, Descartes, and Leibnitz, among others, concurred with Spinoza's dictum that *non omnia hominum causa fieri.*[26] The order of the day was now either to redefine man's place within the universe according to new principles, or at least to rethink his position within the old Great Chain of Being. This, above all, had become the task of "natural history," a discipline then busy defining its own parameters and establishing its scientific status. Contemporary naturalists were swamped by new information and a great many new specimens of hitherto unknown minerals, plants, and animals. The great improvement of the "compound microscope" during the late seventeenth century also made possible the findings of the first microbiologists. They all had to confront now a view of natural "Plenitude"—to use Lovejoy's befitting term—of new scope and dimensions.[27]

It was then realized by the gentlemen-scholars of the time that the boundaries of humanity were not as clear-cut as had once been assumed. The discussion concerning the humanity of the American Indians, for instance, was decided as early as the first half of the sixteenth century by the authority of State and Church, with the papal Bull of Paul III (June 9, 1537) and Charles V's "Leyes nuevas" of 1542.[28] Their humanity was above all a precondition for their christening. After all, affirming the humanity of various barbarian tribes on the European continent had been a necessary and known practice of the Church for centuries. For the Crown, too, such affirmation—in the case of the South American Indians—was needed mainly for the purpose of weakening the power of the great landlords in the Americas and retaining central authority in the Old World. But such practical and moral concerns were not always relevant.[29] The exact status of the African blacks, for instance, was never clearly defined, nor was it apparent how to rank the already celebrated Hottentots, or even the various apes, chimpanzees, or orangutan. In addition to Hume's remarks concerning the Negroes, observe Rousseau's comments in note no. 10 of his *Second Discourse:* having counted the various kinds of men of different color, size and shape, even those that "have tails like quadrupeds," Rousseau expresses his wonder "whether the various *animals* similar to men, taken by travelers without much scrutiny for beasts...would not in fact be veritable savage men whose race... has not had time to develop any of its virtual faculties." And he goes on to quote at length from a description of the orangutans in the East Indies which occupy—according to common belief, so he says—"a middle ground between the human species and the baboons," but who show in fact "striking points of conformity with the human species and lesser differences than those that would be assigned between one man and another."[30] Almost twenty years later, the Scot Lord Monboddo repeated Rousseau's analysis of the higher apes, and even the Swiss theologian Charles Bonnet was filled with awe facing these beings "resembling man so nearly that the characters which distinguish them seem less the characters of species than of mere varieties."[31]

Professional naturalists were no less confused. In fact, the problem of the orangutan was first presented to an amazed reading public in 1699 by Edward Tyson's book, *Orang Outang sive homo sylvestris, or The Anatomy of a Pygmie compared with that of Monkey, an Ape and a Man.* The book was republished in 1751 and may well have influenced Rousseau, among others. But the most systematic effort to classify all living species and thus properly place man in nature and draw the boundaries of his kind was surely that of the Swedish naturalist Linnaeus. He first published his *Systema Naturae* in 1735 and then continued to revise and republish it, admitting, in fact, at one point, his total desperation at finding or defining *the* decisive morphological human property.[32] Finally Linnaeus came up with a double-column scheme, the *homo sapiens* on the one side and *homo monstruosus* on the other. The first included the "wild man—four-footed, mute and hairy," in addition to the American, the European, the Asiatic, and the African men, interestingly distinguished from one another not only by color and stature but also by outstanding habits and the style of their government. The second included an even more peculiar mixture of fabulous creatures reported either in classical works or in the travel literature of the day—a sad reflection upon contemporary biology, a century after Newton.

It was finally George Louis Leclerc du Buffon, who was to be crowned "the Newton of the new biology." Against the static and abstract system of Linnaeus, Buffon developed the concept and method of *histoire naturelle,* an empirically oriented, developmental approach, seeking to integrate man within the world of living creatures, without abandoning the search for his uniqueness.[33] Like so many during that time, Buffon was particularly obsessed with the link between man and animal. Rejecting Descartes' strict division of the worlds of humans and animals, the new materialism of Buffon and many of his followers emphatically reasserted the links between them. The biological line of investigation then joined the philosophical in opposing the Cartesian orthodoxy. In his turn, the Abbé de Condillac published as early as 1755 his own *Traité des Animaux,* "après avoir fait des observations critiques sur le sentiment de Descartes, et sur celui de M. de Buffon," as the title assures us.[34]

Thus, by the last third of the eighteenth century, France—indeed, all of educated Europe—was vibrating with new theories concerning human divisions and the boundaries of humanity.[35] In 1774, Henry Homes (Lord Kames) published his *Sketches of the History of Man.* A year later, Friedrich Blumenbach came out with his *De generis humani varietate nativa.* And in Switzerland at the same time Johann Kaspar Lavater published his richly illustrated *Physiognomische Fragmente*—gaining immense popularity in Germany as well as in England and France. Physiognomy was indeed becoming popular everywhere at the time, drawing the attention of naturalists, poets, painters and philosophers alike. The new interest had not only been a matter for men long forgotten. In the same momentous year of 1775, Immanuel Kant published his essay *Von den verschiedenen Rassen der Menschen,* and though Herder's magnum opus, *Ideen zur Philosophie der Geschichte der Menschheit* was by then not yet completed, his essay *Über den Ursprung der Sprache* was already in print. Herder, indeed, is an interesting case in point; all his work is diffused with the sense of human diversity and cultural pluralism. From Isaiah Berlin we have learned to see in him a representative of the so-called "counter-Enlightenment," an outsider to the world of typical eighteenth-century thought.[36] But Herder can perhaps better stand for one of its strands. While from the late seventeenth century and during much of the eighteenth, European intellectuals were primarily searching for the unitary essence of man and for his common origin, an emphasis on human diversity and plurality had always been there, gradually even gaining the upper hand. Like Herder, those preoccupied with variety rather than uniformity, in France as well as in Germany, did not usually abandon their universalism. It was more a matter of shifting the balance from system-building to classification, from theory to observation. They were seeking the meaning and essence of humanity, but they now preferred to do so by investigating its limits, not only its core.

We have now come a full circle, back to the men of the Société des Observateurs de l'homme. Not much is known about them. Their society never managed to publish its mémoires; its archive was apparently destroyed, and many of its prominent members have been long forgotten. In such a celebrated reference book as the *Britannica* of 1911, its founder, Louis-Francois Jauffret, or the once well-known *médicin-philosophe* Jean Itard, do not even have an article to their name. A few others, like the enormously productive and prize-winning savant Joseph-Marie Degérando; the notorious world traveler, historian, and ethnographer Constantin François Volney; or the resolute teacher of the deaf and dumb, Abbé Sicard are sometimes mentioned, but they too have otherwise fallen into oblivion.[37] The only one who recently achieved some renewed fame is the physician of mentally afflicted Parisians, Philippe Pinel, saved from anonymity by Michel Foucault.[38]

And it is indeed Foucault who, in *Les Mots et les choses,* maps the epistemological relations between the scientific disciplines of that time and draws our attention to the preconditions that made the emergence of a new "science of man" possible. With the undermining of the hierarchical structure of knowledge crowned by mathematics, "the domain of the modern episteme" could now be best represented as a "volume of space open in three dimensions." In the first of these Foucault situates the deductive mathematical and physical sciences; in the second, the empirical disciplines of biology, economics and linguistics; and in the third, the realm of philosophical reflection. The new "science of man," he explains, though clearly nourished by all three and in its turn relevant for all of them, did not belong to any of these domains. It was as if "floating" within the "open space of knowledge," gaining thereby its independence and also its precariousness.[39]

This, though somewhat obscurely formulated, seems to me to offer an admirable characterization of the prospects as well as the predicament of the project undertaken by the Observateurs. To begin with, theirs was a decidedly interdisciplinary group. They included, for instance, the publicly active group of the *médicins-philosophes* and several other savants, seeking to overcome the traditional split of man between body and soul, the moral and the physical.[40] The practitioners of physiognomy or the adherents of Lamarck's "philosophie Zoologique" clearly belonged to this intellectual milieu, too.[41] But the Observateurs were particularly radical in this respect. In a little-known manuscript written by Jauffret as a programmatic statement for his newly-established association, he emphatically declared that the society "intends to observe Man in his various aspects"—physical, intellectual and moral—but it will nevertheless "endeavor to hold on to *certain limits.*" *"The observation of physical man, for instance,"* he goes on to explain, "includes anatomy and physiology, medicine and hygiene," but the society ought never to lose sight of the fact that *it* wishes to investigate "only that which actually relates to the natural history of man." The special perspective of comparative anthropology, Jauffret assures us, "will allow [it] to absorb the latest and most important research but will also have the advantage of not confusing [its work] with that of the experts for medicine and surgery."[42]

The society has also had precise plans for a number of grand projects: the organization of a journey by sea in order "to investigate man in the great theater of the world," as Jauffret poetically put it; the publication of a complete "Handbook of Signs," a truly "national monument" according to him, that would not only help the "unfortunate"—presumably the deaf and dumb—but would also facilitate communication with "wild peoples" and "enable the philosophers to pursue with surprising ease," to be sure, "the entire history of the emergence of our ideas."[43] Apparently the Observateurs also planned to establish an ethnographical museum, though we know practically nothing about it; and finally, they intended to carry out what was for long known in Europe as the "forbidden experiment,"[44] namely "an experiment about natural man": obtaining the permission of the government, four or six children, half of them boys and half girls, would be placed in complete isolation from birth onward in order to finally observe "the development of their ideas and language."[45]

These were the general outlines of the enterprise. In practice, of course, very few of these plans were carried out. The various members of the society continued each with his own project. Jauffret himself left a number of ethnological manuscripts, among them, for instance, original works on handwriting, and other systems of human signs, such as *Des différents genres d'écriture and Histoire de l'écriture hiéroglyphique.*[46] Degérando continued to work on his study of gesture, interpreting language as a complex sign-system and composing one of the first systematic works on semiotics.[47] Volney continued his ethnological studies of Egypt and Syria, the "savages of north America," and Indians in general.[48] The naturalist Georges Cuvier lectured in the Collège de France on comparative anatomy and pursued his geological and paleontological studies.[49] In addition, the group assembled periodically and, since their meetings were often reported in the Parisian *Magasin Encyclopédique,* we have relatively detailed information about their joint interests.[50] Apparently the Observateurs heard lectures on the "galvanic" effects upon the human organism, perhaps in relation to the vogue of mesmerism at the time.[51] Pinel occasionally presented to them his particularly interesting mental patients; the Abbé Sicard reported on the education of the deaf; they were instructed in the benefits of physical education (despite Rousseau's outspoken opinion against it) and heard about the possibility of treating amnesia. They were once presented with a male and female midget and decided immediately to form not one, but two committees in order to investigate their intellectual and moral character; they were instructed concerning the habits of the Tartars and some remote Siberian tribes, and also discussed the various religions of the Indian sub-continent.

From the historian's perspective they may easily seem eccentric, even somewhat muddled. But their task, it must be remembered, was very intricate indeed. The new human science which they were endeavoring to construct was truly complex. Its object, to go back to Foucault, was not human life, labor, or language but that peculiar being whose consciousness allows him to analyze and, above all, to *represent* the various aspects of his existence.[52] "Anthropology"—as that enterprise was by then often named—was called upon to draw general conclusions about the meaning of humanity and the nature of mankind. But the gap between such ambitions and empirical study of detailed, often outlandish cases was great and the epistemology involved often problematic.

One should not judge them too harshly. After all, the great Kant was likewise entangled in this intricate situation. It is probably correct to say, in the most general terms, that the proper subject matter of his philosophy was man and his reason.[53] In many of his writings, first and foremost in his *Critique of Pure Reason,* he indicated the three major questions which preoccupied him: "What can man know"; "What ought he to do"; and "What may he hope for." On one occasion, however, in the Introduction to his *Logic,* Kant adds a fourth question: "What is Man?" and he then immediately comments: "The first question is answered by *Metaphysics,* the second by *Morals,* the third by *Religion,* and the fourth by *Anthropology.*" "In reality," he adds, "all these might be reckoned under *Anthropology,* since the first three questions refer to the last."[54] One is therefore justified in approaching Kant's single work bearing the title *Anthropologie,* with great expectations.[55] It was, moreover, a subject on which he had lectured, according to his own testimony, "for some 30 years".[56] But this work, in fact, provides no final synthesis at all. It includes an extensive discourse on what one may term "empirical psychology" in the first "didactic" part, and a rather prolonged text on physiognomy, gender differences, and national and racial character in the second part, under the sub-title *Charakteristik*. The work ends with an attempt to explain how reason finally manages to overcome the "rawness" of human nature and direct man to socialize with others for the purpose of "cultivating, civilizing and moralizing himself".[57] This, surely, is not the best among Kant's *oeuvres*. To the end, his remained "*philosophical* anthropology." Kant's profound insights into the nature of man were based, like those of Rousseau and the other *philosophes,* on hypothetical reasoning *("écarter tous les faits.")*[58] The efforts to move from "philosophical reflection" into the realm of the empirical human sciences while holding on to both, seemed to have brought Kant surprisingly close to the discourse of the Observateurs. This was the intellectual predicament of the age.

Perhaps this is why many at the time were so often busy defining the new "Science of Man." The virtually forgotten Swiss scholar Alexandre Chavanne, in his *Anthropologie, ou Science de l'homme,* published in Lausanne in 1788, wrote that "real anthropology is the science of man which observes the constitution of his nature, namely all traits that draw him near the other species and all that distinguishes him from them."[59] This, I believe, is what the Observateurs were really trying to do and it can partially explain their constant search for the "boundaries of Humanity," for "borderline cases", for what one can learn by observing that which we have come to identify as "the other."

The list of lectures arranged for the Observateurs clearly attests to this sort of interest. Sheer luck seemed to have served them even better. While they were beginning their deliberations, Paris was aroused by the appearance of a real Chinese man in its midst.[60] Tchong-A-Sam had been apparently captured by pirates at sea and brought to Bordeaux. Having been moved from town to town for some time, he finally landed in a Parisian hospital and was brought to the attention of Eustache Broquet, an instructor at Sicard's Institut pour les Sourds et Muets. The case was duly reported to the Société, and having received an official permit to "observe" the man, immediately appointed a committee to perform the task. This seems to have been standard procedure. The members of that committee attempted to learn elemental Chinese in order to communicate with Tchong-A-Sam, drawing immediate conclusions about that language's phonetic qualities. They proceeded to try and determine his race, using Blumenbach's categories, and to produce precise sketches of his head and face. Unfortunately, the authorities decided to send the man back "to the East" and the project was prematurely interrupted. Now, Chinese men, as well as Indians and Blacks from America or the West Indies, were not, of course, a complete novelty in Europe of 1800.[61] They were always considered exotic, fascinating, and amusing, but never previously as objects of science. For the Observateurs, and other academics, every human "other" now quickly turned into a focus of research.

This was demonstrated again in the case of Victor, known as "le sauvage de l'Aveyron," a wild child found in the forest of that southern French department in January 1800.[62] The child, in his early teens, was first spotted in 1798 but managed to escape and it was somewhat later, that he was brought to Paris and eventually handed over to the scrutiny of the Observateurs. The society appointed a committee chaired by Pinel and including some of the most illustrious members of the group: Jauffret, Degérando, Cuvier, and Sicard, in whose School for the Deaf and Dumb the wild-child finally found shelter. Victor, as he was subsequently named, aroused a great deal of interest. Inevitably, he was regarded as a specimen of that much sought-after *l'homme de nature,* and soon caused deep disenchantment. Finding him confused and apathetic, experts noted that "except for his human face—what would distinguish him from a monkey?"[63] But the Observateurs seemed to consider the matter differently. They wished to apply their own, presumably more scientific methods of observation to this case, and to use Victor's education (the process of cultivating and civilizing him) as a crucial test case. Soon it was Pinel himself who despaired of the whole affair. He pronounced the child an "idiot" and claimed that this probably was the reason why he had been left by his parents in the woods. The child, he promptly decided, was an impossible object for improvement or education and a hopeless case from a scientific point of view.[64]

But the case was saved for posterity, despite the great reputation of the famous physician, by another Observateur. Jean Itard, himself a physician and one-time student of Pinel, employed by the Abbé Sicard in his School for the Deaf and Dumb, took it upon himself to civilize the young brute. He spent some five years of his life on this project and finally published in 1801 and 1807 a fascinating two-part report about the project, written with a great deal of literary skill and intellectual honesty.[65] Itard made a conscious effort to operate in that sphere between the philosophical theories of Locke, Condillac, or Helvetius, and the praxis of empirical education and medicine. This was an attempt to apply the logic of a "borderline case-study" in order to learn about humanity. Victor was a perfect "other," ready-made material for experimental observation.

Similar concerns lay at the root of the eighteenth-century fascination with remote and foreign tribes. The Observateurs were involved in organizing a scientific expedition to Australia and Joseph-Marie Degérando, a leading member of the society, has left us a detailed work listing the necessary prerequisites for properly executing the anthropological aspect of the task. His *Considération sur diverses Méthodes d'observation des peuples sauvages* is perhaps the first handbook for anthropologists.[66] In it, he lists the prejudices and preconceptions from which one must be freed before embarking on such a project, above all from the influence of obsolete philosophical "systems."[67] He insists on an absolute concern for facts alone. Properly observing the primitives was comparable, he believed, to a "journey back in time."[68] By learning methodically their language and ideas, their habits and institutions, we would become wiser concerning mankind as a whole. The most distant cases, once again, were considered crucial for appreciating the human essence. It is the "other" who alone can help us know ourselves.

Exotic, unfamiliar communities within Europe, were also a target for the scientific spirit of the age. Jews, for instance, though apparently never considered by the Observateurs, could be viewed in this light. To be sure, *they* were never unequivocally considered "others" within Christian civilization, nor were they ever an uncontested element of the European collective *"nous."*[69] As major actors within the still-dominant biblical tale of human history, they surely belonged. As willful religious dissidents for centuries, they were outsiders. But by the late sixteenth century, one can clearly note a change of perspective in some of the literature dealing with them, and a century later this trend could no longer be overlooked.[70] At first, some travelers began to include detailed observations on the Jews in faraway lands and, eventually, local European Jewish communities too were made an object of general curiosity and scientific observation. Common prejudices may have, indeed, threatened to distort such works even more frequently and more thoroughly than those dealing with less familiar human groups, or those less intricately linked with Christian tradition. But a few of the early ethnographers did manage to achieve a fair degree of distance and objectivity. In fact, confusion and misrepresentation were often more conspicuous in this literature than open prejudice. The frontispiece of Lancelot Addison's *The Present State of the Jews in Barbary,* first published in 1675, portrays what might be seen either as the illustrator's "idea of a typical Moor" or, more probably, his image of an Indian in full attire.[71] As a matter of fact, the "Jewish Indian Theory," claiming that the American Indians were descendent from the "Ten Lost Tribes" of Israel, has recently been shown by Richard Popkin to have survived well into the nineteenth century.[72] At first, connecting the christianization of the North American Indians with the millenial expectations of the mid-seventeenth century, it was then also supported (though somewhat hesitantly) by Menasseh Ben Israel, and fully endorsed and propagated by a number of Christian missionaries. The attraction of the theory, making it possible to retain the biblical story of creation as well as the contemporary scientific convention of human "monogenesis," may explain its tenacity during so much of the eighteenth century. As late as our fateful year 1799, in fact, one Charles Crawford published in Philadelphia *An Essay on the Propagation of the Gospel, in which there are numerous Facts and Arguments adduced to prove that Many of the Indians in America are descended from the Ten Tribes.*[73]

All this was apparently not considered improbable at the time and it surely served to add flavor to contemporary ethnography. But the Eighteenth Century also offers a considerable number of rather well-founded, detailed descriptions of the inner life of various Jewish communities in and out of Europe. Jews were sometimes treated as part of a general, human gallery and occasionally their customs were described in studies devoted to some specific cultural habits, such as marriage or burial ceremonies.[74] Early in the century, bibliophiles across Europe could already get hold of one of the many editions of the richly illustrated publication of the French lithographer, Bernard Picart, *Cérémonies et coutumes religieuses de tous les peuples du monde,* including numerous visual and verbal descriptions of Jewish scenes. The book first appeared in Amsterdam in 1723 and enjoyed many editions in various languages throughout the century.[75] At its appearance, however, German readers were already familier with other books on the same topic. Johannes Jakob Schudt's *Jüdische Merkwürdigkeiten* (1714–1718) was aesthetically less impressive, but soon became no less popular. By 1749, Johann Christoph Georg Bodenschatz's *Kirchliche Verfassung der heutigen Juden, sonderlich derer in Deutschland,* richly illustrated with thirty copper plates, also became available.[76] At that time, too, a number of converts to Christianity, published their own more or less reliable sketches. Jews were by then clearly arousing the same kind of embryonic anthropological interest, which we have observed growing during the eighteenth century.

As in the case of others, *their* essential humanity, too, had to be repeatedly reaffirmed. This line of argument became particularly important in the context of impending emancipation. "The Jew is more a man than he is a Jew" ran Christian Wilhelm Dohm's oft-quoted dictum, repeated by Mirabeau and the Abbé Grégoire, indeed by all who championed the cause of Jewish civil equality.[77] The closing appeal of Abbé Grégoire's prize-winning *Essai sur la Régénération physique, morale et politique des juifs,* suffused with Christian allusions, also included this, more timely assertion: Jews "are members of that universal family that ought to establish fraternity among all people."[78] And in his later *Motion en faveur des Juifs,* Grégoire exclaimed: "When are we finally going to bring back into humanity this people, always debased by our discrimination as if it were a creature between man and animal?"[79]

The issue of human boundary was thus never far from the consciousness of the French and German reformers at the end of the eighteenth century.

Indeed, both Dohm and the Abbé Grégoire had interests that far exceeded the case of the Jews. It is rarely realized that before embarking upon his pioneering *Über die bürgerliche Verbesserung der Juden,* Dohm had made plans to write a major work on the history, religion, philosophy, and law of India; translated a number of travel books, and prepared an annotated edition of one of the most highly esteemed travel reports in Germany at the time, Kämpfer's book on Japan.[80] Furthermore, Dohm's original intention with regard to his work on the Jews had been to introduce it with an extensive and detailed exposition of their history. The Jews were clearly—though perhaps not explicitly—a "borderline case" for him. His description of their character was, after all, far from complimentary. But if *they* could be *verbessert* (improved), a powerful proof for the theoretical assumption of human perfectibility would be provided. If *they* could be civilized under new circumstances, then some of the prevailing theories concerning environmental and social effects on man would surely receive strong confirmation. It was exceedingly difficult to prove such theories with respect to savage peoples across the oceans. It was far simpler to use available, local material.

Abbé Grégoire, too, was certain that Jews would make responsible citizens *despite* their obvious shortcomings. For him, too, no doubt they served as a kind of test case—not only for the strength of his Christian compassion but also for the validity of his humanistic concerns. Like Dohm, he also had wider interests as far as the fight for the equal rights of marginal social elements was concerned. By the turn of the century, when once again a member of the legislative body in France, Abbé Grégoire stood at the head of the French anti-slavery lobby.[81] In an extensive treaty on this issue he accuses the slave merchants of having "at one time...seriously affected to doubt whether the Africans could be admitted into the class of reasonable beings," and then proceeds to assure his readers that "from the multiplicity of facts which...attests the identity and unity of the human species, they too were soon obliged to concede the point as no longer questionable."[82] The issue of drawing and redrawing the presumably scientific boundaries of humanity was apparently never far from the surface. It was a constitutive element in the discourse of the time, whether political or purely scientific.

Politics, indeed, may have helped make this matter all the more relevant. In the later years of the French Republic, universality and equality turned out to be a mere embarrassment for those who were running public affairs. By 1800, slowly digesting the experience of the Revolution, Europe was everywhere preoccupied with matters of exclusion. The anti-revolutionary forces were vigorously seeking ways to reestablish legitimate social hierarchies and to restrain the power of the "mob." Clearly, the intellectual apparatus needed for the task was by then easily available. In Germany, the literary Romantics, as well as the "new historians" and a small group of naturalists, were stressing individuality and singularity, busy differentiating among human groups, nations, and races. Conservatives were also making use of the new trends. "The constitution of 1795, just like its predecessors," wrote de Maistre, "was made for man. But there is no such thing as man in the world. In the course of my life I have seen Frenchmen, Italians, Russians, etc.; I know, too, thanks to Montesquieu," he sarcastically adds "that one can be Persian. But as for man, I declare that I have never met him in my life; if he exists, he is unknown to me."[83] Finally, empiricism and the new human sciences, originally conceived as support for the grand ideals of the Enlightenment, were all too often made to serve entirely different goals. During the nineteenth century, they were used and misused in every conceivable way. This is, perhaps, yet another aspect of the manipulation of the Enlightenment message, a reminder of its complex dialectical features.

Notes

1. Among the first to refer to the Société des Observateurs de l'homme was the late nineteenth-century surgeon and anthropologist, Paul Broca in his *Histoire de progrès des Études anthropologiques depuis la fondation de la société* (report read at the tenth anniversary of the Société d'Anthropologie, 8 July 1869; published Paris 1870). Some of the papers of the Observateurs were recovered by Georges Hervé, "Le premier programme de l'Anthropologie," *Revue scientifique* 12 (1909): 520–28; idem, "Les premiers cours d'Anthropologie" *Revue anthropologique* 24 (1914): 255–56. To my knowledge, the fullest modern presentation of the Société des Observateurs is Sergio Moravia, *La Scienza dell'Uomo nel Settecento* (Bari 1970). I have used, and quoted from, the German translation, *Beobachtende Vernunft. Philosophie und Anthropologie in der Aufklärung* (Munich 1973).

2. See Ernst Cassirer, *An Essay on Man. An Introduction to a Philosophy of Human Culture* (1st ed. Yale Univ. Press 1944; 2nd ed. New York 1953).

3. John E. Smith, "The Question of Man," in *The Philosophy of Kant and Our Modern World,* ed. Charles W. Hendel (New York 1957), 3–24.

4. Ibid., 7.

5. David Hume, "An Abstract of a Treatise of Human Nature" (1740), in *An Inquiry Concerning Human Understanding* (New York: Library of Liberal Arts, 1955), 184.

6. Denis Diderot, "Encyclopaedia," in idem, *Oeuvres complètes,* eds. Jules Assézat and Maurice Tourneux (Paris 1875–77), vol. 14, 453; see Arthur M. Wilson, *Diderot. The Testing Years, 1713–1759* (New York 1957) 245, 384 n. 40.

7. For a critical view, see C. B. Macpherson, *Political Theory of Possessive Individualism, Hobbes to Locke* (Oxford 1962); Carol Pateman, *The Sexual Contract* (Oxford 1988).

8. See Macpherson, *Political Theory,* 221–38; Anthony Pagden, *European Encounter with the New World. From renaissance to Romaticism* (New Haven and London 1993), 127–29.

9. Quotes from Peter Gay, *The Enlightenment, An Interpretation* (New York 1977), vol. 2: *The Science of Freedom,* 168.

10. David Hume, *Political Essays,* ed. Knud Haakonssen (Cambridge 1994), 84 (emphasis added).

11. The discussion relies on Pateman's analysis, *Sexual Contract;* see also Sylvana Tomaselli, "The Enlightenment Debate on Women," in *History Workshop* (1985), no. 20: 101–24.

12. See summary and bibliography in Joan Kelly, "Early Feminist Theory and the *Querelle des Femmes,* 1400–1789," in *Sign* (Autumn 1982): 4–28.

13. Quoted in Patemann, *Sexual Contract,* 51–2.

14. John Locke, *Of Civil Government. Second Treatise* (1690), in The Works of John Locke (Chicago: Gateway Edition, 1962), §78, §82, 62–64.

15. John Locke, *Of Civil Government, First Treatise* (1690), §47 (emphasis added), quoted from *Works of John Locke,* vol. 5 (London 1963), 247.

16. Cf. especially Judith N. Shklar, *Men and Citizens. A Study of Rousseau's Social Theory* (Cambridge 1969, 1985); quote is from 1985 edition, 25. Rousseau's quotation is from *Emile* (in English) (London 1948), 322.

17. Translation follows Pateman, *Sexual Contract,* 162. The German original is "Nichts von Sollen, nichts von Müssen, nichts von Schuldigkeit." It appears in Kant's "Betrachtungen über das Gefühl des Schönen und Erhabenen"; see Immanuel Kant, *Werke im Sechs Bänden,* ed. Wilhelm Weischedel, vol. 1: *Vorkritische Schriften* (Wiesbaden 1960), 854.

18. Kant, "Metaphysik der Sitten," in *Werke,* vol. 4: *Schriften zur Ethik und Religionsphilosophie* (Wiesbaden 1964), 433.

19. Ibid., 392.

20. See Franz Neumann, "Introduction," in *The Spirit of the Laws* by Montesquieu (New York 1949), xiii.

21. On Montesquieu, see, e.g., Louis Althusser, "Montesquieu: Politics and History," in idem, *Montesquieu, Rousseau, Marx. Politics and History* (London 1972), 13–109; Raymond Aron, "Montesquieu," in idem, *Main Currents in Sociological Thought,* vol. 1 (Garden City, N.Y. 1968); Isaiah Berlin, "Montesquieu" in idem, *Against the Current* (London 1979), 130–61.

22. Cassirer, *The Philosophy of the Enlightenment* (Boston 1955), 211; see also Isaiah Berlin, "Montesquieu," 130–32.

23. Jean-Jacques Rousseau, *On the Social Contract, Discourse on the Origins of Inequality, Discourse on Political Economy,* tr. Donald A. Cress, introduction by Peter Gay (Indianapolis 1983), 117–18.

24. Ibid., 208.

25. Quoted in Cassirer, *Philosophy,* 216.

26. Discussed in Arthur O. Lovejoy, *The Great Chain of Being. A Study of the History of an Idea* (Cambridge, Mass., 1936), 187–89.

27. See Georges Gusdorf, *Dieu, la nature, l'homme au siècle des lumières* (Paris 1972), 312–16.

28. Lewis Hanke, *The Spanish Struggle for Justice in the Conquest of America* (Boston 1965), 72–73, 91–95; see also Miri Eliav-Feldman, "Guilty Consciences in the Beginning of the Colonial Era" (in Hebrew) *Zemanim* 14 (1984): 4–11.

29. Hanke, *Spanish Struggle,* quotes extensively from Bartholomé de Las Casas (1474–1566), chief protagonist of Indian rights, e.g., his definition of humanity, p. 125.

30. Rousseau, *On the Social Contract,* 203–205.

31. Quoted by Lovejoy, *Great Chain of Being,* 235; see idem, "Monboddo and Rousseau," in *Essays in the History of Ideas* (Baltimore 1948), 38–61.

32. See Gunsdorf, *Dieu,* 335–38, 369–73; Hodgen, *Early Anthropology,* 424–26.

33. Georges Louis Leclerc du Buffon, *Histoire naturelle, De l'homme,* and *De la nature de l'homme,* in his *Oeuvres philosophiques, Corpus général des philosophes français* (Paris 1954); Gusdorf, *Dieu,* 324–42, 372–82.

34. Abbé de Condillac, *Traité des Sensations,* in *Corpus des Oeuvres de philosophie en langue francaise* (Paris 1984), 309–429.

35. The best summary of the relevant literature is George Mosse, *Towards the Final Solution. A History of European Racism* (London 1978), 1–34.

36. See Isaiah Berlin, "The Counter-Enlightenment," in idem, *Against the Current,* 1–24; idem, *Vico and Herder. Two Studies in the History of Ideas* (London 1976).

37. See: R. M. Reboul, *Louis-Francois Jauffret. Sa vie et ses oeuvres* (Paris 1869); Wilhelm Köster, "Joseph Marie Degérando als Philosoph" (Ph.D. diss., Freiburg i.Br., Paderborn, 1933); J. Gaulmier, *Volney. Un grand témoin de la révolution et de l'Empire,* (Paris 1959); H. Daudin, *Les classes zoologiques et l'idée de série animale en France à l'époque de Lamarck et de Cuvier (1790–1830)* (Paris 1926); on the Abbé Roch-Ambroise Sicard, see Harlane Lane, *When the Mind Hears: A History of the Deaf,* chs. 2, 3 (New York 1984), 17–41; Ferdinand Berthier, *L'Abbé Sicard, célèbre instituteur des sourds muets* (Paris 1873).

38. Michel Foucault, *Histoire de la Folie à l'âge classique* (Paris 1961), ch. 8, especially 264–81. Foucault considers Georges Cuvier as the founder of biology; see Foucault, *The Order of Things* (London 1970; reprint 1994), ch. 8, section 3.

39. Foucault, *Order of Things,* 344–48.

40. See e.g., Gusdorf, Dieu, 452–98; cf. George Rosen, "The philosophy and ideology of the Emergence of Modern Medicine in France," *Bulletin of the History of Medicine* 20 (1946): 328–39; and Sergio Moravia, "Philosophie et medicine en France à la fin du 18ème siècle," *Studies on Voltaire and the Eighteenth Century* 89 (1972): 108–51.

41. Lamarck may have been a member of the society; see Moravia, *Beobachtende Vernunft,* 269 n. 2. Much of his work was published at that time, e.g., *Recherches sur les causes des principaux faits physiques* (1794); *Recherches sur l'organisation des corps vivants* (1801); *Philosophie zoologique* (1809).

42. This text, somewhat abridged, appears in Moravia, *Beobachtende Vernunft,* 209–19.

43. Ibid., 215.

44. Roger Shattuck, *The Forbidden Experiment. The Story of the Wild Boy of Aveyron* (London 1980), 42–67.

45. Moravia, *Beobachtende Vernunft,* 215.

46. Published by Georges Hervé in *Revue de l'École d'Anthropologie de Paris,* vols. 19, 20, 21 (1909–1911).

47. See, Degérando, *Des Signes et de l'art de penser considérés dans leur rapports mutuels* (Paris 1800); idem, *De la génération des connoissances humaines* (Berlin 1802); idem, *Histoire comparée des sytemes de philosophie relativement aux principes des connaissances humaines* (Paris 1804).

48. Constantin François Volney, *Oeuvres complètes* (Paris 1860), including *Voyages en Égypte et en Syrie* and *Leçons d'histoire prononcées à l'École Normale.*

49. See Georges Cuvier, *Tableau élémentaire de l'histoire naturelle des animaux* (1798); and *Leçons d'anatomie comparée* (1800).

50. See Moravia, *Beobachtende Vernunft,* 86–87.

51. Robert Darnton, *Mesmerism and the End of the Enlightenment in France* (Cambridge, Mass. 1968).

52. Foucault, *Order of Things,* 348–55.

53. See Smith, "Question of Man," 12–14.

54. Immanuel Kant, *Werke,* vol. 3: *Schriften zur Metaphysik und Logik* (Wiesbaden 1958), 448.

55. Immanuel Kant, "Anthropologie in pragmatischer Hinsicht, " in Kant, *Werke,* vol. 6: *Schriften zur Anthropologie, Geschichtsphilosophie, Politik und Pädagogik* (Darmstadt 1970), 398–690.

56. Smith, "Question of Man," 13.

57. Kant, "Anthropologie in Pragmatischer Hinsicht," 678.

58. Cassirer, *Essay on Man,* 79–86.

59. Alexandre Chavanne, *Anthropologie,* iii, quoted in Moravia, *La Scienza,* 63.

60. See Moravia, *Beobachtende Vernunft,* 88–92.

61. See Stephen Greenblatt, *Marvelous Possessions. The Wonder of the New World* (Oxford 1991); Anthony Pagden, *European Encounter.*

62. See Harlan Lane, *The Wild Boy of Aveyron* (Cambridge, Mass. 1976); Shattuck *Forbidden Experiment.* On other cases of "wolf-children," see J. A. L. Singh and R. M. Zingg, *Wolf Childern and Feral Men* (n.p. 1942; 2nd ed. 1966); Lucien Malson, *Les enfants sauvages* (Paris 1964).

63. Shattuck, *Forbidden Experiment,* 27.

64. See Georges Hervé, "Le sauvage de l'Aveyron devant les Observateurs de l'homme (avec le Rapport retrouvé de Philippe Pinel), *Revue Anthropologique* 21 (1911).

65. Jean Itard, *De l'éducation d'un homme sauvage ou des premiers développements physiques et moraux du jeune sauvage de l'Aveyron* (Paris 1801); idem, *Rapport fait à son Excellence le Ministre de l'Intérieur, sur les nouveaux développements et l'état actuel du sauvage de l'Aveyron* (Paris 1807); both now available in: Jean Itard, *Victor de l'Aveyron* (Paris 1994).

66. F. C. T. Moore, *The Observation of Savage Peoples by Joseph-Marie Degérando* (London 1969), with introduction on the expedition of Captain Baudin; see also Moravia, *Beobachtende Vernunft,* 162–81; apparently Georges Cuvier also wrote instructions for this expedition, found and reprinted by Georges Hervé, *Revue de l'Ecole d'Anthropologie de Paris* 20 (1910).

67. Moore, *Observation,* 61.

68. Ibid., 63.

69. Terminology borrowed from Todorov, *Nous et les autres. La réflexion française sur la diversité humaine* (Paris 1989).

70. The early ethnographic literature on the Jews has often been neglected in the historiography because of the emphasis on anti-Jewish writings; see, e.g., Shmuel Ettinger "Judaism and Jews in the Eyes of the English Deists in the 18th Century" (in Hebrew), *Zion* (1964); Arthur Hertzberg, *The French Enlightenment and the Jews* (New York 1970); Alfred D. Low, *Jews in the Eyes of the Germans. From the Enlightenment to Imperial Germany* (Philadelphia 1979); Miriam Yardeni, *Anti-Jewish Mentalities in Early Modern Europe* (Lanham and London 1990).

71. First suggestion is to be found in Israel Abrahams, *By-Paths in Hebraic Bookland* (Philadelphia 1920), 154.

72. Richard Popkin, "The Rise and Fall of the Jewish Indian Theory," in *Menasseh Ben Israel and his World*, ed. Yosef Kaplan et al. (Leiden 1989), 63–82.

73. Ibid., 72.

74. For examples, see Richard I. Cohen "The Visual Image of the Jew and Judaism in Early Modern Europe: From Symbolism to Realism" (in Hebrew), *Zion* (1992): 275–340; on studies of particular ceremonies, 297 and notes.

75. Ibid., 316–26.

76. Abrahams, *By-Paths,* 160–61.

77. Christian Wilhelm Dohm, *Über die bürgerliche Verbesserung der Juden* (Berlin-Stettin 1783), 28.

78. Abbé Grégoire, *Essai sur la Régénération physique, morale et politique des juifs* (Metz 1789), quoted from ibid., Robert Badiner, ed. (Paris 1988), 174, tr. by author.

79. Quoted in Frank Paul Bowman, *L'abbé Grégoire, Évêque des lumières* (Paris 1988), 26.

80. Robert Lieberles, "The Historical Context of Dohm's Treatise on the Jews," in *Das deutsche Judentum und der Liberalismus* (German Jewry and Liberalism) (Königswinter 1986), 44–69; on Dohm, see also I. Dambacher, *Christian Wilhelm von Dohm* (Frankfurt a.M. 1974).

81. Ruth Necheles, *The Abbé Grégoire, 1787–1831. The Odyssey of an Egalitarian* (Westport, Conn. 1971); M. Ezran, *L'abbé Grégoire—juifs et noirs* (Paris 1992).

82. Abbé Grégoire, *On the Slave Trade and on the Slavery of the Blacks and of the Whites* (London 1815), 3.

83. Joseph de Maistre, *Oevres Complètes de Joseph de Maistre* (Lyon and Paris 1884–87), vol. 1, 74, quoted by Isaiah Berlin, "Joseph de Maistre and the Origins of Fascism," in idem, *The Crooked Timber of Humanity* (London 1990), 100.

10

Otherness and Difference:
The Perspective of Gender Theory

Yael S. Feldman
New York University

There is an obvious connection between the demonization of Woman and of the Jew. After all, Jews have been often stereotyped as feminine, as the "female other" of the groups in a position of control and hegemony. Yet despite this analogy, contemporary Gender Theory has provided little to elucidate the theme of "The 'Other' as Threat." A product of the 1970s, Gender Theory is naturally implicated in the discourse of postmodernism. As such, it is heavily involved in the deconstruction of the basic dichotomy postulated by the binarism of "self and other." Furthermore, to the extent that our theme identifies the other *only* with threat and demonization, it might appear to preclude the tensions and even self-contradictions that have energized debates over the "Woman as Other" for the past fifty years.

Not that the demonization of the female "other" went unexplored. On the contrary—having roots almost in prehistoric times, this ancient tradition (much older than antisemitic demonization) was and still is the basis for feminist challenges in different areas of research. At the same time, however, the philosophical and psychological tradition underlying this "perception," the binary logic of "either/or," has been undergoing severe revisions. For one thing, the "other" can be seen as a "threat" only by the objectivizing gaze of a "subject"—the very construct which postmodernism has been unravelling, decentering, and deconstructing for the past few decades. In the absence of a stable subject, the dichotomy assumed by our topic is thrown into question together with its gendered hierarchy. Thus, while postmodern philosophy has generally decentered the human "cogito" from its privileged position in the Western tradition, gender theory has questioned its historical identification with heterosexual masculinity. This questioning naturally results in a reevaluation of the concept of female otherness. Indeed, one could say that the major contribution of contemporary gender studies has been the destabilization of the automatic identification of otherness with threat, demonization, marginalization, or exclusion. Otherness has shed much of its pejorative connotation and is often viewed as a new definition of female selfhood.

This new positive perception of female otherness has been marked by a lexical shift not surprising for scholars of antisemitism. For precisely such a strategy marked one of the primary "solutions" to antisemitic demonization—the Zionist substitution of "Hebrew" (and later, "Israeli") for the historical target of exclusion, the "Jew."[1] In a similar fashion, the older concept of female *otherness* has been recently replaced by a "sexual *difference*" (particularly in France or by French-inspired theorists), signalling a bold reversal of valorization. Indeed, it is in the semantic space between these two terms that the predicament of gender scholars is located, again reminding us of analogous Jewish dilemmas. Should they refuse the perspective of a privileged male/subject by refuting, denying, explaining, or correcting the "otherness" attributed to the female/object? Or should they, like the Zionists, answer this gaze by upholding, defending, and celebrating their "difference" as their own gynocentric subjectivity?

As we shall see, any choice between these strategies is fraught with pragmatic risks as well as gains. But gender scholars also face a "postmodern" theoretical problem: how is the semantic shift to be conceptualized? Is it a reversal of an androcentric legacy, or a step beyond its categories? Put differently: does "difference" just mark "otherness" as privileged, or does it create a new "space" beyond the self/other dichotomy? Can it function as a third term, as the vaunted postmodernist "elsewhere" "beyond gender" outside the masculine/feminine binarism?[2]

To answer such baffling "postmodern" questions, I wish to propose a brief detour through that *Urtext* of the "Woman Question," Simone de Beauvoir's *The Second Sex*.[3] Considering its decidedly "humanistic" (that is, prepostmodern) framework—it was published in 1949!—we may expect it to offer a stable space for an exploration of the roots of our currently shifting terms. What follows, then, is an outline of these "roots" and the tracing of their offshoots in contemporary gender theories.

Back to Beauvoir: A Stable *Urtext*?

To begin with, *The Second Sex* reminds us that the major common denominator of different descriptions of woman's alterity (as indeed of alterity in general!) is that of *ambivalence*. Whether filtered through Freud's individual psychology or Erich Neumann's "archetypology," or through Beauvoir's own exposition of "myths" about the second sex, the ambivalence of alterity is a constant: Woman is Other, both as Virgin and Harlot (Freud), as the Good Mother and the Terrible Mother (Neumann), as the giver of life and death, as bountiful Nature incarnate and as the menacing embodiment of untamed Nature. In Beauvoir's succinct summary, woman, "the fearsome other," "is all that man desires and all that he does not attain."[4]

It is this position of duality or ambivalence that makes the "other" (in general) a *necessary* foil in the constitution of subjectivity. "The subject can be posed only in being opposed," says Beauvoir, openly reflecting Hegel's speculations on the agonistic formation of self-consciousness: "He sets himself up as the essential, as opposed to the other, the inessential, the object." (To anticipate later formulations *[mutatis mutandis]*, "the subject comes to be[ing] in the field of the other."[5])

Yet, generally speaking, the subject, be it collective or personal, is not alone in the world: "But the other consciousness, the other ego, sets up a reciprocal claim," says Beauvoir, continuing her Hegelian narrative. If there is any potential here for a psychological interpretation (that is, an understanding of this confrontation as internal, as taking place in some mental space), Beauvoir is unaware or perhaps unwilling to acknowledge it, highlighting instead its external, "foreign relations," function. Encounters between cultures, tribes, classes, and private individuals "deprive the concept *Other* of its absolute sense" and make manifest its relativity and reciprocity, thereby opening the path to a mutual, inter-subjective recognition.

Couched in the language of philosophical abstraction, we have here a tension between self-centeredness and reciprocal reflection that is more familiar to us in the garb of the "mirror" metaphor. This age-old, classical image has always had a double function, representing both narcissism (Greek myth, revived by Freud) and mutual specularity (Aristotle). Attended by its obligatory "gaze" or "look," that second meaning was unearthed by Lacan in 1936 *("le stade du miroir")* and newly-reinterpreted by Sartre in 1948 *(L'être et le néant)*. The latter is of particular significance for us because it (metaphorically) dramatizes the Hegelian point which Beauvoir is making: that the looked-upon, objectified "other" has the ontological ability to return the gaze, to say "No" to the objectifying look, thereby gaining his (or her) own subjectivity. Yet, by staying close to Hegel's philosophical discourse, Beauvoir shies away from its metaphorical descendents, especially those coined by Sartre. She does cite Lacan's "gaze" briefly in the discussion of the nursling's "mirror stage" ("It is especially when he is fixed by the gaze of other persons that he appears to himself as being one"), unaware, however, of the potential danger to her Hegelian "Subject" that this gaze harbors. Nor is she cognizant of the gender trouble concealed behind her innocent formulation of "other persons." Using ungendered terms (nursling, infant, child, and "parents"), Beauvoir weaves a seamlessly "neuter" narrative, a balancing act between subjectivity and otherness, separation and attachment. The grammatical subject of this narrative is the ostensibly all-inclusive humanist "he." And although Sartre's Existentialism lurks behind her formulation of the "autonomous subject," his "duel of looks" is never mentioned. Was Beauvoir returning the "look" of her life-long companion whose *magnum opus* preceded her own by several years?

We will never know for sure, except for the clues she has left in her conceptualization of the particular case of Woman's alterity. She keenly reminds us that this reciprocity has "not been recognized between the sexes" (Beauvoir, xxi), with one term set up as the sole essential and its correlative defined as *pure otherness.* This anomaly is further sharpened by comparing women's otherness to that of Jews and "American Negroes": on the one hand women are not a numerical minority like these two groups; on the other they lack even the "memory of former days," before dis-recognition (or oppression) had set in, to which the other two groups have recourse. It is the memory of this past (a foundational myth or collective memory) that makes change possible, "as the negroes of Haiti and others have proved." (Interestingly, the "proof" of the "Jews of Palestine" had not reached her yet in 1949.) Her next observation has however a familiar ring: "Regarding themselves as subjects, they transform the bourgeois, the whites, into 'others'" (Beauvoir, xxii).

Several points of this argument deserve our attention: first, the classification of women's alterity in the same category as racial/religious marginalization (women=Jews=blacks); second, the importance of the past (or at least a memory of one) for restoring balance; finally, the unquestioned premise that by assuming subjectivity one automatically transforms the other party into an "other"—a rather pessimistic perception of the human subject, to which we shall return.

In any case, women have not had this option, nor the problem it arouses. Never having shared the world in equality with the "first" sex, they are likened to the slave in the notorious "master-slave" paradigm, that cornerstone of human relations according to Hegelian (and Marxist) theories. It is this primordial otherness that needs to be repaired if women are to invent themselves as authentic subjects. Daunting as it may sound, this is not a theoretically impossible task if we remember that the "slave" of that paradigm is presumed to progressively gain more access to the means of production and thereby to freedom. Yet Beauvoir's prognosis for women's liberation is guarded, given the "deep-seated tendencies towards complicity," later called "alienation," that she detects in her peers. This leads her finally to ask, "how did all this begin?"—a question that is still very much with us, I am afraid, despite the 800 pages of *The Second Sex* and half a century of deliberation!

From the vantage point of the 1990s, of course, not all of Beauvoir's answers and explanations seem satisfactory. She has been charged by some with "essentialism," especially for her acceptance of biology as a determinant factor of sexual difference, and her concomitant rejection of motherhood as "the crown of a woman's life" (Beauvoir, 582ff). Others have championed her as the first gender theorist *avant la lettre*.[6] On the other hand, she has been criticized for holding up a so-called "masculine" ideal of existential "transcendence" as the goal of women's liberation. "Being like a man" is not politically correct anymore; nor is the insistence on the power of willed, rational intelligence to overcome acquired *unconscious* behavioral patterns. So if I have quoted *The Second Sex* somewhat generously, it is not for the strength of the solutions it offers so much as for the power of its exposition and its diagnostic relevance. Indeed, it is commonly agreed that the various feminisms that have developed in the West in the past decades have all responded, in their different ways, to Beauvoir's challenge.

I would further suggest, however, that by grouping together "the eternal feminine," "the black soul," and "the Jewish character" as three categories of oppressed alterity, she anticipated the contemporary explosion of ethnic/cultural/postcolonial studies which has also left its mark on Jewish studies.[7] For the moment, however, another question is in order: How did Beauvoir's conceptualization of woman as "other" and her anticipation of "multicultural" otherness survive the feminist upheavals of recent decades?

Beauvoir's Daughters: The Atlantic Divide

An interesting clue is offered by historian Karen Offen who in 1988 traced the reception history of *The Second Sex* as part of her outline of the changing definitions of the term "feminism": "Beauvoir's arguments were received with greater enthusiasm in English-speaking countries than in her own," apparently because of the socio-national legacy of French feminism.[8] France developed what Offen labels "relational" feminism, featuring the "primacy of a companionate, non-hierarchical, male-female couple as the basic unit of society," and emphasizing women's rights as *women* (defined mainly by their nurturing capacities). But Anglo-American feminists followed Beauvoir's "individualist" feminism, emphasizing the abstract concept of human rights and "celebrating the quest for personal independence (or autonomy) in all aspects of life, while downplaying... childbearing and its attending responsibilities."[9]

It is this emphasis that eventually won the day with the "explosion" of the "second wave" feminism of the English-speaking countries in the 1960s. Beauvoir's anatomy of Woman's otherness thus inspired a Feminism whose goal was the eradication of all those inequalities blamed on the socio-political alterity of women. This orientation, alternatively called "equal rights," "individualist," "humanist," or "liberal" feminism, reduced the duality and ambiguity of woman's alterity as described by Beauvoir, pre-serving only the pejorative connotation of the concept. Like Beauvoir, however, it equally applied itself to other underprivileged groups (racial and ethnic minorities, social classes). Furthermore, following her famous statement, "One is not born, but rather becomes, a woman" (*The Second Sex*, 301)—yet in contrast to her ostensible "biologism"—Anglo-American feminism developed the concept of *gender* to distinguish between "given" (biological) sexual differences and those gender *relations* that are constructed by social and cultural processes. It is the latter that are responsible for the *production* of perceived dissymmetry, thereby perpetuating *representations* of female otherness.[10]

Ironically, however, the search for the *roots* of the "gender straightjacket" led back to the realm of psychoanalysis, the very discipline whose explanatory power had been dismissed for good reason by the foremother of feminism ("All psychoanalysts systematically reject the idea of *choice* and the correlated concept of value, and therein lies the intrinsic weakness of the system" [Beauvoir, 50]). This was not, however, a return to Freud (whose female psychology had been found lacking, to say the least) but to post-Freudian psychology. Beauvoir herself tried to account for male ambivalence toward the female by the somewhat circular argument that "the source of these terrors lies in the fact that in the Other, quite beyond reach, alterity, otherness, abide" (p. 191). More recent explanations rely on psychoanalytic assessments of early, *pre*-oedipal family dynamics, where the mother rather than the (oedipal) father plays a major role. This so-called "Object-Relation" theory, developed mainly in England, helped Nancy Chodorow, for example, in questioning Freud's oedipal masterplot. In *The Reproduction of Mothering: Psychoanalysis and the Sociology of Gender*,[11] she offers a new definition of woman's alterity. In contrast to girls' identification with their mothers, she argues that boys develop their sense of self in defensive *opposition* to the mother. Their later denigration of the feminine is therefore conceptualized as a *defense* against their earlier identification with the phallic *pre*-oedipal mother. Despite the explicitly psychoanalytic language, I believe that the legacy of Beauvoir's "fearsome other" is quite clear here, as is the [Hegelian] agonistic perception of the construction of [masculine!] subjectivity. What is new, however, is the (quite disturbing) transformation of philosophy's generalized abstract "other" into a "flesh and blood," sociologically (if not biologically) necessary female (m)other. Motherhood is again (as for Beauvoir) the culprit, but on a deeper, *unconscious* level. Since it perpetually reproduces psychological differences between the genders, it of necessity reinforces female otherness: the ostensibly relational, easily malleable ego of woman, the result of mother-daughter identification (and the cause of her attachment needs), as opposed to man's fixed, inflexible ego-boundaries, an expression of separation anxiety, but also the cause of masculine autonomy.

Needless to say, this theory has its problems, not only for its inadequacy to explain "male domination" as it purports to do.[12] No less troubling is the substitution of bedrock "psychological" differences for biological ones. At least one of these differences, the presumed "separation vs. attachment" dissymmetry between the genders, has been recently challenged: "Whereas a woman's relational needs get defined as her 'dependency,' men may disguise their dependency needs because they are being met everyday by women.... [financial] dependence must not be confused with psychological dependency."[13] These shortcomings notwithstanding, Chodorow has had a decisive impact on the perception of female otherness precisely because it made possible a shift in the valorization of "otherness" from negative to positive. Despite the indictment of the institution of mothering (which Chodorow proposes to "fix" by changing child-rearing arrangements; cf. Dorothy Dinnerstein, 1976[14]), her analysis brought to the fore aspects of female psychological growth that allowed for the beginning of a new trend—the celebration of mother-daughter bonding and its concomitant "feminine" identity.

This change of perspective should come as no surprise. By the 1980s Beauvoir's valorization of male subjectivity had come under attack, and with it "liberal" feminism. Labelled "masculinist" or "assimilationist," it has been recently charged with making masculinity a universal norm of liberation and achievement, thereby perpetuating traditional phallocentric dichotomies. Between the publication of Carol Giligan's *In A Different Voice* (1982) and Sara Ruddik's *Maternal Thinking* (1989), Anglo-American gender studies were transformed. Refusing the perspective of the male gaze, that Hegelian/Existentialist legacy already explored and undermined by feminist cinema theorists since the mid-1970s,[15] these "separatist" feminists now embrace their otherness rather than deplore it. If "black is beautiful," so is the feminine. Beauvoir's wish for reciprocity is finally coming into existence, at least in theory—though it is probably not the one she was looking forward to. American women, although not exactly a minority, now extol their *difference* under the banner of cultural pluralism.

The inspiration for this change came, ironically enough, from Beauvoir's own unfaithful "daughters." If we recall the tradition of French matrimonial ("relational") feminism described by Offen, we should not wonder at its latest phase. Here woman's alterity has totally shed its pejorative meaning and has come to signify her particularly embodied and engendered being in the world. These "sexual difference" theorists (Helen Cixous, Luce Irigaray, Monique Wittig et al) celebrate their otherness by privileging the very negativities traditionally attributed to women in Western civilization. In what could be described as an "oedipal agon," Beauvoir's priorities have been turned upside down.[16]

In a massive rewriting of the history of the "mirror" and "gaze" metaphors, those traditional emblems of subjectivity (avoided by Beauvoir, we may note!), Luce Irigaray has exposed the complicity of philosophy itself in the perpetuation of sexual binarism and hierarchy, in the privileging of the masculine, and in the production of female alterity. Her *Speculum of the Other Woman* (1974) is a parodic feminist/deconstructive reading of Freud and Lacan, Plato and Aristotle, Hegel and Descartes.[17] Identifying the specular/speculative tradition as phallocentric (man's eye understood as a substitute for the penis), she rejects its terms altogether, dismissing the theory of her mentor, Jacques Lacan, in the process. Via this dismissal, Beauvoir's invitation to women to attain subjectivity is interpreted as another re-objectivization, because "Any Theory of the 'Subject' Has Always Been Appropriated by the 'Masculine.'" Woman has no gaze, no discourse for her specific specularization that would allow her to identify with herself. Self-identity, self-consciousness, subjectivity are declined by Irigaray as a masculinist obsession with "sameness" and "oneness," the expression of fear of multiplicity. Fluid ego boundaries, metaphorized by female sexuality and anatomy (see *This Sex Which is Not One* [1977][18]) are the very markers of female difference that she invites us to applaud.

Although Irigaray is hard to pin down, the source from which she derives this positive female difference is none other than the *maternal*—that same biological function that Beauvoir saw as the obstacle on woman's route towards equality, subjectivity, and transcendence. Like Chodorow's followers—though with different emphasis and aims—Irigaray privileges the mother-daughter symbiotic bonding as the root (at least metaphorically) of female empathy and psychological fluidity. Unlike them, however, she uses "otherness" to deconstruct the heterosexual paradigm. Much like Adrienne Rich on the other side of the Atlantic, who went from the reappropriation of motherhood (*Of Woman Born* [1976]) to a "lesbian continuum" (1980),[19] Irigaray moves from the critique of phallocentric essentialism to the idealization of "gynocentrism," of female sexual multiplicity and of homoeroticism. This progression is also reflected in her style of writing: more associative, richly allusive and metaphoric, at times even ungrammatical, it challenges from within the logocentric expository prose of philosophical discourse that *The Second Sex* so dutifully followed. This is *écriture féminine* par excellence, the ultimate exaltation of sexual difference.

The foundational text of this orientation is Helen Cixous's *The Laugh of the Medusa* (1975) which ushered in experimental, disruptive, and unsettling "writing through the body."[20] The declared purpose of this mode of writing was to inscribe an "other" language, alternatively named the "(m)other's voice" or the "discourse of the hysteric,"[21] which is now valorized and idealized. "Feminine writers" (among whom some major male authors are counted) are presumed to lift the lid of repression off female otherness, symbolized by the body and by the hysteric's desire. They thereby challenge the mind-body split and other logocentric binarisms. However, in so doing, they in fact sustain the very dichotomy that *The Second Sex* had set out to undo, which is indeed one of the great ironies of the recent history of female difference.

"Le Féminin" as Postmodernism's "Other"

This irony increases as we probe a little deeper into the ostensible analogy between theories of "difference" on both sides of the Atlantic. In the United States, gender difference was originally conceptualized as a socio-cultural category, never losing sight of its political implications. Inspired by Foucault's analysis of the structures of power and domination operating within the sociocultural system, this orientation has recently yielded an ever-growing differentiation with an emphasis on the particularity of more narrowly-defined social groups. "Woman" was replaced by women; feminism by womanism (black women). "Third World women" and "Women of color," social classes, and diverging sexual orientations—each group insists on a historical and cultural particularism that generic "feminism" or even "gender studies" cannot address.[22] Responding to the postmodern "crisis of representation" by eschewing the universality of the traditional discourses of subjectivity (philosophy and psychoanalysis), these others nevertheless redefine their social space in terms of collective selfhood, often "transforming some other group into 'an other'" (Beauvoir, xxii).

The conceptualization of sexual difference in France is quite different, almost diametrically opposite. To begin with, the basic concepts of "sexual difference" and *écriture féminine* are not as originally "female products" as they may seem to be, nor is the celebration of woman's alterity. As convincingly demonstrated by Alice Jardine *(Gynesis)*[23] and Teresa de Lauretis

(Technologies of Gender), postmodern discourse has habitually named as "la femme" or "le féminin" all those "spaces" external to the [metaphysical, psychoanalytic, social] system from which it tried to deconstruct or unhinge the "humanist" meta-narratives of the West ["Truth," "History," "Man"]. Thus for Lacan, the "Subject comes to be in the field of the Other" precisely because the Cartesian (and Hegelian-Sartrian-Beauvoirian) Subject has lost its mastery, priority, and stability; he is "subject to" (that is, "subjected to") the system into which he is initiated, rather than the subject of it (that is, its agentic manipulator). That power is attributed to the Unconscious, the Other with a capital O, which Lacan genders as feminine (the Other is by definition that which is beyond "the symbolic," outside our system of representation). As for Derrida, his Other is "writing," *écriture*—the archemetaphor for the "endless play of signifiers," the deferment of closure and the dissemination of meaning; locus of all the revisionary and subversive energies deployed in the deconstruction of logocentric signification and phallocentric binarisms. Less consistently but nevertheless in a tangible way, *écriture* is naturally gendered as feminine (and not only because of its grammatical inflection in French).

Thus, while women as such are almost absent from the theories of these leading spokesmen of postmodernism, the abstract notion of the "female other" has come to occupy center stage in their discourse. Even more paradoxically, this ostensible "transvaluation" does nothing for the deconstruction of the hoary dichotomy of male-female. Whether or not we see the "revolutionary" deployment of the "feminine" as a reification of Hegelian Negativity, as has been recently claimed,[24] I believe that this teleology does not expunge "the feminine" of its original negatives. Although marked positively by Derrida, Lacan, Foucault, and Lyotard, the feminine remains entrapped in the old binarism: it is exclusion, absence, lack, unarticulated matter and unrepresentable body, nothingness and even "god," in short, the ultimate Other, "all that [postmodern] Man desires and all that he cannot attain."

In women theorists' attempts to explain this paradox we can predictably detect shades of the demonized female other, the so-called "phallic mother." While Alice Jardine has implied "male paranoia," Jane Flax has gone so far as to take Chodorow's suggestions to their logical extremity or absurdity, claiming that postmodernist deconstruction of subjectivity derives from "the need to evade, deny or repress the importance of early childhood experiences, especially mother-child relationships, in the constitution of the self and the culture more generally" (Flax, 232). If we take Flax's "diagnosis" seriously, we are compelled to face an unflattering scene of competition, of a tragi-comic or even grotesque pathology, that cruelly undercuts deconstruction's aspirations to revise the phallocentric discourse of Western metaphysics and epistemology.

But even if we do not go that far, we may now be in a better position to appreciate the impasse in which French female intelletuals have found themselves: with no recourse to Cartesian subjectivity, and with the feminine taken up by their male peers, they have opted to seize those revolutionary "spaces" of *abstract* feminine otherness and make them their own by re-*embodying* them. Hence the exaltation of female anatomy and female homo-eroticism, the hysterization of feminine writing, and the exuberant celebration of female desire and the maternal function—precisely that demonized, unrepresentable "ghost" that *still* lurks beyond the confines of androcentric "postmodern metaphysics."

Although claimed to be symbolic and iconic rather than literal, this glorification of feminine "difference" exposes its propagators (on both sides of the Atlantic) to charges of "reverse essentialism." In a paradoxical way, it is not a Derridean *différence* (that is, a "third term" outside the traditional binarism of male subjectivity and female otherness) that has been constructed in French "feminine writing," but an exaggerated version of traditional representations of female "otherness." The only difference lies in the reversal of its valorization from negative to positive.[25]

Kristeva's Maternal Semiotic — The De-Demonized M/other?

A way out of this impasse awaits us in the work of Julia Kristeva, who ostensibly conceptualizes the "Other" beyond gender dichotomy altogether. Dismissing *écriture féminine* and "sexual difference" as reinforcing received binary oppositions, she considers as "other" that revolutionary impulse which fractures the Symbolic Order by introducing pre-verbal, pre-oedipal, and unrepresented patterns of signification that she names the "Semiotic" (*Revolution in Poetic Language* [1974]). Although descriptively and functionally similar to the generic "feminine other" of postmodern discourse, its closest conceptual "relative" is Lacan's Imaginary, again with the predictable reversal of its valorization. Like the Imaginary, the Semiotic is derived from infantile bodily and emotional experience, which is naturally available to *both* genders; similarly, it is *contained within* the symbolic order, rather than projected beyond its boundaries (as is the "Other" of postmodernism); unlike it, however, it is perceived as the source of subversive creativity, a potentiality placed high on Kristeva's scale of priorities. Furthermore, by identifying this "maternal other" in the avant-garde writing of Artaud, Mallarmé, Joyce, and other (mostly male) writers, Kristeva insists on its genderlessness. Her theory seems to transcend gender alterity by positioning otherness within subjectivity itself (decentered as the latter may be), irrespective of gender.

Have we finally reached our destination, or rather that of Gender theory? Is Kristeva's maternal Semiotic that "third term" that goes beyond binarism, beyond essence, by paradoxically diving inside? An Archimedean point within the system rather than without? Has she managed to counteract the paranoic demonization of the (m)other by including rather than excluding maternal otherness and difference?

If the reception and dissemination of her ideas are any measure, she may indeed have done just that,[26] ironically at the expense of "feminist political correctness." Her notorious declaration that the task of "third generation" women (not "feminists") is "the de-dramatization of the 'fight to the death' between rival groups and thus between the sexes" ("Women's Time" [1979])[27] readily supports both sides of the irony. But beyond the pragmatic gripe of political feminism,[28] Kristeva's conceptualization does not get around the by now predictable charge of complicity with received representations of feminine (or in her case, maternal) otherness. By relegating, as she does, the question of gender difference to the realm of "metaphysics" (an altogether suspect discourse in her frame of postmodernist thinking, as her "Woman's Time" makes clear), she does not, to my mind, get rid of it. It returns through the back door, so to speak, through the unresolved tension between the commonality of human [infantile] experience and the biological one-genderedness of maternity. Taking both as unquestioned givens, Kristeva is unable to allow both genders an *equal* use of the Semiotic other. It is not by chance that the models of her "revolutionary poetics" are male writers. Their sex/gender distance (difference?) from the maternal protects them, she says, from the risk of psychotic disintegration that would threaten a woman under the same condition (!).

The psychoanalytic underpinnings of this logic are tiresomely familiar. So is the old adage about "the madwoman in the attic." But how are we to account for women's creativity? For instance, for Julia Kristeva's protean fecundity?

It is not my intention to grapple with this question here. Fortunately, Kristeva's amazingly rich and multifaceted creativity seems to belie her own theory. For this visit to the promised land "beyond gender" of her making, turns out to be quite disturbing. Under the guise of a progressive theory, which attractively names its most privileged term after the maternal, Kristeva once again exacts a high price on women's creativity. The inclusion of gender difference within the system fails to obliterate women's partial exclusion. If their access to the site of artistic agency is not totally blocked, it is fraught with grave danger (ironically because it is too close for comfort). In the final analysis, Kristeva's system, ostensibly beyond gender, allows woman to buy her way into its maternal site of energy and excitement only at the cost of preserving intact the existing paternal order.

It should by now come as no surprise that it is "the maternal" that is once again at the heart of this paradox. Inded, it is the ambiguous position of this female-feminine "excess" that emerges as a major parameter for the conceptualization of gender alterity. In some sense, the analysis of "female otherness" carried out by Gender Theory for the past fifty years may be reduced to just that: the anchoring of the general ambivalence towards "woman"—as summarized by Beauvoir—in its ostensible "origin," motherhood. Whether demonized or idolized, concretized or metaphorized, it is this *"excess"* that has replaced Freud's anatomical female *"lack"* (castration) as the marker of sexual difference. United around this single shared premise, different gender scholars are nevertheless divided by their evaluation of its theoretical and pragmatic implications. In fact, the distance travelled by gender studies may be measured by that between Beauvoir and Kristeva on this issue. While the former views maternity critically as the social institution that hinders woman's journey towards autonomy and transcendence, the latter valiantly grapples with the Catholic tradition she has inherited ("Stabat Mater" [1977][29]). In so doing, she is attempting to recast the maternal as the psychological locus of "androgynous" revolution and creativity, thereby redeeming it from an age-old perception of "female otherness."[30]

In the final analysis Kristeva's thematization of Maryology in the midst of the [atheist? to the exclusion of Lacan?] discourse of postmodernism, may signify a "return of the repressed" of yet another dimension of anti-universalist "difference," namely, "religion." Whether and how this veteran difference is a decisive factor in the divergence of responses to otherness among gender theorists, is a question awaiting future research.[31]

My thanks to Eve Tabor Bannet, Nurit Gertz, and Anne Golomb Hoffman for reading and responding to an earlier version of this paper without necessarily agreeing with all my arguments. Special thanks to Anne for her generous comments.

Notes

1. See Yael S. Feldman, "The 'Other Within' in Contemporary Israeli Fiction," *Middle East Review* 22, no. 1 (Fall 1989): 47–53.
2. Selya Benhabib and Drucilla Cornell, eds. *Feminism as Critique* (Duluth 1987), 15.

3. As did others recently, e.g., Judith Butler "Variations on Sex and Gender: Beauvoir, Wittig and Foucault," in *Feminism as Critique,* 128–42; Andrea Nye, *Feminist Theories and the Philosophies of Man* (New York 1988), 73—114; Toril Moi, "Ambiguity and Alienation in *The Second Sex,*" in *Feminism and Postmodernism,* eds. Margaret Ferguson and Jennifer Wicke (Durham, NC 1994), 86–102.

4. Simone de Beauvoir, *The Second Sex* (London: Penguin Books, 1974), 186 and xx, 50ff, 303.

5. Jane Flax, *Thinking Fragments: Psychoanalysis, Feminism and Postmodernism in the Contemporary West* (Berkeley 1990), 126; attributed to both Jacques Lacan and D. W. Winnicott.

6. See Monique Wittig, "One Is Not Born A Woman," *Feminist Issues* 1, 2 (1978); cf. Butler, especially "Gender as Choice," in *Feminism as Critique,* 131 ff.

7. Most relevant is the historical confluence of racism and misogyny, as in Sander Gilman's work on gender in antisemitism and its impact on Freud's theories, e.g., *Freud, Race and Gender* (Princeton University Press 1993). For the problematics of gender within Judaism, see Judith Plaskow, *Standing Again at Sinai* (New York 1990); Daniel Boyarin, *Carnal Israel* (Berkeley 1993); Lynn Davidman and Shelly Tenenbaum, eds., *Feminist Perspectives on Jewish Studies* (New Haven 1995); T. M. Rudavsky, ed., *Gender and Judaism* (New York 1995); Yael Feldman, "'And Rebecca Loved Jacob,' But Freud Did Not," *Freud and Forbidden Knowledge,* eds. Peter Rudnytsky and Ellen Spitz (New York 1995), 7–35. For the symbolization and artistic sublimation of these issues by Israeli creative writers, see Yael S. Feldman, "From Feminist Romance to An Anatomy of Freedom: Israeli Women Novelists," in *The Boom in Contemporary Israeli Fiction,* ed. Alan Mintz (New England University Press 1997), 71–113; as well as idem, *Beyond the Feminist Romance* (New York: Columbia University Press, forthcoming).

8. Karen Offen, "Defining Feminism: A Comparative Historical Approach," *Signs* 14, no. 1 (Autumn 1988): 119–57.

9. Ibid., 136.

10. This transposition of "gender" from grammar to sociology was introduced by Gayle Rubin in "The Traffic in Women: The Political Economy of Sex," in *Towards an Anthropology of Women,* ed. Rayna Reiter (New York 1975), 178–92.

11. Nancy Chodorow, *The Reproduction of Mothering: Psychoanalysis and the Sociology of Gender* (Berkeley 1978).

12. See especially the critique of Iris Young, "Is Male Gender Identity the Cause of Male Domination?," in Joyce Treblicot, ed., *Mothering: Essays in Feminist Theory* (Rowman and Allenheld, 1983).

13. Miriam Johnson, *Strong Mothers, Weak Wives* (Berkeley 1994), 46.

14. Dorothy Dinnerstein, *The Mermaid and the Minotaur: Sexual Arrangement and Human Malaise* (New York 1976).

15. See Laura Mulvey, "Visual Pleasure and Narrative Cinema," *Screen* 16, no. 3 (Autumn 1975).

16. See Sandra Gilbert and Susan Gubar, *The Madwoman in the Attic* (New Haven 1979), for their critique of Harold Bloom's "masculinist" conceptualization of the transmission of literary tradition. They claim that his use of the "oedipal agon" as a paradigm for the relationship between literary generations is not applicable to women writers because they

do not confront strong (female) percursers. My understanding of the short history of French feminism belies this contention.

17. Luce Irigaray, *Speculum of the Other Woman*, tr. by Gillian C. Gill (Ithaca 1985). Cf. Genevieve Lloyd, *The Man of Reason: "Male" and "Female" in Western Philosophy* (Minneapolis, Minn. 1984).

18. Luce Irigaray, *This Sex Which is Not One*, tr. Catherine Porter (Ithaca 1985).

19. Adrienne Rich, *Of Woman Born: Motherhood as Experience and Institution* (New York 1976); "Compulsory Heterosexuality and Lesbian Existence," *Signs* 5 (1980): 631–60.

20. Published in English, Helen Cixous, "The Laugh of the Medusa," *Signs* 1, no. 4 (1975): 875–93.

21. Cixous modelled this ideal after Freud's Dora (*The Portrait of Dora*, 1975).

22. See, for example, Gayatri Chakravorty Spivak, *In Other Worlds: Essays in Cultural Politics* (New York 1987); Teresa de Laurentis, *Technologies of Gender: Essays on Theory, Film, and Fiction* (Bloomington, Ind. 1987).

23. Alice Jardine, *Gynesis: Configurations of Woman and Modernity* (Ithaca 1985).

24. See Drucilla Cornell and Adam Thurschwell, "Feminism, Negativity, Intersubjectivity," in *Feminism as Critique*, 143–62.

25. For a revision of this position, see Luce Irigaray's later work (1984), recently published in English: *The Ethics of Sexual Difference*, tr. Carolyn Burke and Gillian C. Gill (Ithaca 1993). My thanks to Eve Tabor-Bannet who called my attention to this orientation.

26. See Toril Moi, *Sexual/Textual Politics* (New York 1985). For a critique, see Judith P. Butler, *Gender Trouble: Feminism and the Subversion of Identity* (New York 1990).

27. See Toril Moi, ed., *The Kristeva Reader* (New York 1975), 187–213.

28. See Wendy Harcourt, "Feminism, Body, Self: Third-Generation Feminism," in *Psychoanalysis, Feminism and the Future of Gender*, eds. Joseph H. Smith and Afaf Mahfouz (Baltimore 1994), 70–90.

29. Julia Kristeva, "Stabat Mater," in *Kristeva Reader*, 160–86.

30. For Virginia Woolf's earlier "use" of androgyny as a defence against the "maternal anxiety," see Yael S. Feldman, "The Challenge of Androgyny," in *Beyond the Feminist Romance* (New York: Columbia University Press, forthcoming).

31. See David Crownfield, *Body/Text in Julia Kristeva: Religion, Women, and Psychoanalysis* (New York: SUNY Press, 1992).

11

Recurrent Images in French Antisemitism in the Third Republic

Richard I. Cohen
The Hebrew University of Jerusalem

Confronted by an onslaught against the reigning monarchical system, opponents of the ensuing French Revolution found it impossible to imagine internal explanations for the disaster, often preferring various conspiracy theories: the Jews were not among the groups often cited as the source of the revolution. Yet, one hundred years later when critics began fulminating against the return of liberal values, etched out in the principles of the Third Republic, the Jews were high up on the list of those considered responsible for its creation. Even seventy years later, in the throes of growing criticism of the Third Republic and its anti-French character, the Jews and their ideological and political agents continued to be marked out for their destructive impact on the nature of French society. Whereas in 1789 the emancipation of the Jews of France was still very much up in the air, in the wake of the general declaration of the Rights of Man, one hundred years later the Dreyfus Affair riveted French society, provoking a fissure of remarkable dimensions; and just less than one hundred and fifty years later, French society elected in a democratic process Léon Blum, the first professing Jew to become a prime minister in Europe.

Jews in 1789 were seriously divided among themselves on how best to guarantee their rights and privileges: the more traditional elements from Alsace-Lorraine were clearly concerned to preserve their normative and autonomous existence, while the Bordeaux Jews, from Spanish and Portuguese extraction eagerly sought the benefits of becoming full-fledged citizens of France. In the Third Republic, on the other hand, native Jews now highly concentrated in Paris, guardedly rejected antisemitic arguments, during both the Dreyfus Affair and the turmoil of the 1930s, and found themselves at loggerheads with the more aggressive strategies of leftist oriented Jews and those of immigrant background. Appreciation of and reliance on the state and its liberal tradition remained a salient part of its evaluation of the challenges against these hallowed notions.

France and her Jews, from this bird's eye comparative view, underwent in 150 years a major transformation: France struggled throughout this period with the tradition of the Revolution and its heritage, not willing to destroy completely the orientation of the *ancien régime*. Friction between Church and State remained constant, pecking away at the erstwhile agreements enacted by Napoleon. Modernization took hold of larger elements of French society, gradually turning "peasants into Frenchmen" but not without conflict and tension; France's colonial and imperial designs coincided with its great missionary vision that continued its Enlightenment sense of the superiority of French culture, yet France failed to rise to the occasion and succumbed to the hands of the German army in 1870. Political tensions rocked France at different junctures of the nineteenth and twentieth centuries, attesting to the volatile political climate that characterized her emergence from monarchical rule, but the liberal Third Republic lasted longer than any other form of French rule since 1789.

France harbored in its midst a small, mostly unassimilated Jewish population on the eve of the Revolution—it numbered some 40,000—but that element grew in French society to close to 100,000 one hundred years later, and approximately 300,000 towards the close of the 1930s. During the interval, French Jewry emerged in the mind and imagination of French society as a vibrant, and dominant, element with the ability to wreak havoc to the hallowed principles of the *ancien régime*. Indeed, Jewish institutions and leaders showed definite signs of integration and worked to turn their coreligionists into French citizens. This effort did not encompass the majority of Jewish society which remained, until the Third Republic, in Alsace-Lorraine, largely unaffected by the changing nature of French society. Jews in these eastern regions of France persisted in their insular and traditional ways, as the historian Paula Hyman has taught us, more akin to their forefathers during the days of the Revolution than their children in Paris.[1] Yet, during the course of this period, an important element among French Jewry had shown itself to be enamoured by the principles of the Revolution, endorsing them wholeheartedly. Jews were moving to the center stage of the bastions of the French state—the army, the judiciary, political administration, and politics. This move to the center was to be dramatically apparent during the Third Republic. No wonder that the confident Chief Rabbi of France declared on the eve of the Dreyfus Affair that Jews in France see no reason to convert as they face no opposition to living where they prefer to live, enter unhindered into all areas of French society, and can legitimately maintain their religious tradition. Rabbi Debré and many others in leadership positions among French Jewry downplayed the fact that the presence of certain Jews as economic entrepreneurs and major players in the mainstream of political and cultural developments in France had provoked throughout the nineteenth century, among the Left and the Right, recurrent criticism. A century earlier, Abbé Grégoire, writing on the eve of the Revolution, feared the consequences of granting Jews a place in the French state system, where they could legislate to Christians; however, the Revolution, which he strongly supported, removed that hesitation and he himself endorsed total freedom of occupation for Jews.

But the entry of Jews into the state apparatus was not to be taken lightly and aroused antagonism among those who continued to hold high its Christian character and rejected the meritocratic system embedded in the principles of the Revolution. The notion that Jews were "les rois de l'époque," in Toussenel's notorious phrase of 1845, become more than a refrain. It reappeared at various stages in the next hundred years, in literary denunciations and visual caricatures, asserting forcefully that layers of associations continued to be unleashed when conjuring Jewish success and its impact on French life.[2] Moreover, the notion of Jewish domination starkly revealed that the Jewish understanding of freedom of choice, enunciated by Debré, was not shared by certain elements of French society. In this sense, the gradual move of Jews from the backwaters of Alsace-Lorraine to Paris, the hub of political, economic, and cultural affairs, raised the spectre of widespread Jewish penetration into the mainstream of French life.

This essay will thus concentrate on themes that predominated in antisemitism during the Third Republic (that lasted until the fall of France in 1940), taking into consideration the changing nature of the Jews' relationship to and involvement in France during this period. Studies of antisemitism in general, and of antisemitism in France in particular, have often overlooked the developments in Jewish life, seeing them as unrelated to that process. However, it would appear that such an orientation overlooks the inner drama of the interrelationship between the majority society and its minorities. Jews were not passive factors in this process and their actions and responses resonated in the ways the majority society related to them. In this spirit we have highlighted some of the major changes in their demographic situation in the period under study. More was to come. Jewish immigrants from Eastern Europe were to restructure the nature of the Jewish community in the interwar period, bringing both native Jews and French society to encounter a less malleable Jew, more openly expressive of his or her beliefs and opinions, and less prone to accept the dictates of propriety and French centralistic politics. The changing map of the French Jewish population was countered by developments in French politics and society, exacerbated by the economic ills that confronted Europe following World War I.

But let us return to the beginning of the Third Republic, following France's defeat at the hands of the Prussian army and the ensuing soul-searching, part of the aftermath of the war and the Paris Commune. Liberal elements in society utilized the new republican form of government to return to unsolved issues in the revolutionary agenda. First and foremost was their attempt to curb the influence and power of the Catholic Church, especially in the area of education—a perennial area of battle in the French political and cultural scene. From the moment Jules Ferry became the head of the Ministry of Education in 1879, the ministry began its open confrontation with the Church and its hold over the school system. This coincided with Ernst Renan's sharp attack against the French educational system that attributed the French defeat in 1870 to its undeveloped and backward nature. The educational system had remained the last bastion of concerted Church influence in French society. In wresting from its hands the right to grant degrees, to offer religious education in the schools, and by disbanding the Jesuit order, the Ministry of Education closed the gap between the revolutionary zeal for separation of Church and State and the reality.

Opposition to these actions came from wide sections of the society. The Republic loomed in the eyes of its antagonists as a Satanic force, driven by undetermined and behind-the-scenes powers who sought to remove the Church from its role in the State. Now, unlike the days of the Revolution, it was the Jews' turn to become a central player in the imagination of those who ranted against the State's policy. Together with the Freemasons, they were seen as a united bloc that intended to remove the State from Christian influence. In the 1870s Freemasons were constantly attacked by local Catholic groups whose efforts were given legitimacy by the reigning Pope Leo XII, who in 1884 declared that the principles of Freemasonry were opposed to Christianity and were responsible for the anti-Christian atmosphere prevailing in France. In various works directed against the Freemasons, Jews were also attacked. For example, in that of Father Chabauty, the conspiracy theory locking Jews together with Freemasons took on a pseudo-scientific basis: according to Chabauty, Satan dominated the Freemasons and used them to destroy the Christian religion in order to prepare the world for the coming of antichrist. In this apocalyptic vision, the domination by antichrist will also pave the way for the return of the Jews to Palestine and the Jewish domination of the world will commence. Chabauty's original scheme, as the historian Jacob Katz has shown, granted the Jews the ultimate power—they were the ones to command, and the Freemasons were the ones to fulfill their orders.[3] In 1882 Chabauty was also writing in the spirit of Toussenel; in his work entitled *The Jews Our Masters,* he maintained that the secret leaders of Jewry were dominating the nations of the world. They did this through other secret societies who worked constantly to destroy Christianity and the Christian nations. Ultimately the Jews would assume power over all of them. Once again, economic issues intertwined with the tension over efforts to curb the Christian influence in the French educational system.[4]

The failure of the Catholic Bank in 1882 brought in its wake economic duress for many lower middle class French people in the provincial regions. It intensified the demonization of the banker—and the Jewish banker in particular—in French society, popular from the days of Pierre-Joseph Proudhon. Myth and reality joined hands. Jewish figures, who had been mythologized in the works of several great nineteenth-century French novelists for their maleficent activity in banking were now held responsible. The Gundermann archetype, a man of rather inhuman and almost monstrous nature, depicted in Zola's novel *L'argent,* now came to life. He was now not only the foil of James de Rothschild, but he epitomized the efforts of Jewish bankers to destroy the economic livelihoods of "simple" Christians. The crash of the Catholic bank, founded by a former employee of the Rothschilds, supported the grassroots argument that the Rothschilds had joined hands with members of the educational elite to eliminate Catholic influence in French culture and society.[5] Once again the cries of latter-day Toussenels reappeared, based on the impressive growth of Jewish banking firms in France during the Third Republic. August Chirac's *Les juifs, rois de la République* (1883) was soon to have its sequel in one of the most important works of antisemitic writing in France—Edouard Drumont's *La France Juive* (Paris 1886). Riding on the wave of discontent engendered by the battle over religious education and the emerging myth of the all-powerful Jew, Drumont was able to capitalize on traditional dissatisfaction with the liberal ideology of the Third Republic. Adroitly, Drumont weaved together the various threads of Third Republic malaise: Freemasons, the defeat of 1870, educational reform, entrepreneurial banking, the changing physical character of Paris, and the overriding force that encapsulated and engineered these ailments—the Jews.[6]

However, Drumont radicalized the positions assumed by the ideologues on the Left and Right before him by subjugating his notions of Jewish domination to racial categories. His demonic portrayal of the Jewish takeover needs enunciation. In Drumont's depiction, Jewish individuals join together in small groups and gradually usurp every position in the state system, from top to bottom. They do this elegantly, not by violence, but secretly, gradually, and thoroughly. The takeover that began in physical and professional areas would terminate in the extinction of the French way of life and religion. Pitting the "Semite" against the "Aryan," Drumont characterized the former, and especially the "Jewish Semite," as a parasite who can subsist only in a foreign culture which was not its creation. Finance was seen as *the* area of Jewish expertise where the Jew was able to capitalize on the work of others by his parasitic and devious ways. Two unequal forces were at loggerheads: the international Jewish financial network seeking power and domination, and the debilitated French state, merely desiring to maintain its cultural and religious tradition. Drumont longed for the appearance of a strong figure, or "a brave captain" who would risk his life and lead the opposition to the Jewish capitalists and bankers, and bring about a swift "aryanization" of Jewish funds. This would be the beginning of the resurrection of France from its downtrodden situation. Once again we hear the recurrent theme, characteristic of modern antisemitism—the future of French society depended upon the ability of its citizens to curb Jewish influence.

Few antisemtic works rivalled the popularity of Drumont's book in the next generation. But it was during the following decade that his campaign against the Jews was coopted by more central players in French politics and culture. Captain Alfred Dreyfus was, as Barrès put it, "the pretext" of the Affair—but also the symbol of what had transpired among Jews in France during the nineteenth century and particularly during the first generation of the Third Republic.[7] Dreyfus, like many other Jews, had turned to the army as a way of integrating fully into French society. Making havoc of the Revolutionary and pre-revolutionary debates on whether Jews could become loyal citizens and physically capable of fighting for their country, Dreyfus and others opted with pride for military service. As Pierre Birnbaum, the political sociologist has uncovered, these Jewish officers rose in the ranks but maintained themselves a certain Jewish "sociability" and were often the butt of social discrimination among their peers.[8] But Dreyfus was symbolic of other aspects of the demographic and cultural transformations of French Jews: he became profoundly attached to French culture and grew very distant from his Jewish roots. Having moved to Paris he remained part of a social Jewish milieu, educated his children to believe and trust in the Fatherland, but married within the faith and in a synagogue, identifying with liberal but not radical politics.[9]

Grégoire's early premonition was correct. Jewish penetration into the state apparatus was clearly something that went against the grain of French society. Though the Third Republic replaced tradition with meritocracy and liberalism, upholders of the spirit of the *ancien régime* (from clericalists to monarchists to Bonapartists) who continued to wrestle for their "restoration" saw in the uproar over Dreyfus an opportunity to swing France back into their camp. The stakes were much higher than ridding the country of Jewish influence/domination; they were ultimately concerned with the nature of France and its pre-Revolutionary character. In that sense the Dreyfus Affair succeeded in driving French politics and culture to a showdown over the future of the Third Republic. Just as elements of France's right wing perceived the affair as a microcosm of the ills of republican principles, so did the republican forces merge gradually into a united core to reaffirm their commitment to the Revolutionary ideals. A Jewish leader, Isaïe Levaillant,[10] who well exemplified the "success" story of French Jews, having been a Préfet for many years and havnig served in other high-ranking state positions, put this succinctly in 1907:

> The decline of antisemitism began when, in the light of the events, its true character and purpose were revealed to the entire country and even the country's republicans, did not grasp that antisemitism was only a mask for the rejected clericalism to wear, and that disguised as a war against the Jews the battle was really being waged against the Republic. But owing to the lessons of the Dreyfus Affair, and the useful warnings that emerged in characteristic and serious affairs, such as the rebellion at Fort Chabrol and the altercation at the Reuilly barracks, the country's eyes were opened and it saw clearly that antisemitism constituted a danger, not only to a religious minority, but also to all the achievements of modern France.[11]

Yet, as Levaillant himself knew from experience, the nature of the antisemitic attack was also one that could not be simply glossed over and dismissed as part of a general attack against the republican values. Jews in the state system were not to be integrated without a certain demur. This theme, to rise again during the days of Léon Blum's premiership in the 1930s, put a particularly French slant on the antisemitic argument in the Third Republic. The Jews were seen, not only as *les rois de l'époque,* but also as figures who collaborated to destroy the nature of French society in its pristine character. The separation of Church and State in 1905 solidified for some the efforts of the Jews to create a state free of Christian influence and open to liberal ideals and values. For the Jews in France it was indeed a moment of relief. Scanning the few Jewish newspapers during the period of the separation debates, one cannot but notice their strong support for separation. Separation meant for them an opportunity to release France from the hands of the ultramontane forces in the Church, who were without scruples when it came to maintaining their hold over education and dogma. Moreover, Jewish journalists in these newspapers showed no signs of pusillanimity in attacking their arch-rivals—the ultramontane Church forces. Support for separation was also a way to enable less established figures within the Jewish community to extend their influence on internal Jewish affairs.

The separation of church and state in 1905 did not terminate France's struggle over the nature of French society, and antisemitism continued to lift its head in post-Dreyfus France. Just as the Affair did not invent this tradition, it also failed to bury it. Moreover, Jews continued their penetration into those areas of French society that provoked a negative response. Meritocracy had succeeded and Jews saw no reason not to continue their "success story" in the spirit of the Chief Rabbi's remarks on the eve of the Affair. Yet antisemitism appears to have taken a new direction—a less overt expression that continued to percolate down in cultural or social contexts but remained negligible in the political arena. Even in Algeria where it became violent and volatile during the *fin de siècle* and where a plethora of antisemitic newspapers and journals proliferated, the public and "political" manifestations seem to have reached their peak by World War I. The Algerian context shows that even in a colonial situation, the common graph of European antisemitism held sway. First, a rise of antisemitic activity and representation in the 1880s and 1890s, accompanied by some political successes, followed by an overt decline in its political manifestations in the first decade of the twentieth century.[12]

But as war had caused havoc to France in 1870 and unleashed a major *Kulturkampf* that rocked the country for more than half a century, so World War I unleashed dramatic changes in French society. Though France was one of the victors of the war, the country emerged battered and scarred. France was in ruins and desolated, and sorely in need of manpower. In the years following the Great War, France was to be involved in a major reconstruction and, as is well known, opened its doors in the 1930s to millions of immigrants from Eastern Europe, Italy, and elsewhere. Jews from Eastern Europe found in France a new haven, especially following the clampdown on immigration to the United States in 1924. The number of Jews in France soared in this period, changing the makeup of the community. Though they continued to hold the reins of the major Jewish organizations, the Jews *de vieille souche* (native French Jews) had become a minority, and tension among the Jews themselves was often quite sharp. The internal Jewish situation mirrored the developments within French society at large. Whereas in the early 1920s the French had shown themselves exceedingly open to immigrants from Eastern Europe, Italy, and other countries, the large numbers of foreigners began to grate on the hospitality tendered by French society in the latter part of the decade. Expressions of resentment against foreigners and Jews were heard at that juncture, especially from Action Française, the popular right-wing organization, and its vociferous leader Charles Maurras. However, the organization's anticlerical position pushed the Vatican to excommunicate its Catholic members in 1926, thus limiting its impact on French politics and on the tide of antisemitism. The clash between universal, humanistic values, and the attraction of a nativistic, authoritarian movement was well expressed years later by Jacques Maritain, the French philosopher and Catholic intellectual, in his memoirs. Maritain recorded the impact of the Church's position on his political and social thought:

> Today more than ever, I bless the liberating intervention of the Church which...exposed the errors of the *Action française,* following which I finally examined Maurras' doctrines and saw what they were worth. There began for me then a period of reflection devoted to moral and political philosophy

in which I tried to work out the character of authentically Christian politics and to establish, in the light of philosophy of history and of culture, the true significance of democratic inspiration and the nature of the new humanism for which we are waiting.

Nevertheless, the 1920s showed the resilience of the Masonic-Jewish conspiracy theory, supported by Pope Benedictus XV, and the claim among Catholic newspapers (*La croix, La libre parole,* etc.) that the coalition of Masonic and Jewish forces had determined the outcome of the anti-Catholic legislation at the turn of the century. However, these traditional pockets of antisemitic activity had little public support and were seldom taken seriously by political forces in the French polity; for example, the Left, that had figured prominently in the dissemination of antisemitic literature in the nineteenth century, emerged from the Dreyfus Affair with a more unambiguous attitude to antisemitism, one which persisted during the aftermath of World War I. In this atmosphere, Jewish figures and organizations were buoyed by the lack of controversy engendered by the influx of Jewish immigrants. Native Jews continued to be highly represented in governmental positions, in the prestigious Conseil d'État, in prefectorial positions, and as deputies in the national assembly.[13] Jews played a significant role in the development of new academic and cultural areas—from the sociologist Marcel Mauss[14] to the historian Marc Bloch,[15] one of the founders of the prestigious historical journal *Annales*—and artists of Jewish origin found Paris a most congenial ambience for their creative endeavors.[16] Jews, of native and immigrant birth, continued to sense that the Republic offered them the freedom to create and was an essential ingredient in their makeup. Even for those, like Marc Bloch, who were deeply integrated into French society, conversion was out of the question and seemed totally irrelevant. One could still invoke Rabbi Debré's optimism of the old adage "Hereux comme Dieu en France."[17] A historian's assessment that "beneath the surface moderation of the twenties...there remained a reservoir of antipathy to Jews in France, often stagnant and scarcely visible," was based more on supposition than on hard evidence.

The tide changed toward the end of the 1920s and the beginning of the 1930s. A complex of issues joined together to exert pressure on the idyllic postwar atmosphere and to bring back some of the recurrent images in French antisemitism. Immigrants and refugees provoked increasing opposition from French workers, who were losing their jobs in an era of unemployment and growing economic depression. Even before the rise of Hitler to power in Germany, the cry against immigrants assumed a nationalistic orientation. Voices from both the Right and Left called for measures to curb refugee settlement. By 1934, for the first time in French history, a law was passed that discriminated against naturalized French citizens: naturalized foreigners were barred from practising law for ten years following the receipt of their citizenship. This was to be the beginning of a general rejection of the open door policy of the 1920s. German refugees, many of them Jewish, were no longer to receive preferential treatment, a position even supported by influential Jewish figures involved in refugee questions. Jewish attachment to the state code knew no bounds.[18] However, Jewish support of stringent immigrant legislation failed to make an impression upon the recrudescence of antisemitic arguments that accompanied the growing anti-immigrant attitude. Jews were singled out for threatening the nature of French society and culture, for usurping the jobs of the French, and for subjecting France to Jewish interests. Xavier Vallat in the Chamber of Deputies, Brasillach, Giraudoux, and Bonnard in pamphlets and books called for legislation to prevent Jews from assuming governmental positions—yet in 1936 Léon Blum formed a Socialist-Radical cabinet supported by Communists. Blum's success in the midst of tremendous economic unrest provided food for the right-wing radicals, who now concentrated their antisemitic attacks against him and his alliance with what they considered an arm of Judaism—the communist movement.

But Blum was not only vilified for his political alliances and associations. He unnerved French sensibilities in a more subtle way as well. Xavier Vallat's notorious harangue against Blum in the opening session of the Chamber in 1936 raised the stakes against him by pitting the rational, dispossessed, and cosmopolitan Jew against the rooted and visceral French. He declared:

> I have the special duty here...of saying aloud what everyone is thinking to himself: that to govern this peasant nation of France it is better to have someone whose origins, no matter how modest, spring from our soil than to have a subtle Talmudist.

Vallat noted the historic moment that a Jew rose for the first time to govern France, the "Gallic-Roman country." Vallat's integral provocation points to an essential aspect of the antisemitic discourse during the Third Republic and hints at that of Vichy's as well. Race was a *sine qua non*. France and Judaism were necessarily at loggerheads. Rooted in the soil, Frenchmen derive their strength from a visceral connection to the land and to its traditions. Simplicity was seen as a value, as was the village; the modernized and cosmopolitan city was an aberration. Paris was not France, even though it bustled with the cultural and political achievements of the French. In comparison, in Vallat's pointed remarks, Blum represented the rationalist tradition, distant from the soil and the peasant tradition: the Jew was the epitome of the modern, city personality; foreigners to the Gallic-Roman country, Jews could never really become part of French society. Indeed, Blum's rise to power was accompanied by a tremendous outpouring of antisemitic literature—he was seen as the representative of liberal, parliamentary politics that threatened the very nature of French society. This theme predominated in the late 1930s as antisemitic arguments took on a more radical and vociferous tone. Not only were the Jews to blame for the economic disaster and the corruption of French culture, but they were judged to be responsible for a system which was both impotent and totally alien to the "authentic" French experience. These contentions were heard elsewhere in Europe during the 1930s, but they had a French vintage to them. There were not simply French imports but part of a recurrent conflict within French society. But the radical Right added another timely issue.[19]

Céline's fascist outbursts in 1937–1938 spoke in racial categories about the defeat of the Aryans at the hands of the Jews. His extreme synthesis posited that this confrontation motivated the Jews to involve France in a major international war to guarantee its defeat. Blum's policies were allegedly typical of Jewish strategy. By implicating France with Spain, Blum hoped to weaken France and solidify Jewry's international designs. Though Céline's extremist solutions to the "Jewish Question" were echoed by others (e.g., Brasillach, Drieu La Rochelle, Déat), they did not have significant resonance. Moreover, Céline's attacks did not go unanswered and were not successful in turning back the principles of the Third Republic, that withstood tremendously harsh criticism of its attitude to Jews. Even though the post-Blum years saw an intensification of anti-immigrant legislation, antisemitic legislation did not become a part of it. As long as the system remained intact, Jews were not singled out for discriminatory legislation. But when the system was defeated, as a consequence of the collapse of France in 1940, Jews were earmarked for special attention as the true representatives of the Third Republic. That contention the Jews could not really deny—they were indeed the arch supporters of its principles and ideological battless. They were by no means the *rois de l'époque,* but they were ardent believers in the meritocratic system which the Third Republic attempted to establish.

The reversal in the image of the Jew that transpired in French consciousness since the French Revolution was hard for Jews in the Vichy period to comprehend. Having moved close to the center of French cultural, political, and economic activity, they struggled to understand how they had been recast as major enemies of French society and its institutions. French Jewry to a great extent minimized the importance and prevalence of the recurrent images of French antisemitism during the Third Republic. Instead, their trust and allegiances remained with the spirit of the Revolution that had granted them an emancipation lasting uninterruptedly for 150 years.

Notes

1. Paul E. Hyman, *The Emancipation of the Jews of Alsace. Acculturation and Tradition in the Nineteenth Century* (New Haven and London 1991).

2. See Norman L. Kleeblatt, ed., *The Dreyfus Affair. Art, Truth, and Justice* (Berkeley and Los Angeles 1987), passim.

3. Jacob Katz, *Jews and Freemasons in Europe 1723–1939* (Cambridge, Mass. 1970).

4. On Toussenel and other critics of Jewish economic activity in France, see Robert Wistrich, "Radical Antisemitism in France and Germany (1840–1880)," *Modern Judaism* 15 (1995): 112–21.

5. It should be noted that this atmosphere was not alien to the Pope himself. In 1891 in the famous *Rerum Novarum* encyclical that sought to reestablish relations with more liberal elements in France, expressed reservations about capitalist ventures that threatened the fabric of society. It was, indirectly, pointing an accusing finger at Jewish finance which it regarded with special contempt. See Hubert Bonin, *L'argent en France depuis 1880. Banquiers, financiers, épargnants* (Paris 1989).

6. Apart from the controversy over education, these issues were a high priority on the Left as well. It is commonplace to maintain that nineteenth-century French antisemitism produced many exponents of these ideas on the Left. However, it is of special interest to place Drumont's litany side by side with the pen-and-ink drawings of the Jewish anarchist artist Camille Pissarro. In his *Les turpitudes sociales* of 1889, sent to his nieces in London as a primer in political thinking, Pissarro not only associates the new god of *mammon* with the Jews, but shows the results of this new worship. The poor, emaciated figures begging for a pittance from a Jew, who holds a bag of money close to his chest, are seen in the foreground of a modern park with statues and the recently-built Eiffel Tower, a source of much controversy during those years. The image of the Jew as the "roi de l'époque" had clearly moved to center stage, even in the mind of a Jew himself, albeit one obviously on the periphery of Jewish life. See Linda Nochlin, "Degas and the Dreyfus Affair: A Portrait of the Artist as an Anti-Semite," in Kleeblatt, *Dreyfus Affair*, 98.

7. Quoted in Michael Burns, "Majority Faith: Dreyfus Before the Affair," in *From East and West. Jews in a Changing Europe 1750–1870,* ed. Frances Malino and David Sorkin (Oxford and Cambridge, Mass. 1990–1991), 57.

8. See Piere Birnbaum, *Les foux de la république* (Paris 1992).

9. Burns, "Majority Faith."

10. On Levailant and his career in the French state system, see Pierre Birnbaum, ed., *La France de l'affaire Dreyfus* (Paris 1994), esp. 191–202.

11. Quoted in Richard I. Cohen, "The Dreyfus Affair and the Jews," in *Antisemitism Through the Ages,* ed. Shmuel Almog (Oxford 1988), 300.

12. See Michel Abitbol, *From Crémieux to Pétain. Antisemitism in Colonial Algeria (1870–1940)* (in Hebrew) (Jerusalem 1994).

13. Birnbaum, *Les foux,* passim.

14. Pierre Birnbaum, "French Jewish Sociologists between Reason and Faith: The Impact of the Dreyfus Affair," *Jewish Social Studies* 2 (1995): 1–36.

15. Carole Fink, *Marc Bloch. A Life in History* (Cambridge and New York 1989).

16. See Kenneth E. Silver and Romy Golan, *The Circle of Montparnasse. Jewish Artists in Paris 1905–1945* (New York 1985).

17. Cf. David H. Weinberg, "Hereux comme Dieu en France" East European Jewish Immigrants in Paris, 1881–1914," *Studies in Contemporary Jewry,* vol. 1, ed. Jonathan Frankel (Bloomington, Ind. 1984), 26–54.

18. See Timothy Maga, "Closing the Door: The French Government and Refugee Policy, 1933–1939," *French Historical Studies* 12 (1982): 424–42; Vicki Caron, "Loyalities in Conflict: French Jewry and the Refugee Crisis, 1933–1935," *Leo Baeck Institute Yearbook* 36 (1991): 305–38.

19. Zeev Sternhell, *Neither Right nor Left. Fascist Ideology* in France, tr. David Maisel (Berkeley, Los Angeles and London 1986).

12

The Critique of Judaism in Modern European Thought: Genuine Factors and Demonic Perceptions

Otto D. Kulka
The Hebrew University of Jerusalem

In the introduction to her *Origins of Totalitarianism* Hannah Arendt points to the paradox of the relative unimportance of Jewish existence as a reality and its demonization as a threat in all its world-historical dimensions:

> It must be possible to face and understand the outrageous fact that so small (and, in world-politics, so unimportant) a phenomenon as the Jewish question and antisemitism could become the catalytic agent for first, the Nazi movement, then a world war, and finally the establishment of death factories.[1]

Many past and present explanations of antisemitism have tried to interpret it as an expression of hatred or fear of otherness representing the strange, the weak, or characteristics of social marginality and ostracism. But how shall we explain the perception of Judaism and Jews as a threat identified with the most powerful factors within Western civilization, such as Capitalism and Democracy, Socialism and Bolshevism, Modernity or Anti-Modernism? I agree with Arendt "that the scapegoat explanation remains one of the principle attempts to escape the seriousness of antisemitism and the significance of the fact that the Jews were driven into the storm center of events,"[2] though I cannot accept her interpretation of its causes in the modern era as being connected with the political system of totalitarianism.

The present paper is an attempt at re-examination of a number of concepts fundamental to the study of modern antisemitism and proposes alternative ways of characterizing the phenomenon, its causes, and implications. Its methodological approach can be summed up as a reassessment of the ambivalent meaning of the centrality of the Jewish component in Western civilization. Its retrospective point of departure will be the findings of the historiography on National Socialism, which stress the world historical significance of its anti-Jewish principles as an expression of one of the most grave crises of this civilization—a crisis with the potential to change the course of human history.

Notwithstanding the singularity of National Socialist antisemitism and its "Final Solution," and despite the difficulty in tracing and proving historical continuities, the research of the last decades, particularly of Jerusalem scholars like Shmuel Ettinger, Jacob Talmon (and from a different methodological approach, Jacob Katz), as well as of important works of German historiography since the 1960s, makes it possible to examine the development in a wide historical perspective.[3] We are now able to show the inherent nature of the critique of Judaism as a source of active anti-Jewish ideology in the main philosophical, social and political currents of modern Europe—indeed as part of the process of its secularization since the end of the seventeenth century.

Yet it appears that due to the constant and unique role of the Jewish component in this culture, the rationalization of the anti-Jewish criticism had enormous mythic potential and made it possible not only to identify Judaism with powers and systems such as capitalism, democracy, and socialism, but to postulate a monistic world view that explained the entire course of history as a manichean struggle between the Jews and all other nations.

The Centrality of Antisemitism in National Socialist Ideology and the Crisis of Western Civilization

Many scholarly works written on National Socialism over the past three decades have reached the conclusion that antisemitism played a vital role in ideology and policy of the Third Reich.[4] Of all the ideological and political ingredients that went into the making of Hitler's outlook, antisemitism, in its broadest sense, appears to be not only the one consistent and immutable element, it also bridges such seemingly contradictory leanings as anti-Marxism and anti-capitalism, the struggle against democracy and modernism, and a basic anti-Christian disposition. The same is true of the conceptual bearing and functional significance of these apparent contradictions in the foreign policy and war aims of National Socialism: anti-Bolshevism, conceived as determining the inevitable struggle against the Soviet Union, "anti-plutocracy" and "anti-Democracy" as basic motives for the war against the Western Powers—France, Britain, and the United States.[5] Yet Hitler consistently portrays this ideological war in the international arena as an extension of the struggle that the National Socialist movement had waged, from its inception, against its ideological and political enemies within Germany itself: Jewish Marxism, Jewish parliamentary democracy, Jewish capitalism, and even the "Political churches" and the Jewish foundations of Christianity. In the movement's racial-determinist conception, the Jews stand in an obviously dominant relationship to all these forces and factors as the biological source of doctrines and ideologies whose most radical expression is Bolshevism but whose origin was Judaism's introduction of Christianity into the Western world.[6]

National Socialist antisemitism traced the sense of crisis that dogged the modern world to its domination by "Jewish-Christian-Bolshevik" principles that were based on a universalist "destructive belief" in the unity of the world and the equality of men in all spheres of life. These principles were antithetical to the Nazi Social-Darwinist version of the "natural order," i.e., the inherent inequality of the races and the eternal struggle between them for their very survival. Hence only the restoration of this order—which was conditional upon the absolute annihilation, physical and spiritual, of Judaism—could ensure the future health, indeed the very existence of the human race.

In the name of a struggle against historical principles and forces— alledgedly represented by Judaism—the messianic-political creed of National Socialism was meant to change the course that universal history had taken since the encounter between Judaism and Hellenism and the birth of the Judeo-Christian culture. Yet clearly this aim—unique in terms of its ideological radicalism and harrowing historical realization—was but one aspect of the antagonism intrinsic to Judeo-Christian culture, which throughout its history has both been shaped by and struggled against its Judaic sources. Only in this sense and through this perspective can one attempt to propose an "explanation of the inexplicable" (to use Kafka's phrase on the meaning of the relationship between myth, reality, and history) regarding both the historical and substantive import of the Holocaust.[7]

The Destruction and Restoration of the "Natural Order"

Though the most radical ideological expression of Nazi antisemitism was the apocalyptic vision of humanity's demise due to the triumph of "Jewish Bolshevism"—the traumatic historical event that underlay this development was "Christianity's entry into and destruction of the ancient world." In Hitler's words:

> The sensational event of the ancient world was the mobilisation of the underworld against the established order.... The Jew who fraudulently introduced Christianity into the ancient world—in order to ruin it—reopened the same breach in modern times, this time taking as his pretext the social

question.... Just as Saul changed into St. Paul, Mardochai became Karl Marx.[8]

This, so Hitler believed, was the first assault on the world's "natural order":

Peace can result only from a natural order.... The condition of this order is that there is a hierarchy amongst nations. The most capable nations must necessarily take the lead.... It is Jewry that always destroys this order.... A people that is rid of its Jews, returns spontaneously to the natural order.[9]

Notwithstanding the pronounced distinctiveness of these formulations, there is no difficulty tracing their sources directly to the ramified antisemitic literature of the late nineteenth and early twentieth century.[10] But as we have pointed out, antisemitism reached such a level of radicalization in National-Socialism and through its appalling political realization so thoroughly changed its character that the question of continuity becomes problematic. Nevertheless, the key question that the study of modern antisemitism must address is where the entire process began, or, as Ettinger put it, where are "the roots of antisemitism in the modern era."[11]

It seems to me that late seventeenth-century English Deism—the first philosophical current to express the crisis of faith in Christianity and to offer a rationalist concept of "natural religion" as a radical alternative—is the historical point of departure for the development.[12] Its critique of Christianity arose from the self-exploration of a religious, social, and political system whose radical thinkers tried to delve down to its historical origins and arrived, almost inevitably, at an examination of Christianity's Judaic sources. "Natural religion," as the rational basis of the cultural and social values of the pre-Christian world, was portrayed by the Deists as the antithesis of Judaism, an alternative to it, and the system of ideals that was destroyed by it.[13]

What we have here is a paradigmatic situation in which the inherent logic underlying the radical critique of the Judeo-Christian tradition generated the beginning of that radical revolution that strives, in the name of progress and renewal, to turn back the clock and restore the glories of the past. Yet by the time it reached the final stage of the National Socialist revolution, the original rationalist ideal of natural "religion" had been transformed into an irrational vision of "saving the human race" by reinstating the "natural order" of history.

One can trace an unbroken thread of influence leading from the critique of Judaism by the English Deists to modern antisemitism in the nineteenth and twentieth centuries. As we shall see further on, Ettinger examined this thread of thought in England, France, and Germany over the course of more than a century. He showed that the Young Hegelian radicals of the mid-nineteenth century did not reflect the ideas of the German Enlightenment and not even those of Hegel himself; rather, they demonstrated their direct resort to the critique of religion and anti-Jewish concepts of the English and French Materialists of the preceding century.[14]

Ettinger, whose studies trace continuity in the development of modern antisemitism, stressed the paradox of radicalism in espousing the idea of progress and at the same time, by its criticism of Judaism, perpetuating the hostile *historical stereotype* of earlier ages.[15] I believe that in this context as well, the consciousness of a crisis of the entire epoch of secularism and modernism deserves equal stress. From this point of view, the ongoing trend of criticism of and hostility towards Judaism need not be interpreted as a paradoxical phenomenon at all. Indeed, it may well exist not *despite* the progressive and modernist ideas of the new currents but *because* of them.

Critique of Religion by the English Deists and French Rationalists: The Ambivalence of "Natural Religion" and anti-Christian Antisemitism

Let us now return to Ettinger's historical starting point: the critical initial influence of English Deism. The direct tie between English Deism and French rationalism is commonplace in the history of modern thought, but the same cannot be said of the connection between the critique of Judaism in both these schools. The most prominent example of this approach is of course Voltaire's negative view of Judaism, which many have traced to an unpleasant personal experience with Jewish moneymen—though some believe his anti-Jewish vitriol to be just a tactic in his struggle with the Church.[16] Indeed, the strong connection between the criticism of Christianity and its Jewish roots (and the identification of Judaism and the Bible as the basis of the social-political order) is argued as convincingly by French rationalists as it is by the English Deists. Moreover, given the objective historical circumstances of the mid-eighteenth century, their writings reflect an even more acute crisis whose impact on subsequent developments was so formidable that it may well be regarded as the dawn of the new "Age of Revolution" that would make such a lasting impression upon the modern world.

Capitalism and the "Jewish Spirit": Marx and the Critique of Religion by the Young Hegelians

As we have already noted the next significant stage in the development of the secular antisemitic ideology can be found in the radical thinking of the Young Hegelians. Karl Marx considered the Young Hegelian "criticism of religion" to be "the greatest achievement of German philosophy."[17] Yet the new context in which the critique of Judaism and Christianity appears in Marx's work lumps together the "practical spirit of Judaism" with the rule of capital that had gained sway over Christian society and found its latest expression in moderm capitalism. It was his sense of the keen social crisis brought on by industrialization that prompted Marx to examine the entire history of Christian society from this standpoint. In an attempt to uncover the "root of evil" in a single dominant factor, he arrived (by the same logic as the English Deists) at Judaism: "The practical Jewish spirit has become the practical spirit of the Christian nations." Hence the vision of reforming Christian society is defined as the "emancipation from Judaism," which is also the "social emancipation of the Jew."

Yet here in mid-nineteenth-century Germany, we find that the social and political situation of the Jews had already changed; and for all their historiosophic significance, the words of the young Marx were written at the height of the debate over the highly concrete question of abolishing the long-standing restrictions on the legal status of the Jews.[18] As Eleonore Sterling already demonstrated in her pioneering study on the genesis of political antisemitism in Germany in the first half of the nineteenth century, in this particular situation the conclusions of an abstract historio-theological debate on the character and properties of Judaism were incorporated into discussion of the "essential nature" and traits of Jews of the day.[19] Ettinger for his part believed that what distinguished the Young Hegelians' discussion of Judaism and the Jews was their rejection of the developmental approach associated with the thinkers of the German Enlightenment that "accorded the Jews and their religion a respectable place on the ladder of human-historical development."[20] Whereas the eighteenth-century and early nineteenth-century Enlightenment theorists explained the condition of the Jews and their flaws as a consequence of the persecution to which Christian society had subjected them, "the Young Hegelians viewed these defects as the inevitable result of the immutable 'nature of Judaism.'"[21]

The reappearance of the critique of religion in the mid-nineteenth century was parallel and even symbiotically related to the development of a radical romanticism like that of Richard Wagner, himself influenced by the thinking of the Young Hegelians. Wagner was one of the first to articulate a racial-determinist version of the anti-Jewish doctrine.[22]

The "Conservative Revolution": Wagner, the Existential Import of the Crisis of Creativity, and the "Judaization of European Culture"

Judaism, including all its basic anthropological features, appears at the heart of Wagner's outlook, as a historical fossil whose existence in all spheres of life is marked by the "absence of authentic human qualities, hence its eternal creative sterility." Paradoxically, however, this alien and "inferior" phenomenon, in Wagner's rendering of it, had wrested control of all spheres of life, including the arts, in modern Europe. The cultural crisis in this case was not about the endurance of a conservative regime or the exposure of its roots but concerned the process of disintegration and decline of an organic wholeness of life. It was this crisis and the abstract-rationalist principles of the Age of Emancipation that made possible the rise of capitalism (a creation of the Jews), the emergence of the modern press and Jewry's control of public opinion, of literature (on which it inflicted its sterile style), and above all, music. One could say that Wagner identified the "spirit of Judaism" and the activities of Jews with the epitome of modernism not in the sense of progress and human liberation but as an expression of man's decadence and subjugation.

Following Wagner's logic, the necessary condition for restoration, regeneration or "redemption" was the liberation from the rule of Jewry in every creative realm and walk of life. As with Marx, the elimination of Judaism and an end to Jewish existence are portrayed as "redemption from the curse hanging over them," as the freedom from their destructive role throughout human history. Such liberation would restore the world to its old glory, to the pre-modern (and pre-emancipatory) era, which presumably did not abide the destructive and decadent influence of Judaism. Yet Wagner's gospel of redemption and regeneration also aimed at purifying the Christian tradition of its Jewish components and in its most radical expression signalled a return to the pre-Christian mythological past.[23]

Here again the critique of Judaism and even an extreme antisemitic approach are part and parcel of an attempt at self-examination by a society and culture in crisis which in Wagner's portrayal of it, takes on the existential meaning of a choice between life and death. To illustrate the grave implications of this outlook, it is enough to quote a few lines from Wagner's 1850 piece "Judaism in Music," which Talmon once called a "turning point" on "the road to Auschwitz":

> So long as the separate art of Music has a real organic life-need in it, down to the epochs of Mozart and Beethoven, there was nowhere to be found a Jew composer: it was impossible for an element entirely foreign to that living organism to take part in the formative stages of that life. Only when a body's inner death is manifest, do outside elements win the power of lodgment in it—yet merely to destroy it.[24]

Here we must again pose the question of how important established patterns of thinking about the nature and properties of Judaism may have been in forging the antisemitic attitudes that are characteristic of Wagner and the radical-romantic anti-Jewish school. As we have seen, the dogmatic anthropologically-based patterns of the French and English rationalists, later reformulated by the Young Hegelians, may have influenced Wagner's racist anti-Jewish thinking. The same can be said of the inclusion of historical anti-Jewish stereotypes in his critique of Judaism. But if we take the reflection of the historical situation in his outlook to be an authentic awareness of the existential crisis he portrayed (inter alia, through the moods prevailing in German romanticism), we can assume that these influences were not a decisive causal factor in forging the ideological core of his beliefs. Indeed, following the same logic by which the critique of Judaism emerged in other radical schools of secular thought, Wagner may have arrived at his approach independent of these influences. In any event, it should be mentioned that Wagner's antisemitic ideas were formulated in the climate of pessimism and despair that followed the failure of the revolutions of 1848. Moreover, his protest against the emancipation of the Jews was, as we have noted, a function of his rejection of the principles of the "abstract rationalism" underlying it.[25] Yet such pessimism, along with a romantic longing for regeneration through a return to the values of the past and a rejection of the impact of rationalism, brings us back to an earlier crisis in Germany at the the the time of the Napoleonic Wars—when the Jews were first granted partial emancipation. Indeed, this school of anti-Jewish criticism initially took shape with the consolidation of the German romantic-nationalist movement among a number of its more radical expoments.[26]

Yet even the ideology of the conservative opponents of emancipation, who espoused the idea of the "Christian state," was fuelled by a fear of the destructive influence of Judaism. Naturally, their hostile approach did not view Christianity's roots in Judaism as being the heart of the problem; instead it stressed the antagonistic nature of Jewry's existence within Christian society before the crisis of secularization. Jewry's entry into Christian society and its impact on that society's image were perceived as the infiltration of an alien, antagonistic element, and the imposition of its anti-Christian character on a state and society in whose formative historical development the Jews had played no part. This society was even defined as Christian by virtue of its religious antagonism to Judaism. The critique of the secularization and modernization of Christian society brought in its wake, as one of its explanations and the responses to it, an attack on emancipated Jewry, which was identified with various expressions of modernism. The conservative-Christian school initially saw the possibility of resolving religious antagonism by the conversion and assimilation of the Jews. The later penetration of racist thinking into the conservative ideology changed, however, its perception of assimilation as not merely irrelevant but as a threat to the very existence of non-Jewish society. In this context it should be noted that due to the dialectic of the revolutionary historical situation from which it arose during the first half of the nineteenth century, the conservative ideology of the "Christian state" had radical qualities of its own that justify the use of the term "conservative revolution."

Antisemitism as anti-Christian and anti-Democratic Radicalism:
National Socialism as Political Messianism and as a Dual Revolution

Following these distinctions we can say that the ideological, social, and political manifestations of antisemitism were essentially concentrated in two trends.

First, there was the anti-Christian, radical-rationalist critique of Judaism which identified its shortcomings—especially the Jewish antecedents of Christianity—with the ills of contemporary Christian society. Its point of departure was the consciousness of a crisis of faith and also of corruption and injustice in contemporary political and social systems deriving from the legacy of the rule of religion. The cure for these ills was to be radical change and faith in progress—congruent with the general aim of liberation from Judeo-Christianity as a condition for emancipating man and society.

Second, there was the conservative critique of Judaism, which identified it with the spirit of modernism per se, including the processes of change, secularization, and revolution in all spheres of life. Here a belief in the absolute merit of the basic values of the past, prior to the crisis of secularization and modernism, generated a desire to preserve or restore a historical tradition in which hostility towards Judaism was built into the system.

In essence the two kinds of anti-Jewish criticism, equated the influence of Judaism with the existential causes of the crisis within contemporary society. Yet the first type of critique perceived that crisis as a result of the endurance and further distortion of society's Judeo-Christian character, while the second regarded Judaism as an attack on the survival of the Christian tradition as well as the national organism. There is no doubt that more than being an expression of hostility towards the Jew as an individual or distinct minority in the surrounding society, both these trends express an awareness of the need for self-examination by a society in crisis. In attempting to examine the roots of the crisis, such radical introspection may lead, as one of the possible explanations, to a confrontation with Judaism or to a re-examination of the Jewish component in Western culture—either as one of the elements upon which its culture was based or as an antagonistic factor that defined the particular existence and role of that culture as the heir to Judaism and executor of its mission.

I shall not expand upon this point by drawing on the wealth of extant "classic" antisemitic literature and journalistic commentary from the last third of the nineteenth century. The social, political, religious, and cultural developments and crises of this period in which modern antisemitism developed into a public movement and political organization have already been discussed at length in the scholarly literature. Instead I prefer to dwell on the claim that the diminishing importance of the antisemitic parties towards the end of the nineteenth century, especially in Germany, does not indicate a parallel decline in the basic ideas underlying their critique of Judaism. Rather it suggests the penetration of this criticism into the ideologies of most of the large political parties at the end of the imperial age and during the Weimar era.[27]

The National Socialist ideology also emerged against the background of a sharp sense of crisis and historical upheavals. There was the trauma and outcome of World War I, the dissolution of the empire, revolutions and counterrevolutions, the world economic crisis and collapse of the monetary system; above all the structural changes and accelerated modernization that encompassed all spheres of life in the new democratic Weimar republic were highly conducive to introspection and pondering the reasons for the unintelligible crisis, with one of the possible explanations focusing on Judaism and the Jews. What distinguished National Socialist antisemitism from its immediate predecessors, however, was its tendency to combine the two primary and ostensibly contradictory elements of the critique of Judaism in modern antisemitism: the radical anti-Christian trend, with all its revolutionary implications, and the radical-conservative tendency, with its anti-revolutionary and anti-democratic slant. Moreover, the anti-Jewish element, which was an integral but relatively inconsequential component of the main schools of nineteenth-century political thought, now became a focal feature of an ideology that developed into the political program of a modern totalitarian party aspiring to global hegemony.[28] This ideology, including Hitler's political messianism, became one of the basic motives in the Nazi attempt to change the course of history by eliminating the Jewish foundations of European civilization. For it was these "Jewishly tainted" factors that had purportedly brought humanity to the brink of self-destruction. Only by destroying the regimes and ideologies that embodied the spirit of Judaism and physically annihilating the millions of Jews that comprised its biological source, would it be possible to rescue the human race and restore the harmony that had epitomized the "natural order."

The Mythic Potential of the Jewish Component in Western Culture and the Recurrent Crises of the Secular Age

At the beginning of this paper I noted that the scholarly literature has already established the centrality of antisemitism in the ideology and policy of the Third Reich. In the course of this discussion we have seen that the "Jewish Question" lay at the heart of the gravest and most menacing crisis of Western civilization—an attempt to revolt against the moral core of its very existence. Most works on modern antisemitism, including studies on the background to its National Socialist version, focus on the period beginning in the last third of the nineteenth century with its advent as an organized political movement. We have taken as our point of departure the innovating contribution of Shmuel Ettinger's studies, which explore the critique of Judaism as a source of active anti-Jewish ideology in the secularization process of modern Europe since the end of the seventeenth century.[29] This perspective has also enabled us to stress the decisive contribution of radicalism of both the Left and the Right.

The critique of Judaism and the Jews involved virtually all the phenomena that shaped the modern world—including Christianity, capitalism, and revolution, democracy and socialism; on another plane the Jews were associated with the domination of the modern finance, with domestic and international political systems, and with the press, literature, and the arts. It seems to us that the critique of these concepts by modern antisemitism can best be seen as a reflection of Western society in an age of constant crisis marked by the process of secularization and modernization. This critique of Judaism, which contained both fear and bewilderment over the implications of these changes, could not have arisen had Judaism not been a constant and central component of Western culture.

The radical protest aimed at modern society together with the thirst for rational explanations and solutions undoubtedly expressed an authentic perplexity and sense of far-reaching alienation.[30] The critique of the Jewish elements in Western culture and their influence on modernity was often congruent with other rational or even monocausal explanations of that situation and the perplexities, hopes, and fears that accompanied it. But as a result of the constant and unique role of the Jewish component in Western culture, the rationalization of this anti-Jewish ideology had enormous mythic potential. This fact made it possible not only to identify Judaism with forces such as capitalism, democracy, and socialism, but to postulate a monistic worldview that explained the entire course of history as a manichean struggle between the Jews and all other nations.[31] During the era of secularization in European thought, this potential of mythic rationalization broke free from the standard theological view on the place of Judaism and the Jew in Christian society and in the future course of history. It waxed, waned, and ultimately rebounded with unimagined force, following the same inherent logic of reactions that we have attempted to trace in this essay.

It would, of course, be a dangerous exaggeration to regard modern antisemitism through its various manifestations in deterministic terms. The history of Western society and its self-critical confrontation with modernity should not be read as a history of unrelenting "pan-antisemitism." Yet research into modern antisemitism, and particularly its most radical manifestation in National Socialism, suggests that it would be equally unacceptable and no less dangerous to ignore the significance of the central role which the "Jewish Question" has played in the history of modern Western culture.

Notes

1. Hannah Arendt, *The Origins of Totalitarianism,* 2nd. ed. (New York 1958, viii.
2. Ibid., 7.
3. I shall base my analysis of the historical developments up to World War I mainly on Shmuel Ettinger, *Modern Anti-Semitism. Studies and Essays* (in Hebrew) (Tel Aviv 1978); several chapters of this book appeared in an English translation and are quoted accordingly; Jacob L. Talmon, "European History as the Seedbed of the Holocaust," in *Holocaust and Rebirth. A Symposium* (Jerusalem 1974) 11–75; Jacob Katz, *From Prejudice to Destruction. Anti-Semitism, 1770–1933* (Cambridge, Mass. 1980); idem, "On Jewish Social History. Epochal and Supra-Epochal Historiography," in *Jewish History* 7 (1993): 89–96. Concerning research on National Socialism, particularly in German historiography, see below, n. 4.
4. For these conclusions, particularly in non-Jewish historiography, cf. my study "Die deutsche Geschichtsschreibung über den Nationalsozialismus und die 'Endlösung.' Tendenzen und Entwicklungsphasen 1924–1984," *Historische Zeitschrift* 240 (1985): 599–640; for an extended version see Yisrael Gutman and Gideon Greif, eds., *The Historiography of the Holocaust Period* (Jerusalem 1988), 1–58. On various tendencies in the so-called *Historikerstreit,* see O. D. Kulka, "Singularity and Its Relativization. Changing Views in German Historiography on National Socialism and the 'Final Solution,'" *Yad Vashem Studies* (Jerusalem) 19 (1988): 151–86; and Ian Kershaw, *The Nazi Dictatorship. Problems and Perspectives of Interpretation,* 3rd. ed. (London 1993), chs. 9 and 10.
5. Among others, see Eberhard Jäckel, *Hitler's World View. A Blueprint for Power* (Cambridge, Mass. 1981); Andreas Hillgruber, "The Extermination of the European Jews in its Historical Context—A Recapitulation," *Yad Vashem Studies* 17 (1986): 1–15; idem, "War in the East and the Extermination of the Jews," *Yad Vashem Studies* 18 (1987): 103–32; Ulrich Thamer, *Verführung und Gewalt. Deutschland 1933–1945* (Berlin 1986); Michael Burleigh and Wolfgang Wippermann, *The Racial State. Germany 1933–1945* (Cambridge, Mass. 1991); Philippe Burrin, *Hitler and the Jews. The Genesis of the Holocaust* (London 1994); and in a broad historical perspective, Steven T. Katz, *The Holocaust in Historical Context,* vol. 1 (Oxford 1994).
6. Cf. Klaus Scholder, "Judaism and Christianity in the Ideology and Politics of National Socialism," in *Judaism and Christianity under the Impact of National Socialism,* eds. O. D. Kulka and Paul R. Mendes-Flohr (Jerusalem 1978), 183–95; idem, "Die Kirchen im Dritten Reich" Beilage zur Wochenzeitung, *Das Parlament* B15/71 (10 April 1971).
7. Gutman and Greif, *Historiography of the Holocaust Period,* 36.
8. H. R. Trevor-Roper, ed., *Hitler's Table Talk 1941–1944* (London 1973), 313 (from Hitler's "monologue" of 17 February 1942).
9. Ibid., 314.
10. See Léon Poliakov, *The History of Anti-Semitism,* vols. 3–4 (New York 1978 and 1985); Jacob Katz, *From Prejudice to Destruction;* and Talmon, "European History as the Seedbed"; Hermann Greive, *Geschichte des modernen Antisemitismus in Deutschland* (Darmstadt 1983); Helmut Berding, *Moderner Antisemitismus in Deutschland* (Frankfurt a.M. 1988); Paul W. Massing, *Rehearsal for Destruction. A Study of Political Antisem-*

itism in Imperial Germany (New York 1949); Peter Pulzer, *The Rise of Political Anti-Semitism in Germany and Austria* (New York 1964); Uriel Tal, *Christians and Jews in Germany. Religion, Politics and Ideology in the Second Reich* (Ithaca and London 1975); Reinhard Rürup, *Emanzipation und Antisemitismus* (Göttingen 1975), chs. 3–5.

11. See Ettinger's opening essay of the same name (in Hebrew) in Ettinger, *Modern Anti-Semitism,* 1–27.

12. Shmuel Ettinger,"Secular Roots of Modern Antisemitism," in Kulka and Mendes-Flohr, *Judaism and Christianity,* 43. See, in particular, Ettinger's fundamental study, "Jews and Judaism as Seen by the English Deists of the 18th Century," (in Hebrew), in Ettinger, *Modern Anti-Semitism,* 57–87; for an English abstract see, *Zion,* 29 (1964): i–ii.

13. Ettinger, "Deists," esp. 84–85.

14. See Shmuel Ettinger, "The Young Hegelians—A Source of Modern Antisemitism?," *Jerusalem Quarterly* 28 (1983): 80.

15. Ibid., 82.

16. Ettinger, "Deists," 58.

17. Ettinger, "Young Hegelians," 73.

18. See Nathan Rotenstreich, "For and Against Emancipation. The Bruno Bauer Controversy," *Leo Baeck Institute Year Book,* 4 (1959): 3–36.

19. Eleonore Sterling, *Judenhaß. Die Anfänge des politischen Antisemitismus in Deutschland (1815–1850),* 2nd. ed. (Frankfurt a.M. 1969).

20. Ettinger, "Young Hegelians," 78–79.

21. Ibid., 79.

22. See O. D. Kulka, "Richard Wagner und die Anfänge des modernen Antisemitismus," *Bulletin des Leo Baeck Instituts* 4 (1961): 281–300. For a diverging view cf. Katz, *From Prejudice to Destruction,* ch. 15.

23. See especially the findings of Hartmut Zelinski, "Einleitung," *Richard Wagner—ein deutsches Thema. Eine Dokumentation zur Wirkungsgeschichte Richard Wagners, 1876–1976,* 2nd ed. (Vienna and Berlin 1983), 6–22, 278–84.

24. Richard Wagner, *Das Judenthum in der Musik,* 2nd ed. (Leipzig 1869), 31; Jacob L. Talmon, *The Myth of the Nation and the Vision of Revolution. The Origins of Ideological Polarisation in the Twentieth Century* (London 1980), 208–209.

25. Richard Wagner, *Das Judenthum in der Musik,* 10–11.

26. See Sterling, *Judenhaß,* and Hans Kohn, *The Mind of Germany* (London 1965). A contemporary autobiographical account appears in Heinrich Heine, "Zur Geschichte der Religion und Philosophie in Deutschland," *Heines Werke in fünfzehn Teilen,* vol. 9 (Berlin (n.d.), 275–77, and in his "Ludwig Börne," ibid., vol. 14, 89–90.

27. Ettinger, "Secular Roots," 60.

28. See Ernst Nolte's standard work on Fascism and National Socialism (his latter views in connection with the *Historikerstreit* notwithstanding), *Three Faces of Fascism* (London 1963), 332. On Richard Wagner, see Kulka, "Richard Wagner und die Anfänge"; Talmon, *Myth of the Nation*; on Wilhelm Marr, see M. Zimmerman, *Wilhelm Marr* (New York 1986); and Robert S. Wistrich, "Antisemitism as a 'Radical' Ideology in the 19th Century," *Jerusalem Quarterly* 28 (1983): 88; on the *völkisch* movement, see George L.

Mosse, *The Crisis of German Ideology. Intellectual Origins of the Third Reich* (New York 1964).

29. Apart from Ettinger's pioneering work we might mention Arthur Hertzberg, *The French Enlightenment and the Jews* (New York 1961), Hermann Greive, *History of Modern Antisemitism in Germany,* and Léon Poliakov, *History of Anti-Semitism.*

30. Some of these observations with regard to the rise of modern antisemitism in Germany are discussed in Eva Reichmann, *Hostages of Civilisation. The Social Sources of National Socialist Anti-Semitism* (London 1950).

31. Cf. also Jacob L. Talmon's formulation: "It is no accident that Nazism found it necessary to reinterpret the whole of history as a permanent life-and-death struggle between Nordic Aryanism and the Jewish spirit attributing to Jews a significance and effectiveness which the most extreme Jewish chauvinist would not dream of claiming," "Uniqueness and Universality of Jewish History. A Mid-Century Revaluation, " in idem, *The Unique and the Universal. Some Historical Reflections* (London 1965), 87. Similarly the German historian Andreas Hillgruber: "Der geschichtliche Ort der Judenvernichtung," in *Der Mord an den Juden im Zweiten Weltkrieg. Entschlußbildung und Verwirklichung,* eds. Eberhard Jäckel and Jürgen Rohwer (Stuttgart 1985), 220.

Part II

13

"Europe's Inner Demons": The "Other" as Threat in Early Twentieth-Century European Culture

Saul Friedländer
Tel Aviv University
University of California Los Angeles

In October 1939, close behind the Wehrmacht units which occupied Lodz, a film crew arrived in the city. Under the personal supervision of Joseph Goebbels and the direction of Fritz Hippler, head of the film section in the Propaganda Ministry, the cameras started rolling in the Jewish slums for the production of the ultimate anti-Jewish film, *The Eternal Jew.*[1] Throughout the end of 1939 and much of 1940, Goebbels devoted constant attention to the "Judenfilm"—the "Jew film"—as he called it. On 17 October, he mentioned the film to Hitler, who "showed great interest."[2] On the *same day,* he returned to the topic:

> "Film tests.... Pictures from the "Ghetto" film. Such a thing never existed before. Scenes so dreadful and brutal in their details that one's blood freezes. One pulls back in horror at so much brutality. This Jewry must be exterminated."[3]

> 24 October: "Further tests for our Jew film. Shots of synagogue scenes of extraordinary significance. We are now working in order to make a propaganda masterpiece of it all...."[4] 28 October: "Shot tests for our Jew film. Shocking. This film will be our big hit."[5]

On November 2, Goebbels flew to Poland, first to Lodz:

> "We travel through the ghetto. We get out and observe everything in detail. It's indescribable. These are not human beings any more, they are animals. Therefore, we have not a humanitarian task to perform, but a surgical one. One must cut here, in a radical way. Otherwise, one day, Europe will perish of the Jewish disease."[6]

In Goebbels' diary entry, the otherness of the Jew is absolute, as absolute as the difference between the beholder's world and the "Synagogue," between "human beings" and "animals." The threat represented by the Jew as the quintessential Other is illustrated by increasingly more extreme metaphors. First, the "brutality" of the Jew's beast-like life provokes such horror that "one's blood freezes"; then, the merely horrifying brutishness turns into mortal danger: the Jew as pestilence and disease will bring about the death of Europe if no radical ("surgical") intervention takes place.

In this essay I shall deal with the image of the Jew as a representation of the threatening Other in the Western imagination. I have chosen the early part of the century and particularly the interwar period as the temporal framework and the European Right, mainly the extreme or radical right as ideological background.

Within this context, I shall first turn to the explicit and manifest level of this discourse and consider, initially, what may be defined as a "minimal" perception of the Jewish threat represented in essentially passive terms. This minimal perception should lead to a basic question: was the Jewish peril merely considered as the most extreme aspect of a general threat of otherness or did it carry peculiar characteristics—and that will be my position—which need to be identified? In a second stage, I shall turn to the far more extreme belief in an active Jewish menace, mainly perceived in terms of sinister conspiracy. It should allow us to define the peculiar dimension of the Jew as threat in more precise terms. In the third and last section, I shall attempt to move one step beyond the manifest discourse and point to a latent level carrying images molded not only by the reworking of culturally transmitted stereotypes but also by some of the deepest fears of the contemporary imagination. It is at this level that one may, by way of associations, perceive something of the hallucinatory backdrop of the extermination.

An incidental aspect of the main argument relates to the second stage of my presentation, the manifest discourse on Jewish conspiracies. In this domain I have chosen to dwell on Christian constructs stemming primarily from England and France in order to show how such beliefs arose far beyond the boundaries of racial theories, creating a ready ground of understanding for the later anti-Jewish policies of the Nazis.

"Spiritual Splitting"

Europe's Inner Demons is the powerfully evocative title of Norman Cohn's book about witches and witch-hunts in early modern Europe.[7] It points to the dual aspect of the threat. In order to be perceived as a fundamental threat the Other has to dwell in the midst of the "threatened" community (it has to be an *inner* demon) and it has to partake of some mysterious force, identified with powers external to the group. This composite aspect of ominous Otherness will reappear at every stage of our inquiry.

What, in the most general terms, was actually perceived by the European Right at the turn of the century as the *object* of the threat; as the endangered domain? "The nation," the "race," the "culture," in other words, *partial* aspects of the category opposed to the Other: *the Self.* The ultranationalism of the turn of the century, that of Maurice Barrès for example, loudly proclaimed that the fight for the collective Self allowed no compromises. The Self was totalitarian.[8]

The collective and total Self necessarily implied both a biological and a cultural identity. The two elements were linked, with the Other perceived as a threat to both. Quite characteristically, the official commentary to the Nuremberg Laws referred to the racial-biological effect of race mixing *and* to its "spiritual" or cultural consequences. Wilhelm Stuckart and Hans Globke wrote:

> "The addition of foreign blood to one's own brings about damaging changes in the racial body (*Volkskörper*), because the homogeneity, the instinctively certain will of a body is thereby weakened; in its stead, an uncertain, hesitating attitude appears in all decisive life situations, an overestimation of the intellect and a spiritual splitting. A blood mixture does not achieve a uniform fusion of the two races foreign to each other but leads in general to a disturbance in the spiritual equilibrium of the receiving part...."[9]

Stuckart and Globke were referring to that mysterious entity, to that core of the collective self which was both biology and culture, body and soul. They predicated this entity on racial criteria just as they predicated Otherness, particularly that of the Jew, on racial criteria. But, the exclusive character of the Self was accepted well beyond the confines of racial theory, as was the notion of the indefinable but absolute character of the Otherness of the Jew.

The integrity of the Self was both threatened by outside penetration and, at the same time, unable to benefit from the contribution of the Other. Thus Pierre Drieu La Rochelle, after rejecting the notion that Jews had contributed anything to French culture, insisted that even the most obvious exceptions were no proof to the contrary: "The value of these two half-Jews (Bergson and Proust)," he wrote in his diary, "...does not change any of this."[10]

How far from racial theory, but how firmly anchored this notion of the Jew as essential, fundamental Other could be, was perhaps best expressed by the most representative voice of the German "Conservative Revolution," Ernst Jünger. In his 1930 essay on "Total Mobilization," after having mentioned a number of Germans who, from being the carriers of the internationalist faith in Progress, had turned, in 1914, into staunch supporters of the national cause (every one of them Jews, although Jünger did not mention the fact) he turned to the case of Walter Rathenau. Jünger reminded his readers of Rathenau's central contribution to the war effort and of his call for a "mass insurrection" in reaction to the armistice conditions imposed by the Western powers, but then added: "How is it possible that soon after, he [Rathenau] could offer the well-known observation that world history would have lost its meaning had the Reich's representatives entered the capital as victors through the Brandenburg Gate? Here we see very clearly how the spirit of mobilization can dominate an individual's technical capacities, yet fail to penetrate his essence."[11] Rathenau's "essence," his otherness as Jew, was unveiled by his sudden change of attitude towards the national cause; superficially, he could adapt for a while to the spirit of national commitment, but no more. *Mutatis mutandis* this was true for Bergson and Proust as well: on the surface they could appear as creative contributors to French culture but the real value of their contribution was problematic. As Drieu put it: "about their positive value (*bienfaisance*) many questions remain."[12]

In summary, for the militant European Right, the penetration of the community by the Jew destabilized its essential biological and cultural harmony (Stuckart/Globke), whatever the Jew's apparent contribution to the community may have been (Drieu La Rochelle on Proust and Bergson; Jünger on Rathenau). Moreover, the Jew was a highly adaptable being who could succeed—up to a point—in fulfilling the role of French writer or philosopher, or that of German industrialist or politician, without being either really French or German. The frightening significance of this ability became clear if one considered that, be it in the case of Bergson and Proust or that of Rathenau (or for that matter Maximilian Harden, also mentioned by Jünger), these aliens were capable of reaching the *innermost core* of the culture or *the highest echelons* of influence and power.

The answer to our earlier question regarding the *peculiar nature* of the threatening otherness of the Jew thus becomes partly apparent. Whereas in general the Other's most threatening aspect seems to reside in an identifiable difference, the most ominous aspect of the Jewish threat appeared as related to sameness. The Jews' adaptability seemed to efface all boundaries and to subvert the possibilities of natural confrontation. The Jew was the *inner* enemy *par excellence*. It is this mimetic ability which, as we shall see, will open the way for the most extreme phantasms. At this stage. a general issue of this conference appears with some clarity: is otherness more threatening in its difference or is it more menacing in its sameness?

"They won't get us alive"

Nesta Webster, a popular English Catholic "historian" of the 1920s, abandoned her scholarly studies on the French Revolution as "the state of the world at the end of the Great War seemed to demand an inquiry into the present phase of the revolutionary movement...."[13] One inquiry led to another and her *World Revolution* was followed by *Secret Societies and Subversive Movements* which aimed at uncovering the deep origins of the contemporary upheavals.[14]

At first, Webster seemed to hesitate about the source of evil: "if one Power controls the rest it is either the Pan-German Power, the Jewish Power, or what we can only call Illuminism."[15] Then she moved towards the most plausible solution:

> "If then, one inner circle exists, composed of Illuminati animated by a purely destructive purpose, it is conceivable that they might find support in those Germans who desire to disintegrate the countries of the Allies with a view to future conquests, and in those Jews who hope to establish their empire on the ruins of Christian civilization—hence the superb organization and the immense financial resources at the disposal of the world revolutionaries. On the other hand it may be that the hidden center of direction consists in a circle of Jews located in the background of the Grand Orient, or perhaps, like the early nineteenth-century Illuminati, located nowhere, but working in accord and using both Pan-Germans and Gentile Illuminati as their tools."[16]

Here, in postwar Europe, the traditional anti-Jewish imagery of Christianity reappeared in full force, at the level of popular "history" of the Webster kind and, also in literary works of an entirely different calibre as we shall see further on. In other words the *völkisch* and Nazi representations of the Jewish threat were but part of a much larger discourse on "The Jewish Peril" (this was, incidentally, the title of the English edition of *The Protocols of the Elders of Zion*). Within this vast discourse the militant Christian Right constructed an imagery of Jewish world domination no less lurid than that of the Nazis.

Webster herself was not sure of the authenticity of the *Protocols* but left it "as an entirely open question."[17] About the wave of anti-Jewish feeling passing over postwar England, she wrote: "It has nothing in common with the racial hatred that inspires the "anti-Semitism" of Germany."[18] She nonetheless saw the Jewish danger as a mortal one:

> "If in a world where all patriotism, all national traditions, and all Christian virtues are being systematically destroyed by the doctrines of International Socialism, one race alone, a race that since time immemorial has cherished

the dream of world-power, is not only allowed but encouraged to consolidate itself, to maintain all its national traditions, and to fulfill all its national aspirations at the expense of other races, it is evident that Christian civilization must be eventually obliterated."[19]

The immediate threat which militant Christianity and wide sectors of conservative European society identified with the Jews was obviously that of communist revolution. The brothers Tharaud's horrifying description of Jewish rule in Hungary under Bela Kun's regime, *Quand Israël est Roi,* was published in France in 1922 and translated into English in 1924 from its *64th* French reprinting. Three years earlier Thomas Mann had discussed this aspect of the Jewish threat with Ernst Bertram:

> "We also spoke of that type of Russian Jew, the leader of the world revolutionary movement, an explosive mixture of Jewish intellectual radicalism and Slavic Christian enthusiasm. A world which retains any instinct of self-preservation must act against this sort of people with all the energy that can be mobilized and with the swiftness of martial law."[20]

As for Webster, she obviously had not missed this specific menace: "But now we come to the further question," she wrote in *World Revolution,* "who are the modern *Illuminati,* the authors of the Plot? What is their ultimate object in wishing to destroy civilization? What do they hope to gain by it? It is this apparent absence of motive, this seemingly aimless campaign of destruction carried on by the Bolsheviks of Russia, that has led many people to believe in the theory of a Jewish conspiracy to destroy Christianity...."[21]

But, beyond this immediate aspect of the Jewish conspiracy, part of the European Right and certainly its militant Catholic wing saw the Jewish threat in larger civilizational terms. Let us merely mention one of the most vituperative but also one of the most powerful representatives of the French anti-Jewish literary onslaught, Georges Bernanos, whose *La Grande Peur des Bien Pensants* (1931) was a torrential essay in praise of the most famous and most rabid of French antisemites, Edouard Drumont.[22]

For Bernanos and his peers, the values threatened by what they perceived as an ever-increasing Jewish domination were those of Christian civilization, of the nation as a living organic entity, and of an economy unfettered by the concentrated financial power of "les gros"—the "two hundred families" which both Right and Left identified with the Jews.[23] In other words, the Jewish threat was in part at least, that of *modernity.* The Jews were the forerunners, the masters and the avid preachers of the doctrine of Progress. To their French disciples, they were bringing

> a new mystique, admirably suited to that of Progress, that modern messianism which expects from man only the revelation of the future God.

> In this engineers' paradise, naked and smooth like a laboratory, the Jewish imagination was the only one able to produce these monstrous flowers.[24]

Bernanos' essay ends with the darkest forebodings. In its last lines the Jews are left unmentioned but the whole logic of the text links this apocalyptic ending to Drumont's lost fight against Jewry. The society which was being created before his eyes was a Godless one in which Bernanos felt unable to live: "There is no air!" Bernanos exclaimed... "But they won't get us... they won't get us alive!"[25]

And, for those skeptics who considered Jewish world domination as a mere slogan, Bernanos added some concreteness to the threat:

> "The heroic period of the Jewish conquest described by Drumont is over.... That war was but a child's play. One will witness something quite different when the tiny Jewish beast, after chewing up the American giant's head, will pounce on the Russian colossus, also emptied of its brains."[26]

One of the striking aspects of this second and more extreme set of representations of the Jew as threat is the wide acceptance in various segments of the interwar European Right of the notion of a Jewish conspiracy aiming at the destruction of Christianity and traditional European civilization. This wide acceptance underscores the fact that Nazi representations of the Jew thrust their roots into a deep and fertile soil which already nurtured a variety of weeds belonging to the same poisonous family. Such a shared repertory of images helps to explain the impact of Nazism on German Conservatives and, to a point, on sections of German Protestantism and Catholicism; it contributes to our assessment of the inroads made by Nazi antisemitism into wide spheres of European society and, finally, it cannot but point to some general reasons for the almost total passivity, indifference and partial cooperation in the events that were to come.

Let me return now to the question left previously open, that of threatening difference and threatening sameness. The leadership of the Jewish conspiracy is possibly nowhere, says Webster, which means nowhere to be seen; but, since times immemorial, the Jewish race has not changed either its traditions or its dreams of world power: the essence of Jewry is immutable. In other words, contrary to the rather touching Jewish devil which adorns the program of our conference and who, notwithstanding his horns, his wings and his Jewish nose, seems deeply bored by his "watch on the Seine," the demons of my text are the protean carriers of an evil essence. Thus, cannot we say that for those who feel menaced, Otherness appears as utterly threatening when what they perceive as the most extreme difference in essence and the complete sameness in appearance converge?

"The Night Side of History"

On January 11 and 13, 1939, German radio broadcast a two-part lecture by Walter Frank, the Head of the Reich Institute for the History of the New Germany on "German Science in its Struggle against World Jewry." After stressing that scientific research on the Jewish question could not be pursued in isolation but had to be integrated in the totality of national and world history Frank added:

> Jewry is one of the great negative principles of world history and thus can only be understood as a parasite within the opposing positive principle. As little as Judas Iscariot with his thirty silver coins and the rope with which he ultimately hung himself can be understood without the Lord whose community he sneeringly betrayed but whose face haunted him to his last hour—that night side of history called Jewry cannot be understood without its being positioned within the totality of the historical process, in which God and Satan, Creation and Destruction confront each other in an eternal struggle.[27]

Frank's display of religious imagery appears at first as one more utilization of the worst anti-Jewish themes of Christian tradition. His radio address which was aimed to reach hundreds of thousands of listeners at least, was possibly part of an ongoing effort by the regime to wipe out any remaining shame or sympathy for the victims of the November pogrom. But, no doubt involuntarily, Frank's rhetorical flight also introduced an element sharply dissonant with his own main argument that a global approach to the Jewish problem would solve it successfully. In Frank's last sentence, the

> "night side of history called Jewry" takes on an eternal dimension; this radical departure from Christian tradition is reinforced by what follows: "God and Satan, creation and destruction confront each other in an eternal struggle."

Unwittingly Frank's Manichean vision rekindles a fear which had already surfaced in early Nazi writings including *Mein Kampf:* that the struggle against Jewry was an eternal struggle, a vision from which intimations of defeat had never entirely disappeared.

Strangely enough, the same themes and the same fears appear in the militant Christian discourse. The concluding lines of Webster's book on conspiracy proclaims that

> "individual sects, or races fired with the desire for world domination [the Jews, S.F.] have provided the fighting forces of destruction, but behind them are the veritable powers of darkness in eternal conflict with the powers of light."[28]

Thus it seems that an undertone of pessimism suffuses the vision which the Radical Right has of its struggle against the Jew, a pessimism which gives a sense of desperate urgency to the ongoing campaign, an exacerbated shrillness to its tone and a craving for measures ever more draconian, more cruel and more deadly.

Frank's religious imagery in reference to the Jew is matched by the widespread use of biological metaphors in the non-Nazi discourse of the Radical Right, even if full-blown racial theories were not utilized. "The Jew," Drieu wrote in his diary on 13 October 1939, "must have a biological role in the organism of humanity. The role of a microbe or that of a white blood cell."[29] Webster regularly refers to the Jewish race and so does Hilaire Belloc. But it is Bernanos who crafted the more evocative image when, as we recall, he described "the tiny Jewish beast" devouring the brain of the American giant and ready to pounce on the Russian colossus, also voided of its brain. On the metaphorical level, the various trends of the Radical Right blend into each other.

This unified field of metaphorical representations of the Jew (including both Nazi and other extreme right wing representations) basically comprised, as has often been noticed, two distinct sets of terror inspiring images: the Jew as demon and the Jew as animal or pestilence. For me, it will be recalled, these images are but screens for other representations.

The Jew, as a force guided by a superhuman, Satanic principle, was the Enemy described by Dietrich Eckart in his "dialogue" with Hitler and obviously, time and again, by Hitler himself. It was the apocalyptic threat which Céline denounced in all possible ways in his *Bagatelles pour un Massacre* or, more succinctly, in interviews like the one given to *L'Intransigeant* in February 1938: "The situation?" Céline declared, "it is sinister... The worst is coming, the apocalypse.... The goys will pay for their criminal credulity.... They never see the broader picture in which their Hell is being prepared. Too bad!"[30]

Within this first category of representations the image of the Jew was a direct and extreme product of what Richard Hofstadter has described as the

> "paranoid style" in politics. True believers imagine dark forces and hidden plots and are convinced of the existence of "a vast and sinister conspiracy, a gigantic and yet subtle machinery of influence set in motion to undermine and destroy a way of life."[31]

These paranoid representations include history itself as a conspiracy "set in motion by demonic forces of almost transcendent power."[32] But is not the paranoid construct but a cover for some even more basic delusions? At a deeper level, does the conspiracy theme not carry an imagery of even more penetrating emotional resonance?

When, in his Reichstag speech of 30 January 1939, Hitler hurled his notorious threat of extermination against the Jews, he referred to the Jewish string-pullers and to the potential passivity of the European peoples (whom the Jews could drag into a general war) as if it were a matter of fact. Later commentators have not given much attention to the premise of Hitler's statement although it raises an immediate and unavoidable question: were the European peoples totally unaware of or unable to oppose such Jewish machinations? Were they unable to stave off a general war? The same impending danger was a constant leitmotif in the ranks of the radical right outside of Germany and the same question was left unanswered: why would the European nations be unable to resist the Jewish plots? Why would they be led passively to slaughter?

It seems that we are being presented with the image of a brainless and hypnotized mass of Europeans (and Americans) at the mercy of the Jewish conspiracy. It is the hypnotized Cesare pushed to murder by the evil Caligari, it is Bernanos' mass of Americans and Russians controlled by the Jewish monster which has devoured their brains, it is the hapless cattle slaughtered by sneering Jewish ritual slaughterers in the final scenes of Goebbels's *"The Eternal Jew."* The ritual slaughter sequence of the Nazi propaganda film is barely minutes away from the final sequence: Hitler's Reichstag speech of January 1939, his extermination threat, and the reference to the European nations pushed into the war by the Jews.

Should we close with this set of images at the highest political level of the regime? The highest intellectual level may offer representations no less extreme, but more astonishing given their source. In his 1938 work on Hobbes, *Der Leviathan in der Staatslehre des Thomas Hobbes,* Carl Schmitt described the deadly battle between the *Leviathan,* the great sea powers, and *Behemoth,* the great land powers, and then, turning a Jewish legend about messianic times into carnage and cannibalism, he added:

> the Jews stand apart and watch as the peoples of the world kill one another; for them this mutual "slaughter and carnage" *(Schächten und Schlachten)* is lawful and "Kosher." Thus they eat the flesh of the slaughtered peoples and live upon it.[33]

The other aspect to these images of mortal danger is not one of secret control but of asphyxiation and infection. "L'air manque!" Bernanos exclaimed. Europe will perish from the Jewish disease if no surgical steps are taken, Goebbels prophesied. Here the image is that of asphyxiation, of engulfment, of microbial penetration, of spreading pestilence. Along with the superhuman control, the subhuman threat is looming.

The image of microbial penetration, of spreading disease is closely related to that of teeming masses. In both cases the collective self is threatened by a chaotic, swarming, multitude of beings, be they germs, germ-carrying rats (as in "the Eternal Jew") or the subhumans so profusely described by Nazi propaganda. The mortal danger which these swarms represent is twofold: the infection they carry, and the overpowering and chaotic mass which they embody.

These representations of engulfment obsessed the European Right of the twenties and the thirties and were usually associated with the Jew: swarms of disease-ridden "Ashkenazes," in Giraudoux's words, crossing the French borders, swarms of *Ostjuden* penetrating into Germany, Bolshevik hordes driven westward by their Jewish commissars, an endless stream. The literature produced in the early 1920s by the postwar German *Freikorps,* those fighting squads of the Counter-Revolution who fought against the Bolsheviks in the Baltic countries, against the Poles in Silesia and against *Spartakus* at home, expresses other but related fears of engulfment. These "male fantasies," analyzed by Klaus Theweleit, show a pervasive fear of "the Woman" as the dreaded Other, of engulfment and being torn apart by certain kinds of women.[34] Whether or not we touch here some of the deepest layers of the "Fascist mind" may be questionable. But it is worth noting that in this Free Corps literature, in the writings of these men sometimes considered as the "Vanguard of Nazism," fantasies of the threatening woman often evoke the revolutionary female killer—the masses of revolutionary women blend into the revolutionary masses led by the Jew.

The image of superhuman control and conspiracy, or that of the engulfing masses, were elementary emotional triggers in the most extreme representations of the Jew as the threatening Other. But, as both sets of contrary representations were attributed to one and the same being and because the anti-Jewish discourse indistinctly presented the Jew as either one of these forces, in some sort of simultaneous two-pronged attack on humanity, one last step in our analysis appears to be necessary.

In a paraphrase of Alfred Rosenberg's representation of the Jew, Philippe Lacoue-Labarthe has foregrounded the Nazi ideologue's notion that the Jews were not the contrary of the Aryan type but "the very absence of type." "Hence their power...," Lacoue-Labarthe continues in his paraphrase,

> to insert themselves into every culture and State and then to live a life that is parasitic upon these, constantly threatening them with bastardization. All in all, the Jews are infinitely mimetic beings, or, in other words, the site of an *endless mimesis,* which is both interminable and inorganic, producing no art and achieving no appropriation....[35]

Many of the images of our texts seem to converge in this area of ongoing mimesis. They are the undistorted echo of past representations of the Jew as endlessly changing and endlessly the same, as the manifestation of an inorganic process, as the living dead, the ghostly wandering Jew or the ghostly inhabitant of the ghetto. Thus, the Jewish threat, having become formless and unrepresentable, leads to the most frightening phantasm of all, one in which images of the contemporary world supersede the representations of the past. The formless Jewish threat lurks everywhere; it penetrates everything; it is a pervasive but invisible carrier of death, like the Enemy, squatting in his trenches, like *gas* spreading over the battlefields of the Great War.

Notes

1. For a summary of the literature about the film and of the main aspects of its production and showing, see Itzhak Aren, Stig Hornshoj-Moller and Christoph B. Melchers, *"Der Ewige Jude." Wie Goebbels hetzte. Untersuchungen zum nationalsozialistischen Propagandafilm* (Aachen, 1990).

2. Elke Froehlich (ed.), *Die Tagebücher von Joseph Goebbels. Sämtliche Fragmente*, 4 vols. (Munich 1987), 3: 612.

3. Ibid.

4. Ibid., 619.

5. Ibid., 624.

6. Ibid., 628.

7. Norman Cohn, *Europe's Inner Demons. An Inquiry Inspired by the Great Witch-Hunt* (New York 1975).

8. David Carroll, *French Literary Fascism: Nationalism, Antisemitism and the Ideology of Culture* (Princeton 1995), 23.

9. Wilhelm Stuckart and Hans Globke, *Kommentare zur deutschen Rassengesetzgebung*, vol. 1 (Munich 1936).

10. Pierre Drieu La Rochelle, *Journal de guerre* (Paris 1992), 190.

11. Quoted in Richard Wolin, ed., *The Heidegger Controversy. A Critical Reader* (Cambridge Mass., 1993), 136.

12. Drieu, *Journal de Guerre*, 190.

13. Webster was recently rediscovered in an article by Jacob Heilbrunn on the sources of evangelist Pat Robertson's 1991 book, *The New World Order*; cf. *New York Review of Books*, 20 April 1995.

14. Nesta H. Webster, *Secret Societies and Subversive Movements* (New York 1924), v.

15. Ibid., 402.

16. Ibid., 403.

17. Ibid., 408.

18. Ibid., 401.

19. Ibid., 401.

20. Thomas Mann, *Tagebücher 1918–1921*, ed. Peter de Mendelsohn (Frankfurt 1979).

21. Nesta H. Webster, *World Revolution. The Plot against Civilization* (London 1921), 293.

22. Georges Bernanos, *La Grande Peur des Bien Pensants*, in *Essais et Ecrits*, vol. 1 (Paris 1971), 329.

23. Pierre Birnbaum, *Le peuple et les gros: Histoire d'un mythe* (Paris 1979).

24. Bernanos, *La Grande Peur*, 329.

25. Ibid., 350.

26. Ibid., 329.

27. Kurt Paetzold, ed., *Verfolgung Vertreibung, Vernichtung. Dokumente des faschistischen Antisemitismus 1933 bis 1942* (Frankfurt 1984), 212–13.

28. Webster, *Secret Societies*, 404–405.

29. Drieu, *Journal de Guerre*, 93.

30. Philippe Alméras, *Les idées de Céline*, 136.

31. Richard Hofstadter, *The Paranoid Style in American Politics and Other Essays* (Chicago 1979).

32. Ibid.

33. Carl Schmitt, *Der Leviathan* (Hamburg 1938), 18. For the translation, cf. Susan Shell, "Taking Evil Seriously: Schmitt's Concept of the Political and Strauss's 'True Politics,' " in *Leo Strauss: Political Philosopher and Jewish Thinker*, eds. Kenneth L. Deutsch and Walter Nicgorski (Lanham 1994), 183 n. 22.

34. Klaus Theweleit, *Male Fantasies*, 2 vols. (Minneapolis 1987–89).

35. Quoted in Carroll, *French Literary Fascism*, 285 (from Philippe Lacoue-Labarthe, *Heidegger, Art and Politics: the Fiction of the Political* [Cambridge 1990], 96).

14

Nazi Antisemitism: Animalization and Demonization

Philippe Burrin
Graduate Institute of International Studies, Geneva

History has known many cases of minority groups defined as "others" by majority groups and becoming as a result the targets of discriminatory policies. But very rare are the cases, at least in the modern period, when a minority group has been represented as being, at one and the same time, both so radically different and so threatening that it became the object of an implacable extermination. Such was the monstrous peculiarity of Nazi antisemitism, with Auschwitz its outcome and culmination.

On the eve of the Great War, various strands of antisemitism coexisted in imperial Germany, differing in sources, motives, and intensity, but all fueling defiance and hostility toward Jews. Christian anti-Judaism persisted alongside new forms of prejudice which had been developed in the wake of, and in reaction to Jewish emancipation—socioeconomic, political, and most notably racial antisemitism. Under one guise or another, all these currents contributed to making antisemitism a "cultural code" that informed the self-understanding of many Germans, mostly on the right of the political spectrum.[1] But, even though prejudice and hostility toward Jews were growing, particularly in the social sphere,[2] there is reason to doubt that the situation in Germany was very different from that in France during the same period.[3] The main difference lay in that countervailing forces may have been weaker in Germany—after all, the Dreyfus affair in France ended up with the rehabilitation of the Jewish captain.

As it was, pre-1914 antisemitism certainly played a crucial role in influencing the course of German history in the next decades. Nonetheless, it is difficult to speak in terms of simple continuity or even of a radicalization of previous tendencies. As has already been observed, a multilayered antisemitism was accompanied by rather timid (compared to what would happen later) propositions destined to solve the so-called "Jewish

Question." With a few exceptions, there was a definite reticence to go back on Jewish emancipation; the alternative of assimilation was at least left open by most antisemites.[4] The Jews were certainly seen by many as "others," and even as dangerous "others." But their alterity was not yet systematically defined in radical terms, and the threat they were said to embody remained identified in rather general terms with modernity. Moreover, it was still relativised by the liberal tinge of the pre-1914 period as well as by a feeling of optimism about the place of Germany in the world.[5]

It was the experience of the First World War and the trauma of defeat that ushered in a new configuration, of which Hitler became, in a few years, the most forceful and successful standard-bearer.[6] Ideologically, three elements combined to make Nazism a new phenomenon: a discourse alternating or mixing pseudo-religious and pseudo-biological themes, with the attendant elimination of any remnant of humanism and liberalism; a conception of politics derived from the war experience and inspired by archaic warfare; a mental universe in which a besieged fortress mentality combined with megalomaniac ambitions[7] to steel a fanatical resolve to triumph or die (*Sieg oder Untergang*[8]).

I

In Nazi antisemitism, two main heterogeneous discourses coexisted, but they both had the effect of dehumanizing the Jews and representing them as an existential threat. The first discourse followed pseudobiological lines, and racism was at its core. For the racist, the human world is divided into races as distinctive from each other as different animal species, and the races are locked into a permanent struggle for life, hierarchised according to their achievements: at one end, the Aryan race, bearer of every great civilization, and at the other end, the inferior races, with Jews at the bottom. Racial identity and hierarchy rest on the value of the "blood," which according to Nazi ideology is a mysterious and sacred substance, functioning as a kind of surrogate to the *Geist* (spirit) in earlier bourgeois thought.[9] Accordingly, even a great race can disappear if its purity of blood is not preserved. To rise again from its decadence and conquer the territory it needed, its vital space, the German race had to purge itself of all its racial weaknesses and foreign admixtures, and to increase its biological substance.

In the 1920s, Hitler hammered out the dangers of abortion, of venereal and hereditary diseases, of Malthusianism, pleading tirelessly for purer blood and demographic expansion. His speeches and articles propagated an extraordinarily crude pseudo-biological discourse (articulated in terms of supposed "eternal laws of nature") which was in fact a Social-Darwinist invocation of the right of the strongest, extending zoological notions into the social and political sphere. It is not surprising that such a vision would be stripped of every consideration of traditional decency and morality. In 1928, Hitler declared that the births of all the children killed through abortion would have been of positive value to Germany, even if, at the same time, one killed the German adults deemed incapable of living without medical assistance.[10] This murderous proposition, expressed in a most matter-of-fact way, was logical enough in the framework of a holistic conception which valued the race, not the individual. Could one then expect that somebody ready to kill in cold blood people of his own nation would refrain from murdering an "inferior race"—one, moreover, that was assumed to be the embodiment of a vital threat?

Intellectually, antisemitism seemed to be a subordinate element of Nazi racism—but an element no less central for that, and acutely felt on an emotional plane. In fact, the fight against "racially inferior" elements of the German race, or against "inferior races" like Gypsies and Slavs, would never evoke as passionate a hatred as did the struggle against the Jews. There is little doubt that Jews had a privileged diabolical status in Nazi eyes: they were the anti-type, the negative image of everything the Nazis stood for, with one exception: their alleged purity of blood could serve as a model because of their supposed absolute refusal of miscegenation. The opposition between Aryans and Jews, a nineteenth-century addition to antisemitic tradition, was elevated into an essential dualism, the positive against the negative principle. In contrast to Aryans, the Jews were a race defined as inherently destructive. They were incapable of creating a state or a culture of their own; they could only exploit the other races—it was their way to carry on the struggle for survival. In short, they were, as Alfred Rosenberg liked to say, a "counter-race"[11]: to the Nazis, the notion of race had positive qualities, of which the Jews were totally devoid.

The Nazi discourse, though it sometimes depicted the Jews as the "enemy race" and at other times as a catch-all phrase for lumping together all their political adversaries, had on the whole a remarkable consistency. The Nazis liked to speak of *the Jew*, referring to a type and subsuming under a uniform identity every individual whom they could define as a member of the Jewish race. Hence, there was no need to aim criticisms specifically at *Ostjuden*, although reactions and resentments toward them among the German population could be conveniently exploited.[12] Assimilated Jews appeared especially dangerous to them for being so similar. In the Nazi scheme of things, the Jews no longer had a place of refuge. They were deprived of the option of assimilation opened by emancipation in the nineteenth century, even if they abandoned their identity and relegated Judaism to the sphere of a private religion. They could not even go back to the status of pariahs as in medieval Europe, when their presence had been tolerated, however precariously, because it could be religiously legitimated.

The Jews had become radical "others" and nothing showed this more powerfully than their symbolic expulsion from the human species, the logical result of a massive pseudo-biological metaphorization. At the end of the nineteenth century, antisemites had already denounced the Jews for the *Zersetzung*—the process of decay that their supposedly critical minds and their intellectualism had been fostering against all received authority.[13] But now, even if that old indictment, along with many others, was still in use, the mainstream of Nazi discourse was heading elsewhere: it was in the process of relegating Jews to the animal kingdom.

Two types of metaphor are particularly noticeable here. First, the recurrent image of the parasite, already in circulation in the nineteenth century but never as widespread as after the First World War, was now employed by the Nazis in a literal way. Henceforth, the vocabulary of parasitology was no longer merely metaphorical but used to assert the identity in a naturalistic way: namely the Jew *is* a parasite.[14] Second, they turned to the even more expressive (and certainly more important for its dehumanizing effect) image of the Jews as carriers of infection, germs, bacillus, microbes, etc., which attack the organism and poison it *(verderben, vergiften)*. The association had been made already in the Middle Ages when the Jews were accused of poisoning sources of water, or spreading plagues. But it was now taking on a much more powerful role, commensurate with the medicalization and hygienization of the world in the twentieth century.

Antisemitic theories about Jews as the source of intellectual decomposition or accusations of parasitism were bad enough, but they did not have the same resonance and symbolic potency as the notion of biological infection associated with the Jews. This was especially threatening when the metaphor of infection was applied to sexuality. The *sexualization* of antisemitic discourse was particularly strong in Nazi propaganda, best illustrated by the oft-quoted passage of *Mein Kampf* where Hitler describes a young Jew satanically spying on an innocent young German girl and setting out to seduce her.[15]

The "pornographic" label usually given to passages of this kind, and even more to the propaganda of Julius Streicher and his *Stürmer*,[16] fails to grasp the power of such images which were so closely and intensely connected to the obsession with the purity of blood. They created a peculiarly aberrant but symbolically resonant representation. According to the Nazis, the Jews had the capacity to permanently poison the blood of German women with whom they once had intercourse; as a result of a sort of genetic impregnation, those women would henceforward transmit Jewish hereditary characteristics even to children conceived by German fathers. The racist author, Arthur Dinter, had placed that absurd idea at the center of a novel (*Die Sünde wider das Blut*, 1918) which became an immediate best-seller and was intended as a warning against a corruption of blood which would last "for ever." Nazi leaders, beginning with Hitler and Streicher, eagerly and obstinately followed suit.[17] *Der Stürmer,* in particular, made a specialty of fanning fears of contamination and of playing on sensitive spots in the human psyche, when it accused Jews of abducting German children for ritual murder purposes or exploiting German girls for prostitution abroad. But nothing was more likely than the image of blood contamination to evoke the idea of some invisible, pervasive, and far-reaching threat, one which called for measures of removal if not eradication.

Many scholars have stressed the dehumanizing effect and the murderous potentiality of the animalization of Jews by the Nazis through their pseudo-biological ideology.[18] But it is at least as important to underline the peculiarities of the type of animalization they selected in their discourse. Whether intentionally or not, they equated the Jews with organisms like parasites and bacilli, which are among the least anthropomorphous in the animal kingdom and which, moreover, belong to the ordinary *Lebenswelt* of domesticity. In that way antisemitism became all the more dangerous since it obliterated the human face of the victims and tied itself to standard values of hygiene and cleanliness. The French revolutionaries had gone down the road toward regicide, on the mental level, through a process of comparing and then identifying Louis XVI with a pig.[19] The Nazi discourse could even erase the disturbing image of bloody violence such as that attached to the death of a pig by appropriating for their own purpose references to the world of pest control, household cleaning, and medical care.

II

Though Nazi discourse functioned primarily in a pseudo-biological key, it also borrowed form the Christian tradition, with Satan as its central figure.[20] The demonization of Jews could only reinforce their "otherness"—microbe or devil, they were in both cases outside humanity—but more importantly, it elevated to dramatic heights the threat they were supposed to constitute. The destructiveness of the Jew was represented as stemming not only from biological determinism, but also from a free and malicious will to exterminate.

The Nazis in their satanic representation of the Jews relied on strong echoes from Christian demonology.[21] First, every move and action from the Jewish side was seen as the fruit of long-term calculation and premeditation—the "eternal Jew" acted systematically, according to a standard Nazi formulation. The racial miscegenation in which the Jews were shamelessly indulging was not to be attributed, for example, to a quest for assimilation, but to a systematic plan of blood poisoning; it had nothing to do with the impulse of lust, but was "the effluence of satanical plotting and calculation."[22] As Dinter had stressed in his novel: "The German people has been polluted and poisoned systematically."[23] Moreover, the Jews hid behind masks and masqueraded in various roles, some of which could seem quite contradictory, for example, those of capitalists and revolutionaries; but in reality, underneath the appearance of division, they worked together to sap the autonomy of Aryan nations and to destroy their purity of blood. Their chosen methods were dissimulation, seduction, and temptation: lying was their natural element and their favorite weapon. Last, but not least, they sneered at their adversaries and made fun of them whenever they succumbed to their deceitfulness. As Hitler put it in 1928, Germans should join forces rather than persist in divisions which are only "in the interest of a third party: the eternally jubilating Jew."[24] The image of the Jew as a laughing devil was eminently suitable for arousing the murderous hate burning in the minds of fanatical and violent people.

The Jews were presented as operating in a mode which accorded with their satanic nature. They were a world power, an occult force, and exhibited an exterminatory will. The first two elements are well-known, stemming directly from the *Protocols of the Elders of Zion,* that tsarist forgery which became highly popular in Germany after 1918 and spread the idea of a Jewish conspiracy for world domination.[25] But the image of the *exterminatory* power needs to be singled out. The eternal damnation which was the punishment in Christian theology for those who succumbed to Satan's temptation was now replaced by racial and physical annihilation. As in their pseudo-biological representations, the Nazis were keen to see themselves in a kind of "elected" relationship with the Jews: they embodied the principle of good against the principle of evil. Accordingly, they fostered the vision of a Jewish enterprise of annihilation directed primarly against the German race, long before they had themselves acceded to power. Their vision of the deadly enmity of the Jews toward Germany was summed up in 1938 by Himmler when he declared that the Jews "want to destroy us" *(uns zu vernichten).*[26] *"Vernichten":* this was the motivation and the objective of the Jews, according to Hitler, Himmler, and the Nazi leadership. The Jews were aggressors who had passed a death sentence on the German Volk. This worldview, monstrously distorted though it may appear to us, allowed the Nazis to claim that they were acting out of *self-defense* against what was perceived as a threat of annihilation.

The Nazis had a narrative of sorts to justify their asserted victimization. To explain their defeat in World War I, they pretended that international Jewry had fomented a global coalition against Germany (while their "racial brothers" inside the country were of course conspiring to stab in the back the undefeated German army). The Jewish objective was to annihilate the vital forces of the German people, and of the Aryan race in general, by making it spill its best blood on the battlefield. That image of premeditated bleeding was at least as strong and emotionally mobilizing as the image of Jews who were allegedly corrupting and poisoning the German blood. No wonder that Nazi propaganda hammered out the theme: "Globally the extermination plan intended to implicate the Germans as the most prominent representatives of the German race in an extensive war. The war of 1914–1918 was a death sentence pronounced on Germany by world Jewry."[27]

After the German defeat of 1918, the Jews had relentlessly prolonged their assault and succeeded in destroying the old regime, opening the way to the further dislocations jointly operated by Marxism and international capitalism. The Nazis had not the slightest doubt that the First World War had allowed Jews to make great strides in their enterprise of domination because it had brought about the collapse of the Central European land empires, the Bolshevization of Russia, the spread of democracy and Marxism, and not least, the penetration of Western financial capitalism. As a result, Germany was now in the forefront of the struggle, with the Nazis representing themselves as the last stronghold which could still prevent a total victory of the Jews. Their Germanocentric vision could therefore take on overtones of a universal mission. In the early 1920s Hitler would sometimes utilize "internationalist" slogans like: "Antisemites of all countries, unite!"[28]

In this narrative of crisis, three aspects must be underlined. First, the sense of living at a decisive moment, the culminating point of the age-old struggle between Aryans and Jews which had now to be decided once and for all. The time of reckoning had come: it could only be "Either-Or."[29] "Either the Jew annihilates us or we neutralize him. No other issue can be imagined."[30] This belief engendered an atmosphere of the Last Judgment which drew inspiration from a characteristically German apocalyptic tradition reaching back to the Romantic period. It was a mood that had made a potent resurgence at the beginning of the First World War.[31] Among the Nazi leaders, Goebbels was particularly prone to express himself in apocalyptic terms, but the tendency was pervasive.[32] It was attested to in the frequent and quasi-fetishistic use of the word "end," either in expressions (*Das Letzte*[33]), or as a prefix *(Endkampf, Endsieg)* climaxing in the "Final Solution" *(Endlösung)*.

Second, the representation of the final struggle was cast in bellicose terms which revealed just how traumatic the Great War had been for the Nazi leaders, and how decisive were its ideological and psychological legacies. In the mental world of these men, the defeat was a lost battle, but by no means the end of the war. Their mission was to put Germany back on its feet and to equip her for conquering the vital space she needed, without repeating past mistakes, most notably the formation of an opposed world coalition. The Jews, anyway, were waging their war against Germany, a silent but deadly war. In Hitler's words, the open war had been replaced after November 1918 by "a war of slow extermination of our people."[34] He would himself never tire of declaring that in a future armed conflict there would be no new armistice nor a new revolution. But, more importantly, he had a quite distinctive understanding of war: his conception was essentially that of an archaic warfare which knew no moral and humanitarian restraints, which demanded an eye for an eye, blood for blood. "Aug um Aug und Zahn um Zahn" was, in Hitler's approving words, "the most primitive conception of law."[35] Needless to say, primitive here had a positive meaning.

Nazi propaganda offered many instances of death wishes concerning the Jews, usually without specifying practical measures. Such was the case with the image of the knife plunged into the heart of the enemy at the most opportune moment.[36] The death-wish was so pervasive that it came out even when Nazi leaders evoked the possible final victory of the Jews, or an apparently nonviolent solution to the "Jewish Question" such as their concentration in a faraway reservation. Being a race of parasites, how could the Jews survive in the absence of the people they were exploiting? In 1934 *Der Stürmer* put forward the idea of transporting all Jews to Madagascar and interning them in a camp "until they would have destroyed and eaten up one another."[37] Very frequently, expressions of vengeance assumed a prophetic tone.[38] This last feature was spectacularly evident when Hitler declared before the Reichstag in January 1939 that he wanted to be a "prophet": if the Jews ever instigated a new world war, they would be exterminated. One looks in vain for another example in modern history of a chief of state using a public tribune to send a warning to a phantom interlocutor, promising terrible vengeance in case some events happened which were totally outside the control of his intended victim.

Nonetheless, it has to be borne in mind that the Nazi leaders, particularly Hitler, also operated on another more political level which sometimes conflicted with their apocalyptic and vengeful perception of the Jews. Hitler, after all, was not only a "prophet," but also a *"Realpolitiker"*: his grasp of political reality allowed him, in fact, to fare much better than the numerous other *völkisch* prophets and right-wing leaders of his time. To be a "prophet" and a "politician" at the same time was no easy task. Regarding the Jews, Hitler the "prophet" thought in terms of the ultimate struggle and final elimination. However, the "politician" in him was inclined not only to use tactical restraint in the interest of his primordial objective (the attainment of hegemony over Europe) but even to view with some flexibility, though a very limited one, the actual threat of the Jewish arch-enemy and the punishment due, whether it be expulsion, isolation, or extermination.

It seems therefore unwarranted to conclude from a purely ideological analysis that an event like the Holocaust was predetermined by the murderous potential of the Nazi discourse. One should rather say that the road to Auschwitz could indeed only be "twisted" [Schleunes] as long as Hitler operated in a situation where he could still maneuver and draw nearer to his goal without being involved in a world war. In that respect, it is significant that his perception of the Jewish world threat between 1939 and 1941 evolved in a direct relation to the amelioration or deterioration of his — perceived strategic position.[39]

We can see at the level of practical anti-Jewish policy the friction which was produced by the interaction of prophecy and politics. We find a mental world of deadly struggle with its attendant death-fantasies projected against Jewry, and on the other hand, the inclination for calculation and realism. In that regard, it is of the greatest import that the Nazi leaders came to express very early on the idea that the Jews in Germany should be treated as hostages: a representation which joined together the image of a *Weltfeind* (the idea was to apply pressure on "international Jewry" by menacing their racial brothers), the conception of a *Kampf* in its archaic version of reprisals according to the *lex talionis,* and a flexible political approach.[40] After 1933, the idea of Jews as hostages or pawns emerged again and again. Hitler continuously oscillated between the desire to have them leave Germany as soon as possible, even if they had to go to Palestine, and the wish to keep them close at hand for pressure and retribution purposes. After 1938, he tried to obtain some other form of control over "international Jewry" by attempting to internationalize the "Jewish Question" and rally European states around the idea of concentrating Jews in a far-distant reservation. Only in 1941 did he resolve to exterminate them.

Whatever the precise date of that decision, it is sufficient for our purpose to stress here the context which surrounded the full-scale carrying out of the genocide. From the moment that the Russian campaign became a war of attrition and that the United States entered the fray, the room for diplomatic maneuver narrowed dramatically to the point of disappearance. Everything was therefore dependent on a military success which could only be had, if at all, at the price of a protracted effort and a substantial bleeding of Germany. The "politician" no longer had much of a role and the scene was now free for the "prophet" who could give himself over to the dark fantasies of the *Sieg oder Untergang* mentality.

Here we can grasp the consequences of the Nazi vision of the Jews as the world enemy. From the start, Jews symbolized many things the Nazis wanted to destroy in Germany in order to achieve the resurrection of their country. At the same time the Jews embodied the obstacles in the outside world that stood in the way of Nazi expansionist dreams. Hence, the fateful novelty of Nazi ideology resided in the fusion of a consistent racial antisemitism and of an expansionist drive going far beyond what had existed before in German history. This combination carried with it from the start the high probability of a new general conflict, one which was bound to result in the victimization of a minority group, the Jews, who had already been for several years the object of the dehumanizing propaganda of the regime.

The two discourses we have emphasized in Nazi antisemitism, the pseudo-biological and the pseudo-religious, with their attendant consequences—the animalization and the demonization of the Jews—were fundamentally heterogeneous. But they coexisted nonetheless, mapping out the mental landscape of the Nazis and bringing about a symptomatic oscillation between contempt and fear. Animalization made it possible to think of easily disposing of the Jews—for example, in the discussions at the Wannsee conference, the killing of millions of people was not expected to produce difficulties. On the other hand, there was the image of a demonic Jewish power against which one would have to muster one's last resources and energies in order to resist and triumph over it.

How can we explain that such heterogeneous discourses ended up by joining forces and facilitating the implementation of genocide? In the context of 1941, the two discourses ultimately adjusted to each other in an implacable way. The Jews within Hitler's grasp were killed like a pest, but their death was inscribed within the framework of all-out struggle with the satanic power of world Jewry, who had succeeded in enlarging the war and was therefore menacing Germans with annihilation. Toward the end of 1941 when the machinery of extermination was gathering speed, Hitler referred several times in private talks with his entourage to the extermination, using a double level of language which perfectly reflects the dual symbolic dimension of the genocide.

On the one hand, he used various kinds of justifications for the killing, all of which postulated the inhuman nature of the Jews and so could help to repress guilt feelings. Some justifications were drawn from the Social Darwinist conception of the struggle for existence and the right of the strongest (should the cat feel guilty for eating the mouse?). Others were taken from the well-equipped stock of animal metaphors (the Jews were bacilli which the body rejected in a healthy reaction of self-defense).[41] At some point, speaking about the actual process of extermination, Hitler used a surgical image which deserves to be quoted:

> You must act quickly; it does not help to extract a tooth by a few centimeters every three months—when it is extracted the pain goes away.[42]

There is no need to emphasize this remarkable reversal of victimization. Hitler evoked the (inexplicable) pain that Germany or German Europe was going to feel when the European Jews would be pulled out from its midst. But the several millions of human beings whose death was in fact talked about were allotted the cold numbness and miniscule concreteness of a tooth.

On the other hand, Hitler also linked the extermination to the hardening struggle with "international Jewry," his demonized enemy. He recalled several times, even in public speeches during 1942, his "prophecy" of January 1939, and on one occasion quoted his favorite proverb:

For the first time the others will not be the only ones to lose their blood, but for the first time the authentically ancient Jewish rule will apply: "eye for eye, tooth for tooth!"[43]

Hitler was fully committed to the logic of a racial war: he was trying to weaken "the Jew" by spilling his precious blood in order to make him expiate the German blood spilled on the battlefield. In recalling his prophecy, he was talking to his enemy, as if he felt the compulsion to let it be known, through a veiled message, what it cost to put obstacles in his way. But in so doing, he was expressing his frustrated anger at a power he could only partially deflect, but which could well, on the other hand, destroy him. The satanic nature of the Jews was definitely confirmed: it was Satan, the laughing devil, that Hitler wanted to reach by killing like a pest the Jews within his grasp.

Notes

1. In this passage I follow largely the convincing case made by Shulamit Volkov; cf. her article "Antisemitismus als kultureller Code," in *Jüdisches Leben und Antisemitismus im 19. und 20. Jahrhundert* (Munich: C. H. Beck, 1990), 13–36.

2. See Werner Jochman, "Antisemitismus im Deutschen Kaiserreich," in *Gesellschaftskrise und Judenfeindschaft in Deutschland 1870–1945* (Hamburg: Hans Christians Verlag, 1988), 30–98.

3. Cf. Stephen Wilson, *Ideology and Experience. Antisemitism in France at the Time of the Dreyfus Affair* (London and Toronto: Associated University Press, 1982).

4. See Shulamit Volkov, "Das geschriebene und das gesprochene Wort. Über Kontinuität und Diskontinuität im deutschen Antisemitismus," in *Jüdisches Leben und Antisemitismus,* 54–75.

5. See, e.g., Geoffrey G. Field, *Evangelist of Race: The Germanic Vision of Houston Stewart Chamberlain* (New York: Columbia U Press, 1982).

6. Cf. Jochmann, "Die Ausbreitung des Antisemitismus in Deutschland, 1914–1923," in idem, *Gesellschaftskrise und Judenfeindschaft,* 99–170; Saul Friedländer, "Die politischen Veränderungen der Kriegszeit und ihre Auswirkungen auf die Judenfrage," in Werner E. Mosse, ed., *Deutsches Judentum in Krieg und Revolution 1916–1923* (Tübingen: J. C. B. Mohr, 1971), 27–66.

7. Victor Klemperer has noted the presence in Hitler's speeches of Caesarian megalomania and a persecution complex; cf. *LTI* (Leipzig: Reclam, 1966), 71.

8. For the background, cf. Hartmut Zelinsky, *Sieg oder Untergang, Sieg und Untergang: Kaiser Wilhelm II., die Werk-Idee Richard Wagners und der "Weltkampf"* (Munich: Keyser, 1990).

9. Klaus Vondung, *Die Apokalypse in Deutschland* (Munich: Deutscher Taschenbuch Verlag, 1988), 208.

10. *Hitler. Reden, Schriften, Anordnungen. Februar 1925 bis Januar 1933* (Munich: K. G. Saur, 1994), vol. 3.

11. Cf. Fritz Nova, *Alfred Rosenberg, Nazi Theorist of the Holocaust* (New York: Hippocrene Books, 1986).

12. Cf. Trude Maurer, *Ostjuden in Deutschland, 1918–1933* (Hamburg: Hans Christians Verlag, 1986).

13. Cf. Renate Schäfer, "Zur Geschichte des Wortes 'Zersetzen,'" *Zeitschrift für deutsche Wortforschung* 1/2 (1962): 40–80.

14. Alex Bein, "'Der jüdische Parasit.' Bemerkungen zur Semantik der Judenfrage," *Vierteljahrshefte für Zeitgeschichte* 2 (April 1965): 130.

15. Adolf Hitler, *Mein Kampf* (Boston: Houghton Mifflin, 1943), 325.

16. Cf. Randall L. Bytwerk, *Julius Streicher* (New York: Dorset Press, 1983).

17. Cf. Fritz Fink, *Die Judenfrage im Unterricht* (Nuremberg: Der Stürmer, 1937), 43–44.

18. Notably Eberhard Jäckel, *Hitler's Weltanschauung: A Blueprint for Power* (Cambridge, MA: Harvard U Press, 1989).

19. Antoine de Baecque, *Le corps de l'histoire. Métaphores et politique (1770–1800)* (Paris: Calmann-Lévy, 1993), 85 sq.

20. On the relationship between Nazism and Christianity, cf. Uriel Tal, "On Structures of Political Theology and Myth in Germany Prior to the Holocaust," in Yehuda Bauer and Nathan Rotenstreich, eds., *The Holocaust as Historical Experience* (New York: Holmes and Meier, 1981), 43–74; see also Michael Ley's approach in terms of the sociology of religion, *Genozid und Heilserwartung. Zum nationalsozialistischen Mord am europäischen Judentum* (Vienna: Picus Verlag, 1993).

21. For the medieval background, see Joshua Trachtenberg, *The Devil and the Jews* (New Haven, CT: Yale U Press, 1943); Joel Carmichael's book, *The Satanizing of the Jews. Origin and Development of Mystical Anti-Semitism* (New York: Fromm, 1992) is unfortunately, not of much help.

22. Fink, *Die Judenfrage im Unterricht,* 44.

23. Bein, "Der jüdische Parasit," 132.

24. *Hitler. Reden, Schriften, Anordnungen,* vol. III/1, Juli 1928–Februar 1929, doc. 13, 31 August 1928, 43.

25. Norman Cohn, *Warrant for Genocide: The Myth of the Jewish World-Conspiracy and the Protocols of the Elders of Zion* (New York: Harper, 1969).

26. Bradley F. Smith and Agnes F. Peterson, eds., *Heinrich Himmler. Geheimreden 1933 bis 1945* (Frankfort am M.:1974), 58.

27. "Das Heer der Welt. Enthüllung der jüdischen Weltverschwörung gegen das deutsche Volk," *Der Stürmer,* 52 (1934), reproduced in *Was soll mit den Juden geschehen?,* 48–49.

28. Adolf Hitler, *Sämtliche Aufzeichnungen 1905–1924,* eds. Eberhard Jäckel and A. Kuhn, (Stuttgart: Deutsche Verlags-Anstalt, 1980), 138, 148, 153.

29. Robert Wistrich, *Hitler's Apocalypse. Jews and the Nazi Legacy* (London: Weidenfeld and Nicolson, 1985), 27 sq.

30. Joseph Paul Goebbels, in his novel *Michael,* cited by Nicolaus Sombart, *Die deutschen Männer und ihre Feinde. Carl Schmitt—ein deutsches Schicksal zwischen Männerbund und Matriarchatsmythos* (Munich: Carl Hanser Verlag, 1991), 280.

31. Cf. Vondung, *Apokalypse in Deutschland.*

32. Cf. Claus-Ekkehard Bärsch, *Erlösung und Vernichtung. Dr. phil. Joseph Goebbels. Zur Psyche und Ideologie eines jungen Nationalsozialisten 1923–1927* (Munich: Kalus Boer Verlag, 1987).

33. See Vondung, *Apokalypse in Deutschland,* 485 sq.

34. *Hitler. Reden, Schriften, Anordnungen,* vol. 3:1, Juli 1928–Februar 1929, doc. 45, 9 November 1928, 22.

35. *Hitler. Reden, Schriften, Anordnungen,* vol. 3:1, Juli 1928–Februar 1929, doc. 45, 9 November 1928, 226.

36. Cf. the well-known passage in Hitler's speech of 29 April 1937 in *"Es spricht der Führer." Sieben exemplarische Hitler-Reden,* eds. Hildegard von Klotze and Helmut Krausnick (Gütersloh: Sigbert Mohn Verlag, 1966), 148. Goebbels used the same expression, *Lenin oder Hitler,* 31, cited by Bärsch, *Erlösung und Vernichtung,* 135.

37. *Der Stürmer,* no. 4 (1934), quoted in *Was soll mit den Juden geschehen?,* 31. Hitler expressed the same idea on several occasions, *Adolf Hitler. Monologe im Führerhauptquartier 1941–1944,* ed. W. Jochmann [Hamburg: Albrecht Kraus Verlag, 1980], 130).

38. For Goebbels, see Ulrich Höver, *Joseph Goebbels—ein nationaler Sozialist* (Bonn: Bouvier, 1992), 173 sq.

39. Cf. Burrin, *Hitler and the Jews. The Genesis of the Holocaust* (London: Edward Arnold, 1994), 79–80.

40. Cf. Herbert A Strauss, "Hostages of 'World Jewry': On the Origin of the Idea of Genocide in German History," *Holocaust and Genocide Studies* 3 (1988): 125–36.

41. *Monologe im Führerhauptquartier,* 1–2 December 1941, 148.

42. Ibid., 25 January 1942, 228–29.

43. Adolf Hitler, "Rede im Sportpalast 30. Januar 1942 in Berlin," in *Der großdeutsche Freiheitskampf,* vol. 3 (Munich: Franz Eher Verlag, 1943), 197.

15

When the Demon Itself Complains
of Being Demonized

Simon Epstein
The Hebrew University of Jerusalem

In the face of a wave of antisemitism, the Jews and their liberal allies generally employ an extensive arsenal of polemics. Some of their arguments appeal to logic. Antisemitic literary efforts are analyzed and their historic and scientific falsehood is demonstrated. The Jewish contribution to civilization and progress is also highlighted. Other arguments, appealing to compassion, evoke the past misfortunes of the Jewish people.[1] Yet other themes take the offensive, attacking both the persons and the political ideas of the antisemites. They stress that antisemitism is a danger for society as a whole (for the nation, for democracy, for one social class or another) and not only for the Jews. All these elements can be found, in one form or another, in any Jewish defense system of the modern age, from the late nineteenth century down to the present day.

These counter-campaigns are often concealed by Jewish historiography for both ideological and technical reasons which we cannot deal with in this forum. However they are not unknown to the antisemites, who must brave the fire of an often skillful and massive counter-propaganda. They cannot remain indifferent to the profusion of articles and interventions which portray them in unflattering terms, and which may well tarnish their image and block their progress in public opinion.

Thus they use different types of responses, which could be qualified as "second-strike" responses, since their aim is to neutralize the Jewish protests. Some of these responses are aggressive; they accuse their liberal opponents of having been corrupted by Jewish money and of being manipulated by Jewish power.[2] However, we very frequently also find *defensive and apologetic arguments*. These endeavor to temper the virulence of the anti-Jewish message, to claim that the antisemites merely seek to protect society from an excessive Jewish influence and that they have no intention of persecuting the

Jews. In this light, the antisemites present themselves as innocent victims of a hostile campaign which seeks to distort their words or actions. By presenting their point of view from an acceptable and moderate angle, they are set on showing that they are slandered and not slanderers, persecuted and not persecutors. They complain of being demonized.[3]

Each anti-Jewish wave, whatever its intensity and whatever its developments, gives rise to Jewish protests. These protests, in turn, oblige the antisemites to vindicate and explain themselves before public opinion in their respective countries or before international opinion. There are many examples, but I have chosen in the limited framework of this exposé, to confine myself to a single country (Germany) and to a single period (the last years of the Weimar Republic).

Adolf Hitler and the Condemnation of Anti-Jewish Violence (1930)

Throughout the 1920s there were a dozen or so desecrations of Jewish cemeteries in Germany each year. The Central-Verein, the large German Jewish defense organization, naturally launched energetic protest campaigns: mass meetings, indignant declarations by Jewish and non-Jewish personalities, press conferences, etc. The Jewish militants knew that the desecrations were committed by youngsters and were sporadic and spontaneous. The Central-Verein, however, attributed the responsibility to the general climate of anti-Jewish feeling which the Nazis were trying to foster in the country. The physical violence suffered by Jews was relatively rare at the time, but was denounced vehemently by the Jewish organizations. The Central-Verein thus presented the Nazis as a fanatical, violent party.[4]

The Nazis, in order to counter the accusation, developed three distinct lines of explanation. One, radical, was directed at the most convinced militants. They accused the Jews of despoiling their own cemeteries, with the perverted aim of incriminating the Nazis and discrediting them in the eyes of the public. The desecrations were perpetrated by Jews and formed the lynchpin of a typical Jewish conspiracy.[5] A second approach, more political and more concerned with credibility, accused the Communists of the desecrations.[6]

In 1930 Hitler developed a third line of response, legalistic and respectable: he made no mention of a conspiracy, but rather firmly condemned the desecrations. Thus, when summoned to testify in the trial of sixteen Nazis accused of violence against Reichsbanner militants (June 1930), he loudly voiced his indignation when questioned in relation to violence and particularly to desecrations. He even affirmed that any Nazi found pillaging Jewish cemeteries would be expelled from the party.[7] Indeed, a few days later the Jewish Telegraphic Agency reported that "Hitler expels five synagogue desecrators from his party after they are sent to prison."[8]

The topic reappeared a few months later, after the Nazi victory in the elections of 14 September 1930 (over 18% of the votes). The convening of the new Reichstag, on 13 October, was greeted in Berlin by bands of young Nazis who attacked Jewish stores before being dispersed by the police. The Nazis blamed the incidents on the Communists,[9] but Hitler, in an attempt to give immediate reassurance to the international press, made particularly pacifying statements. "An anti-Semitism that provokes pogroms or indulges in the violent destruction of private property has no place in our political program," he declared to the *New York Times*. He also repeated his decision to exclude from the party any person advocating or practicing violence against the Jews.[10]

The restraint displayed by Hitler throughout 1930 did not concern only the *current acts of violence,* but also the *future intentions* of the Nazis vis-à-vis the Jews. Thus he affirmed to an American paper, at the beginning of the year, that he did not seek to limit the rights of the Jews in Germany; he merely wished to ensure that the non-Jews did not have fewer rights than the Jews.[11] Hitler's statements, quoted in the German press, caused a stir in the extremist fringes of racist opinion.[12] By making overly lenient remarks concerning the Jews, the Nazi leader took the risk of losing the esteem of his most radical partisans—a sure sign of how uncomfortable his position was.

The moderate line followed by Hitler corresponded to an external necessity—to assuage international concern and to build up an image of a serious and realistic statesman. It also corresponded to domestic concerns, dictated by the party's new electoral tactic: to appeal to the middle-class vote, and not to that of the Communist and Socialist proletariat, as Goebbels wished.[13] In order to attract the middle classes, it was necessary to temper the party's revolutionary image and to woo this public through signs of respectability. The Nazis had to present themselves as a party of order, and thus to curb their natural inclination towards violence. Hitler, who constantly proclaimed his faithfulness to the constitution and his respect for law, made sure that the Jews received the benefit of his moderation.

Gregor Strasser: "We do not want to persecute the Jews."

Gregor Strasser did not go as far as Hitler. He developed an argument based on a constant and repetitive rhetorical structure. He began his speeches by affirming that the Nazis had no intention of persecuting the Jews, then completed these words with a qualification which brutally restricted its reach: "but we do demand elimination of Jews from German life" (October 1930); "but we want to liberate Germany from Jewish dominance" (June 1932).[14] Hermann Goering, in 1932, developed the same theme, explaining that the Nazis had nothing against the Jewish religion, and that they were merely trying to protect Germany from an excessive Jewish influence.[15] The *C.V.*

Zeitung, several times in 1932 ironically printed the slogan "We do not want to persecute the Jews" ("Wir wollen keine Judenverfolgungen"), together with descriptions of Nazi physical or verbal violence.[16]

Joseph Goebbels: "The Jews are also human"

Throughout this period Goebbels was far more radical than Hitler in the positions which he adopted on the Jewish question.[17] In his propaganda, however, he had to deal with an argument frequently proffered by his adversaries, namely that Jews are also human, and that it would be unnatural to persecute them.

In response, Goebbels elaborated an explanatory system which appeared in 1927, and which subsequently came into extensive use.[18] Goebbels admitted the truth of the opposing argument ("the Jews are also human, we have never doubted it"), but with a qualification which robbed the concession he had just made of any sense (..."but the flea is also an animal"). This zoological qualification stresses that the category of "human" covers several subspecies, some noble and productive (the Germans), and others harmful and parasitic (the Jews).[19] Other analogies, based on the same principle and displaying the same logic, were also employed. The anthropological analogy, for instance, indicates that the savages in Africa are also human, but nobody would dream of giving them political responsibilities in a civilized state, even though they are "a thousand times more likable" than the Jews.[20] A later analogy, taken from the plant world, uses mushrooms for comparison, there being good mushrooms which are edible, and bad ones which are poisonous.[21]

The effort made to counter the philosemitic argument ("the Jews are also human") shows the impact of this argument on public opinion in the late 1920s and early 1930s. Goebbels' method consisted in endorsing the argument, and then destroying it with a sophism which deprived it of all relevance.

The Nazis in Power and the Denunciation of the "Atrocity Campaign" (1933)

The Nazi rise to power was accompanied by a wave of anti-Jewish violence, particularly after 5 March 1933 (the elections to the Reichstag). Incensed by these events, the Jewish communities outside Germany reacted in two complementary ways: demonstrations and mass meetings, in all capital cities; and the organization of a vast world boycott movement against German goods. Numerous non-Jewish personalities in all countries adopted an anti-racist stand. The wave of protests in 1933 was far greater than any registered in the past, at the time of the Russian pogroms in 1903–1906, or the Ukrainian massacres of 1919.[22]

We now know that however spectacular these meeting were, their effect was limited. Likewise the boycott, for mainly objective and economic reasons, had only a marginal impact on German exports. However, at that time, in March and April of 1933, the Nazis felt the world protest campaign to be threatening and dangerous. It compromised their basic objective, which was to strengthen their power, relaunch their economy and (very prudently) rearm Germany. Thus, they had to restore their image in world opinion. The Nazis were subject to two other constraints, both internal: until 23 March, namely until the voting of full powers by the Reichstag, they had to assuage the fears of the leaders of the Catholic Center; they also had to take President Hindenburg's reactions into account.

Their retaliation to the Jewish campaigns took various forms, like that of the boycott day against the Jewish stores (1 April 1933).[23] However, they also halted the violence and stabilized the situation of the German Jews, who were expelled from public and administrative life, but not from economic life. Domestic economic factors led the Nazis to adopt a relatively moderate policy concerning the Jews, in the summer of 1933, but certainly foreign reactions also played some part.

The Nazi leaders took pains to reassure international opinion throughout the crisis of the months of March and April 1933. Goering, Minister of the Interior in Prussia, constantly made appeasing statements.[24] Hitler intervened to bring an end to the violence.[25] In May he told the Polish ambassador that he regretted the violence perpetrated on Polish Jews living in Germany.[26] In April, Goebbels attempted to reassure the international press.[27] During a trip to London in mid-May 1933, Alfred Rosenberg admitted that "there have been some very regrettable outrages," but explained that the government had taken all the required steps to reestablish order.[28] Out of all the efforts, it was certainly Heinrich Himmler, chief of the SS, who made the most reassuring remarks. Almost immediately upon his appointment as head of the Munich police, he declared to the press that "fundamentally I regard citizens of the Jewish faith exactly in the same way as any other German citizens, and I shall protect the lives and property of Jewish citizens in exactly the same way as those of any other citizens."[29]

Parallel to these statements, the Nazi regime launched a vast campaign on the theme of the anti-German "atrocity propaganda" *(Greuelpropaganda)*. The theme of "atrocity propaganda" was skillfully chosen, bringing to mind slanders made against the Germans in World War I. They had then been accused by the Allies of killing children, of recovering the fat from the bodies, and so forth. These false accusations had left Western opinion in the 1920s and 1930s with a bad taste. Journalists and politicians felt that they had been caught in the trap of a war propaganda which attributed inhuman, demonic qualities to the enemy.

Thus in 1933, German diplomacy explained that the opponents of the new Reich, i.e., the Jews and the Communists, were in the process of relaunching the atrocity propaganda of fifteen years previously. There was an appeal to reason (since the claims had been utterly false in 1914, they must be false in 1933), to pacifism (the true aim of those who perpetrate falsehoods is to provoke a new European war) and to the feeling of "fair play" (the Hitler regime, which is taking its first steps, must be given a chance). Von Neurath, German Minister of Foreign Affairs, warned the world "against permitting the baneful war-time spirit of vilification to flare up again."[30] In addition the Nazis brought strong pressure to bear on the German Jewish organizations so that they would join their voice to the official denials.[31]

The German counter-protests were far from universally convincing. However, they did succeed in perturbing certain sectors of opinion, especially on the pacifist and liberal left, and gave rise to violent debates in several countries. The partisans of a firm position against racist Germany encountered many objections. Were they not exaggerating the extent of the persecutions? Were they not demonizing Germany once more, when they should be making every effort to establish a lasting peace among all the nations, beyond the differences of regime and the political differences?

Conclusion

As the persecutions intensified, each successive stage was accompanied by an explanatory system (combining justification and camouflage) aimed at the outside world. The arguments advanced were of course radically different from those proffered to the German population at home or to the Nazi parties in the world. The Nazi rhetoric and, more generally, the antisemitic rhetoric in all countries and in all ages, must therefore be analyzed at different levels and from different perspectives.

Our natural tendency, however, is to focus upon the most brutal and cruelest anti-Jewish themes. Attracted by extremes, we neglect the apologetic and civilized forms by which the same message is conveyed. Such an approach is certainly prejudicial to our understanding of the phenomenon. For it is precisely the moderate expressions which allow antisemitism to spread its influence, to gain ground within the "silent majorities" and to overcome any resistance to its progression.

242

Demonizing the Other: Antisemitism, Racism, and Xenophobia

Notes

1. In the late nineteenth century, the Inquisition was cited in this context, as were the Russian and Ukrainian pogroms in the 1920s and 1930s. Since 1945 the references focus only on the Holocaust.

2. The model of this type of reaction is of course the campaign against the Jewish "Syndicate" during the Dreyfus Affair.

3. As a recent example of this tendency, we may look at Jean-Marie Le Pen's campaign during the French presidential elections of April 1995, where he stood for the Extreme Right *Front national*. Le Pen and his supporters repeatedly complain of having been demonized. More than that, the theme of the tactical demonization of the extreme Right has become a part of French public discourse about Le Pen. It is generally said that it was a tactical blunder to demonize Le Pen's movement. See "Appel aux Français" by Jean-Marie Le Pen, April 1996. About the public debate on the demonization *(diabolisation)* of the Front national: *Le Nouvel Observateur*, 15–21 July 1996. On the "victimization" of the *Front national:* Pascal Bruckner, "La démagogie de la détresse," *Le Monde*, 23 June 1995.

4. Many publications exist on the desecrations of Jewish cemeteries in the last years of the Weimar Republic. Inter alia, the Central-Verein published two: *Unsere Maßnahmen zur Bekämpfung der Synagogenschändungen*, Berlin, 1929; *125 Friedhofsschändungen in Deutschland 1923–1932—Dokumente der politischen und kulturellen Verwilderung unserer Zeit*, Berlin, 1932. For examples of Nazi reactions to the Central-Verein campaigns, see *C.V. Zeitung*, 22 August 1930.

5. See, for instance the *JTA Daily News Bulletin*, 8 November 1930 which quotes the *Völkischer Beobachter*. On this theme, see the Central-Verein's publication: *Anti-Anti, Tatsachen zur Judenfrage*, (Berlin 1929), card 20. See also a retrospective article published in *Der Stürmer*, January 1937, no. 2.

6. See the *JTA Daily News Bulletin*, 27 March 1930, which refers to an article in the *Völkischer Beobachter*.

7. On the Schweidnitz trial, *C.V. Zeitung*, 20 June 1930. Hitler's first testimony, December 1929, before the Schweidnitz tribunal: *C.V. Zeitung*, 20 December 1929.

8. *JTA Daily News Bulletin*, 25 June 1930. On the actual desecration and the arrest of the culprits, see *JTA Daily News Bulletin*, 19 February 1930 and 26 March 1930.

9. *Der Angriff,* 16 October 1930.

10. *New York Times*, 15 October 1930. Hitler told the London *Times* (15 October 1930) that he had nothing against "decent Jews, but if Jews associated themselves with Bolshevism, as many unfortunately did, they must be regarded as enemies."

11. Quoted in *C.V. Zeitung*, 7 March 1930.

12. On the entire affair, see *Die Neue Welt*, 4 April 1930; *Le réveil juif*, 21 March 1930.

13. For a good analysis of the modifications in the Nazi electoral strategy in 1929 and 1930, see Dietrich Orlow, *The History of the Nazi Party*, vol. 1 (University of Pittsburgh Press, 1969).

14. Speech to the Reichstag, 13 October 1930, reprinted in the *New York Times,* 18 October 1930; speech broadcast 14 June 1932 for the general election campaign of July 31: *JTA Daily News Bulletin,* 16 June 1932; also: Gregor Strasser, *Kampf um Deutschland* (Munich, 1932), 262 and 384.

15. *JTA Daily News Bulletin,* 16 June 1932.

16. For instance, *C.V. Zeitung,* 24 June 1932, 15 July 1932.

17. As shown, for instance, by a comparative reading of the *Völkischer Beobachter* and of *Der Angriff* in Berlin.

18. See the *C.V. Zeitung,* 23 September 1927.

19. Joseph Goebbels, *Der Nazi-Sozi—Fragen und Antworten für den Nationalsozialisten* (1932). Goebbels also developed a neighboring theme there, that of the "white Jews."

20. Text reprinted in *Paix et droit,* January 1932.

21. For instance, an illustrated brochure distributed in 1938 by the editors of *Der Stürmer.* Even later, Nazi propaganda was to spread the theme of "devils with a human face" throughout occupied Europe.

22. The world Jewish action was widely reported by the Jewish Telegraphic Agency, and by the press of the different countries.

23. The *Völkischer Beobachter* remained relatively discreet on the "Jewish question" in the first three weeks of March 1933. It was completely unfettered after March 23, once full powers had been voted to the Hitler government.

24. *JTA Daily News Bulletin,* 6 March 1933, 7 March 1933, 24 March 1933, 27 March 1933; *New York Times,* 26 March 1933.

25. *JTA Daily News Bulletin,* 13 March 1933.

26. Ibid., 8 May 1933.

27. Ibid., 10 April 1933.

28. Ibid., 15 May 1933.

29. Ibid., 13 March 1933.

30. *New York Times,* 27 March 1933.

31. See the texts reprinted in three languages in: Jakow Trachtenberg, *Die Greuelpropaganda ist eine Lügenpropaganda sagen die deutschen Juden selbst; Atrocity propaganda is based on lies say the Jews of Germany themselves; La propagande d'atrocités n'est que mensonges déclarent les Juifs allemands eux-mêmes* (Berlin, 1933). On the pressure brought to bear on Jewish leaders, see *JTA Daily News Bulletin,* 28 April 1933, special bulletin.

16

"All poets are Yids":
The Voice of the "Other" in Paul Celan

John Felstiner
Stanford University

The demonization of the Jews can be illustrated by a certain joke that stems from Czechoslovakia but that could have come from almost any country on earth. It is early morning, the butcher shop is not open yet but a long queue has formed. After some hours a party official shows up: "Any Jews waiting here?... Go on back home!" More time goes by, and the official shows up again: "Any non-party members here?... Go on home!" Then yet more waiting, until finally the official returns and announces: "You all might as well leave—there won't be any meat today." At this a voice pipes up: "Wouldn't you know it? The Jews always get the best deal!"

The privilege of being Jewish has often seemed a mixed blessing, in the eyes of Jews as well as of their grudging hosts. While evolving a book on the German-speaking poet Paul Celan (1920–1970), I settled some years ago on a title: *Paul Celan and the Strain of Jewishness*. The double sense of "strain" was to catch both the persistence and the difficulty, both the trace and the trauma of being Jewish for this writer from Czernowitz, Bukovina, the eastern outpost of the former Austrian empire; a poet who at age thirteen endured Romanian Iron Guard antisemitism, then Russian occupation, SS Einsatzkommando 10B, overnight loss of his parents deported to Transnistria, nineteen months at forced labor, Soviet takeover again, and exile in Paris with literally nothing left—only a mother tongue that had turned into the murderers' tongue, passing through what this poet called "the thousand darknesses of deathbringing speech."[1]

Because he wrote poems that exacted almost too much from his language and his listeners, Paul Celan is still not a familiar figure outside of Germany, even among literati. Over the years, when I would tell someone that I was working on a writer named Celan who lived in France, often they did not recognize the name and took me to mean Céline—Louis-Ferdinand Céline (1894–1961), famous for his novel *Voyage au bout de la nuit* (1932) and infamous for his vituperative fascist antisemitism. This mistake is rather ironic, since Celan was a dogged, rawly sensitive Jewish survivor, whereas Céline was a perfect instance of demonizing the Other. In 1937 he published *Bagatelles pour un massacre* (Trifles for a Massacre), which would "demand the expulsion of racially impure aliens [*étrangers*] and preach a new crusade against them."[2] Céline's antisemitism provides a full modern textbook case. He urged Aryan supremacy, cited the *Protocols of the Elders of Zion,* saw an international Jewish capitalist, Communist, and Masonic conspiracy along with Jewish influence in the arts and professions, spoke of "Hollywood the jewess," "Moscow the yid," and "Negrified Jews"; he reviled Léon Blum, and blamed Jews for obstructing a Franco-German alliance, for thwarting his own career and love life, and even for preempting his own pariah status.

Most of the papers for this conference quite properly take up the tradition that Céline exemplifies. Our main subject is the demonizing of the Other in history, psychology, art, folklore, and elsewhere, and that demonizing could well be my focus in literature. Within the Anglo-American canon alone, this would entail a comparative survey from Chaucer to T. S. Eliot and above all Ezra Pound, including Anthony Trollope, Henry James, Henry Adams, F. Scott Fitzgerald, Theodore Dreiser, Ernest Hemingway, Graham Greene, H. L. Mencken, e.e. cummings, and others. But rather than survey the agents of antisemitism, which the *Encyclopaedia Judaica*'s able articles by Harold Fisch (for England) and Hillel Halkin (for the United States) begin to do, I am concerned with a victim of antisemitism. I will limit myself to the representative case of Paul Celan—that is, to his own experience and his bitter voicing of otherness.

This experience also involved his aligning himself with vilified or alienated Jews such as Baruch Spinoza, Heinrich Heine, Gustav Landauer, Rosa Luxemburg, Franz Kafka, and Osip Mandelshtam. And as a translator, Celan brought foreign voices, voices of otherness, into his mother tongue: Emily Dickinson, Guillaume Apollinaire, Mandelshtam. In addition, I will explore how the idea of the Other and the term itself came to mark the very aim of Celan's writing: the *Du,* the addressee his lyrics sought, as well as the revelatory strangeness of true poetry and even its movement toward the "wholly Other," the God we cannot grasp.

The voice of the Other will not be found in Paul Celan as simply articulated as it is, for example, in Margarete Susman's *"Die Andern"* (The Others, 1953), which rhymes its title word tellingly with *wandern* (wander):

> Among the peoples of the world
> We are eternally the Other.
> We greet you only as we wander
> In human and in deepest plight,
> In death in common we unite—
> Only in life are we the Other.[3]

Celan's wartime lyrics frequently give voice to the Other in biblical terms. "Black Flakes" speaks of "Ya'akov's heavenly blood blessed by axes," and in "Russian Spring" he asks: "And must I still wrestle with Ya'akov's angel?" Two other 1943 poems, drawn from Psalms, mark a specifically Judaic exile: "By the Waters of Babylon" and "Out of the Depths."[4]

Celan's *"Todesfuge"* (Deathfugue) from 1944, the best-known poem to emerge from the Jewish catastrophe, nervily adopts the voice of the quintessential Other, death-camp inmates whose commandant favors *Rüden* (hounds) over *Juden:* "he whistles his hounds to come close / he whistles his Jews into rows has them shovel a grave in the ground / he commands us play up for the dance." In that last command, *spielt auf nun zum Tanz,* a sudden harsh staccato is heard, the Nazi voice itself overrides the victims' voice. Celan can hear Jewish prisoners actually echoing, citing, the voice that brutalizes *them*—and this may be the most desperate signal of otherness. When it happens again, Celan's own voice get agitated in the only recording he made of *"Todesfuge"*:

> He shouts jab this earth deeper you lot there you others
>   sing up and play
> he grabs for the rod in his belt he swings it his eyes
>   are so blue
> jab your spades deeper you lot there you others play on
>   for the dancing

It's as if the poet himself were abruptly possessed by some memory of the SS vocally brutalizing *ihr einen ihr andern,* "you lot there you others."

After the war, Celan's bitter anger stayed close to the surface. "Late and Deep" (1948) again sets the victims' voices against what are this time Christian vilifiers:

> We eat the apples of muteness...
> We swear to the world the sacred oath of the sand...
> They cry: Ye blaspheme!
>
> We've known that a long time.
> We've known that a long time, but what does it matter?
> You grind in the mills of Death the white meal of the
>   Promise,
> you set it in front of our brothers and sisters—...
>
> You warn us: Ye blaspheme!
> We know that too well.
> Let the guilt be upon us.

A long history is encapsuled here: the Chosen People's desert wandering, the Church's inquisitional condemnation, the Jews' attrition in Auschwitz. Celan's sarcasm, mimicking the fatal words "Let the guilt be upon us" put in the mouths of first-century Jews by Saint Matthew, has nothing to do with self-hatred, nothing to do with the internalized guilt that has bedevilled Jews of earlier generations and our own.

Paul Celan felt enough hatred from outside himself, though he never spoke in detail about the trauma of the Nazi-ridden years. In 1952 he was invited to Germany's postwar literary gathering of Group 47, but was told that his *"Todesfuge"* sounded like "singsong straight out of a synagogue."[5] The next year Claire Goll, widow of the Alsatian-Jewish surrealist Yvan Goll whom Celan had befriended and translated, vented a spurious charge that Celan was plagiarizing her husband's work. In 1957, I'm told, on a Cologne street-corner, Celan heard a German behind him say "What's this Jew-pig doing holding up traffic?"[6] And in Bonn for a reading, he found a caricature on his lectern: "There's the Jew at the Wailing Wall again. Just look how he bites at his chains!"[7] Meanwhile from Germany, neo-Nazi vandalism and recrudescent antisemitism, plus reports about Nazis in government or having fled to Arab countries and South America, exacerbated Celan's sense that "race-madness" *(Rassenwahn)* was still extant, as the 1956 death-camp documentary *Night and Fog* had to say—in Celan's translation.

In the spring of 1957, around Easter, Celan composed one of his most caustic poems, entitling it *"Tenebrae"* after the Good Friday service during which candles are extinguished one by one to dramatize the Crucifixion, when (as Matthew says) "there was darkness over all the earth," *Tenebrae factae sunt*. Celan again bears witness to the voice of the Other, the victims' "we." His poem begins as if Jesus' Passion provided a model for Jewish suffering:

> Near are we, Lord,
> nearby and graspable.
>
> Grasped already, Lord,
> clawed into each other, as if
> each of our bodies were
> your body, Lord.

But in fact Celan drew that image of excruciation, "clawed into each other," verbatim from a firsthand description of Jews suffocating in the gas chamber that had recently appeared in Gerald Reitlinger's *The Final Solution*.[8] And the next lines in Celan's *"Tenebrae,"*

Pray, Lord,
pray to us,
we are near,

echo not the Passion narrative's tragic affirmation but Chaim Nachman
Bialik's "Heavens...You pray for me!" after the 1903 Kishinev Easter
pogrom. The speakers in Celan's poem then add "blood, it was / what you
shed, Lord," to "your body, Lord," and this eucharistic imagery hints at anti-
Jewish blood libels, claims of desecrating the Host and killing Christ.

Despite the bitter ironies in Celan's *"Tenebrae,"* well-meaning German
exegetes have praised it for reconciling the Crucifixion with Jewish
suffering. The philosopher Hans-Georg Gadamer derives a universal
existentialism from the poem: "Each of us is alone and forsaken as the dying
Jesus on the cross," he says, finding a "commonality between Jesus and
us."[9] But this poem's "we" does not migrate into Gadamer's "us." Jewish
agony bespeaks not commonality but otherness.

Around 1958 Celan began to feel the mark of Jewish otherness as acutely
as at any time since the war. (In this connection, we may remember that Elie
Wiesel's *Night* and André Schwarz-Bart's *The Last of the Just* first came out
in Paris in 1958 and 1959.) In 1958, Celan's "encounter"—he reserved that
term for the deepest shock of recognition—with another stigmatized Jewish
poet, Osip Mandelshtam (1891–1938), gave him a way to realize otherness
brilliantly. To begin with, Celan saw a kinship on many personal counts.
Mandelshtam–the name means "almond stem," which to Celan meant
"Jewish stock"—had worked as a translator and had once attempted suicide.
Each grew up close to his mother and because of his father harbored
ambivalence toward Judaism. After a groundless plagiarism charge,
Mandelshtam embraced "the proud title of Jew."[10] This nexus may account
for Celan's belief that Mandelshtam was murdered by Germans (like his own
parents) rather than lost in Siberian exile, as was generally believed.

Over the course of a year, while writing almost no poetry of his own,
Celan as translator brought a piercingly strange voice into postwar Germany
by taking on (and taking over) the voice of this "ruined man" Mandelshtam,
whose country (Celan said) had "wasted" him. The fierceness with which
Celan gave his very best to Mandelshtam, transmuting Russian lyrics into his
own idiosyncratic German, testifies to blood-brotherhood. "Time saws me
like a coin," Celan found it in Mandelshtam to say, and also this: "And am
and stay alone on every pathway."[11]

Just as Celan's Mandelshtam translations were about to be published in
July 1959, he invented another form for realizing his otherness by way of
language. Having travelled with his family to Sils-Maria in the Swiss alps,
he composed a prose fiction called "Conversation in the Mountains," a sort
of folktale where "Jew Little" meets "Jew Big"—*Klein* and *Gross*—and they

schmoose for a while. This tale opens: "One evening when the sun, and not only that, had gone down"—and as Celan's verb here is *untergegangen,* very close to *Untergang* (downfall, destruction), we find ourselves in the aftermath of the Jewish catastrophe. "One evening...stepping out of his cottage went the Jew, the Jew and son of a Jew, and with him went his name, unspeakable... he, whom they let live down below where he belongs." Now "the Jew"— rather than *Jude* Celan says *Jud,* which smacks of either German racism or homey Yiddishism–the *Untermensch* Jew Klein, who goes walking in the mountains "with my shadow, my own and alien," turns out to possess something distinctly his own: a gabby tongue. Celan's "Conversation" develops in a German pervaded by Yiddish-like repetitions, run-ons, contractions, inversions, diminutives, interruptions, self-reference and self-correction, and questions answered with questions, all of which are elusive yet vital to render in translation: "a language not for you and not for me—because I'm asking you, who is it meant for then, the earth, it's not meant for you, I'm saying, and not for me...."

What then is the burden of this tale and of its marked lingo? Celan in Czernowitz (like Kafka in Prague) grew up with two degrees of strangeness: a German-speaking Jew in a non-German Christian nation. Yet (again like Kafka) Celan acknowledged his apartness from east European Jewry. "At home we always spoke High German only," he once said; "dialect for me remained—unfortunately—quite distant."[12] That was before the war. In labor camps, he heard and probably learned more Yiddish than he ever would have otherwise. And later he was well aware that Yiddish, after almost a thousand years in Europe, had been obliterated in the mouths of millions of its speakers. So his Jewishly inflected "Conversation in the Mountains" has a redemptive thrust. (Celan once called it a *Mauscheln,*[13] meaning not Yiddish itself but German with a Jewish twist, the jabber that Germans overheard between Jews—*Mauscheln* being an old slur coined from Moishe, Moses.)

Wherever two peoples interact, language—especially the minority language—becomes a sign of difference. In 1954, for instance, Celan called a poem "Shibboleth," the title alerting us to an Israelite tribal password that the Gileadites used at the river Jordan against Ephraimites fleeing back west, who on pain of death mispronounced it "sibboleth." (Judg. 12:4) His poem speaks out against co-optation by Germany's cultural industry:

> they dragged me
> to the midst of the market,
> to where
> the flag unfurls that I
> swore no kind of oath to.

Then the poet tells himself and others: "Cry out the shibboleth / into the alien homeland." Can he pass into the realm of Goethe and Schiller by proving his identity with a Biblical password?

Even if Jews were not set apart by practice—circumcision, Shabbat, tefillin, mezuzahs, matzohs, etc.—their so-called "secret" speech, whether Hebrew or Yiddish, would stigmatize and marginalize them. Since neither language was a primary option for Celan, he could only hold fatefully to his German mother tongue. "There's nothing in the world," he said after the war, "for which a poet will give up writing, not even when he is a Jew and the language of his poems is German."[14] One way for such a Jew to go on writing in German was to make it his own, to give it all those Yiddish turns of speech in the "Conversation." Celan ended this piece saying "I on the way to myself," and a year later he stressed its "paths on which language gets a voice." Beset by antisemitism, Celan insisted through language on his own otherness.

He could also feel helplessly vulnerable. In October 1959, before "Conversation in the Mountains" appeared in print, a review of his recent book *Sprachgitter* (Speech-Grille) showed Celan that his shibboleth was inadmissible. This review in a Berlin daily criticized his "verbal filigree" and "metaphors not won from reality."[15] Even worse, the reviewer surmised that Celan's "origins"—Romanian? Jewish?—loosened his tie to the German language. For someone dedicated since 1945 to purging his mother tongue and just appointed Lecturer in German at the École Normale Supérieure, this pointing at his "origins" must have galled Celan's Jewish and authorial selves alike.

On Christmas eve of 1959, Cologne's reconsecrated synagogue was daubed with swastikas and slogans. Then followed a wave of neo-Nazi outbursts. Celan wrote to his fellow German-speaking exile poet Nelly Sachs: "What can I say to you? Every day, baseness comes into my house, every day, believe me. What is in store for us Jews?"[16]

Very shortly after this, the plagiarism charge dormant since 1953 was suddenly revived. A magazine in Munich strung together excerpts from glowing reviews of Celan's book *Sprachgitter,* undercut by an editor's note refusing to "lick Herr Celan's ass."[17] Then the widow of Yvan Goll wrote to the magazine renewing her accusation, citing "parallel passages" from this "master plagiarist." Her charges were not simply groundless, they involved misquotation and specious chronology. Yet the charge was disseminated and Celan read accounts of it from Germany—*aus Deutschland*! Though the literary community was nearly unanimous in dismissing it, and one magazine compared this charge to the Dreyfus affair, the damage was done.

In letters to his friends, Celan spoke of "the machinations of neo-Nazism...an attempt to destroy me and my poems."[18] He was "one who is *abolished*...by neo-Nazi German 'human beings' and their tools."[19] He called himself "a 'rootless' Steppenwolf with recognizably Jewish features," and he thought of "Harry Heine—who had it much better back then."[20]

The thought of Heine was anything but casual, for Celan allied himself closely with this Jewish poet exiled in Paris who had grave doubts about the *Vaterland*. In 1961 Celan for the first time gave one of his poems an epigraph—from Heine's caustic lines "To Edom" (the Jews' biblical name for their enemies): *Manchmal nur, in dunklen Zeiten.* "Now and then only, in dark times," this epigraph says obliquely, leaving us to recall the rest of Heine's poem about Gentile "tolerance," broken each time "your pious claws / you color with my blood." Celan's poem deals in gallows humor, mixing hard-core antisemitism with Isaiah's word of a Redeemer making the crooked straight:

> ...where's
> my Jew-badge, where's
> my beard you tear out?
>
> Crooked was the way I went,
> crooked it was, yes,
> for yes,
> it was straight....
> Crooked, so grows my nose.

The link here between messianic prophecy and racial antisemitism is particularly telling, since Celan's versification itself would eventually have to grow crooked, dislocating German language, to get straight the truth of his experience.

With Franz Kafka, Celan's affinity grew even closer than with Heine. On the one hand Kafka's own otherness, his ferment of estrangement, made him a presiding spirit for Celan. In the poet's copy of Kafka's diaries I found vigorously marked the passage where Kafka asks, "What have I in common with Jews? I have hardly anything in common with myself" (8 January 1914). And next to a later entry (24 January 1922) in which Kafka feels "terribly abandoned," Celan in May 1968 simply wrote "13.5.68," identifying himself transparently with that abandonment. I believe that Celan at times, out of his own need, saw a tighter bond between Jewishness and estrangement in Kafka than Kafka himself acknowledged. In 1962 Celan signed off a letter to a close friend with this phrase: *'s ist nur ein Jud* ("'Tis but a Jew"). His source is revealing. In Kafka's story "A Country Doctor," which has nothing to do with Jews, some townspeople sing a jeering ditty: "Strip off his clothes, then let him heal, / And if he doesn't, kill him dead! / 'Tis but a doc, 'Tis but a doc," *'Sist nur ein Arzt!*, Celan was signing himself a kin to Kafka—persecuted and mordant: "'Tis but a Jew."

At the same time, and no less essentially, Celan revered the Prague storyteller for the absoluteness of his calling and craft. The last letter Celan ever wrote cited Kafka's remark about achieving "happiness only if I can raise the world into the Pure, the True, the Immutable."[21]

Jews who, unlike Heine and Kafka, suffered persecution or death in some way related to their origins also compelled Celan's allegiance, and they figure often in his poetry: Baruch Spinoza; Rosa Luxemburg and Gustav Landauer, both assassinated in 1919; Mandelshtam, who perished in Siberia in 1938; Walter Benjamin, a suicide in 1940; Isaak Babel, a victim of Stalin's purges in 1941; Stefan Zweig, a suicide in Brazil in 1942; Edith Stein, an Orthodox Jew who became a nun but died in Auschwitz in 1942.

Figures such as Luxemburg, Landauer, and Babel had especial poignancy for Celan, insofar as they thought their Jewishness need not condemn them. He was gripped by Landauer's statement of German-Jewish symbiosis: "My Germanness and Judaism do each other no harm and much good." But since the war, as Celan told Erich Kahler, this seemed a "most tragic" error.[22] Even the approbation and prizes that Celan received from the Bundesrepublik seemed to him German alibis, leaving him more distanced, not less.

Against the hurt, the alienation, that he suffered at German hands, both during and after the war, Celan forcefully reoriented himself back toward Eastern Europe, whence he felt his genuine self derived. This was the Eastern Europe of his lost parents and homeland, of traditional and mystical Judaism, of Russian poetry and revolutionary hope. When the plagiarism campaign struck him, he wrote to his Romanian-Jewish mentor: "Ach you know, I've often asked myself if I'd have done better to remain among the beechtrees of my homeland."[23] In presenting his first book of poems to Erich Kahler, he admiringly inscribed a sentence from one of Kahler's own books: "Eastern Jews were much defamed, and assimilated Jews in western countries greatly contributed to the defamation, wishing to distance themselves from this testimony to their past."[24] And in 1962, Celan jocularly called himself *Russki poët in partibus nemetskich infidelium*, a "Russian poet in the territory of German infidels."[25]

Having already translated Mandelshtam along with Sergei Esenin and Alexander Blok, Celan welcomed Yevgeny Yevtushenko's poem "Babi Yar" (1961), which commemorated the 33,771 Jews machine-gunned by SS troops at a ravine near Kiev in 1941. Celan translated "Babi Yar" and published his version twice during 1962. By an odd twist, where Yevtushenko courageously assumes the identity of the victimized Other—"I believe I am now / a Jew"—his Jewish translator is authenticating his own identity by rehearsing Yevtushenko's words: "Hounded. / And spat on. / And slandered."

A few months after translating "Babi Yar," Celan continued to claim his East European Jewish otherness by seizing on Mandelshtam's newly published exile poems from Voronezh and translating them. He also wrote a lengthy, obscure poem inspired by the Russian anthology *Pages from Tarusa* (1961), which contained many lyrics by Marina Tsvetaeva (1892–1941). Like his poem the previous year with a verse from Heine, Celan's "And with the Book from Tarusa" carried an epigraph. From a poem by Tsvetaeva, who had married a Jew and after Parisian exile hanged herself in 1941, he took a thought that has now become better known than his (or her) poem itself, but one that is always mistranslated. *"Vse poety zhidy,"* Celan's Russian epigraph, is regularly understood as "All poets [are] Jews," or in French versions of Celan's poem, *Tous les poètes sont des juifs*. The source for Celan's epigraph is Tsvetaeva's "Poem of the End" (1924), in which she comes upon Prague's ancient ghetto and reflects on the outcast condition of poets: "In this most Christian of worlds / Poets — Jews!" The point is that Tsvetaeva's (and Celan's) word *zhid*, a popular Czarist epithet, is derogatory, and is voiced ironically by her and him. Yevtushenko's "Babi Yar," for instance, uses three different terms for Jews: in sympathetic contexts, *iudei* and *evrei*, but *zhid* only in the mouth of a pogromist, whose cry Celan renders "Strike down the Jews, save Russia!"

Celan's epigraph, which forms the title of my essay, really says "All poets are Yids." While he himself vividly heard the slur, he may have meant to keep it strange to his German readers, since he printed the epigraph in Cyrillic characters. Whether or not those readers recognized it, Celan's sense was that true poetic calling exposed one to obloquy and persecution.

Throughout the 1960s, having received Germany's two major prizes, the Bremen and the Büchner, Celan in poem after poem went on reclaiming German language from its "thousand darknesses of deathbringing speech." Sometimes, manic-depressive and confined in a psychiatric clinic, he would start as many as nine brief poems a day. At their most striking, his poems attempt to speak truth in the mother tongue by taking the European Jewish catastrophe as a given, as the radical datum of our time. *Mit den Verfolgten*, he began a poem in 1963,

> With the persecuted in late, un-
> silenced,
> radiant
> covenant.

Rooted in that obligation, his "true-stammered mouth" broke and stripped and compressed and darkened German verse, making the once-estranged language strange in a new way, so as to utter what he called "scar-truth," "need-song."[26] But in writing at the cutting edge of postwar poetry, he felt too little solidarity. A 1964 poems ends:

> No one
> witnesses for the
> witness.

Yet, however idiosyncratic and enigmatic and contradictive Celan's verse became, it never gave up reaching toward "an addressable Thou," a listener, indeed, a responsive Other.

Even as Celan "baked wilderness-bread / out of co-wandered language," and "my clambering mouth bit hard, yet again, / as it sought you, smoketrace"—even as the poet's language honed its imagery and rhythms, he held to a messianic aim: "come with me to Breath / and beyond," he wrote in 1966. Celan had been studying Gershom Scholem for a decade, finding in Kabbalah as well as in Meister Eckhart the paradox of an ineffable Nothingness, the paradox that enabled this poet's "un- / silenced, / radiant / covenant" with the dead. And in the Protestant theologian Rudolph Otto's *Das Heilige* (1917), Celan found a sacral term, "the wholly Other," to point the aim of a poetry that would invest the dead with their unheard-of strangeness and their spiritual presence as well.

This utopian need occurred close in Celan's mind to his idea of Israel. Before the war his parents had not emigrated, and after it, their son elected to "live out to the end the destiny of the Jewish spirit in Europe."[27] The Six-Day War stirred him with both pride and anxiety for the threatened state. Finally, in October 1969, he visited Israel. "I think I have a notion of what Jewish loneliness can be," he told the Hebrew Writers Association. Yet he was elated at the revived language and at the autonomous Jewish collectivity, free in its own place. A possibility surged—to transplant himself at last—but this promise seemed to demand more than he could manage. Perhaps otherness was his lot, he was not really up to messianic fulfillment. Perhaps the challenge of Hebrew, though he had a good knowledge of it, threatened to alienate him from his hard-bought mother tongue.

Once back in Paris, Celan for a while wrote avidly to friends and family in Israel, and spoke of returning. While Israel was problematic, Paris was anything but comfortable. An anecdote from early 1970 catches his state of being. In the Métro one day, a friend of Celan's recalls, "Someone jumped out from a group of young people behind us and bellowed down the car, 'Jews to the ovens!' I saw Paul's face tense up and grow sad, his fists clench."[28] Then minutes later in the post office, a clerk noticed Celan's aerogram to Israel and slowly crushed it before tossing it in the outgoing mail.

Around Pesach in April 1970, Celan went into the Seine River and drowned unobserved. Survivors' suicides are each different: Tadeusz Borowski, Piotr Rawicz, Jean Améry, Primo Levi, Jerzy Kosinski... Celan's suicide, whatever its clinical causes, drives home the burden of both being and seeking an Other:

> No one
> witnesses for the
> witness.

Notes

1. Paul Celan, *Gesammelte Werke*, ed. Beda Allemann and Stefan Reichert, with Rolf Bücher (Frankfurt 1983), 3:186. All quotes from Celan's writings are taken from this edition.

2. David O'Connell, *Louis-Ferdinand Céline* (Boston 1976), 107, 114–16.

3. *Jüdisches Schicksal in deutschen Gedichten*, ed. Siegmund Kaznelson (Berlin 1959), 76.

4. Paul Celan, *Das Frühwerk*, ed. Barbara Wiedemann (Frankfurt 1989), 129, 143, 70, 107.

5. Hans Werner Richter, quoted in Milo Dor, *On the Wrong Track: Fragments of an Autobiography*, tr. Jerry Glenn and Jennifer Kelley (Riverside, Calif. 1993), 160.

6. Mariana Birnbaum, interview by the author, 7 April 1990.

7. Peter Jokostra, *Die Zeit hat keine Ufer: Südfranzösisches Tagebuch* (Munich 1963), 174.

8. Gerald Reitlinger, *Die Endlösung: Hitlers Versuch der Ausrottung der Juden Europas, 1939–1945* (1953), tr. J. W. Brügel (Berlin 1956; 2d ed. 1957), 168.

9. Hans-Georg Gadamer, "Sinn und Sinnverhüllung," *Zeitwende* 46 (1975): 321–29.

10. Osip Mandelshtam, "Fourth Prose," in *Selected Essays*, tr. Sidney Monas (Austin, Tex. 1977), 166.

11. This poem, no. 165 in the 1955 edition of Mandelshtam's work, was not fully translated or published by Celan.

12. Paul Celan to Walter Jens, 19 May 1961.

13. Quoted in Marlies Janz, *Vom Engagement absoluter Poesie: Zur Lyrik und Ästhetik Paul Celans* (Frankfurt 1976), 229.

14. Paul Celan to Israeli relatives, 2 August 1948, quoted in Bianca Rosenthal, "Quellen zum frühen Paul Celan: Der Alfred Margul-Sperber-Nachlass in Bukarest," *Zeitschrift für Kulturaustausch* 32/3 (1982): 230.

15. Günter Blöcker, *Der Tagesspiegel,* 11 October 1959.

16. Paul Celan to Nelly Sachs, 20 February 1960, in *Paul Celan / Nelly Sachs: Briefwechsel,* ed. Barbara Wiedemann (Frankfurt 1993), 29.

17. *Baubudenpoet* 1/3 (1959–60): 62–63.

18. Paul Celan to Alfred Margul-Sperber, 30 July 1960, in "Briefe an Alfred Margul-Sperber," *Neue Literatur* 26/7 (1975): 54.

19. Paul Celan to Petre Solomon, 22 March 1962, in Solomon, "Briefwechsel mit Paul Celan, 1957–1962," *Neue Literatur* 32/11 (1981): 65.

20. Paul Celan to Margul-Sperber, 8 February 1962, in "Briefe," 56; Paul Celan to Reinhard Federmann, 14 March 1962, in Federmann, "In Memoriam Paul Celan," *Die Pestsäule* 1 (September 1972): 21.

21. Paul Celan to Ilana Shmueli, 12 April 1970. Kafka's diary entry: 25 September 1917.

22. Paul Celan to Erich Kahler, 28 July 1965, in *Der Georg-Büchner Preis,* 133.

23. Paul Celan to Margul-Sperber, 30 July 1960, in "Briefe," 54.

24. Erich Kahler, "Origin and Metamorphosis of Jew-Hatred" (1939), in *Die Verantwortung des Geistes* (Frankfurt 1952), 79.

25. Paul Celan to Reinhard Federmann, 23 February 1962, in Federmann, "In Memoriam," 18.

26. Paul Celan, *Eingedunkelt und Gedichte aus dem Umkreis von Eingedunkelt,* ed. Bertrand Badiou and Jean-Claude Rambach (Frankfurt 1991).

27. Paul Celan, letter of 2 August 1948, quoted in Rosenthal, "Quellen," 402.

28. Franz Wurm, "Erinnerung an Paul Celan," *Neue Zürcher Zeitung,* 23 November 1990: 40.

17

The Popular Image of the Jew in Modern Poland

Yisrael Gutman
The Hebrew University of Jerusalem

I

In 1983 the Polish Jewish writer, Henryk Grynberg, who lives in the United States and writes in Polish, published an article in which he claimed that "nothing anti-semitic was ever invented in Poland—almost everything came from a centuries-old Western European tradition."[1] Franciszek Ryszka, the Polish political scientist and historian of attitudes towards Jews in Poland also regards antisemitism in his country as a part of pan-European phenomenon that developed in the context of European culture as a whole.[2] Yet many people—and not just Jews—see East European peoples in general, and the Poles and Romanians in particular, as nations in which an extreme form of antisemitism was rooted and developed.

Sebastian Haffner, in his book on the meaning of Hitler, tells us that "young Hitler was an Austrian who saw himself not as an Austrian but as a German" but "the habitat of Hitler's antisemitism was Eastern Europe."[3] Not only Haffner but also the eminent German historian, Friedrich Meinecke, in *The German Catastrophe,* points to the East as the source for Hitler's antisemitism[4]; while the Israeli historian of Polish Jewish origin, Raphael Mahler, who dealt extensively with the history of the Jews of Poland, refrains, in his essay "Antisemitism in Poland," from presenting it as an unusually strong and consistent phenomenon, asserting that

> the character of antisemitism in a given country can be explained only in terms of the specific social, economic, and political forces operating within that country. Racial, religious, and mystical theories of antisemitism are inadequate to explain the peculiar developments in individual countries. An analysis of the special character of Polish antisemitism, therefore, must be related to the social and economic evolution of the country and to the special role of the Jews in Polish history.[5]

It is widely accepted that the increased antisemitism that developed from the last decades of the nineteenth century to the end of World War I and the Holocaust—a wave of modern, political, and racial antisemitism—was present in various European countries (in the western part of the continent as well as the eastern), and almost simultaneously apparent in countries with different political systems and enjoying differing levels of socio-economic development. Still, it is possible to point to substantial differences between anti-Jewish argumentation and acts of antisemitism in Western Europe and those in Eastern Europe. There is also a discernible regional difference in the nature of Jewish community reactions and in their methods of response to such waves of hostility.

When analyzing the phenomenon of growing antisemitism, it is important to differentiate between those moods and tendencies that reflect a hostile attitude towards the Jews as a result of superstitions based on religious and socio-economic background, and attitudes and arguments whose base is ideological and political; it is rather the latter that became increasingly apparent during the evolution and realization of extreme nationalistic political trends in European countries.

II

In his article "The Significance of Hungarian Jewry," Jacob Katz described ways in which the methods whereby the Jews were integrated into the wider community differed among European peoples at a time of rising national consciousness in the nineteenth century. He explains that the Hungarian national awakening of the second half of the nineteenth century, which was guided by the ambition to adapt to the development patterns of Western Europe, generated considerable openness towards assimilation into the Magyar nation and spirit on the part of various minorities, including the Jews[6]; in Poland, enslaved and divided at that time, a significant change also took place, in great part as a result of the failed uprising against the Russian occupation in 1863. The conclusion reached by nationalistic circles among the Poles was that there was no practical chance of liberating Poland through military uprisings which depended upon the nobility. They therefore envisaged the need to evolve a long-term plan for developing Polish national vigor in all its forms by fostering national consciousness, encouraging rapid economic and cultural development, and preparing for any political change that might allow the removal of the burden of occupation from the country. During this process, which was aimed first and foremost at winning the peasantry to the national cause, the question of the Jews also arose. There had already been Polish leaders who advocated the recognition of the Jews as an integral urban component in Poland's national texture. Following the defeat of the January 1863 revolt the current called Warsaw Positivism, which had a lot of influence on cultural trends, supported the assimilation of Jews into Polish culture and suggested that they should be encouraged to participate in the general national effort.[7] The leaders of this tendency ignored almost totally the ethnic and spiritual vitality of the large Jewish community in Eastern Europe. They assumed that Jewish life, religion, and customs were deeply backward and required far-reaching reform. The reformers also failed to evaluate properly the extent to which the various classes were locked into their social positions, which were feudal in character and reinforced by religio-cultural determinants including language, norms of behavior, strangeness and hostility. This dichotomy, manifested in the divided social structure, is not an exclusive Polish phenomenon, but also manifests itself in other nations and mixed populations in eastern and southeastern Europe. In the case of Polish Jews, who constituted a large percentage of the population in the country's towns and cities, there was no social stratum available that was willing and able to integrate and assimilate them in one way or the other.

There was therefore almost no chance that the Jews would abandon their traditional unifying frameworks in significant numbers. The tiny group of Jews who did assimilate were drawn from among the pioneers of the country's economic modernization drive, the newly affluent, and a segment that had made their way into the Polish intelligentsia in the nineteenth century. In the course of a generation or two, they mostly deserted the Yiddish language, their traditional world, and often even their religion. For Polish Jews, unlike their German coreligionists, assimilation did not, therefore, function as an avenue for them to "escape the ghetto" and as a lever for radical change in the whole Jewish society, but rather became a process of detachment and abandonment of Jewish links.

The effort to crystallize the Poles into a single national entity intensified in the last two decades of the nineteenth century. At the head of this attempt stood mainly people who had despaired of the hope that Poland's national salvation would come from external forces supportive of the "Polish cause," and those who opposed socialism or integrating Poland in a multinational structure. These people believed in the right to "national egoism" and ethnic exclusiveness.

It soon became clear that Jews had no place in this ethnic unity. Proponents of extreme and refined nationalism considered the Jews strangers and as citizens whose duty it was to support Polish nationalistic ambitions and aims. At the beginning of the twentieth century, Roman Dmowski, the ideological leader of the Endecja movement, made it clear that the Jewish mentality was foreign to the Polish people and could be harmful, that Jewish assimilation should therefore be denied and their penetration into the main artery of Polish culture must be stopped. Already in 1881 there had been an anti-Jewish pogrom in Warsaw. There were few casualties, but it made evident the existence of a popular antisemitic current among the masses. Demagogic anti-Jewish preachers emerged in its wake, airing their views publicly or in writing. More than a few of the Polish clergy supported this crude and often brutal hostility. The strong connection between Polish nationalism and Catholicism contributed to the blend of nationalistic political antisemitism based on deep-rooted popular anti-Jewish sentiments which gained strength at the turn of the century.

The failure of assimilation as a way out for the masses does not mean that the Jews were untouched by modernization and new ideological trends. The end of the nineteenth century sees the start of a period of dynamic change in Polish Jewry, especially among the youth. More and more would turn to Jewish nationalism, especially in the form of Zionism; to a modern, cultural, even secular, renewal of Jewish languages, particularly Yiddish; and to socialism in a Jewish context as well as a desire for Jewish cultural autonomy. Naturally, Jewish nationalism, though it did not harbor territorial ambitions of its own, and was not irredentist, could scarcely avoid conflicts of various kinds with the new Polish nationalism. When the Russian Duma confirmed the establishment of municipal government in Polish cities and the Jews demanded representational rights on the eve of World War I, things came to a head with a serious confrontation during the Warsaw elections for the Fourth Duma. The results of the election were seen, not without reason, as a blow to the Polish representatives, leading Dmowski and his nationalist camp to declare an economic boycott against the Jewish population countrywide. The boycott and the wave of hate that accompanied it can be seen as the beginning of an active antisemitic campaign throughout the country, which was to continue in various forms in independent Poland between the wars.[8]

III

Our image of the "other" as belonging to a separate ethnic and religious group is not always based on personal acquaintance and knowledge, but rather on a collection of views, concepts, and positions that are passed on, received, and internalized. In pre-World War II Poland there had been daily contact between the Poles and the Jews for hundreds of years, especially in the economic sphere. There can be no doubt that generalizations or habitual images of the "other" were often contradicted by direct human contact. Generally, the bizarre-looking Jew, unusual in his dress, language, education, food, and the prevailing lifestyle in his separate community, attracted contempt and tended to be seen as part of a homogeneous body with a strange and negative mental world. Daily life created relations based on humane intimacy, but these only served to establish the well-known argument that the "good Jew" is an exception and the majority of Jews are despicable.

The Jews were strongly associated with the charge of deicide, classified as non-locals and considered as not belonging despite the fact that, as one Polish researcher pointed out, the Jews have been in Poland "since the dawn of civilization." The Jews were associated with commerce and petty trade, areas that were considered unproductive in the undeveloped Polish market, and they were regarded as inferior to Poles in the social hierarchy and class structure. Alexander Hertz, whose book *Jews in Polish Culture,* published in 1961, is rich in apt sociological diagnoses, shows that the Jew who made his living by leasing and small trade was regarded as having the traits of "a cheat," "a crook," "a bloodsucker." Hertz suggests, however, that small traders in any primitive market structure tend to have such an image attached to them.[9]

Furthermore, the good qualities that Jews were occasionally admitted to possess, such as diligence, family values, and solidarity amongst themselves, were seen as being exhibited only towards other Jews and never towards non-Jews. The Jew, whose culture and mental world were considered by Gentiles as unfamiliar and incomprehensible in Poland, aroused suspicion and repulsion; rooted local prejudices resulted in his being seen as an individual linked to dark and demonic forces. Hertz noted that there was little research done on the image of the Jew in Polish culture and folklore. Ironically, the first comprehensive work on the subject—according to Hertz—was done by a German Nazi and published in July 1942 in the quarterly *Die Burg,* in Kraków.[10] The piece includes a collection of Polish phrases and sayings. The writer, Joseph Sommerfeldt, doubtless had his own reasons for writing the article, and his racism is evident in his commentaries. Nonetheless, he collected, with impressive precision, 477 Polish proverbs and sayings connected to Jews, and only rarely do they mention Germans or others alongside the Jews. By studying this work I have learned that it embraces certain prominent and recurrent motifs, and that Jewish stereotypes are often used to illustrate extreme and ridiculous situations. The Jew's many nicknames are emphasized, as is the argument that a Jew cannot change and "always remains a Jew," that he is incapable of working the land, that he is a deceitful loan shark, and so on. But these sayings, for all their contempt, do not express violent hostility.

Polish literature often dealt with Jews. One of the main motifs was the exotic aura that surrounds the Jew's character and the customs of Jewish society; another recurrent motif is the relationship between Poles and Jews and the issue of how to integrate or repel them in the context of creating a modern society. Since the end of War World II, the fact of the extermination of the Jews has become a key issue in Polish literature, exposing the tension between the two sides since that fatal period. It is worth noting that this literature is by no means unequivocally anti-Jewish. In other words, along-side expressions of anti-Judaism, Polish literature contains many works and many prominent writers who show sympathy, affection, and interest in Jews and their world.[11] Two contrasting examples belong to Polish romanticism's greatest figures—Adam Mickiewicz and Zygmunt Krasiński. Mickiewicz's epic *Pan Tadeusz* contains one of the most positive and impressive figures of a Jew in European literature, and his work is filled with expressions of warmth, appreciation and strong empathy towards the Jews and their place in history; Krasiński, on the other hand, the descendant of a high noble family, regarded even converted Jews as alien corn, and tacitly expressed views later embraced by modern antisemitism. It seems to me that this duality is one of the trademarks of the national literature, and it left its mark on the Poles, especially the Polish intelligentsia.

I will not, in this general review, go into the complicated and emotionally charged issue of World War II, the Holocaust, and its impact upon the relations between Jews and Poles.[12] The phenomenon of antisemitism in Poland requires a distinction between traditional popular anti-Jewish sentiment and political struggles (such as the violent anti-Jewish campaign undertaken by members of the anti-Soviet Polish right-wing underground in the first years after World War II). One should also note the brutal anti-Jewish line of Communist elements from the mid-1950s, which reached its peak in persecutions that caused the remnants of the Jewish community, including those who were loyal to the regime, to flee after 1968.[13]

In the wake of the restoration of Polish independence in the late 1980s we often come across descriptions of the present situation as one of "antisemitism without Jews." I think that such a representation does not do full justice to the complexity of the changes occurring in Poland. A common opinion is that antisemitism is still rife in Poland, even if it is only simmering under the surface and merely boils over once in a while. According to systematic polls that are currently being conducted, two main motifs are still apparent in Polish attitudes towards Jews: one has to do with religious superstitions (the accusation that Jews were God killers); the second is the continuing tendency to see the Jews as members of a group possessing secret powers that conspires against government and society behind the scenes while supporting its members at the expense of others. However, there is a slow but steady decrease in anti-Jewish sentiment. Arabs and Germans are often seen today in a far worse light by the average Pole.[14]

The change is most apparent among the younger generation and the intelligentsia. The question of Jews and of Polish attitudes towards them is often raised and dealt with by the intelligentsia, with penetrating and daring criticisms heard from, among others, Franciszek Ryszka and Jan Błoński.[15] A segment of the Catholic church is also disinterring the past and propounding an affinity with Jews and Judaism on a spiritual and human level. The fascination with Jewish matters is expressed through a multitude of new publications and translations, through the interest shown towards Israel and Jewish communities around the world, and in the desire to achieve a normal, even friendly, relationship with the Jews. During the election campaign for the Polish parliament, movements that tried to exploit antisemitic slogans were roundly defeated.

It was essentially in the period between the two world wars that antisemitism gained real force in Poland. Indeed, these two decades saw an unprecedented increase in antisemitism in Europe and around the world. Poland, finally independent and eager to assert its sovereignty over its territory, faced minority groups that amounted to a third of the general population. In this atmosphere, the "Jewish question" became a constant issue. Parties that were openly supportive of antisemitic sentiments—among whom the Endecja (the National Democrats) were most prominent—claimed that the Jews were longstanding enemies of Poland, had acted against her during her oppression at the hands of foreign powers, and were responsible for her failures and defeats. They further presented Jews as obstructing Poland in her attempt to fulfill her nationalistic ambitions after 1918, and suggested that international Jewry regularly conspired against Poland in the world arena. Even if we ignore the irrational obsessions of the majority of Endecja's members, we may assume that most Poles believed that Jews were harmful to Poland's economy, that there were too many Jews in Poland, and that they interfered with Poland's drive to modernization. In short, the Jews were aliens and a burden on Poland. It is true that Polish socialists and liberals condemned antisemitism, but they did not represent the prevailing opinion. It should also be stated that, during the 1920s and early 1930s, the Polish parliament was sensitive to the norms established by the leading Western democracies, and this helped to contain the anti-Jewish trend.

Antisemitism reached its peak in Poland after the death of the highly respected Polish leader, Marshal Józef Piłsudski, in 1935. Piłsudski had never used antisemitism to win support, but after his death his successors adopted an anti-Jewish line that had a discernible impact upon public life.

They developed close relations with Nazi Germany, gave their blessing to discrimination and to an economic boycott of the Jews. They claimed that there were too many Jews in Poland, insisting that the expulsion of the Jewish masses was one of the most urgent issues on the Polish political agenda. Such actions encouraged an outburst of popular hatred against the Jews. By now Jews were not just aliens: they were also considered *superfluous*. Moreover, although the Polish government still condemned violence against the Jews, traditional antisemitic elements—especially the radical pro-Fascist groups—emphasized that the exodus of the Jews would only be precipitated by violent action. This wave of persecution came at a time when emigration was limited and almost impossible so that the Jews were therefore caught in a dead end situation.[16]

Some Poles still expressed antisemitic opinions and stood beside the Jews in their struggle against this wave of hostility: reputable university teachers resigned their positions in protest against the confining of Jewish students to "ghetto benches"; socialist youth joined Jewish groups in an organization that defended them against pogrom-like extremist attacks.

All in all, antisemitism in its gravity and results during the late 1930s in Poland does not approach that manifested by Nazi Germany. Anti-Jewish activity in Poland was indeed despicable, but still operated in a manner which is sadly not uncommon in the history of human society. Nazism, its policy, and its actions are beyond the boundaries of anything that can be called human and therefore cannot serve as a basis for comparison.

Indeed, comparison is neither possible nor justifiable: Poland and the rest of Eastern Europe was, for most of this period, not ruled by fully totalitarian governmental systems. Moreover, the Third Reich was unique in being dominated by racist anti-Jewishness as its main ideological principle. Was there not an ideological element in the antisemitism in Poland, Romania, Hungary, and Russia? Were those countries' intellectuals not supportive of it? This was indeed the case. However, we need to differentiate carefully between the various types of antisemitic phenomena that manifested themselves at this time. Regular outbursts of mass antisemitism were, as far as we know, most apparent in Eastern European countries. However, only Nazi ideology classified and judged people in biological racist terms, and claimed to offer humanity a new revolutionary order and a new age. In this new order the Jew was the *absolute* enemy, who had to disappear, since there was no place for him in the world which the Nazis were trying to forge.

The anti-Jewish ideologies of Eastern Europe, brutal and cruel though they might be, were different. They saw the Jews as aliens, as a disturbance and an obstacle to national goals. The Jews were certainly marginalized in cultural life and the economy, there were voices calling for their exile, and they often served as the scapegoats for political failures. However, the Jewish question in Poland was always regarded as a primarily domestic issue; their destruction was not seen as an integral part of an overarching scheme for radically changing civilization. Eastern European antisemitism, at its peak, demanded the expulsion of the Jews (or most of them), it did not recoil from violence and pogroms, but it was incapable of planning and implementing the "Final Solution."

Notes

1. Henryk Grynberg, "Is Polish Anti-Semitism Special?," *Midstream* 3/29, (August–September 1983).

2. Franciszek Ryszka, "Antysemityzm," *Polityka* (Warsaw), 16 April 1983.

3. Sebastian Haffner, *Anmerkungen zu Hitler* (Munich 1978), 16.

4. Friedrich Meinecke, *Die deutsche Katastrophe, Betrachtungen und Erinnerungen* (Wiesbaden 1946), 91–92.

5. See Raphael Mahler, "Antisemitismus in Poland," in *Essays on Antisemitism*, ed. Kopel J. Pinson (New York 1946), 145.

6. Jacob Katz, "The Uniqueness of Hungarian Jewry" (in Hebrew), in *The Leadership of the Hungarian Jews in the Trial of the Holocaust* (Jerusalem 1976), 13–24.

7. On the Positivist trend in nineteenth-century Poland, see Stanislaus A. Blejwas, *Realism in Polish Politics: Warsaw Positivism and National Survival in Nineteenth Century Poland* (New Haven 1984); Adam Bromke, *Poland's Politics: Idealism vs. Realism* (Cambridge 1967); Andrzej Walicki, *The Slavophile Controversy: History of Conservative Utopia in Nineteenth-Century Russian Thought* (Oxford 1975).

8. Roman Dmowski and his activity as the leading figure of the National-Democratic movement in Poland is little known in the West, as his many books and articles were not translated into English. The only biographical work about him (which covers only a short period in his life and political activity) is Alvin Marcus Fountain II, *Roman Dmowski: Party, Tactics, Ideology 1895–1907* (New York 1980). Among the biographies and comprehensive monographs dealing with the movement which have appeared in Polish see Roman Wapiński, *Roman Dmowski* (Lublin 1988); idem., *Narodowa Demokracja 1893–1939* (Wrocław 1980).

9. Aleksander Hertz, *The Jews in Polish Culture* (Evanston Ill., 1988).

10. Dr Josef Sommerfeldt, Referent für Judenforschung an der Sektion Rassen- und Volkstumforschung am Institut für Deutsche Ostarbeit Krakau: "Die Juden in den polnischen sprichwörtlichen Redensarten," in *Die Burg,* Vierteljahresschcrift des Instituts für Deutsche Ostarbeit Krakau, Heft 3, (Krakow, July 1942) 313–54.

11. On the image of Jews in Polish literature, see Henryk Markiewicz, *Literatura i historia* (Kraków 1994) 15–35; Magdalena Opalski, "Trends in the Literary Perception of Jews in Modern Polish Fiction," *Polin, a Journal of Polish-Jewish studies*, 4 (Oxford 1989): 70–86; idem, *The Jewish Tavern-Keeper and his Tavern in Nineteenth-Century Polish Literature* (Jerusalem 1986); M. Opalski and I. Bartal, *Poles and Jews, A Failed*

Brotherhood(Hannover–London 1992); Artur Eisenbach, *Wielka Emigracja wobec kwestii żydowskiej 1832–1849* (Warsaw 1976).

12. For a wider insight on the subject, see Yisrael Gutman and Shmuel Krakowski, *Unequal Victims, Poles and Jews During World War II* (New York 1986); David Engel, *In the Shadow of Auschwitz, The Polish Government-in-Exile and the Jews, 1939–1943* (Chapel Hill and London 1987); idem., *Facing the Holocaust, the Polish Government-in-Exile and the Jews, 1943–1945* (Chapel Hill and London 1993).

13. See the essays of Krystyna Kersten, *Polacy–Żydzi–Komunizm, Anatomia półprawd 1939–68* (Warsaw 1992).

14. For the image of Jews in folk culture, see Alina Cała, *The Image of the Jew in Polish Folk Culture* (Jerusalem 1995).

15. See Jan Błoński, *Biedni Polacy patrzą na getto* (Kraków 1994). See also the polemics following Blonski's article, "The poor Poles look at the Ghetto," in *My Brother's Keeper? Recent Polish Debates on the Holocaust*, ed. Antony Polonsky (Oxford 1990).

16. This period was precisely presented by Emanuel Melzer, *Political Strife in a Blind Alley: The Jews in Poland, 1935–1939* (in Hebrew) (Tel Aviv 1982); idem, "Polish Diplomacy and Jewish Emigration during 1935–1939," in *Gal-Ed* (On the history of the Jews in Poland), vol. 1, (n.p., n.d.), 211–49.

18

Mass Death under Communist Rule and the Limits of "Otherness"

Steven T. Katz
Boston University

Mass death is not a new reality. Over the centuries this tragic phenomenon has manifest itself in many times and places. An integral feature of this history of large-scale violence is what I shall call, "otherness." That is, the victimizer stigmatizes and stereotypes the victim in various ways in order to legitimate the violence that is then unleashed.

What is worthy of note is that this distancing process takes many forms. The historical record reveals cases where the "Other" is created on the grounds of class, sex, color, race, religion, ethnicity, and nationality. So, for example, the majority of Stalin's victims were identified as "class enemies." The most notorious example of such class war was directed at the *Kulaks,* though his entire massive campaign against the peasantry as represented by his forced drive to collectivize agriculture, was based on the notion of class (and his desire for national modernization). Likewise, the extraordinary event that was Kampuchea was defined by the application of a radical communist ideology in which class was everything. Nationalism—connected usually to other factors such as religion, ethnicity, race, or color—has also played its part in justifying oppression and death—as a decisive ingredient in Stalin's exile of the minority nationalities during World War II and in his assault on the Ukraine in the early 1930s.

The Kulaks

Let me begin, then, with the category of class as it was applied in Stalin's infamous campaign against the Kulaks.[1]

Two fundamental facts about this defining event of the Stalinist era can be highlighted at the outset of our analysis: A) Stalin murdered only a minority of the Kulaks. He could have murdered them all, but he explicitly, consciously, chose not to do so. B) Stalin's primary target in this violent confrontation, for all its deadly severity, was a contingent, "socially alien," identity, that by definition, could be altered.[2] Whatever neurotic fears energized and accompanied this convulsive anti-peasant policy, what was elemental in this unstinting war was the Kulaks' self-interested class loyalties that had to be broken down. This coercive policy was judged necessary for the general good, as defined by socialist theory, to prevail. (Stalin was *not* alone in holding this position. It was *the* view of almost the entire Bolshevik elite, including Trotsky—differences existed only as to how best to accomplish this "progressive" policy.)

The need for this policy was the immediate consequence of three related socialist imperatives. First, there was the axiomatic requirement that called for the elimination of all "capitalist" classes which threatened socialist hegemony. Second, only the collectivization of agriculture, following upon the shortages and economic chaos of 1927 and the 1928 confiscations of grains—which Stalin interpreted as pointing the correct way to future policy—could end the severe grain crisis that led to food rationing in the cities in 1928–29. In 1928, grain acquisitions by the government, despite the new use of coercion fell 2 percent below the poor levels of 1927. This failure was symptomatic of the enduring and recurring structural weakness of Soviet agriculture. There was the decline/absence of draft power (horses and oxen, and later, tractors), the inherent limits of communal land tenure, and the inefficiency of subsistence farming; the variety of problems posed by the need for assured acquisition of grain by the state, faulty pricing mechanisms, inadequate distribution and marketing networks; finally, there was the "capitalist greed" on the part of the Kulaks. As Stalin came to understand this weakness he was convinced that only the complete and permanent collectivization of agriculture could remedy this deeply unsatisfactory situation. Only the forced collectivization of the Kulaks and other peasants could provide the needed capital, primarily in the form of grain exports that were to be squeezed out of the newly created collective farms. This capital was required for the massive and rapid industrialization of Russia called for by socialist theory. This had indeed been the governing ideological understanding of Trotsky and the so-called "left" throughout the 1920s, but now it was adopted by Stalin as his own point of departure.

In addition, ideological compulsions aside, the leadership acted to overcome the national economic crisis that now directly involved both rural and urban sectors. Inflation, which was due in large part to a shortage of grain, dramatically eroded real urban wages between 1928 and 1932, while farm wages declined by nearly half in the same period. Though the Bolshevik leadership had in large measure created the present crisis, something dramatic had to be done to overcome it. At the Sixteenth Party Congress held in April 1929, against the background of another grain crisis, the First Secretary's demand for collectivization (a demand typical of Stalin's Bolshevik voluntarism) became Party policy. This transformed the situation, as Stalin later said, from "a policy of limiting the exploiting activities of the Kulaks to a policy liquidating the Kulaks as a class."[3] There would now be an end to accommodations and vacillation. Stalin had convinced the Party Congress—and there were considerable segments within the Party that required little convincing—that there was only one reasoned option that it could choose and that there could be no turning back once this course was selected. The uncompromising treatment of the Kulaks, their exemplary victimization, would set the pace for the collectivization of the whole of the peasantry. This decision would send the appropriate message to the entire agricultural sector, particularly the middle peasantry: the State would not countenance any deviation from or interference with its grand political objective. "We must deal the Kulak such a blow," Molotov announced, "that the middle peasant will snap to attention before us."[4] The country was ill-prepared for the draconian measures that were about to ensue, as was the state apparatus that had to carry out these extraordinary initiatives. But they would come to pass. Between late 1929 and March 1930, in a mere five months, the percentage of all peasants living on collective farms rose from 4.1 percent to 58 percent, i.e., from approximately 1.1 million households to 15 million households (12 percent of the total population). By 1934 the percentage of peasants living on collectivized farms had risen to 75 percent. Thus, through the harsh intrusion of the OGPU (Secret Police), a massive metamorphosis of Soviet peasant life, though *not* its genocidal demise, had occurred.

There was no fully genocidal intention behind the assault on the Kulaks as becomes clear from the policy directives governing the entire action against them. Stalin did intervene to stiffen the guidelines recommended by the special Politburo Commission on De-Kulakization that reported in December 1929. But his own more radical version of this transformational program, published in the name of the Central Committee on January 5, 1930 under the title "On the Tempo of Collectivization and Measures of State Assistance in Collective Farm Construction," still allowed for a tripartite distinction among Kulaks. The first category of Kulaks was held to be composed of hardened, unrepentant reactionaries and anti-Soviet counter-revolutionaries. Such individuals were to be separated out, jailed, or exiled to the Gulag, and if necessary, shot. Their families were also to be exiled. It is estimated that 50,000 to 63,000 households (averaging between 4.2 and 6 persons per family, a maximum of 300,000 to 378,000 persons) fell into this class. The second category to be established, recognized the existence of less recalcitrant, though still "potentially" dangerous Kulaks and their families who were also to be exiled, though to less distant and less harsh conditions. Approximately 112,000 households (672,000 persons at a maximum) were identified as belonging to this second subdivision. The third and largest group established by Stalin's edict was comprised of the less affluent, less politically active Kulaks who constituted the majority, estimated at 75 percent, of all Kulak families. There were between 650,000 and 800,000 households (between 3,900,000 and 4,800,000 persons at a maximum) in this category. They were to be settled in their own *raion* (area), but, on Stalin's insistence, outside of the collective farms. In any event, this three-part organizational plan that involved the active participation of tens of thousands of armed personnel, provided the national blueprint for the program of collectivization.

When the Kulak relocation program actually took place, elements of a class war were unleashed, involving "a positive orgy of violence which were later referred to as 'excesses.'"[5] At the same time, the conditions of exile and resettlement were much harsher than those proposed, however cynically, in the relevant official legislation. As a result, the removals actually carried out amidst the chaotic conditions extant in the countryside (often by overzealous and ill-disciplined district level authorities) created more exiles dispatched to more distant northern locations, more deportations to labor camps, and more "executions" than originally envisioned. Officially, it was at first reported that a total of 240,757 Kulak families, approximately 25 percent of Kulak households, some 1 to 1.5 million people, had been exiled. Later this total was revised upwards to 381,000 families, or nearly (at a maximum) 2.3 million persons. The final number, when all the deportees are included, was probably more than double this estimate, involving upwards of 5 million individuals. These deportations were also the cause, directly and indirectly, of between one and two million deaths, with a disproportionate number of the dead being children who were unable to survive the appalling living conditions (including severe food shortages and wretched weather that existed during the transport and the first years of resettlement).

These horrors and the enormous damage they did to the agricultural infrastructure of the country brought about a public outcry and monumental disorder in the countryside, including the accelerating slaughter of animals with the greatest losses taking place in February and March 1930. Even Stalin, in direct contradiction to his own desire to force the tempo of collectivization, felt constrained to criticize the deportations in his hypocritical essay, "Dizziness from Success."[6] In addition, new guidelines were issued limiting the number and types of Kulaks to be deported. However, this respite from forced collectivization was temporary. A second wave of dekulakization now occurred with the result that while "only 26 percent of peasant households participated as Kolkhoz members in the spring sowing of 1930...between January and March 1931...the figures rose sharply from under 30 percent to 42 percent."[7] And this process continued throughout the second half of 1931 so that "over half the peasant households of the Soviet Union were collectivized by the end of the 1931 sowing, and more than 60 percent by the end of the harvest season."[8] By the spring of 1933 collectivization was a fait accompli and Stalin ordered the cessation of any further forced deportations in support of it.

As a result of these extreme governmental actions, the Minister of Agriculture was able to announce by 1931 that the Kulak population (using the term very broadly), *in terms of class membership,* had declined from 5.4 million in 1928 to its then present size of 1.6 million. Four years later, in 1935, an official document described this class constriction in even more dramatic terms: the 1928 Kulak population of 5,618,000 had been reduced to 149,000 on January 1, 1934. It must be stressed, however, lest serious misunderstanding of what was occurring should arise, that this precipitous drop in class affiliation, involving approximately 5.4 million individuals, does not equal a corresponding loss of life, i.e., every lost unit of class membership is not equivalent to a death. The number of Kulak deaths, from all causes, as a consequence of these tyrannical removals is estimated, as already noted, at between 1 and 2 million. This is to recognize that despite the ferocity of the attack upon the approximately 5.4 (to 5.6) million persons identified as Kulaks in 1928, somewhere between 63 and 81.5 percent of this original group—some 3.4 to 4.4 million individuals—*remained alive.* This statistical conclusion is in line with Stanisaw Swianiewicz's researches. He estimates that of the Kulaks who were deported, one-third perished, and this is consistent with Robert Conquest's more recent calculation that 25 to 30 percent of the Kulaks died in or, as a consequence of the deportations.

But millions of Kulaks and other peasants were deported and lived. Millions of others were not deported at all. In other words, the Kulaks were not subject to a state orchestrated campaign of physical genocide. Consider, in support of this judgment, the overall aggregates of peasant population: in 1929 it is estimated that there were circa 25,900,000 peasant households throughout the Soviet Union with an average of 4.2 persons (at a minimum) per household, or 108,700,000 peasants. By 1938 the number of peasant households had declined to circa 19,900,000, or (at an average of 4.2 members) 83,600,000 individuals, a deficit of 36 million persons. But of this 36 million decline, nearly 24.5 million are projected to have changed their status by moving to the cities or towns, in itself a major testimony against genocide, leaving a net loss of about 11.5 million or approximately 7.5 to 8 percent, up to 1937. Even when another 3 to 3.5 million peasant dead are added to the figure of 11.5 million to account for those imprisoned in this period but who died after 1937, making a total of up to 15 million peasant casualties, the loss rate comes to only 11 to 12 percent of the total peasant population. Or put the other way round, eighty-eight percent of the peasants, even on the highest responsible estimates of loss, survived.

This constrained, very carefully calibrated interpretation of Stalin's crusade against the Kulaks is not intended to lessen the evil nature of his campaign.

Nor again, does it challenge the identification of Stalin as a mass murderer of unrivalled proportions. The criminality of Stalin's behavior towards the Kulaks, and against Russia's peasantry more generally, remains a supreme example of political malevolence. At the same time, however, its discrete empirical morphology and ideological particularity cannot be ignored—despite the temptations of facile historical and phenomenological comparisons—without making truth a casualty. For the class war against the Kulaks never escalated into total annihilation, a war of all against all. The dialectic of history, in Stalinist terms, required the forcible social transformation of the Kulak as a necessary part of its internal and immanent self-development and as an unavoidable imperative in class evolution, but it did not require more than this.

The Case of the Ukraine

The next substantial category that I would like to discuss at some length is nationalism. This is important in itself as a cause of large-scale violence in the modern era. Here, two instances of persecution and mass death generated by nationalist ambitions and their suppression during Stalin's reign are highly instructive: the famine in the Ukraine in 1932–1933, and Stalin's deportation of seven national groups during World War II.

There are two main lines of scholarly interpretation concerning what actually happened and why in the Ukraine.[9] The first of these emphasizes the nationalist dimensions of the event. On this reading, both the indigenous Ukrainian population and the Soviet ruling class knew that the Ukraine, as recently as 1918, had been independent and that it wished to be politically independent again. Accordingly, the confrontations after 1918 in this region are seen as defined by the collision of two competing claims to sovereignty, one nationalist and the other putatively internationalist, though increasingly a cover for Russian national chauvinism.[10] For Stalin, the ultimate objective is assumed to have been the full integration of the Ukraine into the larger, ideally homogenized Soviet state. Anything less was dangerous. In practical terms it would interfere with the Bolsheviks' control of the agricultural market—including the essential issue of grain collection and distribution, a circumstance that often divided the local leadership. There was also danger from the geopolitically divisive character of all nationalist aspirations. Accordingly, Stalin on this reading consciously decided on a deadly campaign—most accurately described by the political category of internal colonialism—to eradicate this recurring threat to Soviet hegemony. Beginning with the purge of Ukrainian academics, as well as political and cultural leaders that began in April 1929, Stalin set in motion a movement that would eventually consume millions of Ukrainians.[11]

The object of the entire terror campaign was allegedly to bring about the complete annihilation of Ukrainian nationalism—a goal that was also consistent with the larger policy of the socialization of agriculture. Much like Hitler's later strategy in Poland for example, (and elsewhere in Eastern Europe), Stalin sought to expunge local autonomy and all manifestations of cultural or political independence in order to facilitate continued domination from Moscow. Here, as in many other cases, (e.g., Cambodia, Nigeria, Sudan, and most recently in Rwanda) the purpose of state-organized violence is the maintenance of political control.

Given the importance of the independent, economically autonomous peasantry in the Ukraine's socio-economic structures, the First Secretary's plan for the extermination of Ukrainian identity also required a crusade against the national intellectuals and "proto-capitalist" strata.[12] As Semen O. Pidhainy has described it, Stalin had to move against "Ukrainian nationalism's social base—the individual land-holdings."[13] "Only a mass terror throughout the body of the nation—that is, the peasantry—could reduce the nation to submission."[14] As long as the *selianym* existed, a euphemism for all free Ukrainian peasants, nationalist (and capitalist) sentiment would remain: both needed to be crushed.

The dominant method used to achieve this collective submission to socialism and elimination of the base of Ukrainian national sentiment, was once more to be the forced collectivization of the agricultural sector. At the same time, such a centralized agrarian policy gave the Communist Party, in the form of the All Union Commissariat of Agriculture, control over the region's grain supply. It was the task and responsibility of this Commissariat, in conjunction with Soviet planners, to calculate, coordinate and organize the yearly grain harvest and to set the state exactions to be levied and collected. When this direct control was expressed in an overly demanding target for grain exports from the region—ostensibly justified by the increased program of industrialization that was to be financed by the agricultural surplus—it effectively translated into a man-made famine in the Ukraine in 1931, that grew worse in the next two years. For example, in 1931 the procurement quota for the region was set at 7 million tons out of a total of 18.3 million tons (much of which had been lost to inefficient collective harvesting).[15] Such a level of national procurement almost certainly spelled trouble for the local community. Matters of food supply only got worse in 1932 when the procurement total was again set at 7 million tons while that year's harvest, due to drought, inefficiency and a decline in the number of acres sown—the latter partly in protest to Stalinist policy—came in at the very reduced level of 14.7 million tons. The local leadership, in the face of the total decline in tonnage, managed to persuade Moscow, at great cost to itself in the suspicions of disloyalty and nationalism that this awakened, to reduce the quota to 6.6 million tons.[16] But even this reduced sum was still far too high to make it possible to avoid massive starvation. Stalin, however, despite the mounting death toll, did not believe that the harvest was too small both to feed the Ukrainian people and to provide sufficient grain for export. Instead, already intensely suspicious of Ukrainian separatism and fearful of local disloyalty, he chose to interpret the failure to meet the inordinate quotas set by the central agencies as deliberate acts of "sabotage." The peasants, he concluded, were no better than "wreckers" of the socialist dream. In a deliberate act intended to punish the population of the Ukraine—which he justified as socialist self-defense—he continued to export grain from the region (if at a lower rate)[17]: 1.73 million tons in 1932 and 1.68 million tons in 1933, compared to 5.2 million tons in 1931. It was this export of grain, given the greatly reduced supplies, which turned an already grave situation into the catastrophe of mass death.

Increased pressure was now also applied against the peasant "class enemy" and against local party officials. Over a third of the new Ukrainian Communist Party members and candidate members were purged (37.3 percent) and 75 percent of local Soviets and members of local committees were replaced, with many being arrested for failing to produce the required quota. Pressure was also applied against those involved in local agricultural middle management with 3 percent of these officials arrested in the second half of 1932 for sabotaging Bolshevik policy[18]; and there was pressure against all channels of Ukrainian self-sufficiency—economic, cultural and nutritional. On December 14, 1932 the Central Committee of the All Union Communist Party accused the leadership of the Ukrainian Communist Party "of tolerating a Ukrainian nationalist deviation in its ranks," and then proceeded, on January 24, 1933, to replace it with a new ruling clique headed by Pavel Postyshev.[19] At the same time, it is argued, all available food aid to the stricken population was consciously denied, existing grain reserves in the region and elsewhere were not made available, the importation of food was stopped at the border of the Ukraine. Meanwhile Stalin, in an act of depravity, continued as already noted, to export more than 3 million tons of grain in 1932 and 1933. As a result there was massive intentional starvation throughout the Ukraine which peaked in 1933 and 1934. Of a peasant population of more than 25 million, about 20 percent, (up to 5 million) plus 500,000 to 750,000 persons in the urban areas of the Ukraine, died from lack of food and related medical problems in this period.[20] In some areas the death rate was as low as 10 percent, in others the rate was nearly 100 percent, the variations depending largely upon local agricultural and ecological conditions, such as the ability to find fish, wildlife, or other sources of nutrition. In many places this also led to cannibalism and infanticide in a desperate effort to cope with the lost grain harvests.

This is the *nationalist* version of the Ukrainian famine, interpreted as an intentional, man-made "genocide." It views Stalin as killing five million or more Ukrainians, plus hundreds of thousands of additional individuals belonging to other ethnic groups such as the Volga Germans and Kuban Cossacks. The goal was to simultaneously decapitate opposition to agricultural collectivization and to eradicate Ukrainian and other nationalist aspirations.

If we accept this nationalist interpretation of Ukrainian history, at least for the sake of argument, what are we to conclude about these events as an instance of genocide? This is certainly neither irrelevant nor a trivial question given the scale of the human losses involved and the evil will which directly caused these losses. There can be no doubt about the horror of this vast collective tragedy. But even five million deaths do *not* constitute in this case the technical crime of genocide and for all of its murderous ferocity and demographic enormity the event is not comparable to the Holocaust. The ruthless campaign against Ukrainian nationalism that destroyed a majority of the indigenous Ukrainian cultural and political elite (as well as a significant segment of the peasant population of the region) is better categorized as an instance of nationalist conflict and internal colonialism.[21] Stalin did not intend to exterminate the entire population of the Ukraine.

This conclusion finds support from the relevant statistical indicators. Though the human carnage was enormous (approaching the number of Jewish victims during the Second World War) the portion of the Ukrainian peasant population lost was somewhere in the region of 20 percent, while the losses for the Ukrainian population as a whole were in the area of 15 percent.[22] These demographic results resemble the figures for population decline in those Eastern European countries overrun by the Nazis, and in both cases the numbers do not indicate that a policy of total population eradication was pursued. Had Stalin in the Ukraine sought to pursue a genocidal war, given the destructive possibilities that lay open to him, more than 15 percent of the population would have been done away with. But more people were not killed because amidst the murderous toll there was still some restraint. The fact is that Stalin did not want to eradicate the people of the Ukraine, he wanted to exploit them. Eliminating the whole of a vanquished 'helot' population makes no more sense than slaughtering one's slaves. However, eliminating a conquered people's controlling elite, leaving it leaderless, anxious, and vertiginous, is a rational, functional strategy. This is a policy long pursued by conquerors to achieve enduring subordination of the subjugated and the political stability of an empire. It is certainly not a humane imperial strategy nor a program to be recommended as a form of empire maintenance, but neither is it genocide.

This judgement is confirmed, ironically, by the heartrending condition of the children, especially infants and the newborn. Throughout the Ukraine, youthful corpses lay strewn across the landscape—the entire territory had become a necropolis for children under 11 and 12 who were unable to obtain enough nourishment to stay alive. Yet, even here in the midst of the most intense human suffering, the relevant population statistics require careful decipherment. The latest demographic data indicates that fewer than 760,000 children died, largely from starvation, between 1932–1934.[23] This represents, depending on one's estimation of other relevant demographic variables, between 6 percent and 33.5 percent of the age cohort, and a significant percentage of the total population decline.[24] But, recognizing the great tragedy that occurred here, even the maximum loss of 33.5 percent does *not* support a genocidal reading of this event. For, on these numbers, at least 66.5 percent of Ukrainian children survived. Moreover, once the famine passed its peak in May 1933, the surviving 2 out of 3 children were not singled out for further harassment and worse. Most of those who managed to live through the crisis of 1932–1933 survived.

This historical outcome regarding children is not trivial. What makes the Ukrainian case non-genocidal and different from the Holocaust is the fact that the majority of Ukrainian children were *permitted to survive.*[25] Even the mountains of evidence pertaining to Stalin's evil actions produced by the proponents of the nationalist genocide thesis (for example James Mace and Robert Conquest) does not indicate either any intent or motive that would plausibly justify the extermination of the general Ukrainian biological stock. The number of Ukrainian children who died (or on the intentionalist reading were murdered) was almost as high or even higher than the number of Jewish children who were exterminated in the Nazi Holocaust. But their deaths represented something wholly different from what the murder of Jewish children at Auschwitz and Treblinka represented and intended. In the Ukrainian case, the aim of the violence and death was national enfeeblement and political dismemberment. In the Shoah the focused object, given its racial determinants, was physical genocide. Stalin intended that after the famine there should still be Ukrainians, though not Ukrainianism. Hitler intended that after Auschwitz there would be neither Jews nor Judaism. The loss of every child in both contexts was, to echo the talmudic Sages, the loss of a world. The death of each child was an act of equal immorality. Nonetheless there is an important, non-reductive, phenomenological difference to be drawn between mass murder (including children) and complete group extinction; between a war for political and territorial domination (including children) and a war of unlimited biological annihilation.

Deported Minorities in the Soviet Union

The case of the deported Soviet national minorities is also instructive as to the nature of massive state violence and its limits. The post-1940 removals of seven national groups en bloc in the USSR under the turbulent and catalytic circumstances of a world war (swelling the demographic pool of Gulag inmates by over 1.3 million) requires separate analysis in the present context.[26] Do these deportations—an organized state action against identifiable collectives—qualify as acts of physical genocide?

The deportation of the four northern Caucasian peoples, the Karachay, Balkars, Chechens and Ingushi, can be analyzed as a unit. All shared four defining attributes in addition to geographical contiguity: (a) all belonged to non-Russian ethnic groups; (b) all were Muslim; (c) each had a considerable history of opposition to Tsarist and Russian rule and would have preferred political independence from the Russian State.[27] (The overt political uprisings of the Chechens, Ingushi, Balkar and Tatar populations in 1929–30 and again in 1939–40 speak decisively to this cardinal issue); (d) each experienced various forms of persecution and coercion under both the Tsars and the Soviets. In addition, each of these national communities was relatively small in size compared to the larger national blocs that comprise the Soviet Union and or in comparison with the Jewish population of Europe in 1939. It is worth recalling that Khrushchev, in his famous anti-Stalinist speech at the Twentieth Party Congress, acknowledged the importance of the *size* factor when discussing the fate of the Ukrainians under Stalin who, unlike the small Muslim nations, could not be deported because they were too numerous.

The second group of national deportees, comprising Kalmyks, Tatars and Volga Germans, was more ethnically and religiously diverse, though their historical and socio-political experience under the Tsars and their Soviet successors was much the same as that of other exiled peoples. National and religious prejudices, continued misrule, occasional severe eruptions of violence and the suppression of ethnic or national aspirations marked their internal colonial status within the Empire. The Kalmyks were ethnically Mongols and practicing Buddhists. On the other hand, the Tatars were an ancient and historically independent Turkic-speaking Muslim people annexed to the Tsarist Empire in 1783. The Tatars had a strong national self-consciousness and harbored fervent national aspirations. The Volga Germans, by contrast, were a distinct community that had settled in Russia in the second half of the eighteenth century in return for economic advantages. Clearly separate in ethnic and religious identity from the surrounding people among whom they lived, they too sought national autonomy, achieving this valued status under the Soviet re-organization that established the autonomous German Volga Soviet Socialist Republic in 1924. (A similar political concession had been made to the Kalmyks in 1920, the Balkars, Chechens, and Karachay in 1922, and the Ingushi in 1924). The national position of the Volga Germans was obviously anomalous and especially sensitive during the Nazi occupation of their territory after 1941.

Between 1941 and 1944 all seven of these national groups were forcibly relocated and their autonomous republics effectively dissolved.[28] In addition, the more disparate Greek population of the Black Sea and Sea of Azov regions was dispersed and resettled in stages during the 1940s.

The rationale employed by Stalin to justify the exile of these national populations involved four major elements. (a) They were said to have resisted and to have continued to oppose the forced socialization of agriculture. (b) They harbored unacceptable minority nationalist aspirations. (c) They were in potentia, if not also in fact, pro-Nazi.[29] (d) They were targeted, as part of Russia's expansionist industrial and agricultural plans, to supply part of that laboring population which could be redeployed in underdeveloped, geographically isolated areas of the Soviet Empire. Another not implausible reason has also been advanced for at least some of the removals in the area of the Crimea—namely that Stalin harbored sinister geopolitical designs on Turkish territory after the war. The Muslim and Turkic populations of the borderlands were perceived as a possible threat to this expansionist ambition.

Regarding the truth of these differing charges and pretexts, the following details should be noted.

(A) Collectivization

All seven of these minority nationality groups opposed the injudicious policy of collectivization from its beginnings in 1929, suffering substantively and even abysmally as a consequence. The programmatic confiscations of property and the rigorous socialist remaking of the countryside (which included the exile of many individuals from these ethnic blocs to Siberia and the camps of the Gulag) won few friends for the revolutionary agricultural effort in these communities. Throughout the inhospitable mountain terrain of the North Caucasus region, minority uprisings in opposition to this vast, transformational schema occurred. They were put down with great ferocity by the Red Army. As early as 1929, 40,000 Balkars were either exiled or died of famine as a direct result of compulsory collectivization. In this same period, as an integral part of the same violent confrontation, 30,000 to 40,000 Tatars and approximately the same number of Chechen-Ingushi were deported. This was only the beginning of the terror. In the partially government-induced famines of 1932–33, tens of thousands of the minority populations would die. (Some scholars have suggested that this desolate event can also be seen as an immensely hostile governmental act to punish and break minorities unreconciled to implacable socialist imperatives.) Yet, even after such punishing measures, these minority peoples continued, if in a less activist mode, to resist the collectivization program. After the Nazi invasion of Russia in 1941 this opposition, at least in certain border areas, once again became more direct and explicit. In response, Stalin, under the banner of national self-defense in time of war, finally put an end to resistance against what had become the hallmark of his commitment to the socialist transformation of Russia.

(B) The Nationalist Issue

The undisguised desire for autonomy and independence by these minorities threatened the dismemberment of the Soviet state. With the Nazi occupation of large parts of the USSR, its dissolution became more than an idle and distant possibility. Though the Soviets had sought to limit and control earlier geopolitical threats through the creation of "autonomous" national republics in the 1920s, this compromise did not remove incremental pressures for more complete independence. Nor did it strike a workable, satisfactory balance between "center" and periphery. As a result the nationality issue would not go away, nor was the unequal and unfair distribution of power between the majority and the minorities appreciably altered.

Transfiguring the meaning and significance of this territorial threat was Stalin's instinctive and parochial Russian nationalism. The dying Lenin, as early as 1923, had privately recorded his extreme unhappiness with Stalin's illiberal approach to the nationality question. The minorities, he wrote, suffered "from invasion of their rights by this typical Russian man, the Chauvinist, whose basic nature is that of a scoundrel and oppressor."[30] The defining considerations in this critical situation, cannot however, be reduced to one of individual psychology, however perverse. Socialist theory recognizes the absolute *moral* priority of class over national interests. "There are cases," Stalin wrote, "when the right of self-determination conflicts with another, a higher right—the right of the working class.... In such cases—this must be said bluntly—the right of self-determination cannot and must not serve as an obstacle to the working class in exercising its right to dictatorship."[31] In the event, under the cover of this ideological justification, almost the entire national minority leadership was purged in the 1930s and 1940s. For example, the political leadership of the Chechen-Ingushi Republic was destroyed in 1937, with many of the Republic's 14,000 "leaders" arrested and murdered. Similar repression occurred in the Balkar, Karachay, and Tatar areas and among the Kalmyks.[32]

Such a proletarian, anti-nationalist ideology logically aspires in its maximalist form to ethnocide (or perhaps a more accurate term would be 'politicide'). If national identity threatened the class unity of the international working class and its champion, the Soviet Union, then such divisive self-consciousness, with all its attendant features of language, religion, national literature, particularistic calendars, and schooling, must be forfeit. At its most radical, this was precisely what Stalin's systematic design of national expatriation sought to accomplish. The Stalinist program of complete cultural conversion through migration (to the extent that there was such a conscious plan) directly and indirectly caused up to 500,000 deaths. It is therefore a paradigmatic instance of ethnocide facilitated through mass murder. But it was neither intended, nor did it become in practice, an example of physical genocide, i.e., the complete physical extermination of a minority nation. The intent was to destroy a variety of minority cultures and the political ambitions built upon them, rather than to murder all the members of a specific people. The growth in the minority populations after removal and the initial period of transition is incontrovertible evidence as to the non-genocidal intentions of the Stalinists.

Two additional aspects of Stalin's assimilationist, "internationalist" agenda, with regard to the national minorities (despite his arbitrary, chauvinistic equation of socialism with Russian national culture) throw light on the non-genocidal character of these deportations. First there is the much discussed Stalinist project of forced Russification of indigenous cultures. Such a far-reaching scheme could be proposed and pursued precisely because the indigenous peoples were not to be eradicated. By comparison, the Nazis had no comparable program for Jews because there was no need to re-educate a people who are about to disappear. There was no point in recreating their linguistic base if they were all shortly to be corpses, no need to convert them religiously and to remake them culturally, if they were soon thereafter to be immolated. Stalin's efforts at acculturation, his ideal of assimilation, was precisely the reverse of Nazi policy towards the Jewish people. Jewish assimilation was seen as an enormous threat by Hitler to be fought without compromise for it allowed the Jew to conceal his real nature and to disguise his unalterable bio-metaphysical characteristics. It made the Jew all the more dangerous in the socio-political, economic and sexual realm, with all the attendant negative racial consequences. For this reason Hitler's anti-Jewish crusade necessarily entailed complete Jewish *dis-assimilation*. For example, every Jew had to insert the name Sarah or Abraham into their given name and mark their often indistinguishable appearance through the wearing of the yellow star. Above all, any sexual contact and intermarriage with non-Jews was strictly prohibited.

If we consider the persecution of the intellectual and leadership elites among the Soviet national minorities, both before and after deportation, then the objective of ethnocidal domination rather than unrestrained physical genocide becomes even more clear. In the case of the Kalmyks there was an assault against the Buddhist religious leadership. "The purge destroyed the entire Kalmyk intelligentsia, which had never been large. The majority were charged with bourgeois nationalism, or with working with foreign countries. As many as 5000 persons were liquidated. The entire priesthood, the most highly educated section of the population, which in 1926 numbered about 3,000 persons... was liquidated. All Buddhist temples and all sacred treasures were destroyed."[33] For the Chechens and Ingushis this entailed:

> Arrests [that] continued until the beginning of 1938. The chief sufferers were the new national intellectuals. The leading Party members among the North Caucasians, including all members of the Party oblast committees, the national parliament, the government, scientists, writers, journalists, etc., were among those arrested. The leading national intellectuals were charged with organizing a "counter-revolutionary and bourgeois nationalist center" in Chechen-Ingushetia, whose members were alleged to have engaged in preparations for an armed uprising against the Soviet regime in 1922–23, in sabotage, in organizing terrorism, etc. All of the 137 persons accused of belonging to the counter-revolutionary center were members of the Communist Party, and 60 percent of them had been educated in special Communist training schools.[34]

In the particular instance of the Balkars and Karachay, "the NKVD struck first at the remnants of the pre-revolutionary non-party intellectuals."[35] Then at their national cultural institutions:

> On the pretext of liquidating "the consequences of the sabotaging activity of these enemies of the people," meaning the "bourgeois nationalists," the "Pan-Turks," "the Pan-Islamites," and the Trotskyite and Bukharinite elements in the North Caucasus, the entire national literature, both original and in translation, was destroyed, including all school textbooks and teaching aids; all fiction, including translations from the Russian and world classics; almost all scientific, technical, and agricultural literature; all historical and philological literature; all works of reference and dictionaries; and all Party and Soviet literature, including translations of Marx, Engels, Lenin, and Stalin. By the first half of 1938 everything in the North Caucasus under the name of "culture, national in form and socialist in content" had been destroyed. So that no trace might remain of this "form," the Kremlin in 1939 "recommended" to the peoples of the North Caucasus and later to all the Turkic and Moslem peoples of the USSR that they adopt the use of the Russian alphabet instead of the Latin.[36]

A similar tale could be told in the case of every national bloc that was deported, as well as in the case of other minority nationality groups that were not uprooted but subjected to other forms of state pressure.

What these measures demonstrate is that though Soviet cultural hegemony recognized few limits to its chauvinistic self-aggrandizement, Stalinist extirpation of the cultural and political elites was the converse of a program of total extermination. Stalinism annihilated the leadership in order to *preserve* the mass, if in a culturally altered state.

The continued existence in reduced circumstances of hundreds of thousands of these uprooted peoples is certain proof that Stalin did not intend their complete liquidation. In their new eastern environments they were put to work primarily, though not exclusively, in agriculture. A considerable minority segment of this now available manpower was enlisted in ongoing mining and industrial projects, such as the difficult task of building the railroad system in the Lake Issyk-Kul region. The explanation for this pragmatic outcome is to be found in Stalin's *Weltanschauung*. Marxist-Leninist socialism, even when crudely interpreted by Stalin, imputed the criminality of the class enemy to an acquired false consciousness created by objective economic and social structures. The threatening "otherness" of the other, having been learned, can also be unlearned. Hence the doctrinal basis for the centrality of political re-education in Marxist-Leninist theory, whatever the deplorable abuses of this dogma in Soviet practice. Even when the internal opposition is most dangerous and its insidious perversions threaten the world-historical victory of the working class, the prime source of danger is the result of an ideological misreading of events, a normative misperception of "what is to be done." For this reason the criminality of the "class enemy," or of the "bourgeois nationalist," however destabilizing and reactionary, is a threat of an altogether different order from that represented by the "racial enemy." In the Manichean biocentric ontology of Nazism where individuals are seen as the biological carriers of essential genetic and meta-genetic attributes, their negative behavior (and being) can never, by definition, be unlearned. The Nazi racial ideology of conflict therefore produces physical genocide rather than repression, socio-economic re-education, the Gulag, national deportations, or mass death.

The stark disparity between Nazi and Stalinist analyses of the type of danger represented by their "opponents," and hence the alternative type of actions deemed appropriate in response, is revealed in the post-exilic history of the deported Soviet national minorities. Stalin possessed the police power and necessary ruthlessness to carry out a program of physical genocide against the minority peoples had he so intended. The decisive fact is that he chose instead a policy of compulsory resettlement and colonial expansion in underdeveloped and underpopulated regions of Russia. As a result, three years after Stalin's death, there were sufficiently large numbers of the deported minority peoples in existence to make their "rehabilitation" both an empirical possibility as well as a Soviet political necessity. Nikita Khrushchev's speech to the Twentieth Party Congress in February 1956 was the highly dramatic beginning of a public recantation of Stalin's past "errors." He spoke of "gross violations of the basic Leninist principles of the nationalities policy of the Soviet state," referring to the national deportations of the Karachay, Chechens, Ingushi, Balkars and Kalmyks. This was the start of a series of practical reforms relating to the minority groups, including the official reestablishment of most of their autonomous republics. As a result:

> Of the seven deported nations three resumed their old constitutional status. One has been downgraded; and one was downgraded for a time then restored to its old status[37]; and two others, numbering at least 584,000 in 1936, have had no rehabilitation at all.[38]

The number of minority peoples available for repatriation under this change of policy, allowing for all the imprecision in the relevant demographic statistics, was, in 1953, somewhere between a minimum of 280,000 and a maximum of 603,400, excluding the Volga Germans and Tatars.[39] If we add the German and Tatar population the figures increase dramatically.[40] The 1959 census lists the total Soviet German population at 1,619,000.[41] Though the number of surviving Crimean Tatars is difficult to estimate with precision, their population by the late 1950s was considerable. Roy Medvedev, in trying to reconstruct their national odyssey, suggests that 50 percent of the original 200,000–250,000 deportees died, but this is almost certainly too high a figure.[42] A loss rate of approximately 30 percent (plus or minus 5 percent) appears more in keeping with the data that we have. Building from this post-removal base of between 140,000 and 175,000 their population advanced until it again numbered in the region of 200,000 to 250,000 by 1953. At the same time, the Tatar population in the Soviet Union as a whole grew considerably in the 1950s reaching, according to 1959 estimates, 4,967,700. This was an increase of 15 percent over what it had been in 1939. These aggregates for the Tatar community are all subject to revision, but they indicate the continued existence of this minority group, even under the rigors of exile. When all these population estimates from 1959 are added together, and the required backward demographic extrapolations are made, the resultant sum of survivors reveals that a large percentage of the resettled minorities were *not* murdered by Stalin. Indeed, the total population of the five main minority peoples—excluding the Volga Germans and Tatars—was only 20 percent smaller in 1953 (on the maximum estimate cited above) than it had been in 1939, just two years before the forced deportations began. If we include the numbers for the Volga Germans and Crimean Tatars, the population of the seven deported national groups was in fact greater in 1953 than it had been in 1939.[43] In effect, there were many hundreds of thousands, even millions of minority individuals that Stalin could have killed but did not, as a result of his restraining ideology.

Kampuchea

Let us consider one final case of mass death as a species of class war: Kampuchea. Between 1975 and 1978 Cambodia was a living hell. In many ways the people of Cambodia were the main victims of the Vietnamese war. The radical instability caused and sustained by that misconceived, ineffectively managed adventure spilled over into Cambodia and undermined its native institutions. This made possible the victory, in an extended civil war, of the fanatical communist Khmer Rouge in April 1975. The exact details of what happened next are still uncertain and subject to widely different interpretations. Yet there is no doubt that an astonishing, if unconscionable, revolutionary transformation of the existing social order was attempted, with thousands upon thousands of casualties in its wake.

In making its singular vision real, the Khmer Rouge held that not only must existing class modalities be destroyed but the individuals who had inhabited these outmoded and perfidious structures must be either fundamentally reformed or killed.

In the eyes of Pol Pot, there were three types of enemies: the "capitalists," mainly shopkeepers and traders; the "feudalists," mainly Buddhists, intellectuals, and royalty; and finally, the largest category of all—the "imperialists." They included ethnic minorities who dressed or spoke differently from the Khmer, as well as so-called agents of the CIA, the KGB, or the Vietnamese.

These groups—that is, the persons who comprised them—were, by definition, "enemies of the people" and therefore had to be socially reeducated and remade into productive agricultural labor, or else eliminated. No third way was permissible. Any compromise was a betrayal of the revolution and hence itself a capital crime. Total revolution, the absolute re-creation of the civic and cultural order, the reduction of the body-politic to only peasants and party members, was not a task easily accomplished, and it produced its carnal sacrifices, even in the hundreds of thousands.

Nevertheless, certain distinctive features of this situation need be understood. First, the overwhelming majority of victims came from the majority population. They were not singled out for belonging to specific ethnic stock as in tribal wars in Africa; or for membership in a particular religion as in the Huguenot wars, the Pakistan-Indian conflict, the wartime Croatian massacres of Serbs, the Turkish slaughter of Armenians, or the various persecutions of Jews. True, the Vietnamese, Chinese, and Cham communities in Cambodia were persecuted for being what they were. However, great care must be taken in labeling the persecution of these ethnic minorities as genocide, for they do not appear to have been marked out for complete physical annihilation.

The Khmer Rouge, for example, ordered the eviction of 150,000 (out of approximately 200,000) ethnic Vietnamese living in Cambodia—no matter how long their residence had been—rather than murder them. The later murder in 1978 of most of the remaining ethnic Vietnamese came in the wake of intense Cambodian-Vietnam political tensions between 1976 and 1978 and the attempted assassination of Pol Pot by Cambodian troops believed to be linked to the Vietnamese regime. Again, the undeniable persecution of the large Chinese community (numbering up to 425,000 in 1975) half of whom are said to have died between 1975 and 1978, is not explicable simply as racial prejudice. As Ben Kiernan has shown, it was directly related to class status, i.e., the role of the ethnic Chinese community as an urban "middle class."[44] And even then, "[The] Chinese...were targeted in an indirect way, as the archetypal urban dwellers (and therefore "exploiters"), and they suffered far more from enforced starvation and disease."[45] This conclusion is supported by the fact that the location to which individual Chinese were deported directly impacted on their chance for survival. If they were deported to the now overpopulated northwest region, where conditions were chaotic, food in short supply, due to the massive influx of 230,000 people from Phnom Penh in 1975—overwhelming the original population of 170,000—then the death rate was high. If, however, the Chinese were deported to the Southwest or Eastern Zones, the rates of survival were far higher. This disparity makes clear that there was no central program of Chinese extermination but rather a massively cruel policy in general, that fell disproportionately on city dwellers ill-equipped for their new life in the rugged countryside—among whom the Chinese were again disproportionately represented. Moreover, "there was no noticeable racialist vendetta against people of Chinese origin in Democratic Kampuchea," and the "tragedy of Kampuchea's Chinese was not that they were singled out for persecution by an anti-Chinese regime, but rather that a pro-Chinese regime subjected them to the same brutal treatment as the rest of the country's population."[46]

The case of the Muslim Cham people is still more ambiguous. There is no doubt that many Cham were killed by the Khmer Rouge. However, the larger Khmer Rouge governing strategy towards the Cham appears not to have required the death of all Cham, though it certainly required uprooting the distinctive Cham culture and its social and political manifestations. Ben Kiernan has identified the persecution of the Cham, which appears to be rooted in class distinctions as much as racial or religious ones, as an instance of physical genocide that claimed 90,000 victims out of 250,000 Cham. Michael Vickery, however, has questioned this description noting that, "unfortunately Kiernan has tinkered with the statistics in a tendentious manner in an attempt to prove the case for genocide."[47] Rather than a roughly 34–35 percent loss rate (based on a population of 250,000 in 1975), the actual rate of loss allowing for some natural growth in the Cham population between 1975 and 1979, is approximately 10 percent—and not genocidal. Though one must be cautious here, and no hard evidence exists to support Vickery or Kiernan, these debates should be taken as a warning not to proceed too quickly or casually. Support for Vickery's position comes from the presence of Mat Ly, a Cham, on the standing committee of the People's Representative Assembly since April 1976 and from the fact that many Cham once resettled on the agricultural collectives—their distinctive Islamic culture shattered—were not then singled out to be murdered. Certainly, such acts as forcing Cham women to cut their customarily long hair, forcing Cham men and women to adopt a more conventional manner of dress, to abandon their own language, to eat pork, to give up their copies of the Koran, and the disbursement of Cham villages, are all acts of ethnocide. I note in support of this judgment that in his paper, "Orphans of Genocide," Kiernan acknowledges that: "the documentary case [for physical genocide] is weak."[48] Moreover, and this is not unimportant, the murder of the Cham appears to have varied from location to location. "In parts of the Center and East in particular, there were apparently massacres of Cham as such, but Chams from the Northwest and North assert that they were not the object of any special attention by the authorities and that they survived in the same proportion as other people."[49]

The majority of those murdered in Kampuchea were identified as *ideological* enemies (along class and military lines) and they were eradicated as political opponents. However, even with regard to class enemies there is reason to question the completeness and thoroughness of the purge by the Khmer Rouge. Undoubtedly many bureaucrats, intellectuals, civil servants, artists, and entrepeneurs were executed. But, at the same time, one must take into account the number of individuals—in the hundreds of thousands—coming from these hated classes, who survived both within Cambodia and as refugees in neighboring Vietnam and Thailand. Thus, it is open to serious doubt whether every member of these "socially unprogressive" and "para-sitic" groups was marked out for extermination. The brutal "reeducation camps" established by the new regime—though places of mass death—are significant counter-indicators to those who argue for genocide. These camps did have survivors. The Khmer Rouge did feel themselves successful in at least some small way in transforming the enemy class consciousness of the former bourgeoisie, and so permitted individuals who belonged to "counter-revolutionary classes" to take their place in the new order. For example, it appears that there were considerable numbers of Buddhist monks—there were approximately 80,000 monks in 1975 when the CPK took power—who fell into this category. The same appears to apply in the case of agricultural engineers and doctors who, after time in these "reduction camps," were integrated into the regular agricultural collectives. As a result 50 percent of the physicians remaining in Cambodia in April 1975 survived the Khmer onslaught against society. This, of course, means that 50 percent of physicians died—but in their totality these figures indicate the complexity, the compromise, the mediation that is here at issue. Even the Khmer Rouge did not insist on the death of *all* its class enemies, now remade into farm laborers. The evil of *class* could be shed, transformed, and a productive individual remade out of the former economic oppressor. This is significantly different from the ineradicable stigma of *racial* distinctiveness attached to those, like the Jews, earmarked for extermination under Nazi rule.

Notes

1. In the actual campaign that unfolded after January 1928, the term "Kulak" was used in a variety of ways and, in general, lost much of its technical meaning, becoming equivalent in practice to any peasant whom the regime wished to persecute. For further consideration of this definitional issue see Moshe Lewin, "Who Was the Soviet Kulak?," in his *The Making of the Soviet System: Essays on the Social History of Inter-war Russia* (New York 1985), 121–41; and Dorothy Atkinson, *The End of the Russian Land Commune, 1905–1930* (Stanford 1984), 281–84. At the Fifteenth Party Congress in 1927, Molotov defined a Kulak as a peasant who hired labor and rented land, calculating that 3.7 percent of the peasants belonged to this category. See here also the statistics on the Kulak proportion of the peasantry worked out by Stephan Merl, *Die Anfänge der Kollektivierung in der Sowjetunion* (Wiesbaden 1985), 138–41. His figures for the size of the Kulak population for 1927 and 1929 are 3.9 and 2.2 percent respectively. His Table 29, 140, entitled "Veränderung der Kulakenwirtschaften zwischen 1927 and 1929 nach Regionen" (Changes in Kulak Commerce between 1927 and 1929 according to Region) gives an idea of the nature and size of Kulak market activity between 1927 and 1929. Lynn Viola has also pointed to the many other sorts of "class" enemies undone as part of the program of dekulakization, "The second coming: Class Enemies in the Soviet Countryside, 1927–1935," in *Stalinist Terror: New Perspectives,* eds. J. A. Getty and R. T. Manning (Cambridge 1993), 65–98.

2. I borrow this expression from M. Lewin, "The Social Background of Stalinism," in *Making of the Soviet System,* 122.

3. Vasily Grossman's provocative claim that "Just as the Germans proclaimed Jews are not human beings, thus did Lenin and Stalin proclaim, 'Kulaks are not human beings,'" cited with at least implicit approval by Robert Conquest, is simply an error. Conquest's self-correcting awareness of its incorrectness is, I believe, indicated by the fact that having used the quote he does nothing more with it and quickly moves on. That is, were this putative similarity more than a rhetorical device, Conquest would be obliged to analyze this entire issue more fully. Grossman's remarks are made in his *Forever Flowering* (New York 1972), 144, cited by Robert Conquest, *Harvest of Sorrow* (New York 1986), 129. More recently Alan Bullock, basing himself I suspect on Conquest's view (though no attribution is given) repeats this erroneous description—"Like the Jews under the Nazis

the Kulaks [were]—declared sub-human," *Hitler and Stalin* (New York 1992), 308. The larger principle to be borne in mind in any close analysis of why individuals are killed, is that, contra Conquest and Bullock, one does not have to be "sub-human" to be persecuted or murdered. Human beings are perfectly capable of doing horrendous things to other human beings. The Nazi classification of Jews as "sub-human" *(Untermenschen)*, is a technical notion, not a metaphor, predicated on pseudo-scientific racial theories that have no parallel within the Stalinist (or Marxist-Leninist) orbit.

4. This assumed, however much it was ignored in practice (though far from completely ignored as we shall see), that one could separate a Kulak's status from his person.

5. Lenin's many compromises during the so-called New Economic Policy (NEP) were now to be seen as only temporary concessions to historic circumstance overtaken by new socio-economic actualities. Zhores Medvedev's conclusion in his *Soviet Agriculture* (New York 1987) that NEP was still a viable option is a minority scholarly position.

6. C. Ward, *Stalin's Russia* (London and New York 1993), 42. This new round of shortages were accompanied by significant free-market price rises of grains and other foodstuffs creating further dislocations throughout the national economy.

7. Analyzed in detail by Moshe Lewin, *Russian Peasants and Soviet Power: A Study of Collectivization* (London 1968), 214–50 and 383–405; Naum Jasny, *The Socialized Agriculture of the USSR* (Stanford, CA 1949), 204; H. Holland, "Soviet Agriculture with and without Collectivization, 1928–1940," *Slavic Review* 47, no. 2 (1988): 206–208; Dorothy Atkinson, *The End of the Russian Land Commune, 1905–1930,* 313–45; S. Merl, *Die Anfänge der Kollektivierung,* 230–41, particularly on the issue of tractors, Table 70, 237.

8. M. Lewin, "Taking Grain," 169–73; and L. Volin, *A Century of Russian Agriculture* (Cambridge, MA 1970), 250ff.

9. For an introduction to this event see Bohdan Krawchenko and Roman Serbyn, eds., *Famine in Ukraine, 1932–1933* (Edmonton 1986); Bohdan Krawchenko, "The Great Famine of 1932–1933 in Soviet Ukraine: Causes and Consequences," *Critique* 17 (1986): 137–46; Iwij Borys, *The Sovietization of the Ukraine* (Edmonton 1980); the report to the U.S. Congress, prepared primarily by James Mace, *Investigation of the Ukrainian Famine 1932–1933; Report to Congress* (Washington, DC 1988); R. Conquest, *The Harvest of Sorrow* (New York 1987); and for further sources, Alexander Pidhaina, "A Bibliography of the Great Famine in the Ukraine, 1932–1934," *New Review: A Journal of East-European History* 4 (1973): 32–68. The post-Stalinist work on the famine and its causes is reviewed in the *U.S. Commission on the Ukraine Famine,* 37–68. As one would expect, until the post-Gorbachev era Soviet scholarship on this subject was intensely apologetic in tone.

10. This conflict has been analyzed by Taras Hunczak (ed.), *The Ukraine, 1917–1921: A Study in Revolution* (Cambridge MA, 1971); Hryhory Kostiuk, *Stalinist Rule in the Ukraine* (New York 1961); John Reshatar, *The Ukrainian Revolution: A Study in Nationalism* (Princeton 1952); Arthur Adams, *Bolsheviks in the Ukraine: The Second Campaign, 1918–1919* (New Haven 1963); Basil D. Mytryshan, *Moscow and the Ukraine, 1918–1953: A Study of Russian Bolshevik Nationality Policy* (New York 1956); Bohdan Krawchenko, *Social Change and National Consciousness in Twentieth-Century Ukraine* (New York 1985); James E. Mace, "Politics and History in Soviet Ukraine, 1921–1933," *Nationality Papers* 1 (1982): 157–80; idem., "Famine and Nationalism in Soviet Ukraine,"

Problems of Communism 33, no. 3 (1984): 37–50; idem., "The Man-Made Famine of 1933," in *Famine in Ukraine, 1932–1933,* eds. R. Serbyn and B. Krawchenko, (Edmonton 1986), 1–14; W. Kosyk, "Der Hungergenozid in der Ukraine 1932–1933," in *Jahrbuch der Ukrainekunder* (1983): 89–126; Steven L. Guthier, "The Popular Base of Ukrainian Nationalism in 1917," *Slavic Review* 38, no. 1 (March 1979): 30–47; Andrew P. Lamis, "Some Observations on the Ukrainian National Movement and the Ukrainian Revolution, 1917–1921," *Harvard Ukrainian Studies* 2, no. 4 (December 1978): 525–31; Orest Subtelny, *Ukraine: A History* (Toronto 1988); a number of the essays dealing with Ukrainian history in Anthony Smith and Tamara Dragadze, eds., *National Identity in Russia, the Soviet Union, and Eastern Europe* (London 1992); George O. Liber, *Soviet Nationality Policy* (Cambridge and New York 1992), and idem., *Communism and the Dilemmas of National Liberation: National Communism in Soviet Ukraine, 1918–1933* (Cambridge, MA 1983). For a comprehensive study of Soviet politics in relationship to the "Ukrainian Question," that is relatively weak and underinformed on the famine of 1932–1933, see Robert S. Sullivant, *Soviet Politics and the Ukraine, 1917–1957* (New York 1962).

11. On Soviet opposition to Ukrainian culture and cultural elites see George S. Luckyj, *Literary Politics in the Soviet Ukraine: 1917–1934* (New York 1956); and H. Kostiuk, *Stalinist Rule in the Ukraine,* 47–59.

12. The Ukrainian *selianym* should not be equated with a Russian peasant or serf. The *selianym* was "a free Cossack-farmer before the Russian occupation of Ukraine. For this historical reason Ukrainian farmers had a much stronger sense of private ownership and deeper feeling of freedom and independence," Miron Dolot, *Execution By Hunger: The Hidden Holocaust* (New York 1985), xiv).

13. Semen O. Pidhainy, et al, eds., *The Black Deeds of the Kremlin: A White Book* (Detroit 1955), vol. 1, 205.

14. Conquest, *Harvest of Sorrow,* 219. Repeated in the *U.S. Commission on the Ukraine Famine,* xiii: "crushing the Ukrainian peasantry made it possible for Stalin to curtail Ukrainian national self-assertion."

15. Conquest, ibid., 221f puts the 1931 procurement at 7.7 million tons, with 7 million tons actually collected. This total already indicates a severe decline from the 23.9 million tons harvested in 1930.

16. On the ambiguities inherent in all these grain statistics, see the pertinent observations of R. W. Davies, "A Note on Grain Statistics," *Soviet Studies* 21, no. 3 (January 1970): 314–29; and idem., *The Socialist Offensive,* vol. I, 65–68. On the trustworthiness (or otherwise) of Russian statistics see also Steven G. Wheatcroft's essay, "The Reliability of Russian Pre War Grain Output Statistics," *Soviet Studies* 25, no. 2 (April 1974): 157–80; idem., "A Reevaluation of Soviet Agricultural Production in the 1920s and 1930s," in *The Soviet Rural Economy,* ed. Robert C. Stuart (Totowa, NJ 1983), 37–38; Abram Bergson, *Soviet National Income and Product in 1937* (New York 1953), 7–9; Naum Jasny, "Intricacies of Russian National Income Indexes," *Journal of Political Economy* 55, no. 4 (August 1947): 299–322; idem., "Soviet Statistics," *Review of Economics and Statistics* 32, no. 1 (February 1950): 92–99; Vladimir G. Trevel and John P. Hardt, eds., *Soviet Economic Statistics* (Durham 1972); and Gregory Grossman, *Soviet Statistics of Physical Output of Industrial Commodities: Their Compilation and Quality* (Princeton 1960). Joseph S. Berliner has, likewise, revealed the tremendous fraud in

factory statistics in his *Factory and Manager in the USSR* (Cambridge, MA 1957), 160–81. Cf. also A. Solzhenitsyn's devastating critique of Soviet statistics in his *Gulag Archipelago* (New York 1974–78), vol. 2, 69.

17. Robert Conquest takes the view that Stalin and his bureaucrats knew that it would be impossible to meet the new targets. They understood, he argues, that the notion that the peasants were hoarding grain and that they controlled large stockpiles of food which they refused to release to the market was "a myth" (*Harvest of Sorrow*, 221). Walter Laqueur has however argued, on the basis of post-Glasnost evidence, that: "the punishment thesis has not been proved. There seems to have been no plan to destroy Ukrainian agriculture and to cause the death of millions of people." See his *Stalin, The Glasnost Revelations* (New York 1990), 282 for an assessment.

18. Conquest, *Harvest of Sorrow*, 227ff.

19. Cited from G. O. Liber, *Soviet Nationality Policy*, 166. On these political activities, interpreted from a radical Ukrainian perspective, see H. Kostiuk, *Stalinist Rule in the Ukraine*, 18–37; from a less ideological perspective, also R. S. Sullivant, *Soviet Politics in the Ukraine*, 195–208.

20. This figure concurs with R. Conquest's estimate, *Harvest of Sorrow*, 303 and 306. He gives a "conservative" aggregate of 7 million famine-related deaths in 1932–1933 for all areas affected by the disaster, 5 million of which occurred in the Ukraine. Cf. also his calculations in his essay "The Famine of 1933: A Survey of Sources," in *Famine in the Ukraine*, eds. R. Serbyn and B. Krawchenko, 50. Serhii Pirozkhov, "Population Losses in the Ukraine in the 1930s and 1940s," 89, argues that Conquest overestimates the losses. This would also appear to be the conclusion of V. V. Tsaplin who has calculated excess deaths in the Soviet Union in 1933 at between 3 and 4 million. (I cite this figure from S. Fitzpatrick, *Stalin's Peasants* [New York 1994], 342, n. 88). Alternatively, the figure of 4.5 million to 5 million actual deaths due to the famine in the Ukraine in 1932–33 is supported by the recent (1990) demographic research of S. V. Kulchytskyi, called to my attention by G. Liber, *Soviet Nationality Policy*, 237, n. 23; and by G. Simon, who refers to "at least 8 million people starved" and "at least 4.5 million deaths" in the Ukraine, *Nationalism and Policy* (Boulder 1991), 99. These figures are, as all figures in this article, subject to revision.

21. This is not to deny the logical possibility that nationalist conflicts can become genocidal. It is only to assert that this is not what actually occurred in this particular historical instance.

22. R. Conquest gives the slightly higher figure of 18.8 percent of the total population of the Ukraine, *Harvest of Sorrow*, 306. However, he does not give sufficient weight to various life-saving factors, especially migration, in his tabulation. The total Ukrainian population in this era was circa 32–35 million, some of it resident outside the Ukraine proper since the terror and famine of 1928. A more detailed reconstruction of Ukrainian population statistics will be found in Robert Lewis, et al., "The Growth and Redistribution of Russia and the USSR: 1897–1970," in *Ukraine in the Seventies*, ed. Peter Potychnyj, (Oakville [Ontario, Can.] 1975), 151–75; and S. Pirozkhov, "Population Loss in Ukraine in the 1930s and 1940s," 90–95.

23. Conquest's maximum total of child deaths of 4 million (3 million as a result of the famine, 1 million due to the program of dekulakization), based on currently available evidence, appears to be too high, *Harvest of Sorrow,* 297. Moreover, this total includes non-Ukrainian children, e.g., those of Kazakhstan, thus significantly reducing the number and percentage of child losses in the Ukraine, even on Conquest's numbers.

24. S. Pirozhkov calculates that, "the unborn and dead children accounted for 54.4 percent of total losses (that is, the potential demographic losses of children was approximately 3.1 million people) and direct losses of children and youths aged under 25 represented 13 percent, or 760,000 people," "Population Loss in the Ukraine in the 1930s and 1940s," 89.

25. M. Maksudov estimates that for the entire period 1926–1939, of the 12 million Ukrainian children born, 1.4 million died, "Ukraine's Demographic Losses 1927–1938," *Sucasnist* 10 (1983): 37.

26. The seven are: the Kalmyks, the Chechens, the Ingushis, the Volga Germans, the Balkar, the Crimean Tatars, and the Karachay. The so-called Meskhetians (a mixed Turkicized Muslim population from Georgia) were an eighth category of persons now often included in the lists of deported national minorities. They were not, in fact, a single, identifiable people with a discrete national territory and identity before they were subject to removal. See B. Nahaylo and V. Swoboda, *Soviet Disunion: A History Of The Nationalities Problem in the USSR* (New York 1989), 97.

27. See on these nationalist aspirations, Serge Zenkovsky, *Pan Turkism and Islam in Russia* (Cambridge, MA 1960); Edige Kirimal, *Der nationale Kampf der Krimturken* (Emsdetten 1952); Gerhard von Mende, *Der nationale Kampf der Rußlandturken* (Berlin 1936); Alan Fisher, *The Crimean Tatars* (Stanford 1978), 94–108; Edward Lazzerini, "Godidism at the Turn of the Twentieth Century: A View from Within," *Cahiers* (April–June 1975): 245–77; Alexandre Bennigsen and Chantal Lemercier-Quelquejay, *La presse et le mouvement national chez les musulmans de Russie avant 1920* (Paris 1964); and G. E. von Grunbaum, "Problems of Muslim Nationalism," in *Islam and the West,* ed. Richard Frye (Gravenhage 1957), 7–29.

28. The Volga Germans were the first group deported. Their removal was authorized by a decree on August 28, 1941. The Karachay and Kalmyks were deported in October–November 1943 and December 1943, respectively, while the Chechen and Ingushi were exiled in March 1944. The Crimean Tatars were not removed until the Soviet reoccupation of the Crimea. The actual date of the beginning of their removal was May 18, 1944.

29. On this sensitive question see Joachim Hoffmann, *Deutsche und Kalmyken 1924 bis 1945* (Freiburg 1974); Patrick von zur Mühlen, *Zwischen Hakenkreuz und Sowjetstern: Der Nationalismus der sowjetischen Orientvölker im Zweiten Weltkrieg* (Dusseldorf 1971); and Norbert Müller, *Wehrmacht und Okkupation 1941–1944* (Berlin 1971).

30. V. I. Lenin, *Works,* vol. 40 (Moscow 1950), 356. Further consideration of Lenin's position on the nationality issue is provided by B. Nahaylo and V. Swoboda, *Soviet Disunion,* 50–59.

31. J. Stalin, *Works,* vol. 5, 270, cited by Robert Conquest, *The Soviet Deportation of Nationalities* (London and New York 1960), 105.

32. Conquest, *Soviet Deportation,* 84–87.

33. Dorzha Akbakov, "The Kalmyks," in *Genocide in the USSR: Studies in Group Destruction* (Munich 1958), 34. On the religious anti-Buddhist aspect, more specifically, see the papers by Nicholaz N. Poppe, "Attempted Distribution of other Religious Groups," and Shamba Balinov, "The Kalmyk Buddhist," in *Genocide in the USSR* (New York 1958), 181–92 and 193–96 respectively.

34. R. Karcha, "The Peoples of the North Caucasus," *Genocide in the USSR,* 39.

35. Ibid.

36. Ibid., 40–41.

37. These five include the Karachay, Chechens, Ingushi, Balkars, and Kalmyks.

38. The two were the Volga Germans and Crimean Tatars. The Meskhetians were also not repatriated. However, the Volga Germans were granted cultural privileges such as the opening of two German newspapers, German language radio broadcasts, and the teaching of the German language, B. Nahaylo and V. Swoboda, *Soviet Disunion,* 126; Conquest, *Soviet Deportations,* 143.

39. 1959 is the first year for which census data are available following Stalin's death in 1953. W. Kolarz, *Russia and Her Colonies* (New York 1952), 75, puts the Volga German population in 1941 at 480,000. Of these, 200,000, or nearly 40 percent, were exiled by the Russians while the Germans during their occupation of the region deported the remaining 280,000, or nearly 60 percent, to Germany. A. Sheehy and B. Nahaylo give the higher estimate of 400,000 Soviet deportations. Interestingly, in response to continued protests from this German community within its borders, the Soviets allowed 55,000 Soviet Germans to leave Russia between 1970 and 1979. A. Sheehy and B. Nahaylo, *The Crimean Tatars, Volga Germans and Meskhetians,* 3rd. ed., (London 1980), 5.

I arrive at these numbers as follows. For the maximum I use the 1959 Russian census figures for the Chechens, 418,000; the Ingushi, 106,000; the Kalmyks, 106,000; the Karachay 81,000; and the Balkars 42,000. These total: 758,000 less 20 percent for natural increase (a rough, perhaps too high, concession to population growth) between 1953 (the year of Stalin's death) and 1959. For the lower figure, I have used R. Conquest's estimate of an absolute minimum less the same 20 percent, though Conquest himself, in his final reckoning, favors the less severe tally of 490,000 survivors rather than the extreme figure of 350,000 (in 1959) that I have employed. See Conquest, *Soviet Deportations,* 170. According to NKVD archives the total number of Chechen, Ingush, Karachay, and Balkar deportees between 1943 and 1949 was 608,749 of whom 184,556 "disappeared [*ubylo*] due to various causes." Figures reported by N. F. Bugai, "The Truth About the Deportation of Chechen and Ingush Peoples," *Soviet Studies in History* 30, no. 2 (Fall 1991): 78.

40. The Volga Germans and Crimean Tatars were not included in the policy of return decreed in 1957 because their war record was considered to have been so reprehensible. However, in August 1964 the Volga Germans were politically rehabilitated. Finally in 1967 the Tatars were partially rehabilitated though their Crimean territory was not returned to them. Consult for the particulars of the 1957 act and for developments during the 1960s, A. Sheehy, *The Crimean Tatars, Volga Germans and Meskhetians* (London, 1980), 13. On Tatar resistance to continued Soviet oppression following the institution of Khrushchev's policy of rehabilitation for the other deported minorities see Borys Lewytzkyj, *Politische Opposition in der Sowjetunion 1960–1972* (Munich 1972); and A. Sheehy and B. Nahaylo, *The Crimean Tatars, Volga Germans and Meskhetians.* Further

information on the contemporary fate of the German population in the Soviet Union is provided by Sidney Hectman, *The Soviet Germans in the USSR Today* (Cologne 1980); and Isabelle Kreindler, "The Soviet Deported Nationalities: A Summary and Update," *Soviet Studies* 38, no. 3 (July 1986): 387–405.

41. The 1970 Soviet census gives their total number at 1,846,000.

42. Roy Medvedev, *Let History Judge* (Oxford 1989), 492. This is consistent with the Tatars' own estimate of casualties that has been put at 46 percent during the removals and during their first 18 months in their new surroundings, Sheehy and Nahayalo, *Crimean Tatars, Volga Germans and Meskhetians,* 8. Soviet figures suggest a smaller percentage of casualties, certainly for the deportation phase itself. This Soviet claim is supported by the demographic estimates of A. Fischer who calculated that the Tatar population in 1978 was 450,000 (*Crimean Tatars,* 700) a figure that almost certainly could not have been reached if the loss among the original population of 200,000 to 250,000 was anywhere near as high as 50 percent.

43. In reaching this conclusion I have employed the following statistics for 1953. Crimean Tatars 200,000; Volga Germans, 600,000; the five main minority peoples, 603,400; making a total of 1,403,400. This exceeds the original deportations for these seven groups, on Conquest's numbers, by approximately 67,000.

44. Ben Kiernan, "Kampuchea's Ethnic Chinese Under Pol Pot," *Journal of Contemporary Asia* 16, no. 1 (1986): 26–27. Kiernan gives the figure of 425,000 Chinese in Kampuchea in 1975, and a death rate of 50 percent, 18.

45. Ibid., 18.

46. Ibid., 20.

47. Michael Vickery, "Comments on Cham Population Figures," *Bulletin of Concerned Asian Scholars* 22, no. 1 (1990): 31–33. An accusation to which Kiernan replied, "The Genocide in Cambodia, 1975–79," *Bulletin of Concerned Asian Scholars* 22, no. 2 (1990): 35–40. The earlier Finnish Commission cited a decline of 75 percent in the Cham population, from 200,000 in 1975 to 50,000 in 1979. But the basis of these figures was unreliable and more Cham survived than the 50,000 here indicated, K. Kiljunen, ed., *Kampuchea: Decade of the Genocide* (London 1984), 34.

48. Ben Kiernan, "Orphans of Genocide. The Cham Muslims of Kampuchea under Pol Pot," *Bulletin of Concerned Asian Scholars* 20, no. 4 (October–December 1988): 2. See his summary of the evidence *for* cultural genocide, ibid., 32–33. David Hawk's more recent statement, almost completely derived from Kiernan's work, is even more confused regarding the issue of the appropriateness of the charge of genocide—which he applies. See his essay, "International Human Rights Law and Democratic Kampuchea," in *The Cambodian Agony,* eds. D. Ablin and M. Hood (New York 1990), 129.

49. M. Vickery, *Cambodia: 1975–1982* (Boston 1984), 182.

19

The Flourishing Demon: Japan in the Role of the Jews?

Ben-Ami Shillony
The Hebrew University of Jerusalem

Introduction

It does not often happen that Japanese and Jews are considered together. Hardly any book on Japanese history mentions the Jews, and scarcely any study on Jewish history mentions Japan. Nevertheless, since the end of the nineteenth century, some non-academic Western observers, Japanese Christians and Jewish visionaries, have been speculating about the so-called common origin of the Jews and the Japanese. Although none of the exponents of that theory were versed in either the languages or the cultures of both the Jews and the Japanese, this disadvantage did not hamper them from indulging in the wildest speculations.[1]

Nor has it prevented the emergence of an antisemitic literature discussing the threat which the Jews are supposed to pose to Japan. This literature, which started in Japan in the 1920s, and is still being written and sold there, is not concerned with actual Jews, whom neither the writers nor the readers have ever seen, but with certain aspects of the West which they label as Jewish, such as materialism, pursuit of profit, aggressiveness, cunning, and deceit, but also riches, wisdom, and genius. Books of this kind are usually based on antisemitic Western literature, mainly the *Protocols of the Elders of Zion,* which they often quote. But while Western antisemites regard the Jews as an alien group in the midst of the West, Japanese antisemitic writers regard them as the pivot of the West, the epitome of all that the Japanese admire and fear in Western culture. Thus these so-called antisemitic writings are not necessarily derogatory toward the Jews because they also contain many expressions of admiration.[2]

A popular way of treating the Jews and the Japanese together, which has also originated in Japan, is to depict them as the opposite poles of mankind.

The outstanding example of this genre was the 1970 book *The Japanese and the Jews,* by Isaiah Ben-Dasan (who, the Japanese believed, was a Jew, though this was the pseudonym of the Japanese writer and critic Yamamoto Shichihei). The book, which became a major bestseller and received a literary prize, stressed the contrary attitudes of the Jews and the Japanese toward life. The Jews, whom the author had in mind, were the biblical Hebrews, wandering in the desert on the orders of an omnipotent God, lacking water and security, and later beqeathing their strict morality and fanatic monotheism to Christianity and Islam, and their sense of insecurity to American Jews. They were contrasted with the sedentary Japanese, who have always enjoyed a fertile land, plenty of water, and the security of an island country. The Japanese could therefore afford to be pragmatic, nondogmatic, and tolerant throughout their history.[3]

Most of the historical writing, in English and in Japanese, concerning the two peoples, focuses on the way the Japanese treated the Jews in the twentieth century, especially before and during World War II. The authors of these books have usually pointed out the fact (quite surprising to Western readers) that the wartime Japanese authorities, while adhering to their friendship with Nazi Germany and accepting the tenets of Western antisemitism, actually saved Jews and helped Jewish refugees who fled to Japan or to Japanese-controlled territories.[4] Other writings discuss the changing image of the Jews in Japan. In their 1995 book *Jews in the Japanese Mind: The History and Uses of a Cultural Stereotype,* David G. Goodman and Masanori Miyazawa describe the way in which the Japanese have related to the Jews in the nineteenth and twentieth centuries, in terms of their problematic relations with the West at that time.[5]

In my own book on *The Jews and the Japanese: The Successful Outsiders,* I tried to introduce a different way of looking at these two peoples—not only as cases of cultural comparison and mutual relationship—but also as victims of a similar kind of demonization by the West. Having rejected Christianity, yet nevertheless having prospered in the Western world, the Jews and the Japanese have stirred similar racist phobias and have appeared as the two great threats to white Christian society.[6] In this essay I would like to focus on the way the Japanese have been demonized since their country was opened up by the West in the mid-nineteenth century up to the current trade friction with the United States. Furthermore, I wish to raise the question whether Japan has taken over the symbolic role of the Jews as the flourishing demon in the Western world.

The Dangerous Infidel

Among all the devils inhabiting the imagination of the Christian world, the most pervasive one was the Jewish demon. The Jews were considered to be diabolical, because they were racially different, they had rejected the Gospel, and they had allegedly crucified Christ. Far from complying with their punishment of being expelled and dispersed, they were believed to be living off the wealth of Christians, and scheming to devour the world. By flourishing and amassing wealth, the Jewish demon violated the official moral code, and constituted a permanent threat to the Christian community. In the twentieth century, the Japanese seem to have assumed a similar demonic role. Like the Jews, they were racially different, rejected Christianity, and had succeeded in penetrating the West, becoming rich and strong. They too, seemed to be scheming to take over the world.

Like the demons which Professor Befu has described, these two peoples were seen as being able to assume the figure of a beautiful woman: they modernized quickly, excelled in science and art, and assumed a benevolent appearance. However, like other demons, their diabolic nature could not be fully hidden. Although the Jews and the Japanese tried hard to disguise themselves as Westerners, one could still recognize their demonic features by spotting some ugly elements in their physiognomy, revealing the depravity of their character. The ideological father of modern racism, Joseph Arthur Gobineau, who proclaimed the supremacy of the Aryan race, wrote in 1853 that the "yellow race" had been created by God before he created the white man, as a rough draft for human beings. Therefore they came out extremely ugly, devoid of intellectual curiosity, and interested only in satisfying their base needs.[7]

The Russo-Japanese War, at the beginning of this century, made the Russians fear that their Christian society was under a dual attack, from the heathen Japanese without and from the infidel Jews within. In 1905, following the humiliating defeats on land and sea that the Japanese had inflicted on the Russian empire, the great writer Leo Tolstoy offered an explanation for his country's setbacks. In a letter to a friend, he wrote:

> This debacle is not only of the Russian army, the Russian fleet and the Russian state.... The disintegration began long ago, with the struggle for money and success in the so-called scientific and artistic pursuits, where the Jews got the edge on the Christians in every country and thereby earned the envy and hatred of all. Today the Japanese have done the same thing in the military field, proving conclusively, by brute force, that there is a goal which Christians must not pursue, for in seeking it they will always fail, vanquished by non-Christians.[8]

In these few sentences Tolstoy, otherwise famous for his humanism and morality, expressed the old Christian fear of the flourishing infidel, whose outstanding representatives in his time were the Jews and the Japanese.

A British writer, T. W. H. Crosland, commenting on the Japanese victories on the Manchurian front in 1904, described as follows the physical features of the Japanese in order to illuminate their low morality:

> A stunted, lymphatic, yellow-faced heathen, with a mouthful of teeth three sizes too big for him, bulging slits where his eyes ought to be, blacking-brush hair, a foolish giggle, a cruel heart, and the conceit of the devil—this, O bemused reader, is the authentic dearly-beloved "Little Jap" of commerce, the fire-eater out of the Far East, and the ally, if you please, of John Bull.... It is a grave question whether Japan, with her marvellous gifts of imitation, her extraordinary energy, her cunning rapidity, and her total want of conscience, is in the least likely to become "a world power" of the kind that Europe is likely to find useful or satisfactory. Indeed the only restraints that could be put upon her are the restraints of the Christian religion. Can she be brought to submit to them? Does she desire in her heart to submit to them? Will she ever be other than pagan and heathen and cruel and unconscionable under the surface? The answer is: No.[9]

The Jews and the Japanese have indeed rejected Christianity despite all the efforts to convert them. Yet, they did so for very different reasons. The Jews rejected Christianity because religion for them was very important, constituting the basis of their collective existence. Therefore, apostasy meant for them separation from the Jewish people. The Japanese rejected Christianity because they did not attach much importance to religion, and were put off by the zealotry and alien nature of the Western faith. They did not regard Christianity as essential to modernization and thought they could accept Newton without accepting Jesus. Although in Japan conversion did not carry a social stigma, and all Christian sects made converts there, the number of Christians never exceeded one percent of the population. The great majority of the people preferred to remain with their less-demanding faiths of Shinto and Buddhism. The West, however, regarded the rejection of Christianity by the Jews and the Japanese as a proof of their intellectual obscurantism and moral depravation.

As long as the Japanese were undeveloped and poor, that situation was considered normal. Heathen people were not supposed to attain power, wealth, and prestige. So, when they embarked on their grandiose project of building a "rich country and strong army," most Westerners were sceptical about their chances of success. Rudyard Kipling, the popular British exponent of the destiny of the white man, wrote in 1900: "The Japanese should have no concern with business. The Jap has no business savvy."[10] But when they built a modern industry, defeated China and Russia, and acquired colonies in Asia, the attitude of the West changed from scepticism to resentment. This change was similar to the antisemitic mood that swept

Europe after the Jews had succeeded in entering Western society and advancing in many fields.

Possession of power and wealth, without the constraints of the Gospel, seemed immensely dangerous. In 1895, following Japan's victory over China, Kaiser Wilhelm II of Germany coined the phrase "Yellow Peril." In a letter to his cousin, Czar Nicholas II of Russia, he warned of the growing danger from the East, above all Japan, to Western civilization. The letter was accompanied by a drawing, done by a German artist, which showed Archangel Michael warning the European countries, represented by mythological females, of an approaching storm from the East. In the center of the storm loomed the image of Buddha.[11]

Jean-Pierre Lehmann quotes a newspaper summary of Kaiser Wilhelm's explanation of Japan's victories over Russia in 1905:

> [The Kaiser] added that the fact that these victories had been won by a heathen over a Christian nation did not warrant the conclusion that Buddha was superior to Jesus Christ. If Russia had been defeated it was, in his opinion, due to the fact that Russian Christianity must be in a very sad condition, while the Japanese exhibited many Christian values. A good Christian meant a good soldier...[12]

Antisemites at the beginning of the century were frequently denigrators of the "yellow race." Czar Nicholas II, who condoned the pogroms against the Jews and blamed them for having stirred up the social turmoil in his country, hated the Japanese no less than he hated the Jews. He called the the Japanese monkeys, ridiculed their army, and promised to wipe them out in war in a short time. He believed that the best way to retain his throne was to divert the social unrest in Russia against the Jews at home and against the Japanese abroad. But he grossly miscalculated: the Japanese beat him on the battlefield, and the Jews joined the revolution.

The Inscrutable Intruder

The Japanese entered the Western world as a nation, unlike the Jews who entered it as individuals or as a social group. The only case in which the Japanese entered Western society as individuals was when they emigrated to the West. Although the number of Japanese immigrants to the United States, compared to that of Jewish or other European immigrants, has always been small, the phobias that they stirred were much greater. To the Japanese immigrant who landed in California at the beginning of this century, America was not the country of freedom and equality. Being an Oriental, he could not acquire American citizenship, and he was subject to official and unofficial discrimination. He could not, for instance, purchase land, send his children to public schools, or join a trade union.

The suspicion and animosity that the Japanese immigrants encountered in America, were reflected in the report of the United States Industrial Commission, which stated in 1901 that the Japanese immigrants were:

> more servile than the Chinese, but less obedient and far less desirable. They have most of the vices of the Chinese, with none of the virtues. They underbid the Chinese in everything, and are as a class tricky, unreliable and dishonest.[13]

Although in 1910 there were only 40,000 Japanese in California, less than two percent of the state population, leading newspapers, like the San Francisco *Examiner,* and most community leaders, waged a fierce campaign against them. The essence of the campaign, which was carried on by conservatives, liberals, and socialists, was that the United States should remain a white man's country, and therefore no "yellow" immigrants should be allowed in. One of the spokesmen of that campaign was the writer Jack London.[14]

The result of this constant demonization was the Immigration Law of 1924, which banned all Oriental immigration to the United States. The law established immigration quotas for Occidentals on the basis of their citizenship, but it excluded *all* Orientals on the basis of their race. Therefore a Japanese could not immigrate to the United States, even if he carried a British passport. At the time that this law was passed there were only 111,000 persons of Japanese origin in the continental United States. These people could not be naturalized, but their children, born in America, did acquire American citizenship. This law was in force for twenty-eight years, and was amended only in 1952.

Although the *nisei,* or second-generation Japanese, were Americans, they too were subject to discrimination and could not, for instance, be employed in public schools. Nevertheless, the Japanese community in the United States, like the Jewish community, became a model minority group, with a high level of education, a low level of crime, and a strong upward mobility. They were diligent, ambitious, and imbued with a high regard for hard work and scholastic achievement. Already in 1901, a Japanese chemist, Takamine Jokichi, who had emigrated to the United States in 1890, was the first to isolate adrenalin; and in 1910 another Japanese Americam chemist, Suzuki Umetaro, was the first to extract vitamin B.[15]

Concentration Camps for Japanese Americans

The phobia of the Oriental intruder was stronger than the good behavior of the Japanese immigrants. When Japan attacked Pearl Harbor and declared war on the United States, the worst suspicions seemed to be validated. In popular imagination, the "yellow enemy" from outside blended with the yellow resident from inside into one threatening monster. Although no Japanese Americans were involved in acts of sabotage or treason, the Americans were gripped by the fear that the Japanese in their midst would become a fifth column and assist Japan in conquering the United States. No such fears arose concerning Americans of German descent, despite the fact that 40,000 of them belonged to the pro-Nazi German-American Bund.[16]

In the spring of 1942, President Roosevelt ordered the incarceration of all the 112,000 Japanese Americans living on the West Coast, two-thirds of whom were native-born Americans. All the residents of California, Oregon, Washington State, and Utah, with more than 1/16 of Japanese blood in their veins, were ordered to relocate in ten hastily built concentration camps, dubbed "relocation centers." These people, who had done nothing wrong, were rounded up in a harsh way, some with only forty-eight hours notice, and were allowed to take with them only what they could carry. All the property that they left behind was confiscated. The camps were located in desolate areas, far from places where ordinary people lived. They were surrounded by barbed wire and guarded by armed troops. Those who attempted to flee were shot.[17] No similar action was taken against German or Italian Americans. The distrust in which the Americans held those who were of Japanese descent was manifested by the fact, that Congress unanimously passed all the legislation which supported that act.

The forced incarceration was carried out by the American military. Lieutenant General John L. De Witt, who was in charge of the project, explained the reason for it to a Congressional committe in 1943: "A Jap's a Jap. You can't change him by giving him a piece of paper." This racist attitude was shared by most Americans at that time. Dower quotes a member of the House of Representatives who declared: "Once a Jap, always a Jap. You can't anymore regenerate a Jap than you can reverse the laws of nature." The *Los Angeles Times* phrased it in zoological terms: "A viper is nonetheless a viper wherever the egg is hatched—so a Japanese American, born of Japanese parents, grows up to be a Japanese not an American."[18]

This glaring civil-liberties violation by the United States can be compared to what was done to the Jews of Europe before 1939. Like the European Jews, the Japanese Americans were put in concentration camps not because of what they had done, but because of their race. But, of course, there was a great difference between the two cases. The American "relocation centers," hard and unpleasant as they were, were a far cry from the German concentration and extermination camps. The inmates of the American camps were neither killed nor brutalized, nor forced to work. Food was sufficient, and one could obtain an exit pass. The rationale for the incarceration was also different: while the United States *was* under Japanese military attack, there was no Jewish state or Jewish people who had attacked Germany.

Despite this harsh evacuation into concentration camps, many of the eva-cuees asked to be enlisted into the armed forces, in order to prove their patriotism. At first, General De Witt objected, claiming that "there isn't any such thing as a loyal Japanese." But he was overruled, and in 1943 the U.S Army started forming special Japanese American units. These units were segregated, and they were sent to the European front, as the authorities did not trust them to fight against other Japanese. Ten thousand Japanese Americans enlisted and many of them distinguished themselves in action. The 522nd Field Artillery Battalion, composed of Japanese Americans, liberated the Dachau concentration camp, and the 442nd Regimental Combat Team, composed of *nisei,* became the most highly decorated American unit in World War II.[19]

When the soldiers and the evacuees returned home after the the war, the property that had been confiscated from them was not returned. In many places the local population resented their return, and tried to prevent them from doing so. It was only in 1976, on the thirty-fourth anniversary of President Roosevelt's incarceration order, that President Gerald Ford declared: "We know now what we should have known then, not only was the evacuation wrong, but Japanese Americans were and are loyal Americans"; and it was only in 1988, after intensive lobbying by various groups, including the Anti-Defamation League of B'nai B'rith, that Congress provided a reparation of $20,000 to each of the 60,000 survivors of the camps, a small fraction of what they had lost.[20]

The Demonic Enemy

A victim of demonization may indeed be a demon. Before and during World War II Japan behaved in a demonic way. It invaded China, allied itself with Hitler and Mussolini, and launched a surprise attack on the United States; it oppressed Asian nations, committed horrendous atrocities, such as the rape of Nanjing and the death march of Bataan, brutalized prisoners of war, conducted medical experiments on human beings, and terrorized civilian populations in the occupied areas; it also abducted Korean and Filippino women to serve as slave prostitutes for Japanese soldiers.

Nevertheless, Japan was a lesser demon than Nazi Germany. There was no dictator in Japan who wielded absolute power, there was no totalitarian party, prime ministers were periodically changed, political opponents at home were not executed, and there were no concentration camps for dis-senters. Japan did not engage in genocide and it did not operate exter-mination camps. Jewish refugees who fled to Japan and to Japanese-controlled territories were protected and not surrendered to the Germans. Brutal as Japan's behavior was in the war, it was not based on a racist ideology. Its propaganda emphasized the liberation of Asia and did not claim that the Japanese were racially superior to other nations. Although the promise of liberation can be dismissed as mere propaganda, it revealed a different attitude from that of the Nazis.

Nevertheless, during World War II, Japan's image in the United States was worse than that of Nazi Germany. John Dower has observed that the American press reported Japanese atrocities more often than German ones, while the Holocaust was hardly mentioned until the end of the war.[21] The press made a distinction between the German people, who were considered to be good, and the Nazis who were considered to be bad. But no such distinction was made regarding the Japanese, all of whom were considered to be evil. The Germans, being white and Christian, were denounced for what they did; but the Japanese, being yellow and heathen, were blamed for what they were. In Europe, the Americans were fighting the Nazis, in the Pacific they were fighting the Japs. The Nazis were evil people, but the Japanese were beasts.

Sheila Johnson quotes a marine on Guadalcanal who told John Hersey in 1942:

> I wish we were fighting against Germans. They are human beings, like us. Fighting against them must be like an athletic performance—matching your skill against someone you know is good. Germans are misled, but at least they react like men. But the Japs are animals. Against them you have to learn a whole new set of physical reactions. You have to get used to their animal stubbornness and tenacity. They take to the jungle as if they had been bred there, and like some beasts you never see them until they are dead.[22]

John Dower cites Ernie Pyle, a famous war correspondent, who reported from the Pacific front:

> In Europe we felt that our enemies, horrible and deadly as they were, were still people. But out here I soon gathered that the Japanese were looked upon as something subhuman and repulsive, the way some people feel about cockroaches or mice.[23]

After visiting a camp of Japanese prisoners of war, he commented:

> They were wrestling and laughing and talking just like normal human beings. And yet they gave me the creeps, and I wanted a mental bath after looking at them.[24]

American war propaganda dehumanized the Japanese, portraying them as vermin and mice, in ways not so different from the dehumanization of the Jews by the Nazis. The conclusion in both cases was the same: they had to be exterminated. Dower mentions restaurants in the United States, putting up signs such as: THIS RESTAURANT POISONS BOTH RATS AND JAPS.[25] Admiral William Halsey, commander of the South Pacific Force, called on his men: "Kill Japs, kill Japs, kill more Japs." He also vowed that by the end of the war the Japanese language would be spoken only in hell.[26] This was not only propaganda. The Navy representative on the government committee, which considered how to deal with Japan after the war, recommended the "almost total elimination of the Japanese as a race".[27] This was also the idea of General De Witt, who had removed the Japanese into concentration camps. He explained to a Congressional committee that the reason that only Japanese Americans had been interned was that he was not worried about the German or Italian nationals in the United States, "but the Japs we will be worried about all the time until they are wiped off the face of the map."[28]

This official attitude toward the Japanese freed the troops on the battlefield from any moral restrictions. Charles Lindbergh, who flew for four months in 1944 with the U.S. forces in the Pacific, recorded in his diary:

> It was freely admitted that some of our soldiers tortured Jap prisoners and were as cruel and barbaric at times as the Japs themselves. Our men think nothing of shooting a Japanese prisoner or soldier attempting to surrender. They treat the Japs with less respect than they would give to an animal, and these acts are condoned by almost everyone.[29]

The Atomic Bombs

The systematic dehumanization of the Japanese paved the way for dropping two atomic bombs on them. A long debate has been going on since 1945 as to whether these bombs were necessary in order to defeat Japan, and whether they were the only means to save the lives of the hundreds of thousands of American soldiers who might have died in a land invasion.[30] Yet, there is general agreement that the atomic bombs were dropped, not as a desparate last resort to stop a dangerous aggressor from destroying the United States, but as a stratagem to finish off a beleaguered enemy and to hasten his surrender.

The heinous character of nuclear weapons, which puts them in a different category from conventional weapons, was understood by the people in authority at that time. Fleet Admiral William D. Leahy, President Truman's representative on the Joint Chiefs of Staff, wrote in his diary soon after the dropping of the bombs:

> It is not a bomb. It is not an explosive. It is a poisonous thing that kills people by its deadly radioactive reaction.... In being the first to use it, we had adopted an ethical standard common to barbarians of the Dark Ages. I was not taught to make war by destroying women and children.... Employment of the atomic bomb in war will take us back in cruelty toward noncombatants to the days of Ghengis Khan.[31]

The nuclear weapon had been intended against Germany, and many Jewish scientists were involved in its development, out of a desire to prevent Hitler from dominating the world. Among them were Albert Einstein, who first suggested the idea to President Roosevelt, and the physicists J. Robert Oppenheimer, Leo Szilard, James Franck, Eugene Rabinowitch, and Edward Teller. The threat that Hitler posed to humanity was so great, that any weapon against him was justifiable. But, the development of the bomb took longer than had initially been assumed, and it was operational only in July 1945. This happened after the surrender of Germany, after most Japanese cities had already been destroyed by conventional air raids, and after the Soviet Union had committed itself at Yalta to join in the attack on Japan.

It is doubtful whether the United States would have dropped two atomic bombs on Germany under similar circumstances, for example in March or April 1945, just to hasten its surrender. It is hard to believe that an American president would have unleashed such weapons of mass destruction in the heart of Europe, against a white, Christian nation on the verge of its military collapse. Had the Japanese dropped atomic bombs on two American cities for the same reasons of shortening the war and saving the lives of their own soldiers, no doubt the whole world would have condemned them as war criminals.

Some of the scientists who were working on building the atomic bomb, did feel a moral responsibility for its deployment and objected to the idea of dropping it on Japan. In March 1945, Einstein sent a letter to President Roosevelt, asking him to meet Leo Szilard, who led the scientists' opposition to the dropping of the bomb on Japan. But Roosevelt died shortly afterwards, without being able to do so. After the surrender of Germany in May 1945, Szilard drafted a petition to President Truman, stating that although there was a justification for using the atomic bomb against Nazi Germany, there was no reason for dropping it on Japan. Unleashing such a horrible weapon against the Japanese would constitute an international crime, and would usher in a new era, in which all mankind would be threatened by mass destruction.

This strongly-worded petition was not sent, because Szilard could not gather enough signatures for it. So he drafted a more moderate document, calling on the President not to drop the atomic bombs before Japan was fully warned of their existence. This revised petition was signed by sixty-seven scientists and sent to President Truman. In June 1945, James Franck, Leo Szilard, Eugene Rabinowitch, and others met with Secretary of War Henry L. Stimson and urged him not to drop the bomb on Japan.[32] But all these efforts were in vain. In August 1945 two atomic bombs were dropped on Hiroshima and Nagasaki, after Japan had been given only a veiled warning, in the form of the Potsdam Declaration, which did not even mention their existence.

Auschwitz and Hiroshima cannot be equated. The atomic bombs were dropped on industrial and military centers of an enemy nation, which had itself committed numerous atrocities during the war. The number of people killed by the atomic bombs was not greater than the number of people killed by conventional air raids on Tokyo and other big cities. Yet, Auschwitz and Hiroshima both represented in their differing ways a new kind of a techno-logical mass destruction, which went beyond what was accepted then and today as legitimate warfare. In both cases, these atrocities were committed after a long campaign of demonization and dehumanization.

The "Yellow Peril" Revived

The defeat of Japan in World War II, dispelled its demonic image for about a generation. The American GIs, who arrived in Japan as an occupation force, were met by docile, smiling and polite people, who did not manifest any hostility toward their former foe. Devastated, impoverished, and con-quered, Japan under occupation posed no threat to American interests, so it could again be romanticized as it had been in the nineteenth century, when it was likewise weak and poor. Japan appeared again as the country of Madame Butterfly and the August Moon, cherry blossoms, and color wood-cuts. For about twenty-five years after the war, Japan even enjoyed a positive image in the West. This image was reflected in such novels as James Michener's *Sayonara* (1954), and James Clavell's *Shogun* (1975). Japan was a democracy surrounded by non-democratic communist and military regimes, a member of the Western camp in a strategic part of the world, and a successful capitalist economy in a poor and unstable Third World. The phobia of the yellow peril did not disappear, but it shifted to the Chinese, who for the first time in history were regarded as posing a threat to Western civilization.

This situation started changing with Japan's high economic growth. The United States had intended Japan to become a showcase of capitalism in Asia, in order to counter the rival model of Maoist China. But Japan with her record economic growth and well-organized society outperformed not only the communist Chinese, but also the capitalist Americans. As Japanese products and consumer goods spread across Western markets, Americans and Europeans started to fear that Japan, having lost its military campaign against them, was waging an economic war of revenge with the same goals and tenacity it had displayed in the past.

The improvement of Sino-American relations in the 1970s and 1980s, and the evaporation of the Cold War in the 1990s, shifted the spectre of the "yellow peril" back to Japan. The success of Japanese consumer goods in American markets delivered a blow to American pride, and undermined the position of the United States as the leader of the West. Japan overtook the

United States in fields that had traditionally been considered bastions of American ingenuity. The automobile and the television set, the two great gifts of Uncle Sam to the common man in the twentieth century, became associated with Japan rather than with the United States. The rich businessmen buying up the world, and the wealthy tourists roaming it, were no longer Americans but Japanese. A public opinion poll conducted by *Newsweek* magazine in October 1989, a few years before the breakup of the Soviet Union, revealed that 52 percent of the American public considered Japan to be the greatest threat to the United States, as against 33 percent who thought it was the Soviet Union.[33]

The racist factor magnified this fear. Japan was not in fact the only country competing favorably with the United States, for Germany's trade surplus with it in 1988 was larger than that of Japan. Nor did the Japanese own more American assets than the British or the Dutch. Yet, resentment against Japan was stronger than that against the European countries. A German or Italian automaker selling his cars in the United States was a commercial rival but the Japanese automaker appeared as a dangerous invader. A Dutch company buying American real estate or a French conglomerate buying an American company attracted little attention. But when Sony bought Columbia Pictures in 1989 and Mitsubishi bought the Rockefeller Center in New York City in the same year, an outcry arose that the Japanese were taking over America. Like the scared Californians at the beginning of the century, Americans in the 1980s were obsessed with the fear that the Japanese were bent on seizing their country.

Japan Bashing and Jew Baiting

For many centuries the Jews have constituted the quintessential alien in Western society, the shady peddler of wealth and influence. In recent decades the Japanese seem to have taken over that role and attracted the same sort of suspicion and hatred. In October 1989, France's Prime Minister Edith Cresson told an American reporter that the Japanese "sit up all night long thinking of ways to screw us both, Americans and Europeans. They are our common enemy."[34] This image, recalling the myth of the Elders of Zion plotting to dominate the world, signified a revival of the West's old fear of the flourishing Japanese demon.

The trade friction between the United States and Japan resurrected wartime imagery, which had never been fully discarded. Once again, the immoral little yellow people were taking advantage of America's benevolence and complacency. They were perceived as mounting a treacherous attack on the United States. The rhetoric on trade sounded similar to the language of war. A Republican presidential candidate, talking on the occasion of the fortieth anniversary of Japan's surrender, urged his audience to remember two "facts": "First, we're still at war with Japan. Second, we're losing"; and an American senator described the Japanese decision to export more auto-mobiles to the United States as "an economic Pearl Harbor." A White House staff member commented that "the next time B-52 fly over Tokyo, we better make sure they carry bombs."[35]

Like in the case of the Jews, the success of Japan in overtaking the West in mass-production, high technology and world trade, has been attributed to cheating. The belief in the cheating Japanese, like the myth of the swindling Jew, reassured the bewildered Westerner that the flourishing demon was a mere aberration. Marvin Wolf, in his book *The Japanese Conspiracy,* pub-lished in 1983, wrote:

> The web of plots and secret agreements, the concerted acts and duplicitous maneuvers, the vast conspiracies that have served Japan's goals ever since World War II ended have become that nation's modus vivendi.... The Japanese have demonstrated that their definition of the ethics of free trade are not ours.[36]

Since today it is not politically correct to openly speak about race, those who raise the alarm about the new "yellow peril" resort to cultural arguments. Wolf claimed that the Japanese language actually encourages cheating:

> The Japanese language seems designed for the speaker who wants to deceive. In Japanese, the verb is always placed at the end of a sentence, a syntax that can be artfully manipulated. It permits the speaker to state the subject and object of a sentence first, perhaps at great length. Meanwhile he monitors the reactions of others present and at the very last moment, he inserts the verb. The verb he has chosen may not be the one he originally had in mind, but it now serves his purpose.[37]

For a conspiracy to work in the last quarter of the twentieth century, the conspirators must be assumed to have gained control of the media. Thus, as in the case of the Jews, the Japanese are being accused of using their wealth to buy influence and manipulate Western mass media. In his 1990 book *Agents of Influence,* the political economist Pat Choate claimed that the Japanese have succeeded in sweeping American public opinion to their side by buying up scholars, journalists and government officials.

According to Choate, the Japanese lobby in Washington is the mightiest lobby of all, more influential than other foreign lobbies there:

> For many years, Chiang Kai-shek's China lobby dominated American think-ing on China. The Israeli lobby has a powerful voice in America's Middle East policy-making. The Irish lobby has long helped influence American policies on Northern Ireland. But of all nations, Japan understands best that political power in America is a commodity that can be acquired by the high-est bidder. Of all nations, Japan wields the most striking power over

America's economic and trade policies. And of all nations, Japan succeeds best at using its political strength in America to gain economic benefits for itself.[38]

In his 1992 best selling mystery novel *Rising Sun,* the author Michael Crichton described the Japanese businessmen in the United States as a group of gangsters, plotting to undermine America's society and grab its wealth. His message, voiced through the mouth of the protagonist, an American detective who has learned the language and the culture of the Japanese, is that the United States is at war with Japan, and it should act accordingly.[39]

Many of the arguments against Japan's trade policies may be correct, and Japan is certainly not an angel in its competition for world markets. But describing it as a nation inherently bent on world domination, due to its racial and cultural traits, goes far beyond logical argumentation. As in the case of the Jews, it draws on deep rooted fears of the inscrutable alien, who flourishes in the Christian world without giving up his infidel ways. Japan bashing and Jew baiting derive both from this historic tendency to demonize the successful outsider.

Notes

1. The first to raise this theory was the Scottish businessman in Japan, Norman McLeod, in *Japan and the Lost Tribes of Israel* (Nagasaki: Rising Sun, 1879). A leading Japanese exponent of this theory before World War II was Oyabe Zenichiro. His 1929 book on the Jewish origins of the Japanese was recently republished under the title *Nihonjin no ruutsu wa Yudayajin da* (The roots of the Japanese are the Jews) (Tokyo: Tama Shuppan, 1991). The Israeli who propagated this theory was the engineer Joseph Eidelberg, in *The Japanese and the Lost Tribes of Israel* (Givatayim: Sycamore Press, 1980).

2. Two flagrant antisemitic books are: Uno Masami, *Yudaya ga wakaru to Nihon ga miete kuru* ([If you understand the Jews, you will understand Japan) (Tokyo: Tokuma Shoten, 1986); Ota Ryu, *Yudaya sekai teikoku to Nihon shinko senryaku* [The Jewish world empire's plot to invade Japan) (Tokyo: Nihon Bungeisha, 1992).

3. An English translation of the book (which omitted some parts) appeared as *The Japanese and the Jews* (Tokyo: Weatherhill, 1972).

4. See, for example, David Kranzler, *Japanese, Nazis and Jews* (New York: Yeshiva University Press, 1976); Marvin Tokayer and Mary Swartz, *The Fugu Plan* (New York: Paddington Press, 1979).

5. David G. Goodman and Masanori Miyazawa, *Jews in the Japanese Mind: The History and Uses of a Cultural Stereotype* (New York: The Free Press, 1995).

6. Ben-Ami Shillony, *The Jews and the Japanese: The Successful Outsiders* (Tokyo: Charles E. Tuttle, 1992).

7. Comte de Gobineau, *Essai sur l'inégalité des races humaines* (Paris: Firmin-Didot, 1940), 1: 454–55.

8. Henri Troyat, *Tolstoy* (New York: Dell, 1969), 711.

9. Jean-Pierre Lehmann, *The Image of Japan* (London: Allen and Unwin, 1978), 169–70.

10. Lehmann, *Image,* 123.

11. Ibid., 149–50.

12. Ibid., 171–71.

13. Sheila K. Johnson, *The Japanese Through American Eyes* (Tokyo: Kodansha International, 1988), 8.

14. Roger Daniels, *Concentration Camps USA* (New York: Holt, Rinehart and Winston, 1971), 6, 10.

15. *Kodansha Encyclopedia of Japan* (Tokyo: Kodansha, 1983), 7: 315.

16. Daniels, *Concentration,* 27, 35.

17. Ibid., 74–81.

18. John W. Dower, *War Without Mercy* (New York: Pantheon Books, 1986), 80–81.

19. Daniels, *Concentration,* 147.

20. *Japan, an Illustrated Encyclopedia* (Tokyo: Kodansha, 1993), 1: 663; *ADL Bulletin,* (June 1987): 10.

21. Dower, *War,* 35.

22. Johnson, *Eyes,* 43–44.

23. Dower, *War,* 78.

24. Ibid., 78.

25. Ibid., 92.

26. Ibid., 36.

27. Ibid., 55.

28. Ibid., 81.

29. Ibid., 70.

30. For some of the different views on this subject, see Harry S. Truman, *Year of Decisions* (New York: Doubleday, 1955), 419; Winston S. Churchill, *The Second World War* (London: Cassell and Co., 1954), 6: 552; U.S. Strategic Bombing Survey, *Japan's Struggle to End The War* (Washington: Government Printing Office, 1946), 13; Gar Alperovitz, *Atomic Diplomacy* (New York: Vintage Books, 1965), 226–42.

31. William D. Leahy, *I Was There* (New York: McGraw Hill, 1950), 514.

32. Arthur H. Compton, *Atomic Quest* (London: Oxford University Press, 1956), 27, 233–44; Robert Jungk, *Brighter than a Thousand Suns* (London: Gollancz, 1958), 173–78, 332–46; Michael Amrine, *The Great Decision* (New York: Putnam, 1959), 21, 98, 103, 143–47.

33. *Newsweek,* 9 October 1989, 18.

34. *Newsweek,* 2 October 1989, 27.

35. Dower, *War,* 314.

36. Marvin J. Wolf, *The Japanese Conspiracy* (New York: Empire Books, 1983), 327, 329.

37. Ibid., 107.

38. Pat Choate, *Agents of Influence* (New York: Knopf, 1990), xvi.

39. Michael Crichton, *Rising Sun* (New York: Knopf, 1992).

20

Anti-Jewish Imagery in the Contemporary Arab-Muslim World

Rivka Yadlin
The Hebrew University of Jerusalem

Demonized "others" in modern times are not clearly defined and pronounced as such. They belong to the fuzzy area of stereotyped perceptions, fraught with tangled emotion, surrounded by an aura which transcends the mere words and acts that go into their making. These effusive dimensions derive from the inherently compelling power of narrative, in which stereotyped "others" are the protagonists. Myths and fables, invented and related, are larger than reality and tend to have a suggestive power which transcends commonsense thinking. Storytellers know it, and so do nations, both nascent and old, who develop myths and hang on to them.

The current mythology about Jews prevalent in the Islamic world is an example of this process. There is very little in the Muslim sources, for example, to account for the negative profile of the Jew in contemporary Arab-Muslim journalism, where he is portrayed as a virtual devil, a serpent, an octopus, a Nazi, or a bloody dagger in the heart of humanity. Examining the demonization of the Jew in the Arab world today is not about the basic precepts of Islam or its potential for either dialogue or negation. It is about what interpreters of Islam, Arabism, and local nationalisms in the Arab world choose to pick out of their cultural heritage in the present context. This may include the adoption by Muslim Arabs of Christian antisemitism—its repetition, diffusion, elaboration, and even its reclaiming as part of an Islamic tradition.

Heeding the Word

Narratives are particularly powerful in the contemporary Arab-Muslim world, where language has for centuries exerted a special fascination. Rhetoric in general tends to affect thinking more than reading or other forms of methodological inquiry.[1] This is all the more so where words (the printed word as well as private or public discourse) are aggrandized by the deep love and appreciation of language, its nuances, rhythm, and incantation. From pre-Islamic times, when recited poems would enchant audiences in the market-place, through the miracle of the Qur'an and Sufi mystic chanting in undu-lating human circles, up to the present-day mosque sermons and speeches by charismatic leaders, language has had a powerful, even irrational effect in the Arab world.

From the early stages of socialization, language plays a key role in the politics of family and interpersonal relations, in fighting for supremacy, and in political life in general. This is all the more so in the public domain, where the aggressive mobilization of opinion became a characteristic of Arab states and of Pan-Arabism in the 1950s, and where Islamists are today battling for the soul of the nation. Written and spoken addresses are seen as an effective tool of politics, recognized as such by the powers-that-be in the Arab world. Ample evidence for this may be found in the personal contacts between Arab heads of state, newspaper editors, and leading journalists; in the vigorous campaigns of indoctrination, the draconian press laws enacted at will, the journals closed for not toeing the government line—even in countries enjoying a considerable freedom of speech. Journalists are often reprimanded, muzzled, isolated, or jailed; books are removed from the shelves. The Rushdie affair offered dramatic evidence of how seriously literature and "talk" can be taken by Muslims, but it was only the tip of the iceberg. In Egypt, a little-known author was handed an eight-year prison sentence because of the way he dealt with Islam in a recent novel. Al-Azhar University, anxious to wrest the leadership of Islam from the radicals, removed from the bookstores works by Judge Sa'id al-'Ashmawi, an Egyptian anti-fundamentalist writer. A brilliant but outspoken assistant professor at Cairo University was recently forced to flee Egypt to Leiden. Nasr Hamid Abu Zeid argued relentlessly against an ahistorical approach to the scriptures, pointing out in his *Critique of Religious Discourse* that all trends in Egypt, from the radicals to the government, were party to common religious maxims and vocabulary.[2] Such "heresies" spawned objections to his promo-tion at the university; he received death threats, and faced legal prosecution by both radical and institutional Islam to separate him forcibly (as an "apostate") from his Muslim wife. The liberal essayist Faraj Foda was actually assassinated because of his cutting words, while Nobel laureate Najib Mahfouz, one of whose novels has been banned for decades but still excites heated public attacks, narrowly escaped the same fate.[3]

The Cutting Edge of the Word

The weight that verbal expression carries was explicitly recognized by an Arab political scientist at a recent conference on inter-Arab conflict: "We consider verbal warfare the fiercest and most severe of all wars; moreover, it is the most important potential [weapon] of actual war, perhaps a prerequisite."[4] This is even more the case regarding the conflicting relations with Jews, and the Jewish state in particular. The leadership of the "Hebrew state," according to Hamid Rabi' in 1982, "fully realizes that in the modern world every author is an explosive, every writer a combat commander."[5]

The mindset to which we are referring is clearly revealed in a genre of essays and books sparked by the onset of normalization between Israel and Egypt, which aimed to expose the Jewish/Zionist "assault on the Arab/Egyptian mind." This alledged assault, conducted through words and ideas, is seen as "penetrating" and "poisoning" the Arab mind. It is an attempt to "force" the Zionist narrative (featuring Zionism as a legitimate Jewish national liberation movement) on the Arabs through efforts at cultural rapprochement—including the search for common threads in Jewish and Muslim culture. A suggestion by Western researchers to introduce "mediating ideas" that would encourage common perceptions and more understanding was rejected out of hand by Sayyid Yasin, veteran head of the mainstream Center of Political and Strategic Studies at the Al-Ahram publishing house, and managing director of the elite magazine *al-Siyasah al-Dawliyyah* [International Relations]. Such ideas, thought Yasin,

> strive primarily towards what can be termed as subjection of the Arab national personality. To be accurate, they are not merely aimed at forcing recognition of Israel's legitimacy; more seriously, their goal is to eradicate the ideological, cultural, civilizational identity of Arab society through a carefully-planned cultural assault, consisting mainly of an innocent call to create a common culture and achieve cultural rapprochement through cultural exchange.[6]

Reification through Reiteration

Narratives also derive their suggestive power from repetition to which, by definition, they necessarily and easily lend themselves. The saliency of Israel and American Jewry on the national agenda of Arab states and the existence of conflict makes for the repetition of attitudes and perceptions at all levels of communication. There are the essays by intellectuals, which, though aimed at a limited audience of opinion-makers, bear the cachet of "serious treatment." Journalistic writing appeals to a broader audience, but still claims to be serious reportage and analysis. Then there are well-focused polemical pamphlets appealing to popular emotions; while in the educational system, anti-Jewish texts are still learned—as are other forms of knowledge—by rote and loud chanting, all of it repetitious. In journalistic iconography the message is communicated swiftly and directly, producing loaded symbolism such as the Star of David, that has come unequivocally to signify a major abomination. Anti-Jewish texts are produced in the universities, sanctioned by the halo of academia, and offered for repetition on the university level. A "study of comparative literature" entitled *The Jewish Personality* by Dr. Muhammed Jala' Idris of Tanta University in Egypt tops the routine litany with the statement that Jews "are not human, but something in the form of humans"; considering their despicable conduct, "it is impossible that they belong to the world of sanity; rather they are derangement itself." The study concludes with the "careful" finding that we may assume with "considerable certainty" that "the Jewish personality as presented in the course of [this literary analysis] and based on the findings by psychologists is abnormal and totally irregular, marked by considerable deviation and derangement." Muhammed Abdallah al-Sharqawi published in 1990 *Al-Kanz al-Marsud fi Fada'ih al-Talmud* (A treasure of Talmudic Infamies), the cover of which included detailed illustrations of Jews using Christian blood for ritual purposes. The author was a professor in the Department of Muslim Philosophy at Cairo University. A master's thesis completed in 1990 by a student in the Department of Religion in Cairo University, entitled "The Protocols of the Elders of Zion and Their Threat to the Islamic Call," was reprinted by the department and used as a teaching aid.[7]

There is no doubt that the frequent repetition of ideas and slogans has a cumulative effect. They become a common idiom, almost a maxim, defeating any fresh considerations or reassessment. Even learned essays take the ignominy of the Jews both as an axiom and as a conclusion. There is hardly a discussion concerning Jews, regardless of its basic assumptions or theoretical framework, that does not reach anti-Jewish conclusions. Without any sense of malaise, prominent Arab intellectuals have made rational arguments the handmaiden of predetermined conclusions. Demonizers of the Jew make no secret of their instrumentalist bent—whether theoretical or designed for mobilizing the masses to jihad.[8] Neither do they try to conceal their selectivity in considering the relevant facts—to quote an Egyptian intellectual of the first rank: "God protect us against useless knowledge."[9]

Such frankness is possible precisely because certain negative attitudes toward Jews are taken to be self-evident maxims. Only this can explain how a twentieth-century society can accept and continue to propagate such preposterous fictions as the blood libel—the belief that Jews kidnap gentile children, slaughter them and mix their blood with unleavened Passover bread. It is not only the simple and ignorant who hold such beliefs. A number of recent books continue to accuse Jews of ritual murder, for example *Jarimah fi Harat al-Yahud: Fatirat al-Yahud Ajinah min Dam al-Masihiyyin* (A crime in the Jewish Quarter: Jewish matza is made with Christian blood), published in Cairo in 1992, prepared and prefaced by the popular mainstream writer Adil Hamuda. It appears in *Fatir Sahyun* (Matza of Zion), issued by no less an "authority" than Mustafa Tlas, the present Syrian Minister of Defense.[10] Even more telling is the fact that this "important work" was quoted on 19 February 1991 by the Syrian delegate to the United Nations Commission on Human Rights in Geneva as "unequivocal" evidence of the "historical reality of Zionist racism."[11] The cover of Tlas's work shows the slashed head of a monk, dripping blood—the victim of hook-nosed Jews. This is characteristic of a certain kind of Arab antisemitism, whose model is European. Jews are accused of undermining regimes, of inventing communism, socialism, capitalism, nationalism, democracy, and Freemasonry. Like its European predecessors, this inventory is not only ecumenical, but also contradictory. Even in present day Egypt, after nineteen years of peace and no need to instill belligerent sentiment in the people, the central idea of the *Protocols of the Elders of Zion* still lingers. Nor can it be explained away by the need of the opposition to needle the regime: it was the Egyptian establishment's daily paper *al-Akhbar* that carried an interview with "one of the greatest experts on Israel and Jewish affairs in the Middle East" (a textile merchant) who confirmed the propensity of the Jews to espionage and betrayal.[12]

The very important weekly, *October* "confirmed" that the notion of a worldwide Jewish conspiracy inherent in the *Protocols* was still of contemporary relevance.[13] Similarly, the semi-official daily, *al-Jumhuriyya* interpreted an opinion poll—in which 49% of the sample identified Israel and Zionism as most likely to benefit from instability in Egypt—to mean that despite the peace agreement with Israel, "we still remember the Protocols."[14] Closer to home, a PFLP representative to the recently-elected Palestinian National Council from Khan Yunis stated that a prerequisite for changing the Palestinian covenant was "that [the Israelis] change the extremism included in the Protocols of the Children [*sic*] of Zion."[15]

A Casting Model

Such myths have been incorporated into a communal psyche, which in recent decades has shown its ability to accomodate no less astonishing metamorphoses of classical anti-Jewish libels. A first rank Egyptian journalist like Anis Mansur could seriously claim that Jewish physicians in Egypt tended to specialize in obstetrics in order to abort Muslim women and eliminate future generations of gentiles. The venerable *Al-Ahram* reported in bold headlines that Israel traded the vital organs of Egyptian POWs in the international implant market.[16] Frequent allegations that Israelis deliberately introduced into Egypt debilitating drugs and bacteria remind one of medieval charges of well-poisoning. The Islamist opposition used these libels as weapons in their battle against trade relations with Israel, claiming for example, that the Jewish State was flooding Egyptian markets with vegetables and fruit carrying "grave diseases."[17] Mustafa Mashhur, recently elected as Supreme Guide of the Muslim Brotherhood in Egypt, warned against lifting the Arab boycott of Israel, reasoning as follows:

> Some Jews have been involved in narcotics and counterfeit currency cases and have attempted to spread AIDS or sow sedition between Muslims and Christians. Our Arab countries must protect themselves from this evil which will corrupt our young people, ruin our economy, and spoil all spheres of life.[18]

More recently, a demonic meaning was given to the vision of a New Middle East proclaimed by former Israeli Prime Minister Shimon Peres. The respectable mainstream Dar al-Ahram publishing house that produced the Arabic translation of Peres's book on the subject (seemingly in the spirit of dialogue) had a preface to it reminiscent of the *Protocols.* Surely, only the power of mythic thinking can explain why high-ranking and intelligent Arabs who finally get to visit the Knesset still believe that the [imagined] tapestry of "Greater Israel" stretching from the Nile to the Euphrates has only been removed temporarily. Such myth-making accounts for the indignation expressed by Arab writers over the intention in some literary circles to cleanse from Shakespeare's *Merchant of Venice* the more offensive expressions against Jews.

Imagery as Social Reality: Ideologies and Institutions

The organizing perspective of anti-Jewish myths has become part of social reality as well. The Arab narrative is tightly related to ideological formulations and political programs, deriving its inventory of slander from both Islamic and Christian sources.

Underlying the viewpoint of both Pan-Arabism and Islamism is the assumption that political sovereignty for minorities in the Middle East has no legitimacy. Contemporary Islamists derive this negation from classical Muslim political theory, which would extend protection and tolerance to monotheistic minorities, provided they do not attempt to transcend their legal and social inferiority. These minorities (Jews and Christians) are denied any measure of political sovereignty on principle, since only the Muslim nation is entitled to this and any alternative would undermine the subjection and inferiority of non-Muslims to Muslim rule. This is not only a matter of legal strategy but involves a profound belief in the exclusive cultural legitimacy and superiority of Islam.

Taking as its model the romantic concept of European nationalism, Pan-Arabism rejects the idea of the nation-state—indeed it repudiates any view of the state which denies primordial organic ties to a continuous Arab history. The "civil" variety of nation-state, personified in the Middle East by Israel, is seen as a major threat to the harmony of the Arab nation. Acceptance or even an understanding of Zionism is assumed to contradict the very foundation of Arab existence in its "ideal" full form—at least, as it is defined by Pan-Arabists.

Ideologies do not exist in a vacuum. They reflect a given sociocultural reality, drawing on it to set new agendas that influence public moods and trends. Ideologies thus become social facts in the Islamic-Arab world as elsewhere.

Ideas become even more of a social reality when they are anchored in institutions. This is the case in Egypt with the prevalence of antisemitic attitudes expressed by virtually all major political-ideological trends. In other Arab countries, who enjoy far less freedom of speech, one can find antisemitic attitudes entrenched in *official* institutions. For example, *al-Riyad,* a journal reflecting the views of the Saudi royal family, has carried a vindication of Hitler.[19] Abu Iyad, the late second-in-command in the PLO to Yasser Arafat, stated publicly that the "Jews are the scum of humanity. Will the Jews keep a promise?," he asked, pointing to their alleged refusal to abide by their agreement with the Prophet Muhammed. "Treachery," he argued, "flows in their blood, as the Qur'an testifies. The Jews are the same as they have always been."[20]

The Islamization of Jewish Imagery

The most significant movement currently articulating the demonization of the Jews is the radical Islamist movement that has swept over the Middle East in the last decade. The suggestive power of anti-Jewish myth is reinforced by the sanctity of divine authority, which appeals strongly to the deeply religious Arab society. Much of this religiosity is not about ritual or prohibitions but more like an engulfing sentiment, a total presence, an avid need for identity. The call to prayer, the recitation of Qur'anic verses, the familiar pattern of mosque sermons and tele-preachers— inspiring, calming, and uplifting the masses—all these facets of Islam find willing audiences. Opinion leaders in the Arab world are well aware of the legitimacy and mobilization that can be acquired through Islamic discourse. "Secular ideologies influence only the educated minority," said Dr. Hasan Hanafi, a prominent Egyptian intellectual, "with the masses, they go into one ear and out of the other."[21]

Iraq's Saddam Hussein, the most brazen secularist leader in the region, transfigured himself during the Gulf War into a scion of the Prophet and a

Savior of Islam, endorsed by an Islamic congress held in Iraq (in August 1990) by the Iraqi National Assembly and Iraqi sages and jurists. Cast as the leader of the "clash between the Muslim world and the infidel West" he indeed rallied the enthusiasm of crowds around the Muslim world.[22] The present regime in Egypt is vying with the Islamists for the title of the representative of Islam, flaunting religious conduct, symbolism, and acts to bolster this claim.

Even though most Arabs do not accept the extreme versions of fundamentalism, they are nevertheless partners to their spiritual world and receptive, in one sense or another, to their message. With growing fundamentalist militancy and involvement in politics, the demonization of the Jews and Israel has grown. Radical Islamists, convinced of the futility of all pacts and agreements, declare a "relentless war in which the Jews will be killed and they will be powerless to resist it."[23] Although classical Islam is by no means categorically anti-Jewish—it even provides for tolerance and coexistence with protected minorities—there is in its claim to a monopoly of the truth, an obvious potential for demonization. The Qur'an harbors within its text contempt and condemnation of Jews. One can easily find holy verses and Muslim oral traditions capable of supporting a negative attitude. Such evidence is mobilized by Islamists across the political spectrum to lend divine authority to their antagonism to Jews, and to reinforce the effect of imported European antisemitic materials. Jews are not merely adversaries, but "enemies of Allah" (Sura 41, verses 19, 28) and if the Qur'an does not implicate them in the murder of Christ, it does blame them for the "killing of the prophets" (Sura 2, verse 61). A vague reference in the Qur'an to the transfiguration of some cursed infidels into pigs and apes (Sura 5, verse 60) has become a current reference in Islamist writing. A cassette-recorded sermon originating in al-Aqsa mosque and replayed a few years ago in Acre mosque not only stresses repeatedly that Jews, both ancient and contemporary, are like apes and pigs, but adds dogs as well as donkeys to the imagery. A 1992 Cairo volume entitled *Jews in the Darkness,* reflecting a conspiratorial vision of the Jews, concludes with what must have seemed a relevant verse from the Qur'an: "Thou will find the most vehement of mankind in hostility to those who believe the Jews and idolators" (Sura 7, verse 82).[24] Another volume on the same subject, *The Jewish Impact on the Media and International Institutions,* is similarly prefaced by a Qur'anic passage: "O ye who believe! Take not the Jews and the Christians for friends. They are friends one to another. He among you who taketh them for friends is [one] of them. Lo! Allah guideth not wrongdoing folk" (Sura 7, verse 52).[25] Free permission to reprint is "granted to any Muslim. God will reward him who will publish it or assist in distributing it, and shed his mercy on him, his parents and all Muslims." *The End of the Jews,* published in 1993 uses Qur'anic references to illustrate the ignominy of the Jews. Its cover shows a powerful hand inscribed with the Muslim precept: "There is no God but Allah, and Muhammed is his Messenger." The hand is stabbing a Star of David, the outstretched arms of [Jewish] people drowning in a bloodbath.[26]

Similar messages are diffused in sermons (whether live, printed, televised, broadcast, or videotaped), in books and bulletins, as well as in the extensive educational "alternative" network. These include home circles, private lessons for students, Islamic-sponsored and directed private schools, and dedicated devotees within the official network of education and the media.

The anti-Jewish message is not confined to the ranks of the Islamists. Their voice is both heard and echoed by the mainstream Egyptian media. The semi-official daily *al-Ahram* invoked Qur'anic verses to suggest that Jews spread corruption, did not heed their promises, betrayed their allies, and offended Islam by burning holy books and killing the prophets.[27] The left-wing weekly *Sabah al-Khayr* quoted Sheikh Omar Abd al-Rahman's directive "to kill Allah's enemies by any means and everywhere, so as to be rid of the descendants of the pigs and the apes."[28]

Zionist or Jew?

The political motivation in this and other Arab perspectives is doubtless crucial and perhaps a major trigger in producing demonizing imagery. The main thrust of the attack may very well be against Zionism/Israel. But Zionism is ultimately about a Jewish state for the Jewish people so that the distinction between the two categories is more often than not blurred. The boundaries may be somewhat fuzzy but the imagery fuses the odium of Judaism and Zionism into a potent brew of hostility. Thus Judaism itself is seen as a "corrupt and arrogant *political* power."[29] "*A Jew is a Jew,* and has not changed for thousands of years. He is base, comtemptible, scorns all moral values, gnaws on live flesh and sucks blood for a pittance.... *Let us, then, cast aside this distinction [between Jews and Israelis] and talk about the Jews,*" wrote the editor-in-chief of an establishment elite weekly [emphasis added].[30]

Time and again, and in a variety of sources, the political confrontation with Zionism/Israel is described as transcending the territorial question of Palestine, or the political existence of Israel. Lieutenant-General Sa'd al-Din Shadhili, former Egyptian Chief of Staff, in objecting to Egypt's signing the Nuclear Non-Proliferation Treaty while Israel maintained her nuclear capacity, concluded that "every believer fully knows that there must be a decisive war between us and the Jews, the Qur'an and the Hadith emphasize this."[31] Obviously this viewpoint is more prevalent with the Islamists of all hues. *Al-Sha'b,* a weekly that is the mouthpiece of the relatively moderate Egyptian Muslim Brotherhood, frowned upon "Zionist attempts at religious normalization," following meetings of Israeli Minister of Religion Shimon Shitrit with religious personalities in Egypt.[32] "The conflict between us and the Jews is a conflict of faith and a conflict of existence," said the Supreme Guide of the Brotherhood. "No Muslim who believes in Allah and the day of judgment can betray His trustship [Palestine] to the enemies of the Muslim nation."[33] A bulletin of *al-Jihad al-Islami* in the West Bank and Gaza, dated 15 June 1990, offers a comprehensive presentation of this notion which is current throughout the Arab world:

> [the struggle against Zionism is] essentially historical and cultural, [and] ongoing until the day of judgment. This struggle will never cease; our presence in Palestine is part of a divine phenomenon, based on the total confrontation with Israel as a corrupting international phenomenon, directed against our [Muslim] nation. Jihad [is imperative] for the liberation of Palestine, all of it. Renouncing one inch of Palestine and recognizing Israel is treason against Islam, history, and the [Muslim] nation.... Jihad is all of Muslim doctrine, the Muslim way to victory, and the instrument to rally the nation all over the Muslim fatherland and the occupied fatherland, in particular.... Our enmity towards Israel and the West is ongoing and a matter of doctrine.... There should be a total confrontation with the entire apparatus of Westernizing culture which aims at isolating the masses from the struggle.... Secularism and Westernization are the implication of Western imperialist existence and the grounds for the Western assault on our nation.... Palestinian existence in the occupied fatherland is part of the divine plan.

Conclusion

The stereotype of the Jew as a demonic "other" is still firmly anchored in Arab-Muslim culture today and through constant repetition to a highly suggestible public, it has achieved a wide audience across secular/religious and Left/Right divides. Even in more benign versions such as the series published in *October* by its veteran editor Salah Muntasir, Jews are depicted as freakish, weird, and outside normal human patterns.[34] The furtive quality inherent in the *Protocols* myth has acquired an existence of its own as the portent of a lethal threat embodied by the corrupted Jews.

The Jew in Arab-Muslim perceptions is fixed in a narrative and a plot determined by the self-definition of Muslim Arabs. Jews as individuals, and even more so as a Jewish state, can do little to affect their place in this narrative through a change in their conduct or policy, unless they revert to their prescribed role as a "tolerated" community. In fact, it was the change in that historic role of "protected people" which turned the classical Muslim contempt for Jews to a virulent antagonism. Zionist Jews dared to transcend their "inferiority" and even to win higher status. Having done that, they for-feited the status of "protected people" under Islam and resumed their initial position as rivals. The peace process and Israeli projects concerning a Middle Eastern Common Market simply underline the competitive and subversive threat in the eyes of Islamic radicals and others who fear Jewish influence. Israeli peace policies are seen as disguised attempts to achieve the old goal of controlling the region and the world. The vision of a new Middle East is accomodated in the *Protocols* perspective, and normalization is perceived as a novel effort at subversion. The inner logic of Arab-Muslim narrative prevails.

Self-definitions are notoriously resistant to reassessment or modification. Any change may jeopardize the integrity of the theory as a whole and undermine the sense of self-identity. Changes in cultural self-definition, anchored in national needs and agendas, sustained and sanctioned to protect the fabric of the nation, do not come about readily or for trivial reasons. This is even more evident when this self-definition is endowed with sacred authority. Its features become even more tenacious when perceived as an absolute revealed truth, whether they derive from Muslim precepts or from imported European notions which have been Islamicized.

The confluence of contemporary Islamist zeal and persistent political strife with Israel has turned Arab antisemitism into a potent brand of the ancient prejudice—striving toward the annihilation of the demon. Spilling the blood of Jews seems like a kind of poetic justice to Muslim extremists. "Slay them wherever you find them" (Qur'an chapter 2, verse 191) has become an Islamist logo. The most popular Hadith circulating from the West Bank to London is:

> The Hour [of judgment] will not occur until the Muslims fight the Jews and kill them.... The Jews will seek shelter behind stones and trees, and the stones and trees will proclaim "O Muslim, O servant of Allah, there is a Jew behind me, come and kill him."[35]

Another hadith is quoted in *Falastin al-Muslimah* to support the conclusion that "unremitting war will go on until the corpse of the last Jew in the blessed land."[36] The title of a recent book, *Alam Bila Yahud* (A world without Jews), sums up this murderous rhetoric. Even if the motivation for violent action is social, economic, or political—it is religious indoctrination that provides the intense passion often evident in militant operations.

Arab-Muslim antisemitism has never really been the result of social ten-sions, and there is no visceral revulsion from Jewish individuals as such. "Slay them wherever you find them" is not an immediate concrete injunction to be found on most Arab-Muslim agendas. Without the political conflict, it might very well have become folklore. But the conflict with Israel has not yet been detonated. Despite the expanded peace process, there has been no compromise on the meta-political level, in the sphere of religious and philosophical conceptions. Against this background, stereotypes more easily take root and intoxication with words can corrupt deeds. A leading Arab political scientist, speaking to this issue a few years ago, touched on a core question: "The Arabs do not believe that Israel has a past or a future. It is not important whether this is right or wrong, but they believe it with conviction, and so it becomes political."[37]

Notes

1. Cf. Benny Kraut, "The Possibilities and Limits of Intercultural Learning," in *Approaches to Antisemitism,* ed. Michael Brown (New York and Jerusalem, 1994).

2. Nasr Hamid Abu Zeid, *Naqd al-Khitab al-Dini* (Critique of religious discourse) (Cairo 1992).

3. Najib Mahfouz, *Awlad Haritna* (Cairo, n.d.).

4. Sayf al-Din Abd al-Fattah, "Verbal Warfare," in *So that There Be Not Another Arab-Arab War* (in Arabic) Proceedings of the Fifth Annual Conference, Center for Political Research and Studies, Cairo University, 1992.

5. Hamid Rabi', *Arab Culture Between the Zionist Assault and the Will for National Integration* (in Arabic) (Cairo 1982), 26–27, 85. Rabi' was then a professor of political science at Cairo University.

6. Al-Sayyid Yasin, "The Question of the Cultural Challenge between Israel and Egypt," *al-Siyasah al-Dawliyyah,* April 1983.

7. Reported in the ruling party's religious organ, *al-Liwa' al-Islami,* 29 March 1990.

8. See Rivka Yadlin, *An Arrogant, Oppressive Spirit* (Oxford, 1989), 44–46.

9. Hasan Hanafi, "Hal Yajuzu Shar'an al-Sulh Ma'a Bani Isra'il" (Does religious law permit us to make peace with the Israelites?), *al-Yasar al-Islami* (Islamic Left, Cairo), 1981: 96–97.

10. Mustafa Tlas, *Fatir Sahyun* (Matza of Zion) (Damascus 1986).

11. Permanent Representative of the Syrian Arab Republic to the United Nations Commission on Human Rights, Geneva, United Nations Economic and Social Council, Commission on Human Rights, 47th Session, E/CN.4/1991/80. For a complete U.N. documentation, see World Union for Progressive Judaism, *Human Rights and Human Wrongs,* no. 10, 18–19, 43, 48–57.

12. *Al-Akhbar,* 1 May 1992.

13. *October,* 8 August 1993.

14. *Al-Jumhuriyya,* 20 June 1993.

15. *Al-Hayat al-Jadidah,* Palestinian Authority, 3 February 1996, quoted in Ha'aretz, 5 February 1996.

16. *Al-Ahram,* February 1996.

17. *Al-Sha'b,* 11 February 1993; 3 March 1993.

18. *Al-Sha'b,* 8 February 1993.

19. *Al-Riyad,* 6 October 1986.

20. *Al-Qabas* (Kuwait), 28 November 1989.

21. Dr. Hasan Hanafi, interview, *Rose al-Youssef* (30 June 1980).

22. *Middle East Contemporary Survey,* 14 (1990).

23. Tariq al-Zumur, *Sira'una Ma'a al-Yahud Sira' Mahsum* (Our battle with the Jews is decisive), quoted in Hala Mustafa, *Al-Islam al-Siyasi fi Misr* (Political Islam in Egypt) (Cairo 1992).

24. *Al-Yahud fi al-Zalam* (Jews in the Darkness) (Cairo 1992).

25. Fu'ad Bin Sayyid Abd al-Rahman al-Rifa'i, *Al-Nufuz al-Yahudi fi al-ajhizah al-I'lamiyyah wal-Mu'ssasat al-Dawliyyah* (The Jewish impact on the media and international institutions) (Cairo 1992).

26. Muhammad Izzat Muhammad Arif, *The End of the Jews* (in Arabic), 1993.

27. *Al-Ahram,* 19 April 1993.

28. *Sabah al-Khayr,* 14 December 1993.

29. *Al-Khalij* (United Arab Emirates), 27 August 1989.

30. *Al-Ahram al-Iqtisadi,* 27 September 1982.

31. *Al-Nur,* 12 January 1996.

32. *Al-Sha'b,* 16 January 1996.

33. *Al-Hilal al-Dawli* (London), 16–30 June 1991.

34. See *Ha'aretz,* 9 February 1996.

35. Related in *Bukhari,* a major canonical compilation of Hadith, vol. 2, p. 23; this translation quoted from *al-Khilafah* (London), 23 February 1990.

36. Quoted in *Falastin al-Muslimah* (Manchester, England), December 1988.

37. Muhammad Sid Ahmad to the *Irish Times,* 9 March 1991.

21

The *Protocols of the Elders of Zion:* New Uses of an Old Myth

Dina Porat
Tel Aviv University

This conference has focused on antisemitism not as a phenomenon per se, but within the conceptual framework of the "demonization" of various groups. Its organizers had in mind "the perception of the 'other' as an existential threat menacing the very continuation of the physical, spiritual, cultural, religious or social existence". A further intention has been "to examine the gap between genuine factors which lead to antagonism, such as social, economic or political conditions, religious differences or ethnic origin and the demonic perceptions of 'danger' leading to domination and destruction"; and finally to explore the origins and development of images and accusations leading to the demonization of specific groups, generally a minority or an underprivileged group, paradoxically seen as a threat to the dominant majority.[1]

The *Protocols of the Elders of Zion* are the embodiment of these points, the perfect example of how Jews, as individuals and as a group, could be depicted as the "other"; as the stranger and the outsider, who challenges the social order from within and without, who aims to take over the world and rule it. Thus the Jews are a threat to the status quo and the continuity of the established world order.

Moreover, their outsider status is further accentuated when Jews are identified with elements that are not considered authentic parts of society—whether cosmopolitan, pro-Western liberal, imperialist or communist—as the case demands. These elements frequently constitute a danger in the minds of antisemites and are therefore readily identified with the Jews, or at least considered to be their allies.

However, the *Protocols* cannot really serve as an example to demonstrate the gap between real factors leading to antagonism and the origins of irrational demonizing perceptions. On the contrary, the *Protocols,* both in content and in their use, point to a constant blur between "genuine" sources of demonization (i.e. logical or at least understandable ones) and the irrational ones. It seems that the latter can be no less genuine, if by that we mean authentic and deeply felt. One might go even further and argue that the irrational factors are more genuine and durable than the obvious and logical ones, or suggest that they form together a nonseparable entity.

It is, for example, a fact that the authors and editors of the *Protocols* explain the source of the Jews' alleged talents and powers, especially their capacity to penetrate society and manipulate it, in irrational and demonizing ways. These explanations become, in their turn, new sources of antagonism and hostility, thereby removing the possibility of precisely defining the gap spoken of earlier.

The issue that needs to be addressed is the motivation for publishing today the *Protocols of the Elders of Zion* over ninety years after its first appearance. Are they still relevant, and if so, where and why? Are the new editions currently being distributed an addition to former variations on the basic idea of Jewish world domination, so prominent in former decades? Does the role they play as a tenet of the antisemitic worldview, affecting the relations between Jews and non-Jews, still have the same importance?

Before delving into specific answers to these questions, a short overview of the present situation is required. In the 1990s the *Protocols* are indeed being published in new editions, serialized forms and new translations, from Chile to the Czech Republic, from Moscow to New Zealand and Tasmania. Accusations of scheming to dominate the world are hurled against Zionism and the State of Israel in particular; against world Jewry and worldwide Jewish organizations; last but not least they are used against individual Jews, as integral parts of the same global entity, even when they are mentioned separately. These charges are usually connected to specific current events and changes in different parts of the world. One may say that the revived *Protocols* are a reflection and an explanation of social, political and economic crises, be they in the former Communist bloc, Japan, the Middle East or in the United States.

In the post–World War II era, the existence of Jews is no longer a precondition for the appearance of antisemitic publications and activities. On the contrary, in some of the regions mentioned above, there are very tiny Jewish communities, as is the case with Japan or most of the Arab Middle East; and in the former eastern bloc, post-Holocaust and post-Communist Jewish communities are today very small in comparison to their numbers in the past. In other words, it is the negative image of the Jew rather than the actual Jew that is needed to provoke a reaction. To quote the historian Raphael Vago, a hidden imaginary enemy may perhaps be considered more dangerous than a conspicuous one—therefore the Jewish world conspiracy theory can thrive even where Jewish communities hardly exist anymore.[2]

One may add that it is a tragic irony indeed, that the ashes of once thriving Jewish communities serve now as the background for denying their very destruction and for perpetuating imaginary accusations.

Nevertheless, the *Protocols* have been less published during the past three years than they were between 1989 and 1992, editions reaching a peak during the Gulf War.[3] The question is why have they not been as frequently mentioned recently in antisemitic literature or distributed as much as formerly?[4]

The following thesis could perhaps explain this development. The *Protocols* were part and parcel of the antisemitic literature, which was on the rise, in quantity and intensity after 1989. They reached an unprecedented high point with the outbreak of the Gulf War when Israel was accused of using its ties with American Jewry to manipulate the United States into attacking Iraq. Protecting Israel's security, without the Israeli armed forces having to lift a finger seemed to be a perfect example of the use of the alledged Jewish ability to make the world move according to its wishes.[5]

But if the classical *Protocols* editions subsided in numbers in the following years, their importance did not really wane but simply provided new variations on the underlying central idea—the pursuit of Jewish world domination. Most important among these new forms has been Holocaust Denial, which has been on the rise in all respects during recent years.

Denial of the Holocaust depicts the Jews as a sophisticated and powerful world organization, capable of talking the entire world into believing in a hoax which they invented, even though it lacks any factual basis whatsoever. In other words, Jewish domination of the world is so gripping and total, that Jews may in fact carry out any scheme that they care to design; they have the ability to present any lie and make it pass as a tragic truth accepted by millions. The story of the Holocaust as the Jews present it is the best possible proof that the world is indeed in their hands, because this baseless horror story rewards them with money and sympathy; it provides Jews with the victim status which is an excellent starting point for conducting profitable negotiations and making extortionate demands. Denying the Holocaust also implies that the Jews have a sick and morbid imagination able to invent gas chambers, mass murders and indescribable tortures—in itself a pinnacle of evil.

There is also a striking similarity between the self-image of Holocaust deniers. Norman Cohn skillfully emphasized how the *Protocols* had been presented to their readers as an exposure of a vicious secret hidden from an innocent world public opinion. Entire nations were unaware, for centuries, of the plot being schemed against them.[6] Similarly, Holocaust deniers today claim to be brave souls challenging public opinion and powerful establishments, (controlled and manipulated by the Jews) exposing a truth, hitherto hidden by this mighty people. In that sense, the publishers of the

Protocols and the Holocaust deniers form one front, fighting for the same cause; they are the lone rangers, defending society, ready to sacrifice and to suffer nobly for the sake of truth.[7]

Undoubtedly, the case of the *Protocols* distributors is being strengthened by this vigorous stance of the deniers. The *Protocols* crystallized a certain image of the Jew—well-organized, subversive, stubbornly laboring to reach his target. The deniers strengthen this image, by returning to older stereotypes created by the Christian churches, of the Jew as a liar, a blackmailer, and a cynical, greedy exploiter. Moreover, Holocaust denial strengthens the cause of the *Protocols'* distributors by removing the stigma of mass murder from a work considered to be a "warrant for genocide." Instead those who defend the *Protocols* can be seen as righteous group, leading the struggle of the innocent victims of Jewish machinations.

One might ask whether Holocaust deniers and purveyors of the *Protocols* actually believe in their own propaganda. Are they truly convinced that Jews are indeed engaged in plotting world domination? Do they feel what Hitler once defined as an inner truth that needs no legal or historical proof? If so, they both follow a long line of antisemites who have depicted themselves, ever since the nineteenth century as the victims of Jewish aggression. The Nazis, in fact, turned such self-presentation of themselves as victims into an art. Does this then mean that Holocaust Denial can penetrate modern cultural and political discourse much as the *Protocols* and the idea of Jewish world domination, succeeding in doing before the Second World War?[8] This must remain an open question: but what cannot be contested anymore is that the *Protocols* and Holocaust Denial go hand in hand today as part of the same fight.

A few examples, among many others, from various places could illustrate this point. A reader's letter in the Venezuelan newspaper *El Universal,* justifies Holocaust Denial, and repeats, at the same time, the essence of the *Protocols.*[9] Dr. Franjo Tudjman, President of Croatia, published (before being elected to office) a book described by the late Menachem Shelach as "a bad copy of *The Protocols of the Elders of Zion.*" For his ideas regarding the Holocaust and the Nazi period, expressed in the same book, Tudjman was initially denied an invitation to the opening ceremonies in Washington of the Holocaust Memorial Museum in April 1993.[10] Another example reported by *Libération* concerns a visit by French Holocaust deniers to Iraq, where the Minister of Information lamented the banning of the *Protocols* in France and a member of the group was personally received by Saddam Hussein. It is not surprising that the French deniers' monthly, *Révision,* should have endorsed the *Protocols*[11]—nor that an Egyptian book published in 1987, presents the Holocaust as a "fairy tale" and the *Protocols* as an integral part of the Jewish heritage.[12]

In Italy, too, one finds allegations that the Holocaust is a modern version of the "Jewish conspiracy," voiced in publications and speeches of Catholic integrists, of the extreme Right and Left, and the new national-communists. A good example is an extreme Left magazine *La Lente de Marx* (Marx's Testimony) that dedicated no less than fifty pages to the issue. So, too, is a book by a leftist "revisionist", expressing the conviction that "the Myth of the Holocaust" was invented in order to create the State of Israel, and calling upon the Left not to leave its refutation to the far Right.[13]

The Italian case shows that at least four different political movements, rivals in every other way, treat Holocaust Denial and the Jewish conspiracy in a similar way. This recalls a phenomenon that characterized the *Protocols* from the beginning—the political elasticity which facilitated their use by all kinds of political groups. Holocaust Denial similarly provides a common denominator, with its hard core composed of blacks and whites, religious and secular, Right and Left and many others in between. The fact that the *Protocols* and Holocaust Denial are two sides of the same coin, does not, of course, rule out the possibility for each to be published and disseminated separately.

Let us now examine the contemporary relevance of the old idea of Jewish world domination, in its present variations in different parts of the world. The varieties are indeed many and sometimes surprising, ranging from accusing the Jews of ruling the Ukraine and responsibility for Chernobyl to forcing the Vatican to change ancient theological doctrines concerning Judaism and sign an agreement with Israel. Jews are even blamed for deliberately spreading the Aids virus and for the destruction of the ozone layer.[14]

Apart from the western world, the revival of the idea of world domination is particularly relevant in the former eastern bloc, in the Middle East (despite the peace process), in the American Black community, and in Japan as a response to economic anxieties.

The *Protocols* (which originated in Russia before the 1917 Revolution) have been particularly evident in the ex-USSR where deep changes have been especially traumatic. The Metropolitan Ioann of St. Petersburg, the second highest ranking clergyman of the Russian Orthodox Church stated during a Moscow trial in 1993: "The *Protocols* have not only failed to become outdated, but have actually become more precise and their views are promoted in our day". When Pamyat serialized the *Protocols*, the *Jewish Gazette* which had charged it with antisemitism found itself sued for slander. Following a sensational trial, the Russian court initially ruled that Pamyat's accusation be rejected and its publishers should compensate the *Jewish Gazette*. The *Protocols* were not even mentioned in this verdict, perhaps because the judge had been asked by Alexey II, Patriarch of the Russian Orthodox Church, not to embarrass the church by involving it in the trial. It was only later ruled that it was not within the court's jurisdiction "to determine the authenticity" of the *Protocols*, or whether they were a forgery. Therefore no slander was involved. The court's decision did not change the Metropolitan's opinion.[15]

The renewed interest in the *Protocols* in the former Communist countries is not altogether surprising. It should be remembered that under Communism, it had been banned, even though a *Protocols*-style conspiracy theory had pervaded the Soviet view of Zionism and Israel.

Moreover, the Russian public has not been exposed to Western court verdicts and detailed research proving the *Protocols* to be a forgery. In Russia and in Eastern Europe they can therefore seem to be at least a plausible hypothesis. Antisemites have exploited this situation and the new freedom of speech in order to legitimize their work. A court addressing itself to this issue in Prague in 1993, for instance, did not ban the dissemination of the *Protocols,* out of concern for free speech.

Another theme encouraging the *Protocols'* dissemination has been the role allegedly played by Jewish personalities during the October Revolution of 1917 in founding the Soviet regime, and their imagined responsibility in destroying it seventy years later. Jewish mass immigration to Israel after 1989, as if they were criminals searching for a haven—gave the *Protocols* a new credibility for antisemites in Russia. This chain of historical events supposedly proved that Jews could first build an empire and then break it apart when it no longer served their interests.[16]

On a more serious level, efforts by East European leaders to come to terms with the Holocaust also provoke antisemitic conspiracy theorists. A political leader who visits the Holocaust Memorial Museum or Yad Vashem and expresses remorse regarding his nation's treatment of the Jews during the Holocaust or who simply adheres to democratic western values, risks being depicted by extreme groups as a "Zionist-Jewish stooge," alien to the authentic culture and tradition of his people. Thus, President Vaclav Havel was accused in 1993 by the leading antisemitic Czech publication *Politika* (involved in the publication of the *Protocols*) of being an agent of the "international Zionist-Jewish conspiracy," and the same goes for Boris Yeltsin in Russia.[17]

As Randolph Braham has written, with regard to the dissemination of traditional propaganda works in the post-Communist world of Eastern Europe: "Among the latter, by far most popular has been the *Protocols of the Elders of Zion.…* It has been disseminated in virtually all former communist countries and was serialized in newspapers and issued as a booklet."[18]

Another example of the use of the *Protocols* in contemporary conflicts may be found in the former Yugoslavia. Having assumed power, the President of Serbia, Slobodan Milosevič, tried to establish contacts with

Israel, defining Jews and Serbs as two "chosen peoples" with tragic histories. He emphasized the differences of opinion between him and the Croatian President, Tudjman, who had been guilty of antisemitic utterances and of relativizing the Holocaust. Yet when the fighting in Bosnia started, this pro-Jewish atmosphere was reversed. The media in Belgrade defined the calls of Jewish intellectuals such as Elie Wiesel for international intervention in Bosnia as "anti-Serb", and world Jewry was accused of an "anti-Serb international conspiracy". Indeed, such allegations were followed by the publication of *Protocols of the Elders of Zion* by an unknown publisher in Belgrade in April 1994.[19]

In the Muslim world, too, there is a clear tendency to turn to antisemitic conspiracy thinking when writing about Israel. "Peace with Egypt is a Jewish manipulation dictated by the instructions of the *Protocols of the Elders of Zion,*" is a quotation from an interview with Omar Tilmisiani, Supreme Guide of the Muslim Brothers. In many books published in Egypt one can read statements claiming that the "*Protocols* are a call for the destruction of the world and for Jewish rule everywhere using every possible means."[20] The peace process is frequently described as an attempt on Israel's part to conquer and subdue the Arab world, and the *Protocols* are offered as an explanation for the new situation: "What Israel and world Zionism did not achieve by war, they are trying to achieve by peace", claims the spiritual leader of the Hizballah, Muhammad Hussein Fadlallah. "Satans", he promised on another occasion, "big or small, trying to devour us will not frighten us."[21]

Even the idea of creating a Middle Eastern Common Market, often advocated by Israeli Prime Minister Shimon Peres, is seen by militant Arabs as an embodiment of the *Protocols:* "The Jews are on their Way to Control World Economy", is the title of an article, whose author, attempting to prove his prediction, cites the *Protocols.* In his opinion they are highly relevant in assessing current events in the Middle East, since they provide the philosophic and religious foundations of the Jews' plans to control the economic resources of the world.[22]

As Esther Webman has skillfully shown, the *Protocols* are used in the Middle East, much as they are elsewhere, by rival and even contradictory forces. Thus an Egyptian non-Islamic opposition paper published an article depicting the "Zionist enemy" as threatening the present, past and future of the Arab nation. The author supports his claims with quotations from the Bible and the Talmud as well as from the *Protocols,* a combination of sources often used in the Muslim world to assert that the Jews seek to rule the world.[23]

The Arab-Israeli peace process and the proposed Middle Eastern Common Market were attacked mainly by militant Muslims in the Arab world. Yet the recognition of Israel by the Vatican met with strong criticism from virtually the entire political spectrum. It was depicted as a proof of the success of Zionism, helped by world Jewry, in "Judaizing" the Catholic Church and manipulating its leadership. The various public declarations of the present Pope, John Paul II, denouncing antisemitism, expressing his sympathy for the victims of the Holocaust, his shift of basic doctrines of the Catholic Church regarding Jews, and his establishing relations with Israel, have outraged Muslim extremists. Sheikh Fadlallah, leader of the Hizballah, declared these acts to be "an historic sin against Christ and humanity." Fadlallah even asserted, as if he were referring to the Vatican itself: "If Christ were here now he would have expelled the Jews from the Temple as he did to the thieves."[24] If this were not enough, the Vatican's readiness today to memorialize the Holocaust can only have augmented Arab resentment, given the Muslim predilection to reduce this event to the level of propaganda for the State of Israel and its rule over the Palestinians.[25]

Not only among Arabs, but even more in Iran, the *Protocols of the Elders of Zion* have been published with devotion and regularity. The reason, given by one Iranian daily, is that "it is important for victims of such conspiracies to be aware of 'the essence and aims of these inauspicious phenomena.'"[26] Iranian publications have continued to connect the Holocaust with an anti-Jewish conspiracy theory, especially since the Vatican's recognition of Israel and Steven Spielberg's film, *Schindler's List.* The success of this movie on the Holocaust is considered in Iran as a proof of Jewish world control over the media and film industry in particular. It is perhaps not surprising that Iran, one of the most radical Middle Eastern countries, where the media and propaganda are fully controlled by the authorities, would both believe in and exploit the *Protocols* with such devotion. Typically, the accusations that Iran planned terrorist actions in Buenos Aires or in New York, are themselves dismissed by its leaders as a product of Jewish-Zionist world domination of the media.[27]

The *Protocols,* it is worth noting, although a Western Christian antisemitic fabrication, have steadily penetrated the Middle East since their first translation into Arabic in the 1920s. Their impact has intensified along with the Arab-Israeli conflict, permitting even Holocaust Denial (a theme basically alien to the Muslim world) to be adapted and politically exploited. At the same time, fundamentalist Muslims have radicalized the demonization of Israel and the Jews, using their own religious sources, especially the Quran. This Islamic demonization is expressed by depicting the Jew as negative and incorrigible in every respect, demonstrating the same vile character traits that he had supposedly displayed in Arabia in the days of the prophet Muhammad.

This arbitrary interpretation of their own religious sources is aggravated by the determination of radical Muslims to identify Zionism and world Jewry with America and the West in general. Thus Jews and Zionists become the incarnation of pure evil and especially of all the secular values that radical Islam opposes. Since the fundamentalist goal is to create a new world Islamic nation, Israel stands out even more as a non-Muslim alien state in the area, sustained by world Jewry, behind which the United States and the entire West are struggling against the righteous claims of Islam.

Radical Islam, which began from an anti-Zionist stance and turned increasingly anti-Jewish, has broadened the Arab-Israeli conflict far beyond its territorial-national aspects into a global dimension based on religious concepts. This universalization, along with the reliance on a theory of world Jewish domination, might perhaps be seen as a form of psychological compensation. It can explain away Muslim failures in economic and technological modernization, especially in their conflict with Israel.

Radical Muslims also publish and propagate the *Protocols* outside the Arab Middle East and Iran. In Turkey, for example, the idea of Jewish world domination is disseminated in local propaganda, especially in the *Son Mesaj* magazine, which fantasizes about the conquest of Anatolia by Jews and Zionists or the selling of millions of Muslims into slavery.[28] In Moscow, a Muslim publication called *Al-Kuds,* serialized chapters from the *Protocols.*[29] In most western European countries, too, as well as in Australia, Muslim fundamentalists have initiated editions of the *Protocols.*[30]

Antisemitism, especially Holocaust Denial, has also grown in the Black community in the U.S.A. It is a feature in some of the propaganda of The Nation of Islam (NOI), a Black Muslim movement led by Minister Louis Farrakhan for the last two decades, which is considered today the most extreme among North American Black radical groups. It seems that the more their antisemitic parlance intensifies, the more their popularity among Black students grows.

In a 1991 book, *The Secret Relations Between Blacks and Jews,* sponsored by the Nation of Islam, Jews are depicted as "the principal architects and prime beneficiaries of the African slave trade," and the theory has been endorsed, by widening circles in the Afro-American community, including by Black college professors.[31]

The fact such myths can thrive despite their clear negation by the American Historical Association, shows once again that solid facts and historical research have been subordinated to social and political needs of the present. The Black community needs an explanation as to why most of the American Jewish community has been successful while the Black community has fallen behind. In their publications, The Nation of Islam accuses Jews of manipulating the media against the Black community and causing its economic paralysis.

As part of its antisemitic mythology, it holds that the extent of the Holocaust has been grossly exaggerated and that Hitler's reaction to the Jews was understandable, if they were doing in Germany what they have been perpetuating in the United States. A related historical conspiracy theory has surfaced in other parts of the Black community, purporting to expose a secret history of anti-Black racism in the Jewish community. This extends from the compilation of the Talmud to the establishment of the slave trade and climaxes in the fostering of racial stereotypes in 'Jewish-controlled' Hollywood movies. Such a secret history shares with Holocaust Denial the assumption that Jews control both historical events and their interpretation, substituting themselves as victims for the American Blacks, the Arabs or the Germans.[32] Such theories have adherents well beyond the hard core Holocaust deniers or the Nation of Islam.

The *Protocols* have also found echoes in Japan, where the idea of a world Jewish plot has gained a strong foothold. Books and brochures, videocassettes and the press have disseminated such ideas to a mass audience. In 1986–87 alone, thirty different books promoted the idea.[33] Among the best-known authors were Uno Masami, an active Christian fundamentalist, whose first antisemitic book sold a million copies in a short time; Doi, who described President Clinton as a puppet in the hands of Jewish capital; Ruy Ohta, leader of a very small but active antisemitic political party (the Global Restoration Party) and many others who propagate the idea that Japan faces the immediate danger of a Zionist-Jewish conquest.[34]

Such literary antisemitism is all the more striking since Japan had hardly any direct contact with Jews in its history. One positive exception was the Jewish banker Jacob Schiff, who lent the Japanese government the huge sum of five million pounds (which enabled it to get a far bigger loan) to help it win the war against Czarist Russia at the turn of the 20th century. Japanese attitudes to Jews are not without admiration for their achievements, even when the global Jewish control of financial networks and manipulation of politics is being emphasized, as in the *Protocols,* which were first translated into Japanese in 1924. It is revealing that when the Nazis demanded from the Japanese the 50,000 Jews gathered in Shanghai, the Foreign Ministry decided to refuse the German demand. Instead they set up a ghetto of their own in Shanghai. Apparently, the *Protocols* led them to conclude that the Jews had better be treated with caution rather than with aggression. Thus, Japan, despite its antisemitic theories, saved tens of thousands of Jews during the war.

Michael J. Schudrich, rabbi of the small Jewish community in Japan, divides the "Jewish book boom" there into those who admiringly describe the financial talents of Jews as worthy of imitation and those who see a worldwide Jewish conspiracy to ruin Japan's economy and rule it. This supposed plot by global Jewish-Zionist financiers (who supposedly rule the American economy) and the giant multinational companies, aims to let the value of the yen constantly rise, thus jeopardizing Japan's exports. Once

Japan goes bankrupt, it can be bought out by the Jews. Books that purport to explain and to frighten the Japanese with such ideas, are read more out of concern for the future than with the Jews. Moreover, it is always easier to blame the Jews rather than to openly attack America, the real rival of Japan.[35]

Jacob Kovalio has noted how the basic idea of world Jewish domination has bred a long list of outlandish accusations: thus the Japanese imperial family is allegedly dominated by Jews, since most of the Empress' ladies-in-waiting are Christians; Japan is the last obstacle preventing a Jewish takeover of the planet—all other countries having been subjugated; Shaul Eisenberg dominates Japan's economy; the atomic bomb was invented by Jewish scientists who hated Japan; Alfred Nobel was a Jew—the list seems endless.[36]

As elsewhere, such books which rely on *Protocols'* ideology, also deny or at least trivialize the Holocaust. Masamu Uno claims, for instance, that it was technically impossible to kill six million people; and on the other hand he "understands" Hitler, who had no choice but to eliminate the Jews. Other books claim that 200,000 Jews at the most died during the war; that the Holocaust is a postwar Jewish and Communist invention; that Jews planned the Crystal Night pogrom of 1938 to embarrass the Germans; that Jews died in camps because the Talmud forbids Jews to receive medical treatment from non-Jews, and many other fantastic claims.[37]

Japan's cultural and political tradition is quite different from that of Christian Europe, the cradle of antisemitism. The anti-Jewish literature has not, so far, been translated into social or political action. On the other hand, ordinary Japanese, having a deep respect for the written word, are easily convinced by a popularly written book. They have always been suspicious of foreigners and their current economic concerns readily encourage xenophobia. In the antisemitic literature, the Jew is, of course, an embodiment of the foreigner, especially the Westerner who places high priority on materialism and success. "Unlike western antisemites, who regard the Jews as an alien group in the West", Ben-Ami Shillony writes, "the Japanese antisemitic writers regard them as a central element of the West, the epitome of all that the Japanese admire and fear in Western Culture."[38]

This is also the case with Muslim extremist groups as well, who treat the Jews and Israelis as the avant-garde of the threatening West, alien to the Middle East culture. It is equally true in Eastern Europe, where xenophobes and antisemites regard the Jew as the incarnation of the foreigner, though he has lived there for centuries. It seems that the more the Jew embodies Western, democratic, modern civilization, the more he is considered as a devilishly talented and dangerous "other" by those who reject or cannot compete with these standards.

Notes

1. Vidal Sassoon International Center for the Study of Antisemitism, Jerusalem to participants at the international conference on "The 'Other' as Threat: Demonization and Antisemitism," January 1994.

2. Raphael Vago, in *Anti-Semitism Worldwide—1994,* issued by the Project for the Study of Anti-Semitism (Tel Aviv 1995), 100.

3. See Nicole Zand, "Another Twist in the Great Jewish Plot that Never Was," *Guardian Weekly,* 10 May 1992, (tr. from *Le Monde*), quoting Pierre-André Taguieff on the "spectacular wave of new editions of the *Protocols* since 1989." The interview marked the publication of his scholarly edition *Les Protocoles des Sages de Sion, Introduction à l'Étude des Protocoles, Un Faux et ses Usages dans le Siècle,* 2 vols. (Paris 1992).

4. This conclusion is a result of a survey of the material accumulated in the computerized database of the Project for the Study of Anti-Semitism, Tel Aviv University, and its analysis in the annual reports.

5. See in details and with original texts, Project for the Study of Anti-Semitism and University and the Anti-Semitism Monitoring Forum, *Anti-Jewish Propaganda* (Tel Aviv 1991), 276.

6. Norman Cohn, *Warrant for Genocide, The Myth of the World Jewish Conspiracy and the Protocols of the Elders of Zion* (London 1967).

7. See, as one example, the reply of the exhibitor who included the *Protocols* and Henry Ford's *International Jew* at an African-American history event: "We are here to sell the truth." *Response* (May 1990): 13.

8. Dr. Joel Baromi, minutes of the annual seminar for researchers on antisemitism, Tel Aviv, January 1995.

9. Antonio Diaz Medina, *El Universal,* 15 October 1995.

10. Menachem Shelach, "Not Such a Fatal Attraction" (in Hebrew), *Ha'aretz,* 22 May 1992; see response, Igor Primoratz (in Hebrew), *Ha'aretz,* 9 June 1992.

11. *Response* (Fall 1991): 9; *Droit de Vivre* (September 1993): 1, for this and another blend of French and Belgian Holocaust Denial and the *Protocols.*

12. Wajih Abu-Zikri, *The First Terrorists—Our New Neighbors* (New Egyptian Library, 1987), 14–16.

13. *La Lente de Marx* (June 1994); Cesare Saletta, *Per il revisionismo storico contro Vidal Naquet* (Graphos 1994).

14. Project for the Study of Anti-Semitism, *Anti-Semitism—1994,* 195, quoting the Nation of Islam's tabloid, *The Final Call,* 1994; Pavel Chemeris, in *Za Vol'nu Ukrainu* (For a free Ukraine), 9 July 1992, on the atomic reactor.

15. *Response* (Spring 1993): 2–3; *Jewish Week,* 18–24 June 1993.

16. My thanks to my friend and colleague Dr. Raphael Vago for his help regarding East European issues.

17. *Mlada Fronta Dnes,* 1 December 1993; *Prague Post,* 8 December 1993; *The Russian Order* (organ of the anti-Yeltsin Russian Guard), March 1994.

18. Randolph L. Braham, "Anti-Semitism and the Holocaust in the Politics of East Central Europe," in *Anti-Semitism and the Treatment of the Holocaust in Post-Communist Eastern Union,* ed. R. L. Braham (New York 1994), 11.

19. *Standart,* 1 April 1994.

20. *El-Da'awa,* April 1978, 8.

21. Esther Webman, chapter on Arab countries and the Maghreb, in *Anti-Semitism—1994,* 156.

22. *Al-'Alam al-Islami,* June 1994; Project for the Study of Anti-Semitism, *Anti-Semitism 1994,* 162.

23. 'Ismat al-Hawari, in *al-Wafd,* April 1994; Project for the Study of Anti-Semitism, *Anti-Semitism 1994,* 158.

24. Ibid., 161.

25. *Al-Sha'b,* 22 February 1994; Project for the Study of Anti-Semitism, *Anti-Semitism—1994,* 162.

26. *Ettela'at,* 25 August 1994; Project for the Study of Anti-Semitism, *Anti-Semitism 1994,* 174.

27. Ibid., 175.

28. Project for the Study of Anti-Semitism, *Anti-Semitism Worldwide—1993,* 57.

29. *Al-Kuds,* June 1992.

30. See CRDA (Centre de Recherche et de Documentation sur l'Antisémitisme), report on Islamic fundamentalism in France (1993), 23; a collection from *Journal du dimanche, l'Humanité, France Soir, Le Parisien,* and *Actualité,* August–September 1993; *Libération,* 9 August 1993; *Actualité Juive,* 14 January 1993; on Australia see Jeremy Jones, in *Anti-Semitism—1994,* 229.

31. Robert Rockaway, "Louis Farrakhan, The Nation of Islam and The Jews" (Tel Aviv University).

32. Marc Caplan, report on antisemitism in the United States, in *Anti-Semitism—1994,* 199.

33. Michael J. Schudrich, "Anti-Semitism in Japan," *IJA Research Report,* no. 12, December 1987, 2–10; *Anti-Semitism monitoring reports,* November 1992, 2.

34. Yajima Manji, *The Art of Reading Between the Lines of the Jewish Protocols* (1986).

35. Schudrich, "Anti-Semitism in Japan," 7.

36. Jacob Kovalio, report on antisemitism in Japan, in *Anti-Semitism 1994,* 236.

37. Ibid., 237.

38. Ben-Ami Shillony, "The Flourishing Demon: Japan in the Role of the Jews?" lecture presented at the conference "The 'Other' as Threat: Demonization and Antisemitism," Jerusalem, October 1995.

22

The Motivations and Impact of Contemporary Holocaust Denial in Germany

Wolfgang Benz
Zentrum für Antisemitismusforschung, Berlin

The "Auschwitz lie," an ugly term implying that the National Socialist murder of six million Jews never happened, has become widely known in Germany, thanks to a brochure written by the recently deceased German neo-Nazi, Thies Christopherson. In 1944 this man was detailed for work in the Plant Cultivation Department of Auschwitz. Claiming the competence of an eyewitness, and with the help of right-wing argumentation, he tried to prove that Auschwitz was a pleasant place where prisoners danced and sang at work; newcomers, undernourished on their arrival in the camp, were given time to enjoy being pepped up.[1]

The "Auschwitz lie" is central to the concept of "revisionist" ideology which denies the crimes committed by the German National Socialist state. With this ideology, the Hitler apologists, the old and new Nazis, and the nationalist superpatriots try to repaint the historical picture of National Socialism, or to "decriminalize" German history.

The Federal German government also defines "revisionism" in this way:

Revisionism in a broader sense describes the attempts to correct the alleged wrong depiction of the history of the Second World War and the Third Reich to give a more favourable picture of National Socialism. The right-wing extremist camp largely agrees that essential knowledge about contemporary German history must be revised, particularly in respect to Hitler's sole guilt for the Second World War and the mass murder of Jews in German concentration camps. "Revisionism" in the narrower sense means the denial of the proven historical fact that during the course of the Second World War millions of European Jews were murdered in gas chambers, etc.[2]

One of the authorities on whom the revisionists base themselves is the Frenchman, Paul Rassinier, whose publications caused a scandal as early as the 1960s.[3] Robert Faurrison, an inferior imitator of Rassinier, was a lecturer in literature in Lyon. His supporters called him "professor for the critique of texts and documents" and have celebrated him as a martyr since the university threw him out.[4] Faurisson bases himself on the jurist, Wilhelm Stäglich, author of *Der Auschwitz-Mythos,* which led Göttingen University to deprive him of his doctor's title.[5] Then we also have the American professor of electrical engineering, Arthur R. Butz, and David Irving, once a journalist, who sank to the level of becoming Hitler's apologist.[6] It is noteworthy that all these "authorities," who claim scientific expertise and whose "professionalism" is continually invoked in revisionist publications, have (apart from Irving), no competence whatever. The same applies to the Institute for Historical Review, a revisionist center in California. Not a single competent historian works for this institution. The revisionists merely propagate ideology, and what is more, one that flies in the face of proven historical facts. Nevertheless, these so-called "scientific authorities" write articles and books, the contents of which are circulated for public consumption in leaflets, brochures, and magazines by colporteurs like Ernst Zündel in Canada, Gary Rex Lauck in the United States, Walter Ochensberger and Gerd Honsik in Austria, Manfred Roeder, Udo Walendy, and many others in Germany.[7]

In November 1992, a Mannheim court sentenced retired teacher Günter Deckert to a one-year suspended sentence and 10,000-mark fine for incitement, instigation to race hatred, slander, and insulting the victims of the Holocaust. The defendant had already been found guilty in several disciplinary proceedings (in 1988 he was dismissed from teaching altogether). At the same time he climbed the career ladder in the right-wing extremist NPD, which he joined in 1965. He was elected Federal Chairman of this party in 1991. Deckert was sentenced for organizing a "Revisionist Conference" in Weinheim where he presented a translation and commentary on a lecture given by the American Fred Leuchter, a dubious expert on executions, and a self-proclaimed engineer. At the behest of Ernst Zündel, a notorious Canadian neo-Nazi, he wrote the *Leuchter Report* in which he "proved" that the murder in the gas chambers of Auschwitz were technically impossible. Since 1988, he has been for neo-Nazis a much-quoted "authority." His report introduced a new stage in the campaign to deny the Holocaust and to prettify the history of National Socialism by using natural scientific and technical arguments intended to prove the supposed impossibility of the mass murders in Auschwitz, Treblinka, Maidanek, and other death camps.

In another article, Leuchter deals with the concentration camps in Dachau and Mauthausen, and the euthanasia murder center in Hartheim.[8] Thanks to widespread publicity by the right-wing camp (where the products of this dilettantic fervor were celebrated as a "scientific sensation") these epigones found people willing to accept their political fanaticism as a search for historical truth.

"Natural scientific proofs" are used to devalue and replace established documents (throwing doubt on their authenticity has been a long tradition of the revisionists) in an attempt to undo historical realities. One of the "scientific" speculations concerns the effects of Zyklon B poison gas used in Auschwitz. In addition, calculations were made about the amount of coke used, the capacity of the crematoria in the death camps, and the length of time needed to burn a body. For example, a natural scientist (with a doctorate) "researched" the effects of Zyklon B and how to dispose of it. He claimed that "even with high temperatures, a room full of cyclon B [*sic*] would still be full of gas two hours later." This, he says, proves that reports that the gas chambers in Auschwitz were opened immediately after the death of the victims are false. He concludes that the murders in Auschwitz could not have been carried out on the scale shown in the historical documents. He and other revisionists operate with the argument that a high temperature was needed for the poison gas to develop, and it was impossible to bring this about. And he was not content with theory. He tested his hypothesis in a practical experiment: "A small—doubtless dilettantic—pilot test with two digital thermometers in a more or less air-tight wooden crate occupied by one person, resulted in an absolutely negligible rise in temperature on the wooden floor."

He backed up his result with the argument that for a natural scientist it is "an iron law that an accepted view, theory, etc. can lead to false conclusions where the basic assumptions are wrong—in this case: the impossibility of disposing of cyclon B if used for mass gassings." When asked about the motivation for doing this research, he replied by invoking his "experience of growing alienation between Germans and Jews in the Weimar Republic—mostly caused by Jewish migration from the East"—and his desire to reestablish the ingenuous relationship that was a matter of course between Germans and Jews during the Kaiser period."[9]

Qualified natural scientists called these findings a "mixture of hypocrisy, narrowminded philistinism, clumsily artificial naivete mixed with an apparently natural scientific objectivity."[10]

Modelled on the Leuchter Report, Otto Ernst Remer (a retired major-general of the Wehrmacht, a Nazi under Hitler and one of the protagonists of the neo-Nazi scene since 1945) engaged a private expert when he had to appear before a German court in 1992 for denying the genocide of Jews. A qualified chemist, then employed at the Stuttgart Max Planck Institute for Solid State Research, had written an "Expertise on the Formation and Provability of Cyanide Connections in the 'Gas Chambers' of Auschwitz."[11] The court did not accept the paper, so Remer sent it to "1000 of the most important people in Germany" after having it printed on very expensive glossy paper. With the help of tables, curves, figures and "chemical analyses" this brochure again tried to prove that the murders in Auschwitz were technically impossible. In an accompanying letter, Remer demonstrated his "new" antisemitism with the help of old clichés: "In the age of religious freedom, all of us must oppose the 'Holocaust religion' which the courts have forced upon us. The truth is an original right. An original right for all people. We must not allow a small, powerful minority to destroy our essence, our spirit, our souls with an enforced religion."[12]

These are the methods which the deniers of the Holocaust use and with which they are gaining ground in public discussion because they build both on public uncertainty as regards historical and moral problems and on traditional antisemitic prejudices. The Deckert case is a good example.

On 15 March 1994 the Federal High Court in Karlsruhe granted the appeal by NPD chairman Günther Deckert, ordering that his sentence, passed in Mannheim in November 1992 be reviewed and rejudged by another chamber in the Mannheim Court. The High Court decision caused considerable public protest, although it confirmed that, in contrast to Deckert's claim, the mass murder of Jews in gas chambers in concentration camps under National Socialist rule is a historical fact and need not be proven again. Deckert's sentence was rescinded for formal reasons. The new sentence stated that the previous one had been too generally formulated and there was no proof that the defendant had identified with racist ideology, as is demanded by the law which bans incitement.[13]

Only in June 1994, however, when the substantiation for the new sentence was published did the case become a scandal. The judge described the defendent as a man of "strong character with a sense of responsibility and clear principles" whose political convictions and deeds were "motivated through his striving to strengthen resistance among the German people to Jewish claims based on the Holocaust. The fact was also taken into consi- deration that today, some fifty years after the war, Germany is still subjected to far-reaching political, moral and financial claims growing out of the persecution of Jews, whereas the mass crimes of other nations remain un- atoned which, at least from the political viewpoint of the defendant, is a heavy burden on the German people."[14]

The wave of public indignation was far stronger than that which arose after the sentence in March. The Federal Chancellor called the substantiation a disgrace and the Federal Justice Minister also condemned it. However, she was severely reproached for her condemnation by the *Frankfurter Allgemeine Zeitung,* which at first called for a "calm view" of the matter, then joined the general indignation and protested on principle: Deckert, who denies the mur- der of Jews thus "questions the legality of the Federal Republic."[15] They doubtless meant the violation of the basic historical agreement in the Constitution about a democracy erected on the ruins of the National Socialist state.

However, the Karlsruhe High Court's empathy for the "subjective element" as expressed in its comprehensive substantiation makes clear that the world-view of the judges and Deckert have elements in common. This is of fundamental importance, because we see here the two basic motives for refusing to accept historical reality: wounded national pride, and nostalgia for National Socialist or German nationalist ideals along with old antisemitic stereotypes.

> The politically right-wing defendant is not an antisemite in the spirit of National Socialist racist ideology, which, in the final analysis denied Jews the right to live, rather he condemns the disenfranchisement and persecution that Jews were subjected to by the Germans in the years 1933 to 1945. However, because of his strong national attitude, he bitterly resents the continual Jewish insistence on the Holocaust and the financial, political and moral claims they still make on Germany almost fifty years after the end of the war. Furthermore, the defendant agrees with revisionism, i.e. he considers it necessary to continually do research even into accepted historical theses."[16]

Finally, the substantiation states that "out of his bitter resentment against the Jews, the defendant wanted to arouse 'a strong emotional enmity' also in those addressed in order to strengthen resistance among the German people against Jewish demands derived from the Holocaust."[17]

Furthermore, the substantiation several times calls Jews "parasites" who persistently exploit their situation as survivors or descendants of survivors; whereby it is interesting to note that Deckert never once used the term "parasites." This was introduced by the judges! Deckert had, of course, meant exactly this, as do all deniers of the Holocaust, but he left the conclusion to others. For the purpose of the argumentation was to paint a public picture of "the Jews" who are to blame for causing uncomfortable feelings (guilt and shame), for benefitting from unjustified claims and for disturbing the social peace by refusing to forget the past:

> The fact was also taken in to consideration that today, some fifty years after the war, Germany is still subjected to far-reaching political, moral and financial claims deriving from the persecutions of Jews, whereas the mass crimes of other nations remain unatoned which, at least from the political viewpoint of the defendant, is a heavy burden on the German people.[18]

Denying the Holocaust is thus not simply an expression of nationalist or neo-Nazi eccentricity, but serves as a code for a new antisemitism and for again excluding the Jewish minority from society. The chairman of the Central Council of Jews in Germany commented in reaction to the Mannheim substantiation that "for some time right-wing radical ideas have no longer been expounded out loud in public merely by extreme peripheral groups and figures, but are obviously accepted right in the middle of our society."[19]

The High Court rescinded the Mannheim sentence on 15 December 1994 because of legal errors made "when considering the law." The judge commented that political blindness does not reduce the judicial guilt of persons who close their eyes to historical truth, sending the Deckert case back to the *Landgericht* (regional court) in Karlsruhe for retrial.

Questioning the number of those who died in the Holocaust has a long tradition among its deniers. The "Six-million lie" was already proclaimed by revisionists in the immediate postwar years. Althought the proof for the figure has been presented again and again, the argumentation always remains the same with occasional "new evidence." The aim is to create confusion, deny the facts and replace them with an invented pseudo-reality through supposedly irrefutable evidence presented by self-proclaimed experts and witnesses whose credibility is claimed to be beyond all criticism. In addition to questioning the figure of six million murdered Jews—a figure which has been proven beyond doubt[20]—statistics are repeatedly quoted which have nothing to do with the number of victims, but with the number of Jews living in the world today. From a mixture of all sorts of sources, most of which are not verifiable, it is said that the Jewish population throughout the world was 15.3 million in 1933. The fact that it had supposedly risen to 17.8 million by 1986 supposedly "proves" that the Holocaust did not take place.

The understandable difficulty for historians to calculate the exact number of Jewish victims is taken as a further proof that the Nazi genocide did not take place. Since the number of those killed in Auschwitz turned out to be too high, this was treated as a revisionist triumph, as was the correction of this error. When the commemorative plaque at Auschwitz was removed, the revisionists argued that there had been no mass murders in Auschwitz at all. It is interesting to note that the mistake was based on statements by no less a person than the Auschwitz commandant, SS-Führer Rudolf Höss, who in the Nuremberg war crimes trials spoke of two and a half million people killed in Auschwitz alone (revisionists asserted that he gave this figure only after being tortured).

In fact, the minimum figures of the number of Jews murdered by poison gas in the death camps, arrived at by professional historians and jurists after meticulous research into all sources, are as follows: in Chelmno (Kulmhof) it was 152,000, in Belzec 600,000, in Sobibor 250,000, in Auschwitz-Birkenau one million, in Treblinka 900,000, in Maidanek 60,00 to 80,000. In other words, almost three million Jews were murdered in these larger death camps alone. To these figures must be added the victims of the SS-*Einsatzgruppen* (according to their own figures, they murdered at least 535,000 Jews), those murdered in ghettos and concentration camps, those killed through forced labor, starvation, and ill-treatment of all kinds. The total figure is probably higher than six million.

Let us look at the method used to "prove" the Holocaust a lie. The oldest "source" on which the revisionists base themselves right up to the present day allegedly comes from the Red Cross, an institution which is generally accepted as one of great integrity and independence. Shortly after World War II, the Red Cross is supposed to have declared that the total number of people who were persecuted by the National Socialists on the basis of their origins, their religion, or their political views numbered a mere 300,000.

In December 1950 the Swiss magazine *Der Turmwart* reported that altogether less than one and half million people had been killed by the German National Socialists and their followers. The source of this figure is a report in the *Baseler Nachrichten* dated 12 June 1946, allegedly using "Jewish statistics." In January 1955, a neo-Nazi paper published in Bad Wörishofen, *Die Anklage,* took the issue again in a series of articles. A "universally known North American" was now introduced into the debate as an "expert," and the figure attributed to him was again 300,000 victims.

The Swiss source was also given as "proof":

> In an official report the Swiss headquarters of the Red Cross has now confirmed the data by the American, Warwick Hesters, published in our article: "The Meanest of all Historical Falsifications." The official statement by the Swiss headquarters of the Red Cross clearly states: "Victims of political, racist and religious persecution in the jails, concentration camps, etc. between 1939 and 1945: 300,000."[21]

Encouraged by this apparently serious source, unsuspecting magazines adopted these figures. The illustrated *Das Grüne Blatt* published an article which stated at the beginning: "Since 1946, the Swiss Headquarters of the Red Cross has collected all official reports about war losses in various countries. The present figures make up a total of horror and are a serious warning for all politicians today to do everything possible to prevent such a blood bath ever being repeated." When the total figure of "57 million victims!" (the article's headline) was broken down, the number of Jews murdered was given as 300,000.[22]

However, *Das Grüne Blatt,* in a letter to the director of the Munich Institute für Zeitgeschichte dated 6 February 1956 (who had asked them for the source) dissociated itself from the figure and gave some interesting information on how this article came about:

> We published the article "57 million victims" in view of the remilitarisation now taking place in order to seriously warn all people responsible. We received this article, which is based on figures from the Swiss Red Cross, from our permanent representative in Copenhagen who also represents us in Switzerland and Austria. Up to now, we have never had any problems with

him. We had no problems with this article, except for the one figure it contains—that of the victims killed in concentration camps. It has now become clear that it is obviously false. We have already had a long correspondence with the Member of Parliament, Kalbitzer, because in Switzerland and Germany, *Das Grüne Blatt* was accused of neo-fascist tendencies, which at first caused us to shake our heads and then made us angry. We then pursued the matter energetically, but, unfortunately, this led to nowhere. The basic source was not made known to us. Our Copenhagen correspondent, most of whose family was murdered in concentration camps and is thus completely above suspicion, took the article from the *Wiener Wochenausgabe,* with whom he has an exchange agreement. The *Wiener Wochenausgabe* wrote to him, as he informed us in a letter, that they could not remember whether they had taken it from *Die Tat* or some other publication.[23]

It was no longer possible to clarify who had started this confusion. What is clear, however, is that the originators lacked factual knowledge and that the most elementary rules of journalism were not observed. But what, in fact, were the official figures given by the Red Cross? They never existed, as the head of the Information Department of the International Committee of the Red Cross wrote in a letter to the Director of the Institut für Zeitgeschichte dated 17 August 1955:

> We cannot provide statistics about the losses among military persons, as the International Red Cross Committee does not do such statistical work. On the one hand, the Committee does not have the necessary means, and on the other, the reports from the Prisoner-of-War Centre refer to prisoners, transfer to other camps, release, etc., but do not give an exact picture of the total number of prisoners-of-war. Statistics which could be taken from these sources would demand not only much tedious work, but would provide only an inexact result. Far more incomplete are our figures about prisoners in concentration camps. Even if we were able to provide aid and support to prisoners at the end of the war, it was impossible, despite much effort, to provide help to the same extent as to prisoners of war, because the Committee does not have the same juridical basis for this.... As you can see from this, the figures given in the German weekly are not based on any information provided by the International Red Cross Committee.[24]

This official denial did not impress those who did not want to know. Ten years later, in an open letter to Cardinal Döpfner of Munich published in the NPD newspaper *Deutsche Nachrichten,* the right-wing radicals again quoted figures allegedly given by the International Red Cross. Again, the Red Cross categorically dissociated itself from the falsification:

We want to make quite clear that the International Red Cross Committee in Geneva has nothing to do with these assertions. The statistics about war losses and the victims of political, racist or religious persecutions are not and never have been within its purview. Even if they were prisoners-of-war (which have been protected since 1929 by an international agreement and for whom, as you know, we have a Central Search Service), we would not dare to publish figures, as we fully realise that we do not possess all information regarding this group of war victims. All the more are we obliged to refrain from all estimations in the case of civilians who were not protected at that time by any Convention and thus almost none of them fell under the jurisdiction of the Red Cross.[25]

The daily press, including many provincial newspapers, reported on this October 1965 letter to the Institute für Zeitgeschichte, yet until now, this Red Cross disclaimer has not worried the Holocaust denial propaganda machinery. On the contrary, neo-Nazi authors go to great lengths to invent new "official" figures. Heinz Roth, for example, wrote a brochure distributed in 1973 entitled "Why are we Germans lied to?" in which he states: "Did you know that the doubtless regrettable losses for the Jewish people—according to statements made by the UNO which has no reason to particularly favour any nation—were two hundred thousand?"[26]

An endless number of such examples can be given. The fact that what is claimed to be the source turns out to be sheer invention, the origins of which remain obscure, does not prevent those interested in minimizing the number of victims from continually repeating the source. The method used by revisionist propaganda is to quote these statements again and again, until they are assumed to be a firm part of the source material, are no longer checked, and are considered correct and thus believed.

A leaflet distributed in Germany by the Institute for Historical Review summarizes the present state of revisionist argumentation. Under the title "66 Questions and Answers about the Holocaust," the denial of this genocide appears as a closed system. The introductory question is: what proofs exist that "the National Socialists committed genocide or killed six million Jews?" With the intention of anchoring this pattern of argumentation in public discourse, the answer claims that historiography is based solely on reports of victims who cannot be taken seriously, because they contradict themselves. There are "no other concrete proofs of any kind such as larger amounts of ash, crematoria with the corresponding capacity, leftover clothing, written files, statistical data, lampshades made of human skin, soap made out of human fat, etc."[27]

With the exception of the soap, which long ago proved to be a legend, all the other proofs do exist. Even preserved skin, a product of the most perverse sadism, was found in Buchenwald.[28] The mixture of monstrous but marginal details in the argumentation has the function of making the historical facts as a whole appear unreal. The claim that there are no proofs except the "statements by certain 'survivors,' whose statements are contradictory" saves Holocaust deniers from having to delve any further, let alone look into the facts that have been provided by the perpetrators' own documents, such as SS statistics or concentration camp index cards, or from having to note that there is certainly no lack of material evidence.

They constantly try to give the impression that no proof for the murder of six million Jews exists, as if this were a well-established fact. When asked where the European Jews had gone, the IHR brochure claims "After the war they were still in Europe with the exception of 300,000 who were killed during the war or immigrated to Israel, America, Argentina or Canada. Most of them left Europe only after the war. There emigrants have all been statistically registered.[29]

Another claim is that two million Jews fled "to the farthest regions of the Soviet Union"; they were never within the German sphere of influence and "more than a million" had supposedly immigrated before the war began. The abstruseness of this claim becomes obvious in light of the fact that the sudden flight of such masses of people was quite impossible in Stalinist Russia, nor was there anywhere for them to emigrate. Jewish emigrants did not enjoy freedom of movement. Those who tried to get out were faced with quotas imposed by the countries in which they wanted to settle, and with endless bureaucratic red tape.

In contrast to the crude and vulgar argumentation of traditional neo-nazis, revisionists generally use pseudo-science to present its claims in a respectable language, but the content is the same. The imitation of science by taking over its forms, such as discussions, lectures, seminars and conferences, and the publication of footnoted journal articles and books does not, in itself constitute a serious scientific content. On the contrary, the demand by malevolent dilettantes to exploit their scientific freedom and falsify historical facts is solely designed to create confusion and doubt.

This is all the easier when political emotions are involved, as in the case of the genocide of European Jews. These include a sense of guilt, shame, and a German patriotism which refuses to accept that the Nazi state organized monstrous crimes—accusations sometimes felt by the post–1945 generation to be unjust and unreasonable.

People with such attitudes not only blame the victims (the Jews have "declared war on Germany" is an often-heard phrase), but above all they tend to deny the entire historical chapter. True, aims and techniques of revisionist misinformation have been thoroughly exposed and their arguments refuted in detail.[30] The originators, however, are not impressed because they are only interested in their own ideology. All the more deplorable, if a notable scholar like the historian Ernst Nolte joins their ranks and suggests that the "radical revisionists," as he calls the deniers of Auschwitz, "have presented research which, if one is familiar with the source material and the critique of the sources, is probably superior to that of the established historians in Germany."[31] Nolte, however, refuses to take note of critical research into sources (such as the number of Jewish victims of National Socialism), wherever this contradicts his speculations. He should, therefore, not be surprised, despite his reassurances that he wants objective science, if he is then considered an ideologue and no longer taken seriously as a historian.

In its form and content, revisionist argumentation is completely antisemitic and follows traditional patterns while reinterpreting historical events. The denial of the genocide of Jews has become the principle and motivation of a new antisemitism, as shown by the detailed description of the meeting in Weinheim which featured the U.S. neo-Nazi Fred Leuchter, and the NPD chairman Günter Deckert, reported as follows in the *Franfurter Allgemeine Zeitung:*

> The main thing that happened at that meeting was a continual incitement against Jews. This was obviously the main purpose of the meeting and the ideological glue that bound the people gathered there. For example, there were comments about "a group, I won't say more than that, you know what I want to say," the sarcastic emphasis on Jewish names in humiliating contexts, the evaluation of the liquidation of Jews, not only as a lie, but as an invention of Jews. The Jews are the persecutors: "Stop it and the Holo is finished!" Again and again, it is these comments that give rise to applause, frenetic applause.[32]

Traditional antisemitic stereotypes, like the legend of the world Jewish conspiracy and the claim that "the Jews" secretly exercise power create the link between the old and the new antisemitism. Not surprisingly, the radical right-wing press called the former chairman of the Central Council of Jews in Germany the "new (Jewish-allied) High Commissioner for and over Germany."[33]

The old and the new antisemitism wants to isolate Jews. In autumn 1994, a new charge was brought against NPD chairman Günter Deckert for racial incitement that intellectually and morally continues the National Socialist antisemitism that drove German Jews out of the country. He wrote to a Presidium Member of the Central Council of Jews in Germany stating that the homeland of Jews has been Israel for decades and not Germany. "Would it not be the most natural and obvious thing for you and yours to pack your cases and go where you belong: to Israel."[34]

That is exactly the point where the National Socialists began in 1933, the process which started by isolating Jews from German society, declaring them to be strangers and enemies, disenfranchising them, driving them out and finally murdering them.

Notes

1. Thies Christopherson, *Die Auschwitz-Lüge* (Mohrkirch, 1973, with many later editions).

2. Federal Government answer in response to a question put by MP Ulla Jelpke and the PDS/Linke Liste group, *Bundestagsdrucksache* 12/2470, 27 April 1992.

3. Paul Rassinier, *Was ist Wahrheit? Die Juden und das Dritte Reich* (Leoni, 1963, with many further editions); see also Lothar Baier, *Französische Zustände. Bericht und Essays.* (Frankfurt/M, 1982).

4. Robert Faurrison, *Ich suchte—und fand die Wahrheit. Die Revisionistische These eines französischen Forschers* (Mohrkirch, 1982).

5. Wilhelm Stäglich, *Der Auschwitz-Mythos—Legende oder Wirklichkeit? Eine kritische Bestandsaufnahme* (Tübingen, 1979).

6. Arthur A. Butz, *Der Jahrhundertbetrug* (Nlotho, 1977); others of the same ilk are: Emil Aretz, *Hexen-Einmal-Eins einer Lüge* (Verlag Hohe Warte o.O., 1984); Richard Harwood, *Starben wirklich sechs Millionen?* (Vlothzo, 1975); Erich Kern, *Die Tragödie der Juden. Schicksal zwischen Propaganda und Wahrheit* (Preußisch Oldendorf, 1979).

7. On the dispute with this type of right-wing extremist propaganda, see Dokumentationsarchiv des österreichischen Widerstandes/Bundesministerium für Unterricht und Kunst, ed., *Amoklauf gegen die Wirklichkeit. NS-Verbrechen und "revisionistische" Geschichtsschreibung* (Vienna, 1992); Wolfgang Benz, ed., *Legenden, Lügen, Vorurteile, Ein Wörterbuch zur Zeitgeschichte* (Munich, 1992).

8. Fred Leuchter, *Der zweite Leuchter-Report. Dachau Mauthausen, Hartheim. Erstellt auf Veranlassung von Ernst Zündel, 15. Juni 1989* (Hamilton, Ontario: Samisdat Publishers, 1989).

9. Correspondence between Dr. S. and the author, August–October 1992.

10. Correspondence, Technische Universität Berlin, Fachbereich Synthetische und Analytische Chemie to the author, November 1992.

11. It is also called the Rudolf Report following its publication in 1992 in a "3rd extended and corrected edition" copyrighted by Germar Rudolf, who was fired by the Max Planck Society but continued his activities. In June 1994 he sent the Chairman of the Central Council of Jews in Germany the introduction to an anthology entitled "Licht in die Vergangenheit. Eine interdisziplinäre Gesamtbetrachtung zur NS-Judenvernichtung" which continues the apologetic line of denying the Holocaust.

12. Otto Ernst Remer, disseminator, *Gutachten über die behaupteten Gaskammern von Auschwitz* (Bad Kissingen, October 1992).

13. On 20 May 1994 the German Bundestag passed a law *(Verbrecherbekämpfungsgesetz)* which makes it a crime to propagate the "Auschwitz lie," etc. Up to now, this was only accepted as a legal charge if the denial of the Holocaust was combined with express slander of Jews ("qualified Auschwitz lie").

14. Landgericht Mannheim, Strafkammer 6, Urteil in der Strafsache Deckert vom 22.6.1994, p. 62.

15. *Frankfurter Allgemeine Zeitung*, 11 August 1994, Betroffenheiten; 15 August 1994, Objektive Selbstzerstörung.

16. Substantiation, Deckert sentence, p. 7–8.

17. Ibid., 9.

18. Ibid., 63.

19. Ignatz Bubis, "Alles was Recht(s) ist. Wenn die Justiz versagt: Das Mannheimer 'Deckert-Urteil' und seine Folgen." in *Algemeine Jüdische Wochenzeitung*, 25 August 1994.

20. See Wolfgang Benz, ed., *Dimension des Völkermords. Die Zahl der Jüdischen Opfer des Nationalsozialismus* (Dimensions of Genocide. The Number of Jewish Victims of National Socialism) (Munich, 1991); Franciszek Piper, *Die Zahl der Opfer von Auschwitz. Aufgrund der Quellen und Erträge der Forschung 1945 bis 1990* (The Number of Victims of Auschwitz. Based on the Sources and Research Findings from 1945 to 1990) (Oswiecim, 1993).

21. "Beweis auf der Schweiz: Was nun Herr Staatsanwalt?," *Die Anklage. Organ der Entrechteten Nachkriegsgeschädigten*, 1 April 1955.

22. "57 million victims!," *Das Grüne Blatt*, 6 March 1955.

23. Archive, Institut für Zeitgeschichte, Munich.

24. Ibid.

25. Ibid., International Committee of the Red Cross to Institut für Zeitgeschichte, 11 October 1965.

26. Heinz Roth, *Warum werden wir Deutsche belogen?* (Witten, 1973).

27. "66 Fragen und Antworten über den Holocaust" (Costa Mesa, CA: Institute for Historical Review, 1994).

28. Benz, ed., *Legenden, Lügen, Vorurteile*, 137, n. 7.

29. Benz, *Legenden, Lügen, Vorurteile*, n. 27.

30. Deborah E. Lipstadt, *Betrofft: Leugnen des Holocaust* (Zurich, 1994); see also Hermann Graml, "Alte und neue Apologeten Hitlers," in *Rechtsextremismus in Deutschland*, Wolfgang Benz, ed. (Frankfurt a. M., 1994), 30ff; and Jean-Claude Pressac, *Die Krematorien von Auschwitz. Die Technik des Massenmordes* (Munich, 1994).

31. Ernst Nolte, *Streitpunkte. Heutige und künftige Kontroversen um den Nationalsozialismus* (Berlin, 1993), 304.

32. Volker Zastrow, "Die Verderber der Jugend und das Wunde der Stasse. Verdienste eines befremdlichen Urteils," *Frankfurter Allgemeine Zeitung*, 13 August 1994.

33. Günter Deckert, "Zwischenrufe," in Deutsche Stimme, *Nationaldemokratische Zeitung*, September 1994.

34. "Neue Anklage gegen NPD-Chef Deckert," *Süddeutsche Zeitung*, 12 October 1994.

23

Xenophobia and Antisemitism in the New Europe: The Case of Germany

Robert S. Wistrich
The Hebrew University of Jerusalem

The demise of Communism and the fall of the Iron Curtain in 1989 presented Europe with a golden opportunity to unite and become a great stabilizing force in the world today. Across the Continent, from East to West, a new consensus emerged in favor of democracy, pluralism, human rights, and the rule of law. For a brief, euphoric moment there was a high tide supporting the idea of European integration, the hope that a common European purpose might yet assert itself beyond the selfish interests of the individual nation-states. With the collapse of the Berlin Wall, the common ideals of peace, security, freedom, and prosperity suddenly seemed within reach of millions who had been denied this promise to the eastern half of the Continent. Since that peak, the idea of Europe has seemed to flounder in both East and West.

The bloody nationalist, ethnic, tribal, and religious warfare in Georgia, Armenia, Azerbaijan, above all, in Chechenya and Bosnia has produced the nightmare of controlling ethnic groups and aggressive majorities or militant minorities seeking to eliminate other national groups.

In Western and Central Europe, a new national populism has also asserted itself, which is fundamentally xenophobic in character. The most visible target of the new populist politics has been the influx of immigrants and asylum-seekers from the Third World, or more recently from Eastern and Southeast Europe, into the European community. Almost every Western industrial society in the past two decades has to some extent become multi-ethnic, with significant minority communities in most of its major cities. This has exacerbated fears and anxieties about law and order, jobs, housing and education, not to mention the more irrational reflexes aroused by differences of culture, religion, and race.

In Germany, in particular, there has been a chain reaction of firebombings, vandalism, and murderous assaults on foreigners during the past few years that raise some agonizing concerns.[1] They were well summarized by German President Richard von Weizsäcker, at a mass rally in Berlin on 8 November 1992:

> "Let us not fool ourselves. The events of this year are unprecedented in our postwar history. Malignancy is rife: there have been violent attacks on homes for foreigners, incitement to xenophobic feelings and assaults on young children. Jewish cemeteries have been desecrated, memorials devastated in the concentration camps at Sachsenhausen, Ravensbrück and Uberlingen. We are faced with violent right-wing extremism and an increasing number of attacks on the weak, both on foreigners and on Germans. Arsonists and killers are on the prowl."[2]

Street violence against foreigners had begun to intensify shortly after unification. In October 1991, neo-Nazis and skinheads in the Saxon town of Hoyerswerda besieged 230 foreigners whose hostel they had subjected to a six-day barrage of stones and Molotov cocktails. To the cheers of many local residents, the foreigners were forced to leave and little was done to punish the perpetrators of the violence. In August 1992, police stood idly by while neo-Nazis mounted a two-day siege of hostels where asylum-seekers lived in the Baltic city of Rostock. This sparked a further wave of savage violence by juveniles.

Altogether, through 1992, there were more than 2,500 attacks carried out by neo-Nazis and radical rightists, causing 17 deaths, injuring 600 and severely damaging many refugee shelters. The assaults were primarily directed against Third World asylum-seekers (Africans, Asians, Arabs), Gypsies, Turkish guest-workers and refugees fleeing from the economic and social chaos caused by the collapse of Communism. Though few Jews were direct victims of physical violence, there were many attacks against Jewish synagogues, cemeteries and Holocaust sites. Between October 1990 and the summer of 1992, for example, no less than 367 Jewish cemeteries were vandalized. In Erfurt, the capital of Thuringia, a young neo-Nazi scattered severed pigs' heads in the local synagogue.[3]

At the end of August 1992, a bomb was thrown at a Holocaust memorial site in Berlin, the place from which fifty years earlier thousands of Jewish Berliners had been deported to death camps in the East. Not long afterwards, the Jewish cemetery in Berlin-Weißensee was desecrated. Such incidents sent an alarming message to the small German Jewish community of around 50,000 to 60,000 (about one-tenth of its size when the Nazis came to power in 1933) that its security could no longer be taken for granted. They also suggested a close connection between the dramatic rise in xenophobia *(Fremdenfeindlichkeit)* and the revival of antisemitism in the new Germany.[4]

By the end of 1992 the attacks against foreigners, minority groups and even the physically disabled, had reached a scale not seen since 1945. The most murderous incidents took place against Turkish *Gastarbeiter* ("guest workers") so-called "foreigners" who had in fact lived in Germany for a generation and had contributed much to the postwar German "economic miracle." In the West German town of Mölln a firebombing on 22 November 1992 caused the deaths of a 51-year-old Turkish woman, her granddaughter, and niece.[5] Five more people died following an arson attack on a Turkish household at Solingen in May 1993. According to the BfV (*Verfassungsschutz,* Office for the Protection of the Constitution), in 1993 there were altogether 2,232 incidents of neo-Nazi and skinhead violence, a slight decrease over the previous year.[6] But the overall number of general extreme Right offenses had increased and antisemitic incidents also rose, including 72 violent acts against Jews.[7] Taken in the perspective of the last decade, the figures still tell a shocking story of escalation, especially since unification.[8] There were also more desecrations of Jewish cemeteries than on the eve of the Nazi seizure of power in 1933.

Germany with its six million foreign residents (one-third of them Muslim Turks) and two million asylum-seekers since 1989, has undoubtedly had a special problem.[9] Most of those asking for asylum are in fact economic refugees, wanting entry into Europe's richest welfare state. In 1992, the peak year of neo-Nazi violence, there were 438,000 asylum-seekers in Germany (60% of the total demand within the European community), knocking on the door of an already overstrained economy.[10] The costs of unification, involving huge transfers of capital to salvage the bankrupt East German economy, rising unemployment and indebtedness, created a growing backlash against foreigners in general. The collapse of the entire East German infrastructure after the rapid unification produced not only high unemployment, insecurity and fear of change, but also a deep demoralization.[11] Disoriented by the aggressive new capitalist ethos, despised by their richer West German cousins, feeling cheated by the promises of an economic miracle and suffering from a poor self-image, East Germans had *real* grounds for resentment.[12] Sympathy for right-wing extremism naturally grew on this fertile soil, despite the anti-fascist tradition of the German Democratic Republic. Although there are today very few foreign workers and even less Jews in the ex-GDR, both xenophobia without foreigners and antisemitism without Jews are not difficult to transplant in conditions of crisis.[13]

Violent rejectionism, alienation and bitterness at disappointed expectations, as well as fear of the future, produced a growing need for scapegoats and a growing attraction to the extreme Right. This has been particularly true among young, white working-class males in the bleak concrete wastelands of Dresden, Leipzig, and other East German cities. A certain receptivity to *völkisch* nationalism also exists in areas bordering Poland, arising from traditional anti-Polish sentiments and fear of an influx of asylum-seekers from the East.[14] Much of the most inflammatory racist propaganda came, it is worth noting, from Gary Rex Lauck's NSDAP-AO in the United States and from Ernst Zundel, a German neo-Nazi exile in Canada through his Munich "agent" Bela Ewald Althans, currently serving a prison term for Holocaust denial.[15]

The neo-Nazi movement, whether based in the east or the west, became increasingly entrenched in the skinhead subculture. The skinhead gangs, especially brutal and thuggish in the East, often assume local policing activities, taking over whole neighborhoods and terrorizing opposition into silence. Youth centers and bars are their battlefields and they also serve as recruiting centers. Many skinheads are unemployed or work at marginal jobs, are poorly educated, come from broken homes and have juvenile criminal records.[16] The primitive Nazi-inspired slogans of German nationalism based on blood, race, and the folk community provide them both with a crude ideology and with a new sense of belonging.

After the Rostock attack in August 1992, destructive street riots and firebombings by neo-Nazi groups spread rapidly—encouraged by police laxity and some open sympathy from the populace, especially in former East Germany. These were not spontaneous attacks by small groups of drunken youths happening to fall on chance victims, contrary to the claims at the time of the authorities. They were organized and prepared acts of violence by well-armed gangs motivated by extreme nationalist rhetoric against foreigners and Jews.[17]

The German neo-Nazis have also succeeded in consolidating some of their international contacts with various extreme right-wing organizations in Russia and Eastern Europe. The internationalization of contacts, exchanges and racist propaganda has in general been a growing feature of the neo-Nazi scene, favored by the use of electronic media, difficult to monitor and even harder to stop. Racist and antisemitic materials are now often distributed through computer networks and bulletin board systems; through various public access TV channels and radio programs; or by the production and distribution of video cassettes. There are neo-Nazi telephone networks and hot-lines as well as computer games that spread the new gospel of Holocaust denial.[18] Thus "electronic" fascism helps keep the Nazi poison alive, to circumvent public bans and censorship by the authorities, as well as providing mutual aid between members of neo-Nazi movements across the world.

Neo-Nazis are still isolated and totally outside the political mainstream, confronted by a German State committed to liberal democracy and the rule of law. Neither in official German government circles, nor among the mainstream political parties, the established press, the business community, the bulk of intellectuals, or respectable public opinion, is there much hint of genuine nostalgia for the Third Reich. The kind of limitless national ambition and rampant militarism that provoked two world wars seems well and truly dead.

Even populist ultranationalists in Germany are not openly fascist and outwardly seek to maintain some tactical distance from neo-Nazism. They play by the rules of the democratic game, claim to express the *vox populi* on immigration and to represent a healthy nativist resistance to the "evils" of a multicultural society. They are also occupied with banishing once and for all the burden of German guilt and demonstrating (in Franz Schönhuber's words) that "Germans have given the world far more than Auschwitz can ever wreck."[19] In the case of the *Deutsche Volkszeitung,* the rejection of what is branded as continuous Allied "war propaganda" against Germany, slides over at times into outright denial of the Holocaust.

The implicit belief in an international Jewish conspiracy is what lies behind the accusation on the far Right that the "Zionists" deliberately fostered the "Auschwitz-lie" to squeeze money from Germany.[20] Once this monstrous "Holocaust myth" has been nailed, not only a nationalistic Germany but the entire far-right ideology can be rehabilitated. World Jewry will once again be seen as the aggressors and persecutors, Germans (and Nazis) as the innocent victims. If there were no gas chambers then the greatest stumbling block in the German past to the coming national rebirth is gone. No more *angst,* no more guilt, the "Truth makes you free!"[21] With German innocence reestablished, the road would be open to ultranationalism, fascism and neo-Nazism with a good conscience. Racism can acquire a shiny new gloss without the attached odium of mass murder. Hence, the great and insidious importance that Holocaust denial has globally assumed on the far Right (but also in other circles) in the postwar period.[22]

This is particularly troubling because the reunification of Germany and the demolition of the "wall" separating East from West, has released many of the demons from the racist and antisemitic past. A historically paralysed postwar German national identity seeks new outlets, the lowest strata of society look for the weakest targets available to express their need for self-affirmation and belonging, while foreigners, asylum-seekers and refugees become targets for suppressed rage and hatreds that had been bottled up for decades.[23] Ties of blood and belonging express the regressive popular anger projected against the most *visible* out-groups. With the collapse of the Soviet "enemy," there is in addition an unconscious need for new enemies. Those who are followers of another monotheistic religion, such as the Muslim minorities in Europe, have today to some extent replaced the Jews in the classic role of scapegoat. The "Jewish question" in postwar Germany is objectively quite different from that of Muslims and foreign workers, but at the level of demonization, there are obvious parallels between anti-Islamism and antisemitism in Christian European civilization.[24]

In 1945, the last great teacher of German Jewry, Rabbi Leo Baeck had declared that the era of the Jews in Germany had forever gone. The historic German Jewry that produced such a dazzling galaxy of talent to enrich German medicine, law, the arts and sciences, the economy and politics, was indeed no more. Hitler's diabolical work of destruction had annihilated two-thirds of European Jewry. Of the half million Jews in Germany in 1933, a mere 15,000 had survived the Nazi mass murder by 1945. For a brief moment, until 1948, in the DP camps under Western occupation in Germany, "the surviving remnant" of the Holocaust (mainly refugees fleeing from eastern Europe) lived on German soil. Convinced that Judaism had no future in Germany, they emigrated to Israel or in some cases, to the United States.

Those who stayed were mainly Polish Jews, along with a small minority of assimilated German Jews who had somehow survived the war. They and their offspring would form the core of the new Jewish community in Germany, reinforced in the 1950s and 1960s by some Jewish immigration from Rumania, Hungary, Poland, Czechoslovakia and Israel. Until the collapse of Communism in 1989, the numbers remained relatively stable at around 30,000. Since then, there has been a substantial influx of former Soviet Jews, who today constitute about half of the total Jewish population living in Germany. As a result, fifty years after the Holocaust, there are between 60,000 and 70,000 Jews (including those outside the official community) who have made their homes in a united Germany. This is still only a fraction of the size of the Muslim minority and of the overall "foreign" population in contemporary German society. But it is a significantly new development which cannot be ignored in our context.

It is all the more remarkable when one recalls that only two decades ago, Jews in Germany were often thought of as having a "packed bag mentality," as people in transit, on their way to another place. Not only did they suffer from the feeling that for Germans they were "unwelcome guests" (antisemitism in the 1950s was still quite vehement in the Federal Republic), but they were pariahs in the eyes of Israel and world Jewry by virtue of living in the "land of the murderers."

Not surprisingly, this has created strong inner conflicts, guilt feelings, self-reproach, and even some degree of self-contempt among the survivors and their children. A schizoid frame of mind developed among many Jews in Germany, encouraged by the contradiction between de facto residence and emigration fantasies that were never realized. They lived private lives focused around family and business, maintaining a low public profile and little social contact with German gentiles. Nevertheless, despite this self-ghettoization, reasonably well functioning communities were established—especially in Berlin, Frankfurt, and Munich—thanks to the assistance of the authorities.

It is only in the past decade, that Jews have begun to develop a new self-consciousness and self-image in Germany, an awareness that they are there to stay and that for better or for worse, this is, in fact, their home. This change of consciousness is especially true for younger Jews, born in postwar Germany, though it is often accompanied by a painful self-questioning and pangs of conscience.[25]

Such doubts are invariably connected with the legacy of mass extermination and efforts by many Germans to relegate it to history. Jews were outraged when ten years ago, Chancellor Kohl invited President Reagan to honor the war dead (including SS officers) in Bitburg. A year later, in 1986, members of the Frankfurt Jewish community occupied the stage to prevent the performance of an antisemitically tinged play, *Garbage, The City and Death,* by the late Rainer Werner Fassbinder.[26] Jews in Germany were no less disconcerted by the efforts of Ernst Nolte and some other German historians to relativize the Holocaust.

Equally troubling for many has been the trend in Germany to blur distinctions between perpetrators and victims, to deny the specificity of the Shoah, and to stress German sufferings during and after the war as being somehow comparable to those of the Jews.[27] The many prominent Germans who in May 1995 signed an advertisement in the *Frankfurter Allgemeine Zeitung,* protesting the commemoration of 8 May 1945 as a day of "liberation" for the German people, were clearly voicing this new emphasis on German victimhood. After 1945, they declared Germany had been divided, Soviet oppression had begun in East Germany, and millions had been expelled by terror from their homes in eastern Europe. Forgetting these facts (which as far as they go are, of course, true) was declared incompatible with German national self-consciousness.

Such declarations should not be confused with the vicious phenomenon of "Holocaust denial" (which has its advocates in German Radical Right and neo-Nazi circles, as elsewhere in Europe and America) but they are a form of relativization. So too, are the efforts to dilute distinctions between the victims of genocide, the sufferings of the civilian population and the deaths of soldiers in World War II. This blurring is precisely the effect of the "Neue Wache" memorial on Unter den Linden in East Berlin, dedicated to the "victims of war and tyranny" on 14 November 1993. This monument to "reconciliation" is symbolized by a big bronze cast of a Pietà by Käthe Kollwitz with the mourning mother and widow, crying for her dead son. It may be a classic expression of anti-war sentiment, but it is hardly adequate for rendering the fate of the Jews and Gypsies. Moreover, the role of those responsible for the mass murders appears to be wholly obscured.[28]

This is not an isolated trend in Kohl's Germany, torn between its official cult of remembrance and the longing to forget the Nazi past, widely shared by the mass of ordinary Germans. One cannot deny to the German Chancellor—surely Europe's most consistently underestimated political leader—a certain consistency in these matters. Central to his vision is the desire to "normalize"Germany's past and to legitimize a robust, healthy patriotism as the basis for a positive German identity. This requires an emphasis on the highs rather than the lows of German history, on those forces and elements that forged the Germany of today rather than the factors that caused the specifically German responsibilities for two wars and the Holocaust in this century.[29]

History must therefore be rearranged to show that Germany has always been part of the mainstream history of the enlightened West and to emphasize the coherence and continuity of the German nation. Inexplicably, we are being led to believe, this "noble" Germany was hijacked by Hitler who seized and "occupied" it for twelve terrible years! But the Nazis allegedly had little to do with the broad stream of German history. Such a remarkably benign view guides the exhibits in the new German Historical Museum which seeks to reclaim the German history lost to Hitler. Germany and the Germans were also victims of Nazism and happily they, too, were "liberated" along with everyone else (including the Jews) in 1945. Such myth-making has helped Kohl turn German defeat in the war into "true" liberation and to reposition himself as one of the victors.

This is a tactically sophisticated piece of historical "revisionism" which exactly suits the mood of the German public, both before and after unification. Most Germans feel, after all, that their country has sufficiently acknowledged its guilt for the past, paid off its moral and material debt to the Jews and amply proven its democratic character. "Normalization," a key word in Kohl's vocabulary, thus appears to them as eminently reasonable. They understandably want to feel pride in being German, to enjoy their history without guilt and (more dubiously) to draw a definitive line (*Schlußtrich*) over the Nazi past.[30]

Clearly, most Jews in Germany and elsewhere find it difficult to acquiesce in such a simplified view of German innocence and in this case, they are not alone. One problem for Jews in Germany is that willy-nilly, they continue to haunt the German memory and reminders of their fate are seen by many Germans as an obstacle to achieving that "healthy" national consciousness to which they anxiously aspire. Germans do not want to be constantly reminded by the world of the greatest disgrace in their history. The backlash can produce deep resentment as was provocatively pointed out by Henryk M. Broder in his book, *Der Ewige Antisemit* (1986), when he coined the bitter remark that "Die Deutschen werden den Juden Auschwitz nie verzeihen" (The Germans will never forgive the Jews for Auschwitz"). In other words, the new antisemitism in Germany exists not despite, but rather because of Auschwitz and the guilt feelings that need to be constantly repressed.

The other side of this particular coin is the official "philosemitism" that has been a feature of German attitudes towards Jews and Israel.[31] This has many practical and positive aspects, including the authorities' financial support for Jewish life in Germany, for research institutes in Jewish studies (which have grown recently) and for communal Jewish museums. Since the first postwar German Chancellor, Konrad Adenauer decided on reparations as a means to ease German reentry into the family of civilized nations, the Jews in Germany have been high on the national agenda despite their small numbers. Their status and well-being was seen as a barometer for Germany's transformation into a genuinely liberal democracy. Hence, the constant rhetorical assurances that Germany has recognized its responsibilities to the Jews and the resulting official readiness to memorialize and commemorate the past.[32]

Sometimes, as with President von Weizsäcker's speech to the West German Parliament ten years ago, where he emphasized that "there can be no reconciliation without remembrance," the effect can be cathartic and beneficial. At other times, Germany's *Gedenkkultur* appears to be little more than lip-service—the soothing clichés about not repeating the past, seemingly pale and inadequate, in the light of a growing xenophobia and antisemitism in the present. The wave of anti-foreigner and racist violence which peaked in 1993 (since then the authorities have acted more forcefully to dampen neo-Nazi rampages), undoubtedly strengthened feelings of isolation and marginalization among Jews in Germany.

Future historians may well conclude that the official German philosemitism of the postwar era came to an end on 9 November 1989, with the fall of the Berlin Wall. Symbolically and perhaps inevitably, this day of German unity (a national holiday) has already begun to displace that mark of shame, 9 November 1938 (Night of Broken Glass) when Germany's synagogues went up in flames.[33] What is still a date of mourning for Jews is now seen as a day of joy and liberation for most Germans. Jews who had grown up in postwar Germany are well aware of such ambiguities in their unwritten contract with the new German national state that has arisen since 1990. As long as Germany was divided, its existence in some ways as provisional as their own, there was little need to identify positively with Germany or with "*Deutschtum*" (Germanness). Things are different today as Jews feel a new pressure to define in what ways they are German or not.

A recent book edited by Susan Stern, *Speaking Out: Jewish Voices from United Germany,* (1995) poignantly illustrates some of these dilemmas. One contributor, Ralph Giordano, a documentary filmmaker and author, as well as survivor, explains that he feels "nailed to the country" precisely because of the past and the lessons to be learned from it. Despite his fiercely critical attitude to the smoldering racism in the country, he has developed a sense of belonging and the conviction that Germans will have "enough good common sense not to engage in a new life-and-death confrontation" with the world.[34]

Another survivor, Ignatz Bubis, the leading spokesman of German Jewry today, acknowledges that antisemitism has qualitatively increased in Germany and is more respectable *(salonfähig)* than before.[35] At the same time, he argues that there is no real threat to democracy and Germany's commitment to the European Union has in no way been weakened by unification.

But above and beyond the question of antisemitism, the mere fact of living in the land of the Holocaust automatically reinforces a sense—uneasy and diffuse—of Jewish identity. For some, like the author Rafael Seligmann, this negative definition which identifies the Jews as a community of victims, is harmful. In Germany, it can be more destructive than in Israel or the rest of the Diaspora, because the community is much more fragile. Seligmann even believes that for Jews "to become identified with the Holocaust to the exclusion of all else...would be the ultimate triumph of Adolph Hitler."[36] At the same time, he does see an important function for Jews in Germany—"to sound the alarm whenever there is a need to make people aware of the dangers at hand—which is the case at the moment."[37]

The great difference between the demonization of Jews in Nazi Germany and in the postwar era must nevertheless be borne in mind. Since 1945, in the western half of Germany, antisemitism has never been state policy and the hard core of antisemites have had little long-term impact on political parties or public consciousness. The classic antisemitic stereotypes of Jews as deicides, usurers, international bankers, cultural subversives, and as the driving-force of Communism, have lost most of their political relevance, although as a popular prejudice, antisemitism remains remarkably stable.[38] It also needs to be remembered that in East Germany, the Communist regime did at times use antisemitism (in the guise of anti-Zionism) as a political weapon though on balance less frequently than in the Soviet Union or Eastern Europe. However, the demonization of foreigners, in Germany as in most European states in the 1990s, is a cultural reality as a direct result of population movements, social and economic difficulties, and political changes. The attitude to Jews despite some parallels, is qualitatively and quantitatively different in historical, sociological and ethical terms. Historically, antisemitism has had an unmistakably Christian background in Germany and in most of Europe, tied as it is to the unique status of Jews as "chosen people" in Christian eyes, condemned to servitude and segregation by the Church and secular rulers for many centuries. Since the Emancipation, however, Jews became an integral part of European culture (even subsequently reshaping it) especially in the German-speaking countries of Central Europe. This is not the case with migrating foreigners against whom the core of current xenophobia is directed.

Moreover the Jews, unlike the foreigners in Germany today, were for centuries a remarkably homogeneous group with a highly developed national-religious identity. Under conditions of assimilation in the nineteenth and twentieth centuries they became prime movers of intellectual and cultural trends towards enlightenment, liberalism, and democracy in German society, without altogether losing their own group identity. Their identification with an idealized Germany was specially intense. None of these factors have any real analogies when one examines the heterogeneous nature of other minority cultures in Germany and Europe today. Indeed the rise of Islamic fundamentalism among Muslim minorities in France, Germany, and Britain, suggests an opposite trend on the part of a section of the Muslim population to the integrationist philosophy which characterized the Jewish minorities in western and central Europe before the Shoah. Finally, when contemplating the Holocaust itself, the incomparability of antisemitism with present-day xenophobia is even more transparent. There have admittedly always been xenophobic elements in antisemitism but the Nazi drive to exterminate *all* Jews was sui generis and went far beyond the simple hatred of the "alien" and the "unlike". There is a very considerable difference between personal prejudice, social and institutional discrimination and mass murder, even if all these phenomena can be placed along one psychological spectrum and seen as respective stages in a historical continuum of hatreds.

Such distinctions do not however mean that antisemitism and racial xenophobia cannot constitute overlapping (though not interchangeable) categories in contemporary Germany—or in neighboring lands. Neo-Nazis, racists, and antisemites often demonize Jews, Muslims, Gypsies, and migrants from Asia and Africa in equal measure.[39] Indeed, in the new reunited Germany, it is fair to say that Turks, Gypsies, and asylum-seekers have borne the brunt of the anger, fear, and anxieties of the population. They, and not the Jews, are the prime targets of racist violence, it is they who are considered as *inassimilable* minorities and still largely denied the rights of citizenship.[40] Jews, by contrast, have been spared most of the physical abuse and insults reserved for foreigners and asylum-seekers—though Holocaust memorial sites and Jewish cemeteries have been extensively desecrated. Thus Jews are still a *symbolic* target, especially for the far Right, but seem almost "invisible" compared to those "aliens" who are more numerous and outwardly different in the eyes of the average Germans.

This difference applies even to Russian Jews who "look" more like Germans than Turks do, and seem to be regarded as a more desirable or assimilable minority. Their social integration is more obviously encouraged than that of Muslims—an attitude clearly linked to the legacy of the past.

The burden of the Shoah similarly helps to explain why the German State is noticeably harsher in its treatment of public antisemitism than in its general response to xenophobia: the German government does not wish to anger Israel, world Jewry, or critically-minded non-Jews who would unreservedly condemn Germany for its failure to make amends for the past. Such constraints do not apply to the same degree towards "foreigners," who in any case are more visibly unpopular among the German population. Thus guilt-feelings, a sense of obligation and international politics tend to override xenophobic sentiment in the case of Jews but not in dealing with "real" *Ausländer*.

Finally, it must be remembered that Jews in Germany are formally *citizens* and far more obviously German by culture (in German eyes) than Turks, Vietnamese, Gypsies, or Africans. They look, sound, and are in fact more German than the demonized "others" in contemporary Germany. Even, when they too are new immigrants, they pass more easily as German. Sander Gilman has summed it up well in a recent book: "Jews no longer define difference in Germany, while difference is still defined by the image of the Jew."[41]

Notes

1. See, for example, *Sunday Times,* 29 November 1992, 16; *Daily Telegraph,* 26 November 1992; *The Times,* 28 November 1992, 10, 14; December 1992, 6–7. Also *Newsweek,* 21 September 1992, 26; and *Der Spiegel* 2 (1992), 36–48.

2. Quoted in *The German Neo-Nazis: An ADL Investigative Report* (New York 1993), 1.

3. Tom Reiss, "Strange World of Germany's Neo-Nazi Youth", *Wall Street Journal,* 17 December 1992. Also Murray Gordon, "Racism and Antisemitism in Germany: Old Problem, New Threat," *Congress Monthly* 60, no. 3 (March/April 1993): 3–7.

4. According to the leader of the German Jewish community, Ignatz Bubis, there is no great difference between the two phenomena. Quoted in Jeffrey M. Peck, "The 'Ins' and 'Outs' of the New Germany: Jews, Foreigners, Asylum Seekers," in *Reemerging Jewish Culture in Germany. Life and Literature Since 1989,* eds. Sander L. Gilman and Karen Remmler (New York and London 1994) 130–31.

5. *The Times* (London), 24 November 1992, 15; "Fanatics of Fire", *Newsweek,* 4 January 1993, 30.

6. Figures quoted in Institute of Jewish Affairs, London, *Antisemitism: World Report 1994* (London 1994), 38.

7. Ibid.

8. These are official figures from the Office for the Protection of the Constitution. See *Response* (Wiesenthal Center World Report) 14, no 2 (Summer 1993): 2 for a more detailed breakdown.

9. "Germany: Including the Auslanders," *Newsweek,* 28 June 1993.

10. See Steve Vogel, "The Politics of Hate," *American Legion Magazine,* April 1993.

11. Cornelia Dieckmann and Mario Kessler, "Right Wing Extremism and Anti-Semitism after the Transformation: The Case of the New German States," in *Antisemitism in Post-Totalitarian Europe,* 259–71.

12. For West German arrogance to their Eastern cousins, see *Der Spiegel,* 11 February 1991, 81.

13. Dieckmann and Kessler, "Right Wing Extremism," 262. They note that less than 1% of all the GDR's residents were foreigners and that they had virtually no contact with East Germans outside the workplace. The Jewish community of East Germany has been estimated at between 2,500 to 3,000. The Communist regime claimed to have uprooted anti-semitism but pursued an aggressively hostile policy to Israel and Zionism. Until shortly before its demise it refused to accept any responsibility for the Holocaust or to pay reparations to Jews outside the country. This contrasted sharply with the West German policy of material restitution since the early 1950s.

14. Ibid., 14.

15. For the Zundel-Althans connection, see the controversial documentary film *Beruf Neo-Nazi* by Winfried Bonengel. Zundel, a German who emigrated to Canada to escape military service, made a living as a commercial artist and expert in retouching photos. An open admirer of Hitler and a Holocaust denier, he sells tapes of speeches by Nazi "greats" and videocassettes abroad to a neo-Nazi constituency. Very media-conscious, he shows off his "concentration camp" pajamas in the film. On Zundel's Holocaust denial, see ADL, *Hitler's Apologists: The Anti-Semitic Propaganda of Holocaust "Revisionism"* (New York 1993), 37–40. Althans, a tall, blond, much younger neo-Nazi ran a sales and publicity company in Munich, offering among other things "action shots" of paramilitary neo-Nazis to the media for a price. He also acted as a German booking agent for British Holocaust denier David Irving. For some of these connections and a good general picture of the neo-Nazi subculture in Germany, see Michael Schmidt, *The New Reich* (London 1993).

16. ADL, *German Neo-Nazis,* 4.

17. Husbands, "Neo-Nazis in East Germany," 6.

18. Ibid., xiv.

19. Quoted in Dieckmann and Kessler, "Right Wing Extremism," 268.

20. For Holocaust negation, see Gil Seidel, *The Holocaust Denial* (Leeds 1986), and Pierre Vidal-Naquet, *Les assassins de la Mémoire* (Paris 1987). This is, of course, an *international* phenomenon, with particularly active branches in Britain, France, and the United States.

21. Michael Schmidt, *The New Reich,* 197. The great popularity of David Irving on the German far Right derives from this need for psychological liberation. He gives them a clean conscience about their past. As a relentless British defamer of Churchill's reputation and now as a Holocaust denier, his "truth" is grist to the neo-Nazi and far Right mill in Germany.

22. For a valuable analysis, see Roger Eatwell, "The Holocaust Denial: a study in propaganda technique," in *Neo-Fascism in Europe,* eds. Luciano Cheles et al. (London 1992), 120–46.

23. See, for example, Sander L. Gilman, *Jews in Today's German Culture* (Bloomington and Indianapolis 1995), 27–31.

24. See the remarks of Professor Dr. Bassam Tibi, Göttingen, published in "Briefe an die Herausgeber," *Frankfurter Allgemeine Zeitung,* 17 January 1995, Nr. 14, 9. An enlightened Muslim, Tibi objects to attempts to compare the persecution of Jews in Germany before the Shoah with discrimination against foreigners today. He sees such efforts as part of the dominant multiculturalist ideology which relies on a concept of "right-wing extremism" *(Rechtsextremismus)* emptied of real content. The German Jews before the Shoah were persecuted in their homeland (i.e., Germany), in which they were not only full citizens but also represented the most enlightened part of German culture. The situation of the Muslims and other minorities who have come from abroad and are not regarded as citizens or as part of German culture, is quite different in its premises and consequences.

25. See the essays in *Reemerging Jewish Culture,* eds. Gilman and Remmler, especially Rafael Seligmann, "What Keeps the Jews in Germany Quiet?," 173–83.

26. See my essay on the Fassbinder controversy, in Robert S. Wistrich, *Between the Redemption and Perdition. Anti-semitism and Jewish Identity* (London and New York 1990) and Johann N. Schmidt, "'Those Unfortunate Years': Nazism in the Public Debate of Post-War Germany," The Inaugural Paul Lecture, The Jewish Studies Program, Indiana University, 1987.

27. Frank Stern, "Jews in the Minds of Germans in the Postwar Period," The 1992 Paul Lecture, Indiana University.

28. Jane Kramer, "Letter from Germany. The Politics of Memory," *The New Yorker.* 14 (August 1995): 48–65.

29. Ibid., 58.

30. Rodney Livingstone, "Germans and Jews," *Patterns of Prejudice* 29, nos. 2 and 3 (1995): 45–59.

31. On the background, Frank Stern, *The Whitewashing of the Yellow Badge. Antisemitism and Philosemitism in Postwar Germany* (Oxford 1992).

32. In a more bitter, ironic vein, Henryk Broder wrote in *Der Spiegel,* 17 April 1995: "When Jews are concerned, German institutions spare no effort and no cost. No matter whether Jews are first to be murdered or afterwards to be memorialized, the objective is followed with persistence, tenacity and a sense for the gigantic."

33. See Julius H. Schoeps, "Vier Thesen zum 9. November 1989," *Semit* 3/90, 17.

34. Ralph Giordano, "Auschwitz—and Life! Why I Have Remained in Germany," in *Speaking Out. Jewish Voices From United Germany,* ed. Susan Stern, (Chicago, Berlin, Tokyo, and Moscow 1995), 47.

35. Ignatz Bubis, "Notes and Reflections on Jews in Germany," *Speaking Out,* 63–64.

36. Rafael Seligmann, "German Jewry Squawking at the Approach of Danger," *Speaking Out,* 165–81.

37. Ibid., 180.

38. See Jennifer L. Golub, *German Attitudes Towards Jews. What Recent Survey Data Reveal* (New York 1991). Surveys between 1990 consistently showed that around 20% of all Germans have negative feelings towards Jews. The stereotype of the crafty, avaricious Jew, and resentment of Jewish influence in the world, along with accusations that Israelis and world Jewry try to profit from German guilt feelings, were fairly

common. Surveys also noted a high correlation between aversion to Turks, Arabs or Blacks, and prejudices against Jews.

See also *Der Spiegel*, 3–4 (March 1992): 41–66, which found in 1992 that one in eight Germans had antisemitic attitudes. No less than 44 per cent felt that "racial purity" was vital to the Germans.

39. Jeffrey Peck, "The 'Ins' and 'Outs' of the New Germany," *Reemerging Jewish Culture in Germany*, eds. Gilman and Remmler, 136 suggests the following hierarchy of *Ausländer* (foreigners) according to color. At the top are white Americans, French, Dutch, and Scandinavians; followed by Germans from the GDR, "ethnic Germans" *(Aussiedler)* from Eastern Europe, by Poles and other East Europeans. Then come the "real" *Ausländer* such as Turks, Blacks, Pakistanis, etc.; followed by Asian foreigners, like the Vietnamese. At the bottom of the pile are Sinti and Roma (so-called Gypsies), of whom the lowest are Gypsies from Rumania and ex-Yugoslavia. The Jews, by contrast, are "white" and able to assimilate into the general population. Being non-Christian and in origins non-German, does not really bring them together with Turks, Blacks, and others. Nevertheless, the rise of xenophobia does affect Jews.

40. Sander L. Gilman, *Jews in Today's German Culture*, 27–31.

41. Ibid, 38.

Index

Printed in the USA/Agawam, MA
April 9, 2013

574297.114